Cultural Intermediaries

JEWISH CULTURE AND CONTEXTS

Published in association with the Center for Advanced Judaic Studies of the University of Pennsylvania

A complete list of books in the series is available from the publisher.

Cultural Intermediaries

Jewish Intellectuals in Early Modern Italy

Edited by
David B. Ruderman and Giuseppe Veltri

PENN

University of Pennsylvania Press
Philadelphia

Publication of this volume was assisted by a grant from the Herbert D. Katz Publications Fund of the Center for Advanced Judaic Studies, University of Pennsylvania.

Printed in the United States of America on acid-free paper

10 9 8 7 6 5 4 3 2 1

Published by
University of Pennsylvania Press
Philadelphia, Pennsylvania 19104-4011

Library of Congress Cataloging-in-Publication Data

Cultural intermediaries : Jewish intellectuals in early modern Italy / edited by David B. Ruderman and Giuseppe Veltri.
p. cm. — (Jewish culture and contexts)
Includes bibliographical references and index.
ISBN 0-8122-3779-X (cloth : alk. paper)
1. Jews—Italy—Intellectual life—16th century—Congresses. 2. Jews—Italy—Intellectual life—17th century—Congresses. 3. Jewish scholars—Italy—Congresses. 4. Jewish learning and scholarship—Italy—History—Congresses. 5. Jews—Italy—Social conditons—Congresses. 6. Italy—Ethnic relations—Congresses. I. Ruderman, David B. II. Veltri, Giuseppe. III. Series.

DS135.I8C86 2004
305.5'52'089924045—dc22 *2003070527*

Contents

Introduction

David B. Ruderman

This book chronicles in novel and original ways the lives and thinking of ten Jewish intellectuals, nine of them from Italy and one from the Ottoman Empire. All of them lived roughly in the same time period, from the end of the fifteenth to the early seventeenth century, an epoch of spectacular demographic, political, economic, and cultural changes for European Jewry. Almost all of them were highly educated in traditional Jewish sources as well as in Western philosophy, science, and literature. Their broad cultural exposure was facilitated by living in intellectual centers such as Florence, Mantua, Pisa, Naples, Ferrara, and Salonika, where books were readily available and social contacts with non-Jewish intellectuals were not uncommon. In the relative openness of cultural exchange in which these individuals participated, their reading habits and cultural tastes were clearly stimulated and challenged by the intense circulation of knowledge between Jewish communities, Ashkenazic and Sephardic, as well as between Jews, Christians, and those conversos inhabiting a space between both faith communities.[1] Given the dramatic mobility of persons and printed books, and the growing positive, albeit ambiguous, reception of Jewish ideas and texts among some elite Christian circles, these Jewish savants were encouraged to enlarge their intellectual horizons, to correlate the teachings of their own tradition with those outside of it, and to rethink the meaning of their religious and ethnic identities within the intellectual and religious categories common to European civilization as a whole.

Such transformations were, however, gradual, subtle, and often taken with considerable risk. The Christian world, even its most daring voices of toleration and change, was hardly ready to accept Jews and Judaism on an equal footing in its midst. A long tradition of subordination and discrimination still persisted in this period and beyond. One might even argue that such events as the Jewish expulsions from Spain and Portugal in 1492 and 1497, Luther's vilification of Jews, the burning of the Talmud, the ghettoization of Italian Jewry, and the Spanish and Portuguese Inquisition were clear signs of an intensification of hatred rather than its diminution or even modification. Intellectual awareness, curiosity about, and even appreciation of the "other" on the part of Jews and Christians could often accompany the most bleak and debilitating social reality. Knowing more about the Jew did not necessarily mean rehabilitating or improving his economic or political status. Christian study of Jewish exegesis and theology as well as Jewish awareness of Christian and pagan wisdom could still remain, and most often did remain, unrelated to any radical adjustment of social and political attitudes.

The engaging intellectual profiles created especially for this volume by the participating authors were first presented in oral form at a conference organized at the famed Herzog August Bibliothek in Wolfenbüttel, Germany, in September 2000. The intimate surroundings of the precious library enabled a small group of scholars to reflect deeply and widely about Jewish intellectual life in early modern Europe. The participants were from Israel and the United States, but primarily from Europe, representing—in age and in religious and cultural background—a wide diversity of perspectives and understandings. One might thus argue that the results of those deliberations now presented in these essays represent the work of a relatively new generation of scholars and a novel reading and interpretation of these thinkers and their writing. While the study of early modern Jewish culture and society has already made considerable strides in the last forty years or so,[2] these essays convey a sense of freshness, the opening of new vistas of inquiry, and the impressive degree to which the writers display a profound mastery of Hebraic sources as well as the larger intellectual context of European civilization.

Although published only twelve years ago, a similar anthology of essays on Jewish cultural life in Italy edited by this author might be compared with the present volume.[3] Besides myself, three others in the present volume were represented in the earlier collection of studies (Harrán, Weinberg, and Idel). The other eight scholars—Lelli, Hames, Veltri, Jacobs, Guetta, Miletto, Shear, and Gutwirth—represent a younger generation of researchers engaged in academic centers of Judaic studies in Italy, Germany, France, Israel, and the United States. In my introduction to the earlier volume, I felt the acute need to justify an entire collection devoted to the subject of Renaissance and baroque Jewish cultural and intellectual history, written almost exclusively by American and Israeli scholars. This new volume testifies to the remarkable growth and diversity of the field, the considerable awareness of and interest in Jewish civilization on the part of European historians in general, and the impressive crop of scholarly books and essays on the subject that has appeared in recent years with which these essays engage. There is hardly a reason any longer to justify the appearance of this volume but only to celebrate the maturation and creativity of a still-blossoming academic field.

* * *

The volume's focus is on Jewish intellectual life, particularly the complex social and cultural roles of a certain type of Jewish scholar in this era. From the outset, it raises two essential problems. First, are we entitled to speak about a coherent era for Jewish cultural and social history, roughly demarcated by the span in which these scholars lived—the sixteenth and seventeenth centuries—which most historians now call the early modern period? Does this era exhibit sufficiently common social structures and intellectual markers that allow us to speak of a distinct cultural epoch encompassing the diverse social settings of Jewish life from the Renaissance to the late baroque and from Western Europe to the Ottoman Empire and Poland/Lithuania? While a few historians have attempted to address this question—most notably, Jonathan Israel[4]—for others, the question remains open. And some prefer simply to ignore it, choosing to link this period with the late Middle Ages[5] or simply calling it "Renaissance" or even "baroque."[6] This volume is not the appropriate forum for addressing the question comprehensively. Its subjects, mostly connected with Italy, provide too narrow a sampling of intellectual voices outside of Italy, ignoring altogether Jewish intellectual life in Eastern Europe. But the intellectual profiles that are represented below do invite us to raise the question, at least tentatively. To what extent do these thinkers share a mentality, a self-image, an approach to Jewish and non-Jewish sources, and even a conscious sense of living in a unique age set apart from earlier ones? Are the individuals described in these pages themselves products of what we might call early modern Jewish culture? No doubt this introduction and the essays themselves probe these questions from a variety of perspectives.

From this, my second problem follows: What do we mean in this book by the "Jewish intellectuals" we describe? This is also a difficult question to answer unambiguously, given the fact that the authors do not approach their individual subjects with a shared and precise understanding of what constitutes a "Jewish intellectual" in this period. To begin by stating the obvious, the abstraction "Jewish intellectual" in any era of Jewish history might mean rabbi, halakhic scholar and decisor, preacher, religious thinker, philosopher, kabbalist, or even, in some cases, Hebraic teacher engaged with non-Jewish elite circles. However we might essentialize this role, many of the characteristics prevalent in previous ages can be located in the era in which these men thought and wrote. In other words, Jewish intellectuals of early modern Europe have much in common with their counterparts in other Jewish societies from antiquity until the fifteenth century. But, as this book hopes to illustrate, there is also something unique about the nature of Jewish intellectual life in the two centuries or so described here. To begin with, the intellectuals treated in these pages were not known especially for their expertise in Jewish legal matters. They were primarily engaged in the study of Jewish thought, as Adam Shear calls it in relation to Judah Moscato,[7] that is, in disciplines outside the traditional bounds of the halakhah such as kabbalah, rhetoric and historiography, scholastic and Neoplatonic philosophy, magic, medicine, the sciences, and even music. In trying to fathom why they were especially interested in and gained intellectual stature in these nonconventional and non-halakhic fields, we are simultaneously beginning to address the first question as well regarding the unique texture of Jewish culture in early modern Europe.

By way of an introduction to the essays that follow, I offer a sketch of recent notions about Jewish intellectual and cultural history in this era that might contextualize and draw out some of the unifying links between the thinkers treated below. I make no claim to be comprehensive; my emphasis reflects my own personal view as well as my own suggestions on how these essays might be read together in pointing to a collective cultural profile of an era.

I begin with two ideas recently put forward in two essays by Moshe Idel. One could also note that his important contribution in this volume follows directly from these earlier articulations, as we shall soon explore. In the first place, Idel proposes to look at the history of sixteenth-century kabbalistic thought through the notion of mobility.[8] Given the demographic upheavals that characterize Jewish life from the late fifteenth century on, specifically the movement of Jewish émigrés from west to east, it stands to reason that intellectual life reflects these calamitous and disruptive changes. The peripatetic scholar's wanderings surely influence the fluidity and reformulation of his thinking in the ever changing social and intellectual settings in which he works. Idel, in focusing exclusively on the kabbalistic scholar, also demonstrates the tensions between fluidity and adaptation with standardization and stabilization, the latter the ultimate conservative reaction to the radical nature of the former.

In a larger sense, mobility—intellectuals on the move, the notion of the refugee scholar, his encounter with new surroundings, the inevitable clashes emerging from the meeting between new and old intellectual elites, and the restructuring of Jewish social and intellectual life in the wake of this dynamic movement—clearly represents a leitmotif of our period and a crucial component for understanding cultural change in early modern Judaism.[9] The mobility of intellectuals is surely not unique to Jewish culture, but given the relatively dramatic uprooting of Jewish populations in this period due primarily to expulsions, this factor weighs heavily in assessing Jewish cultural change. Its importance is well exemplified in the intellectual formation of such figures as Amatus Lusitanus, Yoḥanan Alemanno, Elijah Delmedigo, and Leone Ebreo. The upheaval of the Spanish expulsion and its aftermath is critical in understanding the evolution of Lusitanus's and Ebreo's intellectual life. The restless wanderings of Alemanno and Delmedigo profoundly affect their professional careers and their writing.

Idel's second idea is hardly new but is well articulated by him in the context of Italian Jewish life, especially in such Renaissance centers as Florence, Venice, and Mantua.[10] It challenges the notion that Jews are fully free agents in constructing their own culture but rather are often shaped by the cultural tastes and intellectual agendas of Christian patrons and elites. If one looks at the interests of such figures as Delmedigo, Alemanno, and Ebreo, treated below, and the intimate relations these figures forge directly with Pico della Mirandola or indirectly with the larger intellectual ambience of Florence, their intellectual profiles are surely the direct products of these unique cultural encounters. This would even be more obvious in the case of the Italian Jewish playwright Leone Sommi, not treated in this volume,[11] or his colleague Salamone Rossi, the composer discussed below. In the case of these latter two, they simultaneously address two separate audiences of Jews and Christians; they are obliged to adopt two separate but interrelated identities; their bifurcated and ambivalent existences undoubtedly create personal tensions and internal struggles in correlating or integrating the one social world with the other. Are these dramatic cases typical or exceptional?[12] How might we compare them with analogous roles of medieval Spanish Jewish courtiers, for example? And are the Jewish intellectual contemporaries of Rossi, fellow

Jewish elites in Mantua such as Azariah de' Rossi, Judah Moscato, and David and Abraham Provenzali to be cast in the same mold? While the relationship between patron and Jewish subject is not as obvious in the case of these four, are their cultural interests fashioned directly by the larger political and social elites of Mantuan society? Given the intellectual and cultural interests of the Gonzaga family and their retinue, are we to understand the emergence of these Jewish polymaths in the same light as those employed directly by Christian patrons and courts?

The emphasis on Christian patronage as a factor in Jewish intellectual life needs to be balanced by an earlier and highly influential view of the historian Robert Bonfil. For Bonfil, one cannot reduce Jewish cultural production in this era to the pull of external influences alone. Bonfil demonstrates that the typical Jewish intellectual of this period was not marginal or peripheral to the Jewish community and its cultural concerns. Rabbis and communal leaders were at the center of intellectual creativity and cultural dialogue with the non-Jewish world, as the cases of Yeḥiel Nissim da Pisa, the Provenzali family, Judah Moscato, and many others illustrate. By seeing Jewish intellectual life as merely a reflection of the larger cultural milieu, a servile imitation of larger cultural trends orchestrated by the Christian elite, one distorts the nature of Jewish culture in this era and falsely dichotomizes the internal versus the external forces shaping Jewish identity, Bonfil argues.[13]

No doubt, Bonfil is right in underscoring the autonomy and "self-fashioning" of Jewish culture and in balancing the centripetal and centrifugal forces that determined Jewish culture in this era or in any era. But has he fully resolved this issue of patronage for Jewish culture, a theme of particular resonance for Renaissance cultural formation in general? Would such subjects as the kabbalah, in its particular adhesion to magic and philosophy, or rhetoric, grammar, and history be so important to some Jewish intellectuals if not for the regnant cultural tastes of their Christian interlocutors? Is Judah Messer Leon, for example, the author of the first Hebrew rhetorical handbook and the teacher of Yoḥanan Alemanno, driven by internal and conservative needs of his community or by the political and cultural forces of elite Christian society in proposing a radically new educational agenda for Jewish students?[14] As for the Provenzali a century later, discussed below, is rhetoric important to them as a value in its own right or as a simple defensive strategy, a mere tactical concession to a current fashion, provided only to preserve and strengthen the Jewish loyalty of their students? The case of Azariah de' Rossi, as Joanna Weinberg argues eloquently below, is even more complex. Is he primarily a Jewish apologist and polemicist with Christianity or is he indeed a true intellectual enamored equally of Christian and pagan books along with Jewish ones?[15] Does the writing of his highly learned tome reflect primarily his commitment to defending Jewish interests or to his more human quest for truth, no matter what the religious or ethnic source? Perhaps these two components of his identity cannot ultimately be severed from each other. These are not easy questions to answer unequivocally in the cases of Messer Leon and de' Rossi, as well as countless others, and the way their positions are interpreted by contemporary scholars often reflects their own subjective choices in privileging one factor over another.

Another facet of Jewish intellectual life in this era given prominence in recent scholarship is the role of Jewish doctors in shaping Jewish culture. If one includes in this category the privileged place of magic, occult philosophy, and the study of nature among Jewish intellectuals, the numbers, particularly in Italy, are not insignificant. Of particular importance is the number of rabbis also trained as doctors in Italy from the late sixteenth century on, particularly after the medical school of Padua and later other medical schools begin to accept Jewish students in larger numbers and with growing regularity. Jewish graduates of Italian medical schools together with converso doctors trained in Spain and Portugal ultimately shape a kind of informal fraternity of mutual professional and cultural interests, an elite trained in Latin studies and the natural sciences, that leaves its mark on Jewish culture, especially in Italy. Among the figures treated in this book, Alemanno and del Medigo, Leone Ebreo, Joseph ha-Kohen, the Provenzali, and, of course, Amatus Lusitanus exemplify the significance of this kind of professional training in the formation of Jewish civilization in this era.[16]

One might argue that all of the aforementioned dimensions of Jewish intellectual life in early modern Europe—mobility, patronage, the centrality of the rabbi as cultural producer, and even the mediating role of the Jewish magician/doctor—are not unique to this period and can also be located in ancient and medieval settings. This cannot be said of the next factor: the formation of Jewish intellectual life in an age of print. The print revolution long ago produced an entire subfield among European cultural historians. Only in recent years have scholars of the Jewish experience addressed the issue with the same insight and intensity.[17] The mass printing of books in Hebrew leaves its demonstrable impact on Jewish reading practices in a manner not unlike that of their Christian contemporaries. Nevertheless, one can also point to a number of culturally specific ways in which the printed book affected the production and dissemination of Jewish thought and literature. Beginning with the selection and publication of Hebrew books in a print shop, the era of the printed book unleashed new forces unexpected and unanticipated, including the reconfiguration of classic Jewish legal texts on pages surrounded with medieval commentaries; the collaboration between Christian printers and their Jewish associates; and the migration of regionally based writing such as those produced by Sephardic or Italian Jewish authors to parts far and wide, especially "invading" the relatively isolated communities in Ashkenazic Europe.[18]

Particularly relevant to the subject of this book is the impact of printed books on the scholarly Christian world. Recent scholarship has argued that from the sixteenth century on, Hebrew writers increasingly wrote with Christian as well as Jewish readers in mind. One of the clear results of the Catholic Church's efforts to censor Jewish books was to make Jews more sensitive to articulating themselves without defaming Christianity. In other words, the transformed conditions of the production and dissemination of Hebrew books helped to shape and transform social attitudes toward the "other," at least with regard to the Jewish side.[19] The remarkable popularity of Leone Ebreo's *Dialoghi*, regardless of the language in which it was originally written, could not be unrelated to the sanitized and respectful way in which Judaism and Christianity appear side by side. If the author had meant to polemicize with Christianity, as some argue, it went unnoticed to the many readers of this popular philosophical text.[20] In a similar manner, Azariah de' Rossi's erudite tome, whatever its apologetic or polemical purposes, presents Christianity and pagan learning in a most respectful manner. While some Jews objected to its conclusions, de' Rossi's Christian associates even thought the author could be induced to convert to Christianity.[21] Other Hebrew writers who discuss Christianity, such as Elijah Delmedigo, do so in veiled language, fully sensitive to the need to obfuscate any offensive statements.

As the case of Leone Ebreo makes clear, another result of the success of the printing press was the enhanced availability among Jews of books in the vernacular. Ebreo intended to write for a readership of both Jews and Christians, and later writers such as Jacob Mantino, Abraham de Balmes, Leon Modena, Simone Luzzatto, and David de' Pomis followed suit. In the early modern period, Jewish authors felt the need to alter public opinion by addressing an audience beyond their own coreligionists. In this new age of printing, whether they wrote in Hebrew or in Italian or Latin, they assumed that Jewish culture was becoming "an open book." And the book culture of printing shops, translators, editors, and readers became an essential factor in the consciousness of any serious Jewish scholar, as the cases of Amatus Lusitanus and Azariah de' Rossi make abundantly clear.

Beyond the direct impact of the new technology is a growing cultural awareness on the part of Jewish intellectuals of the multiple sources of human knowledge and experience. Bombarded by new books in print, they, like other readers, look beyond their own religious heritage to expand their cultural horizons, to integrate and correlate the vast range of sources and ideas now available to them with those of their own intellectual legacy. I have in mind the image of the *ḥakham kolel* as articulated so boldly by Judah Messer Leon. For him, learning alone without rhetorical skill does not make the wise man in Jewish society. The role of the Jewish intellectual, as he understands it, is to retrieve all of world literature as a means of restoring and recuperating what was once Israel's alone. I would contend that for Messer Leon and other Jewish scholars, this means more than a rhetorical strategy or a kind of orthodox apologetics, as one scholar has argued.[22] For the Jewish intellectuals documented in this book, no external sources, no matter what their provenance, are prohibited. Alemanno masters the art of magic;[23] his student Abraham Yagel reads and copies Cornelius Agrippa.[24] The Ottoman Jewish scholar Joseph Taitaichak regularly cites the Christian scholastics,[25] while Tobias Cohen discovers the library of the Paracelsians.[26] The great polymaths, from Abraham Portaleone to Judah Moscato and Azariah de' Rossi, make erudition in multiple sources an aesthetic value in itself, even where integration of so vast an array of sources and ideas seems impossible. The impression Moshe Idel draws from studying Moscato's highly technical and convoluted sermons, that the Jewish center of gravity appears in danger of collapsing due to the sheer weight of the authorities that its erudite author chose to cite, might also characterize the writing of some of his other contemporaries.[27] Certainly, in the case of Abraham Yagel, the uninhibited citation of pagan authors, specifically Hermes and the "ancient theologians," might have theological consequences as well in making the insights of the Torah and the pagan philosophers virtually equivalent, as he readily admits.[28]

Given the new intellectual style of the Jewish savant of the sixteenth and seventeenth centuries, the encyclopedia becomes a newly enhanced vehicle of presenting multiple truths and multiple sources without prioritizing one over the other. Surely this genre of writing is preferred by Alemanno and Yagel, but also by Joseph Delmedigo, David de' Pomis, and Abraham Portaleone.[29] And if Adam Shear is correct, Moscato's commentary on the *Kuzari* also exhibits an encyclopedic form of presentation.

This same tendency to gather disparate sources under one intellectual roof, so to speak, defines kabbalistic studies in Italy, as Moshe Idel has argued and continues to argue in his essay below. Scholars in Italy study kabbalistic sources autodidactically in a highly individualized manner. There is no definitive curriculum of study and no institutionalized way of transmitting specific kabbalistic texts and doctrines. Moreover, the kabbalah is never studied in isolation but always correlated with other sources of knowledge.[30] Even the untamed and mythical Lurianic corpus is translated into an occult philosophy, made to cohere to other esoteric and occult ways of thinking through the interpretive "grid" of Italian Jewish kabbalists. Surely this kind of "strong reading" employed by the kabbalistic scholar could be powerfully explosive and unsettling.[31] In this respect, Jewish and Christian scholars in early modern Europe had much in common in their exploration of new worlds through ancient esoteric texts. As Anthony Grafton has pointed out, the ancient heritage of these texts harbored many mutually subversive ways of defining cultural self-identity in relation to the "other."[32] For Jewish as well as Christian students of the kabbalah, the sheer combination of an elastic and pliable hermeneutic conjoined with other ancient Christian and pagan texts could potentially produce a most unstable and radical reinterpretation of Judaism and Christianity.

Another by-product of the new reading and interpretative practices of Jewish intellectuals in early modern Europe was their apparent need to write in differing styles for differing audiences. Perhaps this situation is hardly unique for this period, if one takes into account Leo Strauss's notion of the direct relationship between persecution and the style of self-presentation in reading the Maimonidean corpus and other ancient and medieval writing.[33] Nevertheless, as Perez Zagorin and others have argued, the early modern age was the quintessential epoch of dissimulation, an age when the fear of political suppression obliged authors and publishers to camouflage their true intentions in the public forum of the printed book.[34] Surely, the controversy over how to read Elijah Delmedigo's Hebrew and Latin writing has much to do with the author's conscious effort to obscure his true intentions from his readers. A similar observation could be made about Leone Ebreo's classic. And more than a century later, the Venetian circle of Leon Modena, Simone Luzzatto, and Joseph Delmedigo also wrote in a manner meant to obscure their authentic positions. Modena could simultaneously critique and defend the oral law, as Talya Fishman has well argued.[35] Simone Luzzatto could offer a full-fledged skepticism while presenting himself as a man of faith, while Joseph Delmedigo could juxtapose ideas both critical and receptive to kabbalistic theosophy.[36] In hiding their actual intentions, they appear to deviate from and even subvert traditional normative values. At the very least, among these three highly influential thinkers in close association with one another, there is undoubtedly a crisis of conscience, a breakdown of cohesion between Jewish authoritative texts and other sources of knowledge. Such thinkers are as complex in the presentation of their true selves as Bodin, Rabelais, Campanella, and Bruno. Particularly when they write in two different languages for two distinct audiences, as in the case of all three, their messages are often altered and their ambivalences are even more apparent.

My final consideration is of a different sort. The Jewish scholar of our period lived and worked in a new social setting where previous religious and cultural boundaries were blurring and even breaking apart as new social opportunities for the exchange of ideas and dialogue were emerging. I refer first to the new forms of intellectual sociability within the Jewish community itself: the new intellectual fellowship of Jewish medical graduates mentioned above, along with the swelling number of converso physicians appearing in Italy and northern Europe;[37] the new structures of social interaction manifested in the proliferation of *ḥevrot*, voluntary confraternities, and their creative restructuring of Jewish time and space, to borrow the language of Robert Bonfil;[38] and also the social and cultural intermingling of Jews and former conversos "rehabilitated" and reintegrated into the Jewish communities of Italy, the Ottoman Empire, and the North.[39]

But I am also referring to an even more decisive phenomenon: the new social encounters between Jews and Christians and their converso mediators. In these new settings, rules of social and intellectual engagement are reformulated and adjusted, and new possibilities and challenges for cross-cultural dialogue emerge. We might begin by noting a relatively new phenomenon from the late fifteenth century on: the emergence of the Jewish scholar who sees his role secondarily—or, in some cases, primarily—as a teacher of Christians.[40] Though it is clearly not a "mission" idea to inculcate the larger world with Jewish truths one might nevertheless uncover the kernel of the idea that not only is it permissible to teach non-Jews, but that through such encounters, the teachings of Judaism will circulate more widely among non-Jewish populations. While grounded in the Maimonidean notion of an ultimate universalization of the Jewish notion of the one God, Judah del Bene's much later embrace of the Catholic mission as a means of propagating the truths of Judaism is surely a manifestation of a new consciousness and a new realignment between Judaism and Catholicism in early modern Italy.[41]

No doubt such personal interactions between Jews and Christians were often accompanied by hesitation, self-doubt, and even criticism in light of the lurking dangers such intimacy might entail. This is certainly the case in the unique relationships Pico developed with Elijah Delmedigo and Yoḥanan Alemanno, discussed fully in the chapters of Lelli and Hames. Elijah Levitas's long-standing relation with Egidio of Viterbo emerges in a context similar to that of the Pico circle: the search for Christian truths embedded in Jewish writing, especially its esoteric variety.[42] But these more publicized encounters are only the tip of the iceberg. By definition, it would seem, a Jewish intellectual, at least in Italy, could expect to engage in conversation on a regular basis with his Christian counterparts who might turn to him for Jewish instruction. Such meetings were often conducted under duress and recrimination, as the life experiences of Joseph ha-Kohen and Azariah de' Rossi with conversionary pressures amply suggest. Nevertheless, the terms under which Jewish intellectuals were meeting with their counterparts in the Christian community were clearly changing.

The teacher-student relationship was not the only way in which Jews and Christians engaged. They also met in courtly settings, on university campuses, and in print shops. The process unleashed in the Florentine circles of Pico and Ficino extended to other Italian centers, such as Mantua and Venice. It intensified well into the seventeenth and eighteenth centuries in the Amsterdam circles of Menasseh ben Israel and Orobrio de Castro and even to the London associations of Jewish and Christian Freemasons.

The ultimate result of these accelerated social encounters between Jewish and Christian intellectuals along with the rapid dissemination of Jewish scholarly books in Hebrew and other languages was the emergence of a relatively unprecedented phenomenon: an emerging community of Christian scholars who claimed expertise in Hebraic books and Jewish learning. Over the course of several centuries, this community insisted on translating Judaism into a language accessible and meaningful to Christians alone, independent and oblivious to Jewish sensibilities. From the postbiblical library that Flavius Mithridates translated for Pico in fifteenth-century Florence to the pathbreaking Hebraic scholarship of Münster, Buxdorf, and von Rosenroth in the sixteenth and seventeenth centuries, the Jewish scholar found himself, as time went on, in the increasingly uncomfortable position of being displaced or being ignored. Although in the beginning of this period, the Jewish scholar, or at least a recently converted Jew, was indispensable to the process of Christian self-discovery, by its end, Christians had claimed sufficient mastery of Hebrew and adequate knowledge of Jewish sources to reflect on Judaism through their own resources and their own abilities.[43]

In the Middle Ages, the Jewish intellectual was a primary mediator between Islamic and Christian culture; his expertise in Judaism per se was less important than his ability to translate and transmit the Western classic tradition in Islamic garb into the Latin West. In the early modern period, Elijah Delmedigo and Jacob Mantino, acknowledged experts of the Aristotelian tradition, represented the last of this dying breed. Instead of classical and Islamic sources, Christian scholars, as we have said, became increasingly fascinated by the Jewish sources of Western civilizations, from Pico's library of medieval Jewish exegetes to Reuchlin's kabbalistic sources, from Abendanda's Mishnah to Buxdorf's *Kuzari* and other Christian appropriations of Maimonides' political views.[44] But paradoxically, the role of the Jewish intellectual was not necessarily enhanced by this new appreciation of Judaism, but rather diminished. Instead of relying on Jews for this knowledge, Christians reclaimed the prerogative of Jewish literacy for themselves.

For the Jewish scholar of early modern Europe, Christian Hebraism became a new factor in his intellectual and psychological development. He now had to live with the unsettling fact that Christians, to an unprecedented degree, could master his traditions without recourse to Jews. The Jewish intellectual could ignore his Christian rival, could choose to collaborate with him, or could even embrace his assumptions, at least partially, in studying Judaism. As in the case of Pico and his Jewish interlocutors, Jewish responses could vary from outright condemnation, for Elijah Delmedigo and Leon Modena, to open embrace, for Flavius Mithridates.[45] And from Pico, Johann Reuchlin, and Sebastian Münster in the fifteenth and early sixteenth centuries, to Benjamin Kennicott, Robert Lowth, and Johann David Michaelis at the end of the eighteenth century,[46] Jews faced a formidable challenge that would continue to plague them for centuries to come. They were no longer the sole arbiters of the sacred texts of the Jewish tradition, and certainly not of the Hebrew Bible. In the new cultural space populated by Christian Hebraists and converts, Jewish scholars were surely losing their hegemony over the interpretation of their own texts and their own traditions. Henry More, to cite only one ludicrous example, could presume to speak authoritatively about the cabbala (with a *c*) without having examined any original kabbalistic text and certainly without having encountered a Jewish kabbalist.[47]

In the intellectual world that we have inherited from the most learned of these Christian Hebraists, their notion that Jewish learning and Jewish texts are hardly the sole possession of Jews alone has increasingly left its mark on modern academic life, and particularly the academic study of Jewish culture in the great universities of the world. The significance of Talmud Torah without Jews might appear to be a natural and expected consequence of the ambience created by the secular university. Yet from the perspective of traditional Jewish culture, it might appear abnormal and bizarre. It is indeed the legacy of early modern culture, which first transformed the seemingly abnormal into the normal as the religious and ethnic affiliation of the Judaic studies scholar became thoroughly irrelevant. To what extent the new scholars of Jewish civilization—especially those in North America and Europe, the legitimate descendants of the first Christian Hebraists—have transformed the way Christians perceive Jews and Judaism, and the way Jews perceive Christians and Christianity, and how each group perceives its own identity in our own new century still remains an open question for those who will follow us.

* * *

Having offered these general observations about the distinct nature of Jewish intellectual life emerging in early modern Europe, I now turn to the individual essays that make up this volume, offering a preliminary orientation to each while highlighting their connections to the larger picture I have proposed as well as to one another.

Fabrizio Lelli's study of Yoḥanan Alemanno represents the first of three essays related to the particular cultural ambience of Neoplatonism, humanism, and magic that characterized Florence's intellectual circles. Alemanno is particularly important because of his special relationship with Pico della Mirandola, a relationship built on their mutual interests in magic and kabbalah. Lelli situates Alemanno's Hebrew biography of King Solomon both in the literary contexts of humanist production and the rhetorical curriculum proposed by his own Jewish teacher Judah Messer Leon. But Alemanno's work, as Lelli skillfully shows, is more than a biography of an ancient sage; it describes Alemanno's self-perception as a perfect teacher of mundane and divine knowledge to Pico and other illustrious students. In opening the book with the imposing figure of Alemanno, we are already introduced to an extraordinary scholar whose claim to fame rests on his ability to impart Jewish arcane knowledge to a Christian elite circle.

Harvey Hames's study of Elijah Delmedigo nicely parallels that of Lelli in treating the other Jewish pedagogue of Pico. Delmedigo, like Alemanno, possessed a similar sense of self-importance because of his expertise in Aristotelian/Averroist texts that enhanced his intellectual status in the Christian world. But Delmedigo, unlike Alemanno, was hardly at ease with his Christian interactions. Especially in his Hebrew philosophical work *Beḥinat hadat*, composed in Crete after he had essentially concluded his contacts with Pico and his Christian interlocutors, he offers a rather negative assessment of Neoplatonism, Christianity, magic, and the use of the kabbalah by Christians for their own spiritual purposes. Challenging previous scholarship regarding Delmedigo's commitment to Averroës or to philosophy in general, Hames sees this Jewish philosopher as ultimately espousing a complete commitment to Jewish law and the commandments while questioning the need to rationalize the Jewish faith. Philosophic notions could be utilized to critique Christianity, but they play no role in establishing the truth of Judaism for Delmedigo.

Giuseppe Veltri's essay on Leone Ebreo reevaluates his famous *Dialoghi d'amore* as a work of Jewish philosophy, situating its origin in the same circles of Pico and especially Ficino, to whom Leone is particularly indebted. While the consciousness of being a Jew informs his speculations, this seems not to have offended the cultural sensibilities of his many Christian readers. Even Leone's understanding of the Jewish origins of Aristotelian and Platonic notions seems to have left his readership untroubled. For Christian readers, Veltri argues, the philosophical import of the book was not great, despite the fact that Jewish readers attributed significance to its intellectual contribution. If he was polemicizing with Christianity, as some have claimed, his arguments were too pale to be noticed or to cause offense. Christians generally ignored the Jewish origin of the author to enjoy a pleasant, understandable, and aesthetically pleasing text. Like Delmedigo and Alemanno, Leone held himself in high esteem because of his status in the Christian world, as his Hebrew poem cited by Veltri testifies. He had succeeded, like no other Jewish author in the Renaissance, in translating Jewish knowledge into a universal key in such a way as to temporarily mitigate the tension between Judaism and Christianity.

In sharp contrast, Leone's contemporary Joseph ha-Kohen, the subject of Martin Jacobs's essay, expressed in his writings the cultural tension of living as a Jew in a Christian world. In Jacobs's account of his reliance on two Italian historians—Paolo Giovio and Andrea Cambini—to construct his historical narrative of the Hapsburg and Ottoman Empires, it is his deep sense of Jewish identity in conflict with the Christian majority that shapes his understanding of the past and present. Ha-Kohen attributes divine intervention to the fall of Constantinople or to the military defeats of Andrea Doria; God punishes Christian leaders for their poor treatment of the Jews. Despite ha-Kohen's access to the new historical sources that he employs, his failure to integrate them into his own historical understanding is evident, and his modern appreciation of history and geography is mediated through his powerful sense of alienation from Christian society. As Jacobs puts it, ha-Kohen well illustrates the ambivalent status of a Jewish intellectual who had access to new printed sources of knowledge but whose negative social interactions with Christian society, especially the painful apostasy of his own brother, drove him to see historical events differently from the way his humanist counterparts did.

Yeḥiel Nissim da Pisa offers a different kind of cultural ambivalence from that of Joseph ha-Kohen, in the portrait offered by Alessandro Guetta. His modern consciousness, Guetta argues, emerges in his critique of the old-style rationalism of the Aristotelian schools to which he still remains indebted, together with his fascination with kabbalah, magic, and the intellectual interests emanating from the Florentine ambience. Like Hames's Delmedigo, Yeḥiel ultimately prioritizes the observance of ritual commandments over any speculative philosophy. Unlike his Jewish contemporaries Ovadiah Sforno and Moses Provenzali, Yeḥiel had given up wrestling with Aristotelian notions of Judaism. His Jewish theology emerges ambiguously between philosophy and kabbalah and with a clear awareness of the importance of the positive content of ritual observance. The eclectic and oscillating character of his reflections patently reveals the complexity of his negotiations with the intellectual styles and sources of his cultural world.

On the surface, one might discover the same complexities and oscillations in Azariah de' Rossi's astonishingly erudite and massive *Me'or einayim.* Yet in Joanna Weinberg's estimation, his remarkable mastery of three civilizations—the Jewish, the Christian, and the pagan—reveals a consistent mode of inquiry: the unrepentant search for truth. De' Rossi is surely a committed Jew, fully aware of the pitfalls and lurking dangers for Jews living in the Christian society he inhabits in Mantua. But in contrast to Joseph ha-Kohen and Yeḥiel Nissim da Pisa, he is neither alienated from his cultural surroundings nor fragmented in the way he understands truth. He writes in Italian for Christians and in Hebrew for Jews, but ultimately does not erect barriers between his Jewish and non-Jewish realms. It is his commitment to scholarship that moves him to correct simultaneously ancient Jewish and Christian sources. As Weinberg puts it, he not only absorbs the scholarly legacy of his non-Jewish environment; he makes it his own. His citations of Petrarch and Virgil reveal a personal connection to the Italian classical heritage; his disquisition on the inscription of the cross suggests that no intellectual subject, even gazing on Christian religious images, remains outside his scholarly purview.

De' Rossi's Jewish contemporaries in Mantua, David and Abraham Provenzali, offer a related but somewhat more ambivalent attitude toward their cultural surroundings. In Gianfranco Miletto's study of a broadsheet they circulated in order to raise support for a Jewish academy in Mantua, their broad cultural commitments are apparent. They reveal a genuine commitment to an expanded curriculum of Jewish studies fully integrated with the humanities and the sciences. The kind of erudition that de' Rossi displayed on every page of his scholarly works was surely an ideal to which they aspired. But the intellectual integration they sought was tempered by the instability that the Counter Reformation had injected into Jewish-Christian relations through the recent burning of the Talmud and in the erection of a new ghetto system throughout Italy. The school they proposed was meant not only to expand cultural horizons for Jewish students but to safeguard their souls from the enticement offered by a Christian university. But ironically, as Miletto convincingly argues, their program unconsciously reflects the values and pedagogical ideals of Jesuit education. That combination of wide-ranging learning accompanied by special attention to the inculcation of proper religious and moral attitudes marked their vision and that of their Christian counterparts. In distancing themselves from the encroachments of Christian society, they were paradoxically drawing closer to it in shaping a kind of Jesuit/Jewish mentality.

Their Mantuan neighbor Judah Moscato, the subject of Adam Shear's essay, presents another example of the robust and complex intellectual world of sixteenth-century Jewish society. Like de' Rossi, the Provenzali, Judah del Bene, Abraham Portaleone, and other contemporary members of this Jewish elite, Moscato displays a remarkable erudition in classical, medieval, and Renaissance thought. He moves easily between Renaissance humanist interests in rhetoric and grammar to Maimonidean philosophy in his encyclopedic commentary on Judah Halevi. By writing a massive interpretation of a medieval text, he redefines the notion of a classic in Jewish culture to include medieval writings. Moreover, he produces not a mere reiteration of Halevi's philosophy but a Renaissance version of the author, a synthesis of medieval scholasticism, Renaissance Neoplatonism, and humanism, along with a strong sense of Jewish particularism and cultural confidence. Moscato, like the other thinkers treated in this volume, is an expert in Jewish thought, not in legal rabbinics. His rabbinic role is that of a cultural mediator, of locating correspondences between differing Jewish viewpoints (Halevi and Maimonides) and between Jewish, Christian, and pagan civilizations. In this sense, Moscato aligned himself with the values and priorities of Azariah de' Rossi.

Don Harrán's dual perspectives on the other de' Rossi of Mantua, the musical composer Salamone—as a Jew among Jews and as a Jew among Christians—broaden and deepen our examination of Mantuan Jewish culture at the end of the sixteenth century. Salamone was clearly different from the other thinkers in this volume, because of his musical specialization. But in the duality of his professional and personal lives, and in his obvious contacts, both social and intellectual with Jewish thinkers, he shares with them a lifestyle and intellectual commitments. His actual collaboration with Leon Modena, on the one hand, and the evidence of musical interests of Abraham Portaleone and Judah Moscato, as reflected in their writings, on the other, suggest his sense of connectedness with the others described in this book. Harrán masterfully shows how Rossi's great success as a composer and performer was complicated by his Jewish identity, and how his Jewish perspective might have informed even his most secular compositions. His movement between two cultures, as Harrán puts it, combines but never fuses the poles of his activities and life. His associations with Jews and Gentiles and with Jewish and European culture are always shifting and vacillating, remarkable for their degree of integration against the backdrop of social discomfort and cultural tension. Rossi's world surely parallels the various degrees of integration and dissonance we have encountered in the lives of ha-Kohen, de' Rossi, Leone Ebreo, and the others.

In turning to Amatus Lusitanus, we finally encounter an intellectual whose social and cultural existence was not shaped solely on Italian soil. Despite Lusitanus's residency in Ferrara, Eleazer Gutwirth sees him especially in his Iberian and Ottoman contexts. Lusitanus is primarily a Portuguese exile who writes for and reflects the world of Ottoman Jewish reading communities. Gutwirth laments that Lusitanus has been treated only in a fragmented and incomplete way, primarily by historians of his medical writings. To reconstruct him from a multidimensional viewpoint, Gutwirth explores his social contacts with other Jews and conversos, especially the way his professional medical writings reflect his larger cultural concerns. When one reads his medical observations imaginatively and broadly, as Gutwirth demonstrates, Lusitanus's larger social and cultural interests are manifest. What emerges dramatically are his strong ties to Spain and Portugal; his Jewish and converso cultural habits; his secular use of Jewish texts; his reading tastes and fascination with books, editions, editors, and authors; and especially his sense of history and chronology in the medical histories, all of these overshadowing his narrow professional interests as a physician. In moving beyond Italy, Gutwirth is able to demonstrate Ottoman Jewish humanism, differentiating Lusitanus's cultural experience from that of the others in this volume but also connecting their intellectual priorities with his. His chapter underscores the close connection between humanism, medicine, and Jewish identity, which is also exemplified by several other thinkers included in this volume.

In closing this volume, Moshe Idel departs from the book's format of focusing on individuals to consider the broader question of cultural transmission, that between Safed and Italy. He argues—against the grain of previous scholarship—that the ultimate impact of the creative revival of kabbalistic writing in Safed is hardly its "triumphant conquest" of Italian Jewish culture, but rather its transformation through the intellectual "grid" and the "strong reading" of those Italian Jews who first came into contact with it and virtually reinterpreted it. In their reading, they transposed a mythical, theurgic, and messianic kabbalah into an occult philosophy, closer to Neoplatonic and magical ways of thinking, and more in line with Renaissance and early modern European thought. In Italy, the particularistic systems of Luria and Cordovero became more universal, more open to Christianity, more positively inclined to philosophy. Despite Safed's negative assessment of Christian kabbalists, Lurianic texts and notions were paradoxically embraced and disseminated by them. Thus the ultimate product of Safedian creativity and spirituality and its impact on both the Jewish and Christian worlds can only be appreciated through the prism of Italian Jewish reading and reinterpretation, through the transformative transmission this lore underwent through its Italian Jewish mediation.

Idel closes this essay by returning to an old scholarly question that he had addressed in the past: whether one can speak of a Jewish Renaissance in Italy. Previously, Idel had answered the question by demarcating between an early period (1470–1550), primarily in Florence, of cultural contribution and consumption among Jewish kabbalist thinkers, and a later period, after 1550, primarily of consumption. In his present formulation, however, Idel sees the filtering and adaptation of Safedian kabbalah as a creative function of Italian Jewish thinkers long after 1550. By bringing together divergent forms of knowledge and creating a new complex interplay between their own culture and that of Safed, they performed a mediating role not unlike that of Pico and other Christian intellectuals in Renaissance Italy.

We might add in concluding that in viewing the cultural role of Italian Jewish thinkers as essentially reinterpreting and reconfiguring Safedian kabbalah, Idel reinforces more generally the centrality of Italy in the restructuring of Jewish intellectual life in the sixteenth and seventeenth centuries. Rather than a mere transit stop between West and East, or a passive dumping ground of the cultural remains of the stronger cultures of Jewish émigrés, Italy assumes, in this perspective, a clear and unique cultural role in its natural tendencies toward correlation, integration, and reinterpretation.[48] By defining the primary characteristic of Italian Jewish thought as one of cross-cultural dialogue between disparate Jewish identities and between Jewish and Christian ones, and of translation and transmission of one cultural language into another, we have perhaps captured the most enduring legacy of the intellectuals described in this book and their contribution in shaping Jewish intellectual life in early modern Europe.

Notes

1. The possibility also existed for interaction with Muslims, especially for the ones living in the Ottoman Empire, but this does not seem to be a significant factor in the cases of the thinkers treated in this volume.

2. This is not the place to offer full bibliographical references. For books in English until 1995, see the subsection on the early modern period in D. Ruderman, "Medieval and Modern Jewish History," in *American Historical Association Guide to Historical Literature* (New York, 1995); also see the bibliographies in R. Bonfil, *Jewish*

Life in Renaissance Italy (Berkeley, Calif., 1994), and in A. Foa, *The Jews of Europe After the Black Death* (Berkeley, Calif., 2000); and *Storia d'Italia: Gli ebrei in Italia*, ed. C. Vivanti, 2 vols. (Turin, 1996). For additional references, see the next note.

3. I refer to D. Ruderman, ed., *Essential Papers on Jewish Culture in Renaissance and Baroque Italy* (New York, 1992).

4. J. Israel, *European Jewry in the Age of Mercantilism 1550–1750*, 3d ed. (London, 1998). See also J. Edwards, *The Jews in Christian Europe 1400–1700* (London, 1988); and R. Bonfil, "Lo spazio culturale degli ebrei d'Italia fra Rinascimento ed età barocca," in *Gli ebrei in Italia*, ed. Vivanti, pp. 413–73.

5. See Foa, *The Jews of Europe.*

6. See Bonfil, *Jewish Life in Renaissance Italy*; and the earlier work of C. Roth, *The Jews in the Renaissance* (New York, 1959). On Jewish culture in the baroque period, see G. Sermoneta, "Aspetti del pensiero moderno nell'ebraismo *italiano* tra Rinascimento *ed* età barocca," in *Italia Judaica: Gli ebrei in Italia tra Rinascimento ed età barocca* (Rome, 1986), pp. 17–35; D. Ruderman, *A Valley of Vision: The Heavenly Journey of Abraham ben Hananiah Yagel* (Philadelphia, 1990), pp. 65–68; and Bonfil, "Lo spazio culturale."

7. See Adam Shear's essay in this volume.

8. M. Idel, "On Mobility, Individuals and Groups: Prolegomenon for a Sociological Approach to Sixteenth-Century Kabbalah," *Kabbalah: Journal for the Study of Jewish Mystical Texts* 3 (1998): 145–73.

9. See, for example, N. Canny, ed., *Europeans on the Move: Studies in European Migration 1500–1800* (Oxford, 1994); S. Cavaciocchi, ed., *Le migrazioni in Europa secoli XIII-XVIII* (Florence, 1994); H. Kamen, *Early Modern European Society* (London, 2000), pp. 40–51. See also Y. H. Yerushalmi, "Exile and Expulsion in Jewish History," *Crisis and Creativity in the Sefardi World 1391–1648*, ed. B. Gampel (New York, 1997), pp. 3–22.

10. M. Idel, "Jewish Mystical Thought in the Florence of Lorenzo il Magnifico," in *La cultura ebraica all'epoca di Lorenzo il Magnifico*, ed. D. Liscia Bemporad and I. Zatelli (Florence, 1998), pp. 17–42.

11. On Leone Sommi, see, for example, D. Harrán, "Jewish Dramatists and Musicians in the Renaissance: Separate Activities, Common Aspirations," *Musicologia Humana: Studies in Honor of Warren and Ursula Kirkendale*, ed. S. Gmeinwieser, D. Hiley, and J. Riedlbauer (Florence, 1994), pp. 291–304; Bonfil, "Lo spazio culturale," pp. 457–72.

12. Bonfil sees them as exceptional. See the previous note.

13. In addition to Bonfil's *Jewish Life in Renaissance Italy*, see his *Rabbis and Jewish Communities in Renaissance Italy* (Oxford, 1990); idem "The Historian's Perception of the Jews in Renaissance Italy: Toward a Reappraisal," *Revue des études juives* 134 (1984): 59–82.

14. Note the contrasting positions in R. Bonfil, introduction to the facsimile edition of *Nofet ṣufim* (Jerusalem, 1981), with his later essay "The Book of the Honeycomb's Flow by Judah Messer Leon: The Rhetorical Dimension of Jewish Humanism in Fifteenth-Century Italy," *Jewish History* (Frank Talmage Memorial Volume) 6 (1992):21–33.

15. For a different reading of de' Rossi, underscoring his apologetic and polemical concerns, see R. Bonfil, "Some Reflections on the Place of Azariah de Rossi's *Meor Enayim* in the Cultural Milieu of Italian Renaissance Jewry," in *Jewish Thought in the Sixteenth Century*, ed. B. Cooperman (Cambridge, Mass., 1983), pp. 23–48; Bonfil, ed., *Kitvei Azariah min ha'-adumim* (Jerusalem, 1991), pp. 11–129.

16. See, especially, D. Ruderman, *Kabbalah, Magic, and Science: The Cultural Universe of a Sixteenth-Century Jewish Physician* (Cambridge, Mass., 1988); Ruderman, *Jewish Thought and Scientific Discovery in Early Modern Europe*, 2d ed. (Detroit, 2001).

17. See, for example, M. Lowry, "Printing and Publishing," in *Encyclopedia of the Renaissance*, ed. P.F. Grendler (New York, 1999), 5:161–69, and the extensive bibliography listed there, beginning with E. Eisenstein, *The Printing Press as an Agent of Change* (Cambridge, 1979). On print in Jewish culture, see the summary and bibliography of A. Raz-Krakotzkin, "Print and Jewish Cultural Development," in *Encyclopedia of the Renaissance*, ed. Grendler, 3:344–46.

18. See the bibliography of Raz-Krakotzkin in the previous note, and note, especially, E. Reiner, "The Ashkenazic Elite at the Beginning of the Modern Era: Manuscript versus Printed Book," in *Jews in Early Modern Poland (=Polin)*, ed. G. Hundert (London, 1997), 10:85–98.

19. On this, see the Hebrew book of A. Raz-Krakotzkin, *The Censor, the Editor, and the Text: The Catholic Censor and Hebrew Printing in the Sixteenth Century* (Jerusalem, 2004).

20. See G. Veltri's discussion of this point below.

21. See J. Weinberg, "Azariah de' Rossi: Towards a Reappraisal of the Last Years of His Life," *Annali della Scuola Normale di Pisa* ser. 3, 8 (1978):493–511.

22. I refer to Robert Bonfil's later analysis of this book, "The Book of the Honeycomb's Flow," mentioned in note 14 above.

23. See M. Idel, "The Magical and Neoplatonic Interpretations of the Kabbalah in the Renaissance," in *Essential Papers*, ed. Ruderman, pp. 107–69.

24. See Ruderman, *Kabbalah, Magic, and Science*, pp. 144–50.

25. G. Sermoneta, "The Philosophical Scholastic Literature in the Book *Porat Yosef* of R. Joseph Taitaichak" (Hebrew), *Sefunot* 11 [=Sefer Yavan 1] (1971–78): 135–85.

26. See Ruderman, *Jewish Thought*, pp. 229–55.

27. M. Idel, "Judah Moscato: A Late Renaissance Jewish Preacher," in *Preachers of the Italian Ghetto*, ed. D. Ruderman (Berkeley, Calif., 1992), pp. 41–66.

28. See Ruderman, *Kabbalah, Magic, and Science*, pp. 139–60.

29. See A. Melamed, "Hebrew Italian Renaissance and Early Modern Encyclopedias," *Rivista di storia della filosofia* 40 (1985):91–112; and see Adam Shear's discussion of this genre below.

30. In addition to his essay below, see M. Idel, "Particularism and Universalism in Kabbalah, 1480–1650," and "Major Currents in Italian Kabbalah between 1560 and 1660," both in *Essential Papers*, ed. Ruderman, pp. 324–44, 345–72.

31. The terms "grid" and "strong reading" are employed by Idel in his essay below.

32. This is a central theme of A. Grafton (with A. Shelford and N. Siraisi), *New*

Worlds, Ancient Texts: The Power of Tradition and the Shock of Discovery (Cambridge, Mass., 1992).

33. L. Strauss, *Persecution and the Art of Writing* (Glencoe, Ill., 1952).

34. P. Zagorin, *Ways of Lying: Dissimulation, Persecution, and Conformity in Early Modern Europe* (Cambridge, Mass., 1990).

35. T. Fishman, *Shaking the Pillars of Exile: "Voice of a Fool," an Early Modern Jewish Critique of Rabbinic Culture* (Stanford, Calif., 1997).

36. See Ruderman, *Jewish Thought*, pp. 118–84.

37. Ibid., 100–117.

38. See R. Bonfil, "Changes in the Cultural Patterns of a Jewish Society in Crisis: Italian Jewry at the Close of the Sixteenth Century," in *Essential Papers*, ed. Ruderman, pp. 401–28.

39. See, generally, Y. Kaplan, *An Alternative Path to Modernity: The Sephardi Diaspora in Western Europe* (Leiden, 2000).

40. See, for example, D. Kaufmann, "Elia Menaḥem Chalfan on Jews Teaching Hebrew to Non-Jews," *Jewish Quarterly Review*, o.s., 9 (1896):500–508; D. Ruderman, *The World of a Renaissance Jew: The Life and Thought of Abraham ben Mordecai Farissol* (Cincinnati, 1981), pp. 98–106.

41. See R. Bonfil, "Preaching as Mediation Between Elite and Popular Culture," in *Jewish Preachers of the Italian Ghetto*, ed. Ruderman, pp. 67–88; and Ruderman, *Jewish Thought*, pp. 185–98.

42. See E. Weil, *Elie Levita: Humaniste et massorete (1469–1549)* (Leiden, 1963).

43. On the phenomenon of Christian Hebraism in early modern Europe, see, for now, F. Manuel, *The Broken Staff: Judaism Through Christian Eyes* (Cambridge, Mass., 1992); and Y. Deutsch, "A View of the Jewish Religion: Conceptions of Jewish Practice and Ritual in Early Modern Europe," *Archiv für Religionsgeschichte* 3 (2001):237–95, and the extensive bibliography he supplies in his notes. See also A. Coudert and J. Shoulson, eds., *Hebraica Veritas? Christian Hebraists and the Study of Judaism in Early Modern Europe* (Philadelphia, 2004).

44. All these examples are described by Manuel in *The Broken Staff*.

45. See, for example, Ruderman, *The World of a Renaissance Jew*, chap. 4.

46. On Kennicott and Lowth, see D. Ruderman, *Jewish Enlightenment in an English Key: Anglo-Jewry's Construction of Modern Jewish Thought* (Princeton, N.J., 2000), chaps. 1–2. On Michaelis and Christian critiques of the Masoretic text, see E. Breuer, *The Limits of Enlightenment: Jews, Germans, and the Eighteenth-Century Study of Scripture* (Cambridge, Mass., 1995).

47. See D. Katz, "Henry More and the Jews," in *Henry More (1614–1687): Tercentenary Studies*, ed. S. Hutton (Dordrecht, 1990).

48. Compare D. Ruderman, "At the Intersection of Cultures: The Historical Legacy of Italian Jewry," in *Gardens and Ghettos: The Art of Jewish Life in Italy*, ed. V. Mann (Berkeley, Calif., 1989), pp. 1–23, written in response to I. Sonne, *Hayahadut haitalkit: Demuta umekoma betoledot 'am Yisrael* (Jerusalem, 1961).

Chapter 1

Biography and Autobiography in Yoḥanan Alemanno's Literary Perception

Fabrizio Lelli

A peculiar feature of humanism and the Renaissance was the high social prestige attributed to knowledge. During the fifteenth century, Florence, Naples, Urbino, and Milan were visited by many scholars who risked long and dangerous journeys to meet illustrious humanists whose intellectual influence extended far beyond the borders of these cities. The specific value attributed by humanism to the individual led to the actual glorification of literary figures and teachers, who were often hired by rich Italian courts seeking universal renown for their cultural achievements.

A significant paradigm is that of Francesco Filelfo, who was capable of converting his profound knowledge of Greek and his rhetorical skills into a very precious merchandise. While in Florence, as a professor of Greek, he attracted throngs to hear his lectures on ancient Greek authors. Among his patrons were the most influential men in the city, including Cosimo de' Medici and Leonardo Bruni. An interesting account of Filelfo's self-perception is provided by his letter book,[1] an extraordinary example of the humanistic autobiographical genre. Of his warm reception by the Florentines, he writes: "I like Florence for many reasons. First of all, because it is a beautiful city. . . . In addition to this, the whole population is well disposed toward me. Everybody respects me and holds me in high esteem; everybody praises me. My name is known to everybody."

A highly cultured Jewish teacher named Yoḥanan Alemanno was a younger contemporary of the humanist Filelfo. Very similar to him in terms of his vast culture and his profession, he seems to have shared the same feelings when exalting Florence and its supreme authority, Lorenzo de' Medici. At the beginning of his commentary on the Song of Songs, entitled *Ḥesheq Shelomo* (Solomon's desire), dedicated to Giovanni Pico della Mirandola,

Alemanno presents Lorenzo as the most perfect of all princes and Florence as the most beautiful of all cities, since it warmly welcomes foreigners, and its inhabitants are tolerant toward them. Among the seven virtues Alemanno attributes to the Florentines, their curiosity and thirst for knowledge are probably the most remarkable ones.[2]

In such an environment, the role of a cultured teacher like Alemanno was significant. Wealthy Jewish families, who measured themselves against the styles of life of the non-Jewish milieus, displayed their high social position by hiring distinguished preceptors for their children. The rich banker Yeḥiel Nissim da Pisa hired Yoḥanan as a tutor for his children Isaac and Samuel. Thanks to the renown of the da Pisa family, Alemanno's fame spread all over Italy. Therefore, even when he became the target of the charges of those Jews who did not appreciate his unorthodox style of educating their children, his name was so well known that disciples came from other cities specifically to study with him. Such is the case of David ben Judah Messer Leon, who moved from Naples to Florence to study kabbalah with Alemanno, despite his father's anti-kabbalistic attitudes.

From this initial evidence, it appears that the role of Alemanno was not perceived differently from that of other contemporary humanists. But on what documents can we rely to better understand this perception? Our analysis of the issue depends mostly on Alemanno's works, which, like other humanistic autobiographies, offer considerable information concerning the life of the author. Can we define them as biographical documents? Since for Alemanno, as I have tried to demonstrate elsewhere,[3] rhetorical skill is almost tantamount to speculative training, an analysis of his self-perception must necessarily be based upon the evaluation of the philosophic content as well as literary characteristics of his works.

Concerning the latter, we may raise the question first of whether a biographical genre existed in Jewish literature of the Renaissance[4] or, to extend our inquiry to the whole humanistic cultural environment, whether such a genre can be identified in fifteenth-century literature in general. It is well known that a specific genre defined as "biography" did not exist during the Renaissance, although humanists gave importance to the literary production known from classical tradition as *vitae*. The revival of Greek and Latin studies made it possible for humanists to read biographical works composed by Xenophon, Plutarch, Cornelius Nepos, and Suetonius. The medieval tradition of the lives of the saints, still highly esteemed in the fifteenth century, was also an influential model for humanists, who could have recourse to both pagan and Christian traditions to mix the classical invitation to virtue or reprobation of vice, contained in the rhetorical setting of the ancient lives, into Christian examples of faith.[5]

Among the specific characteristics of fifteenth-century life writers, one of the most significant was their tendency to make simultaneous use of imaginary elements and motifs drawn from real history. In this they followed the well-established tradition, already popular in Florence in earlier centuries, of building fictitious stories around historical personages, as in Boccaccio's tales, infusing them with a strong moral connotation. The accounts of the deeds of actual heroes of the classical and the medieval world could coexist alongside the legendary biographies of personages of classical mythology, as well as the main characters of the widely diffused French epic production, often derived, in turn, from the medieval reinterpretation of the classical mythological tradition.

From this point of view, Boccaccio's great interest in biographical traits in his *Decameron* is not at all surprising; it should be borne in mind that he was one of the first scholars to compose works such as *De casibus virorum illustrium* (On cases of famous men), *De claris mulieribus* (On famous women), and, even more important, *La vita di Dante* (The life of Dante). While in the tales of the *Decameron*, biographical data depend on the moral models of virtue to be followed, classified according to specific subjects (love, fortune or misfortune, and so on), the biographies of famous men and women were classifications of legendary or historical personages. If the former can be said to be based on rhetorical models inspired by collections of examples of virtue such as Valerius Maximus's *Factorum ac dictorum memorabilium libri* (Books on memorable sayings and deeds), the latter can be seen as hagiographic rereadings of Plutarch's or Cornelius Nepos's biographical works. Boccaccio's *Vita di Dante* is even more striking, representing the exemplary life of a contemporary figure chosen by the author as a paradigm of political activity, moral virtue, and intellectual skill.

Another distinct feature of fifteenth-century biographies consists in resorting to autobiographical introspection. In many cases, the domains of biography and autobiography overlapped, the former being just a metaphorical garment for the latter. In this case, the main models drawn from pagan antiquity were Caesar's third-person *Commentaries*; Augustine's *Confessions*, from classical Christian tradition; and, from the recent past, the lives of the Provençal poets, which had influenced Dante's *Vita nova* (New life). Therefore, albeit not precisely defined as a genre in itself, Italian humanistic biographical writing, connected to historiography, was based on pagan and Christian models, on classical Greek and Latin, and medieval French and Italian writers.

If we now turn to the Italian Jewish cultural milieu of the fifteenth century, we notice that some of the previously mentioned features of humanist biography appear in the same terms in Hebrew letters, such as David Messer Leon's treatise *Shevaḥ nashim* (Praise of women), a work clearly influenced by Boccaccio's *De claris mulieribus*. As a matter of fact, Jewish literature had long known specific forms of biographical and autobiographical text production. In addition to the historical narrative sections of the Bible, dealing with the lives of the patriarchs, prophets, and kings,[6] and their midrashic interpretations, we may but recall the distinctly medieval genre of the mystical autobiography. The latter model appears in several works, often anonymous, where revelations received from God or other intermediate supernal powers are adapted to the chief characters, whose lives become significant paradigms of mystical experience in which historical reality merges with religious imagery. A case in point, influential in the development of Italian Jewish literature, is represented by Abulafia's prophetic commentaries, in which the author, while explaining the different stages of his mission to be carried out against a historical background, associates prophetic revelations with his own career.[7]

In the fifteenth century, we observe the continuation in Italy of the Spanish poetic genre of praise to patrons and contemporary important figures, both Christian and Jews, containing references to biographical deeds of the dedicatees. One such example is Avigdor of Fano's praise of women: in his composition, real biographical data are interwoven with fictitious elements drawn from other literary registers, which, in the case of Avigdor, are well represented by the Bible.[8] This genre, emerging in Spain under the influence of Arabic poetry, which had relied on Aristotelian poetics conceived as the art form for praise or blame, had a more direct precedent in Tuscan fourteenth-century literature, as I have shown elsewhere.[9] The biographical character poetically portrayed became an example of virtue or vice; especially in the fifteenth century, it took on the same function as a painted portrait.[10] In the fifteenth century, Italian Jewish traders created a new form of autobiographical literary production, represented by travel journals, seemingly inspired by the contemporary travel literature produced by non-Jews for trading purposes. The most outstanding diary, describing a journey to the Holy Land, is by Meshullam da Volterra;[11] not dissimilar in content, but shaped according to the more common genre of the epistle, is Obadiah of Bertinoro's *Letters from the Land of Israel.*[12]

Yet the first Jewish scholar who seems to adhere to the humanist revival of biographies of ancient historical figures is Yoḥanan Alemanno. He relied on this literary genre to write about an ancient Jew whose life may have paralleled those of the pagans in antiquity. In the following passage from his introduction to the above-mentioned commentary on the Song of Songs, Alemanno explains to his reader why he has decided to compose a biography of Solomon, the putative author of the biblical book:

> I shall not, however, amplify this discussion further, because I am very well aware, my son, that you are a wise and understanding man, a Jew who is not used to such long stories about a man and his deeds, and who might say that listening to the bleating of this flock of Solomon's virtues wearies the mind. You may say, "All these virtues are already recorded in the book of Chronicles. Why must you recount his statutes and teachings? Praise the Lord with graceful, noble words, for He is awesome and praiseworthy."
>
> Listen, therefore, to my replies to anyone who would seal his ears from hearing more:
>
> First, I greatly envied those among all the nations who praise their idols and compose about a single man whole hosts of books as long as the chronicles of the kings of Israel and Judah combined; while we the community of Jews, do not know how to give two or three particles of praise to one of the holy men of our people. I have, therefore, opened my mouth to glorify and praise King Solomon, may he rest in peace, with many praises. I took it upon myself to put them into a book in an order that will make apparent to all the nations that we have a heart like them.[13]

King Solomon is the perfect personage to be described through rhetorical patterns partly derived from the Bible, partly from the lesson Alemanno learned from contemporary humanists. Solomon is not a prophet, but a man, with all his virtues and vices, who, thanks to his culture, was able to attain the final human goal, the achievement of *devequt,* the cleaving to God. His totally human character was not completely perfect. That is why he had to choose, like Pico della Mirandola's ideal man, whether to raise himself to superior knowledge or to degrade himself to the level of an animal. By praying for knowledge, rather than for worldly power, Solomon was able to reach a high intellectual degree, since unsurpassed. Thus, the biography of the man Solomon is the paradigm for any Jew who wishes to lead his intellectual soul to cleave unto God. Only after acquiring a full mastery of the sciences, including practical art, politics, and magic, which were so important in the Platonist Ficinian environment, could a Jew become a *ḥakham kolel*, a universal wise man, capable of attaining supernal bliss. In the description of Solomon's path to knowledge, Alemanno reveals his own didactic study program, making use of the biographical rhetorical device to build up a whole Jewish educational system, partly inspired by contemporary humanistic models diffused in northern Italy.[14]

Solomon's biography clearly represents the account of the life of a biblical personage infused, like Boccaccio's or Petrarch's biographies of ancient men, with highly moral connotations. Solomon is described as a king, like many historical kings dealt with in ancient and contemporary non-Jewish biographies, as well as a saint. Alemanno's biography of King Solomon can therefore be said to have been compiled according to classical rhetorical and hagiographic patterns. The representation of Solomon's moral qualities and deeds is shaped according to the dominant biographical cliché followed by humanists, who generally did not intend to portray lives as lived, but rather as instances of a particular model or a rhetorical object. Thus, history and praise were inextricably bound together, analogous to the ancient literary subgenre of the *effigies*, or portrait, which also inspired Renaissance artistic iconographies of real or legendary figures of the past. In describing the literary character of Alemanno's work, should we recall the different attitudes of Suetonius and Plutarch toward biographical description—Suetonius stressing deeds, Plutarch emphasizing characters?

We do not know for sure whether Alemanno's sources also included classical works, but it is evident that he might have had access to those biographical works through Petrarch or Boccaccio, while he could have been motivated to compose a life of Solomon by his teacher Judah Messer Leon's rhetorical analysis of Scripture, as reflected in his celebrated handbook *Sefer nofet ṣufim* (Book of the honeycomb's flow). There Messer Leon highlighted the rhetorical meaning of the biographical example to emphasize virtues or vices.[15] Messer Leon combined the above-mentioned views expressed in Aristotle's *Poetics*, reread through the Arabic mediation of Avicenna and Averroës, with a broad knowledge of classical rhetoricians whose works circulated widely among humanists.

In the third book of *Sefer nofet ṣufim*, the author deals with the various moral characters that can be represented in fiction. This human variety of moral attitudes is classified according to the periods of human life. Thus: "beginning, then, with the character traits of young men, we say: young men are they who have moved past two heptads in age on the way to three. It is characteristic of them that they will make a choice of some kind and rush off toward whatever it is they desire: and the bodily lusts that chiefly govern them are those ascribed to the influence of the planet Venus. The young are given to sudden change."[16]

This description of the characteristics of youth is reminiscent of Alemanno's description of adolescence. Noteworthy is the theme of the two heptads, that is, the two periods of seven years that should be completed in order for a boy to pass to adolescence. We can recognize this very common pattern of life periodization, inspired by neo-Pythagorean motifs, diffused through Arabic works, chiefly in Averroës, and in Dante as well as in Pico della Mirandola's *Conclusiones* (Theses), where the link between the period and the planet governing it is clearly established.[17] If we take into account Alemanno's passage from *Ḥay ha-'Olamim* (The immortal), where he deals with the disciplines that should be studied during adolescence, the affinities with such conceptions are evident. According to Alemanno, the period between four and eighteen years of age (that is, a period of two heptads, starting from the first steps in the child's education) falls under the patronage of the Sun and Mercury, both planets presiding over primary education. Basing himself on Plato, known through Averroës, the author maintains that this period of human life must be fully devoted to education, since, as already shown by Messer Leon, "the young are given to sudden change" and during adolescence their intellect is more receptive. What interests me is the initial passage of the description of the education of the teenager. After asserting that this is the best period to delve into specific subjects aimed at distinguishing true from false, Alemanno recalls the exemplary model of Moses, who, according to his legendary biographies, as an adolescent left Egypt for Midian, where he was to study the local sciences and introduce them to the Jews.[18] We have here a clear example of a rhetoric biographical *effigies*/portrait adapted to the most outstanding figure of the Jewish religion, inspired by the rational tradition of Plato, Averroës, and Messer Leon on the one hand, and the Jewish literary tradition of the midrash on the other. So far, we have what we have just defined on the basis of the humanistic approach to biography, namely, a fictitious biographical example structured to be a paradigm of moral perfection for the reader. If we proceed in our interpretation of Alemanno's passage, we discover that this example[19] is then associated with Alemanno's autobiographical self-perception.

Like Moses, who left Egypt for Midian in order to study foreign disciplines, Alemanno left his residence during adolescence and moved to Florence. As he himself asserts, every young Jewish man should be sent to Florence to enter into the cultural activities of a prosperous city, where the atmosphere provided by the beauty of the site, in addition to the social habits of the inhabitants and their intellectual achievements, fosters the proper education of a young person's mind. Thus, the abstract model of Moses, a rhetorical biographical *topos*, is applied to the author himself, who becomes the effective paradigm to be emulated.[20]

We are here confronted with the complicated issue of Alemanno's autobiographical self-perception. In his attempt to lay the basis for the perfect education of the Jew, yearning for the final goal of *devequt*, this philosopher does not limit himself to presenting *effigies* of perfect lives of men in the past. In his time, when an active life was the prerequisite for any speculation, he could not help but put forward historical examples drawn from personal experience: like contemporary humanists, he depicts Lorenzo de' Medici as the perfect paradigm of political and intellectual skill (recalling such works as Niccolò Valori's *Vita di Lorenzo* [Life of Lorenzo de' Medici]), and the Florentines as gifted with every practical virtue (seemingly inspired by contemporary *laudationes* composed by humanists such as Leonardo Bruni). Consequently, he considered his personal status to be very high, thus linking his life to the biographical career of outstanding ancient figures such as Moses or Solomon, and comparing himself with the most renowned scholars of his time, such as Pico.

The first passage we have quoted from his commentary on the Song of Songs is one proof, among many others, of his high self-esteem. He was the first Jew to look for foreign biographical models to describe the praiseworthy life of King Solomon. His tendency to refer mostly to meetings with important non-Jewish politicians or scholars as a result of his knowledge, which made them eager to learn Hebrew or delve into difficult problems arising from the interpretation of the Hebrew Scripture or the kabbalah, is well documented in all of Alemanno's works. With the exception of the rhetorical description of the first meeting with Pico in the introduction to his commentary on the Song of Songs, which we will take into consideration later, other meetings with contemporary humanists are described in Alemanno's works as ordinary events that the author emphasizes to flaunt his important acquaintances before his Jewish audience. In Alemanno's treatise *Ḥay ha-'Olamim*, we find an interesting anecdote that reveals the author's curiosity for contemporary events, especially those in a non-Jewish environment. While dealing with madness and its relation to magic (a medieval theme that will recur, for example, in Agrippa's *De occulta philosophia* [The occult philosophy], where, by the way, the subject is formulated in a similar way to that of Alemanno),[21] Alemanno relates what Pico della Mirandola told him he had personally experienced in Milan. Pico had met a madman who was convinced that he was the pope and who had publicly excommunicated the duchess of Ferrara, Eleonora d'Aragona, in the cathedral of Milan. The event took place in 1491, on the occasion of the wedding of Beatrice d'Este, daughter of Eleonora d'Aragona, to Ludovico the More. Alemanno confirms Pico's story by adding that Paride da Ceresara, a famous humanist alchemist working at the court of the Gonzaga, had told him of the same event.[22] Paride da Ceresara, famous mainly for having been one of the intellectuals responsible for the Hermetic program of decoration of Isabella d'Este Gonzaga's study room in Mantua, is also quoted by Alemanno in the introduction to his kabbalistic treatise, contained in a Parisian Hebrew manuscript (Bibl. Nat., hebr. 849). There, Ceresara is described as an alchemist who, according to Alemanno, supposedly succeeded in finding the secret of eternal life.[23]

In this tendency of the author to stress autobiographical accounts, we can perceive the same rhetorical approach we had observed in his description of legendary characters. When in the introduction to his commentary on the Song of Songs, he reports on his first meeting with Pico, in 1488, Alemanno stresses his role as a wise teacher, though speaking as a devoted servant to the count, thus adhering to the rhetorical pattern of the profession of modesty prescribed by the ancients and by Messer Leon. Yet the dimension of the historical event, which, in Alemanno's words, was to be so significant in the development of his career, is set in a kind of mystical frame, devoid of clear references to space. Its only temporal data seem connected to the sudden manifestation of a portent, not dissimilar to a revelation received from supernal realms. Referring to Pico as a divine cherub,[24] Alemanno states:

> When I came to take shelter in the shadow of this cherub, crowned with divine lights, a prince perfect in knowledge, the Lord, who shields him and his intelligence day and night and is never separated from him, stirred his mouth and tongue to ask me if, in my vain life, I had seen any brilliant light among the commentators on the Song that is Solomon's that would distinguish between the various things that are so confusingly mixed in it.
>
> I said, "Ah, my Lord, the wisest of the wise have commented upon it, but not many of them have understood or explained it profoundly. Yet from God come solutions, new and old; He graced me with a few of them twenty years ago, and they are at my home."

He said, "Please let me hear too, for I have labored over all the commentators who have written in Greek and Latin, but I am not satisfied about the correct order of progression to be found in it."

So I, as a servant before his master, read out its arrangement which I had established among its symbols and, praise to the living God! He thought of me as of someone who has found a great treasure. . . .

This is my lord, called Count Giovanni della Mirandola and I am Yoḥanan, son of Isaac of Paris, called Ashkenazi, in Hebrew, and Aleman in the language of the people among whom I live.[25]

The lexicon of the passage has been heavily borrowed from prophetic books, thus creating in the reader of the original Hebrew text the feeling that he is witnessing a sort of portentous event, transpiring in a remote dimension far from the mundane world. However, if the use of prophetic terminology is mainly due to the teaching of Messer Leon, who advised the Jewish writer to make use of prophetic verses or sections of the Bible, we could also conceive of this passage as indebted to the tradition of the poetic lives of the Provençal poets known as *razos*, best represented in Italian literature by Dante's *Vita nova.* In this work, too, the life of the poet is construed according to a symbolic periodization. Temporal dates are reported only to hint at a supernatural order of events, while apparently mundane events are freed from any spatial connotation. Dante's dimension of the dream and its link to an abstract reality fraught with symbols recall Abulafia's autobiographical perception. Both authors obtained revelations through a degree of divine reality that may be identified with the philosophic conception of the active intellect. Both authors charge dates with almost eschatological meanings (let it suffice to recall the importance for both of the year 1290).

It is not certain that Alemanno knew Dante's *Vita nova,* which circulated widely among humanist scholars. Be that as it may, Alemanno's autobiographical description shares significant elements with the thirteenth-century philosophic literary tradition. As mentioned earlier, Alemanno's ideal life is divided, according to Arabic models, into periods of seven years, thus reaching its peak at its thirty-fifth year: in *Ḥay ha-'Olamim,* both the life of the man aiming at perfection and Alemanno's life are shaped according to this periodization. Thus, like Dante's *incipit* of the *Comedy*—taking place on a metaphysical dimension, when the mundane life of the real author has reached its peak, that is, his thirty-fifth year—Alemanno's *incipit* of his Hebrew composition, a work also sharing significant literary features with Dante's *Vita nova,*[26] has its starting point in 1470, when the author, aged thirty-five, receives a vision from above. In that afflatus, he is called to play the role of a prophet who will speed the universal redemption of the Jews (a mission similar to Dante's redemption of himself and then of all the sins of mankind). Like Dante, whose ultramundane journey takes place in 1300 and who finds himself in a dark forest, symbolic of his intellectual sin and Reason's difficulty in finding God's light without His grace, Alemanno affirms that in 5230, another round year, corresponding to 1469/70, he was wandering in the darkness of the *galut*, when he decided to repent and ask for universal forgiveness from above, so that the light of God, obscured by the intellectual sins of mankind, could shine forth once again. The symbolic temporal data of the redemption are linked in both cases to the biographical activity of the two men, who, thanks to their new prophetic powers, will set their souls free from corporeal ties, ascend to God, and, after returning from their supernal journey, will propagate the message received from above to all men, thus bringing about complete redemption.

To a certain extent, Alemanno's life, like that of the child chosen by God in *Ḥay ha-'Olamim*, tended to perfection from the beginning. In order to reveal his birth date, Alemanno resorts to a formula whose letters' numerical value is 194, corresponding to the Christian year 1433/34: the expression is *ḥanan Elohim*. The meaning of the whole passage from *Ḥay ha-'Olamim* (f. 12v) is that "God shed His grace" upon the child destined to perfection from birth, but the reference to Yoḥanan can be understood on the basis of the etymological affinity between the author's name and the formula. Thus, biography and the building of a stereotypical life according to classical and medieval rhetoric models, associated with legendary figures of the past, are linked to an autobiographical approach springing from a strong prophetic self-perception. Instead of the mystical prophetic perception of Abulafia, Alemanno chooses the more humanistic role of a prophet acting as a perfect teacher of mundane and divine knowledge.

In Alemanno's notebooks (*Liqqutim*), we find numerous references to his self-perception. The author records an episode that shows us his deep curiosity with contemporary culture. He reports that one of Pico's "servants," as he terms him, read his palm, which "tells about me . . . from the past and for the future. It indicates a grievous pang on the occasion of great honor without much use. An appetite to see every wonderful thing . . . Many promised to benefit me, but they did not keep their promise. All these have come to pass. These are the ones that have not happened until now: . . . of wealth and honor. To die away from my place and my homeland. Further he told me . . . a wonderful passion always to invent new things, in sciences and behavior and in all things."[27]

At the end of this description, we find a sad note: the palm reader foresees that Alemanno will die far from his homeland. We do not know where Alemanno's homeland was or where he ended his days. Recently, Moshe Idel has assumed, on the basis of a letter sent from Jerusalem to Italy,[28] that Alemanno may have died in the Holy Land. If Idel's interpretation is correct, the prediction of the palm reader would have been only partly true. Alemanno would indeed have left his birthplace, Italy, but would have died in his real homeland, the Land of Israel. What is more interesting in the document supporting Idel's assertion are the words used by the author to define Alemanno. These confirm that Alemanno's contemporaries attributed to him the same esteem that was an essential part of his humanistic self-perception. The writer informs his Italian Jewish correspondent that "this year two Ashkenazi wise men came to Jerusalem, one of them being *haḥakham hashalem hayashish Yoḥanan*" ("the perfect old sage").[29]

Notes

1. F. Filelfo, *Epistolae* (1477; published Venice, 1502).

2. See A. Melamed, "The Hebrew 'Laudatio' of Yoḥanan Alemanno in Praise of Lorenzo il Magnifico and the Florentine Constitution," in *Jews in Italy: Studies Dedicated to the Memory of U. Cassuto on the 100th anniversary of His Birth*, ed. Ḥ. Beinart (Jerusalem, 1988), pp. 1–34; F. Lelli, "Umanesimo laurenziano nell'opera di Yoḥanan Alemanno," in *La cultura ebraica all'epoca di Lorenzo il Magnifico*, ed. D. Liscia Bemporad and I. Zatelli (Florence, 1998), pp. 49–67.

3. See F. Lelli, "Retorica, poetica e linguistica nel *Ḥay ha-'Olamim* (L'Immortale) di Yoḥanan Alemanno" (Ph.D. diss., University of Turin, 1992), partly published in Y. Alemanno, *Ḥay ha-'Olamim (L'Immortale)*, vol. 1: *La Retorica*, ed. F. Lelli (Florence, 1995).

4. On this issue, see "Biographies and Autobiographies," in *Encyclopaedia Judaica* (Jeusalem, 1972), vol. 4, cols. 1009–15, partly edited by the editorial staff, partly by Joseph Dan. It is worth observing that this brief overview of the Jewish biographical genre finds its most important evidence in Renaissance Italian Jewish literature. According to Dan, Abraham Yagel's sixteenth-century *Gei ḥizzayon* (A valley of vision) should be considered the first autobiography "to be written in Hebrew by a minor writer about a comparatively trivial life. The focus is not on any major historical event, nor on the author's participation in a noteworthy adventure. . . . Earlier works belong more to the field of historiography as they were written as personal experience (Dan, "Biographies," col. 1011). Alemanno's significant biographical data

scattered throughout all his works contrast with Dan's assumption, since they date to an earlier period than Yagel. It is worth recalling that Yagel admired Alemanno and possessed at least one of his autobiographical manuscripts. Probably the recourse to the autobiographical genre was also due to Alemanno's influence upon him. On Dan's assessment of Yagel, see also J. Dan, *Hasippur ha'ivri bime habenayim* (Jerusalem, 1974), pp. 217–21. On Yagel's *Valley of Vision* and on its role in early modern autobiography, see *A Valley of Vision: The Heavenly Journey of Abraham ben Hananiah Yagel*, ed. D. Ruderman (Philadelphia, 1990), pp. 23–27, who strongly disagrees with Dan's assessment. On Alemanno's quotations in Yagel's works, see M. Idel, "The Magical and Neoplatonic Interpretations of the Kabbalah in the Renaissance," in *Jewish Thought in the Sixteenth Century*, ed. B. D. Cooperman (Cambridge, Mass., 1983), pp. 186–242, esp. 224–27.

5. On Renaissance biographies, see E. Garin, *Ritratti di umanisti italiani* (Florence, 1967); N. Mann and L. Syson, eds., *The Image of the Individual: Portraits in the Renaissance* (London, 1998); see also T. F. Mayer, "Biography and Autobiography," in *Encyclopedia of the Renaissance*, ed. P. F. Grendler (New York, 1999), 1: 226–29.

6. Among the biblical books, Nehemiah can be considered an autobiography. However, the first known biography of a historical figure is that of Saadiah Gaon, which was written by his two sons at the request of Ḥisdai ibn Shaprut. See bibliographical references in "Biographies and Autobiographies," *Encyclopaedia Judaica*, col. 1009.

7. See M. Idel, "Abraham Abulafia's Works and Doctrines" (Hebrew) (Ph.D. diss., Hebrew University, 1976); idem, *The Mystical Experience in Abraham Abulafia* (Albany, N.Y., 1987).

8. See Avigdor of Fano's *'Ozer nashim* (Women's supporter), in A. Neubauer, "Zur Frauenliteratur," *Israelitische letterbode* 10 (1892): 97–105, esp. 101–3.

9. On this and other issues concerning Renaissance poetic imagery and iconography compared with those of Jewish fifteenth-century literature, see F. Lelli, "Jews, Humanists, and the Reappraisal of Pagan Wisdom Associated with the Ideal of *Dignitas Hominis*," in A. Coudert and J. Shoulson, eds., *Hebraica Veritas? Christian Hebraists and the Study of Judaism in Early Modern Europe* (Philadelphia, 2004), 1–3.

10. I attempt to analyze the relationship between iconographic rhetoric in Renaissance and Jewish literature in the chapter mentioned in the previous note.

11. On travel journals in fifteenth-century Italian Jewish literature, see. A. Veronese, "Il viaggio di Meshullam ben Menaḥem da Volterra," in *Viaggitori ebrei: Berichte jüdischer Reisender vom Mittelalter bis in die Gegenwart*, ed. G. Busi (Bologna, 1992), pp. 45–66.

12. See *From Italy to Jerusalem: The Letters of Rabbi Obadiah of Bertinoro from the Land of Israel*, ed. A. David (Ramat Gan, 1997).

13. A. M. Lesley, " 'The Song of Solomon's Ascents' by Yoḥanan Alemanno: Love and Human Perfection according to a Jewish Colleague of Giovanni Pico della Mirandola" (Ph.D. diss., University of California, 1976), p. 53.

14. See Alemanno, *Ḥay ha-'Olamim*, pp. 29–55.

15. See A. Melamed, "Rhetoric and Philosophy in Judah Messer Leon's *Sefer Nofet Ṣufim*" (Hebrerw), *Italia* 1, no. 2 (1978): vii–xxviii.

16. *The Book of the Honeycomb's Flow: Sēpher Nōpheth Ṣuphīm by Judah Messer Leon*; ed. I. Rabinowitz (Ithaca, N.Y., 1983), p. 377.

17. See M. Idel, "The Study Program of R. Yoḥanan Alemanno" (Hebrew), *Tarbiẓ* 48 (1979/80): 303–31.

18. See Alemanno, *Ḥay ha-'Olamim*, pp. 149–51, 155–56.

19. This example recalls the model of Solomon in Alemanno's commentary on the Song of Songs, which was also construed through having recourse to a periodization of human life.

20. See Idel, "The Study Program"; see also Lelli, "Umanesimo laurenziano."

21. See Cornelius Agrippa, *De occulta philosophia libri tres*, ed. V. Perrone Compagni (Leiden, 1992), pp. 220–27.

22. See F. Lelli, "L'educazione ebraica nella seconda metà del 400: Poetica e scienze naturali nel *Ḥay ha-'Olamim* di Yoḥanan Alemanno," *Rinascimento*, 2d series, 36 (1996): 75–136, esp. 113–14 n. 31).

23. For further references to Paride da Ceresara's acquaintance with and his interest in Hebrew and Jewish studies, see Lesley,"The Song," p. 271 n. 20, 287, n. 20. Another humanist who had connections with Alemanno was Alberto Pio, Pico's nephew (see Lesley, "The Song," p. 270 n. 19).

24. On Pico as a cherub, see F. Lelli, "Yoḥanan Alemanno's Intellectual Relationship with Giovanni Pico della Mirandola," paper delivered at the Center for Advanced Judaic Studies, University of Pennsylvania, Philadelphia, 6 October 1999.

25. Lesley, "The Song," pp. 28–29.

26. See A. M. Lesley's review of my partial edition of Alemanno's *Ḥay ha-'Olamim*, which appeared in *Renaissance Quarterly* 52 (1999): 778: Lesley correctly points out that the "coupling of popular and scholarly presentations [of the issues dealt with in Alemanno's work] produces an effect like that of poems from the time that were written to be accompanied by learned commentaries, such as Benivieni's *Canzone d'amore* with Giovanni Pico's commentary." I would add to Lesley's remark that in his commentary, Pico follows the tradition of the Provençal *razos*.

27. See Lesley, "The Song," p. 6.

28. The letter, included in the Ms. Firenze, Biblioteca Medicea Laurenziana, Plut. II, 35, cc. 30v, 30v–31v, was sent from Israel to Abraham of Perugia. A. David ("A Jeusalemite Epistle from the Beginning of the Ottoman Rule over the Land of Israel" [Hebrew], in *Chapters in the History of Jerusalem at the Beginning of the Ottoman Age*, ed. Y. Ben-Porat [Jerusalem, 1989], pp. 39–60) has recently attributed it to the kabbalist Abraham Eliezer Halevi.

29. See David, "A Jerusalemite Epistle," p. 56.

Chapter 2

Elijah Delmedigo: An Archetype of the Halakhic Man?

Harvey Hames

"And the person who urged me to this point is the noble master, Pico della Mirandola, who is given to speculation of the highest sciences, is a very intelligent man, a worthy philosopher, a lover of truth, of whose like I have not seen in these times."[1] Thus wrote Elijah Delmedigo in the introduction to his commentary on Averroës' *De substantia orbis*, written at the behest of the famous count of Mirandola as a result of their discussions in 1485. In late 1486, Pico, then in Rome, presented his *Conclusiones*, in which he was able to couple the philosophy of Averroës with statements such as: "Averroës and Avicenna cannot disagree fundamentally on whether the physicist receives composite bodies from the metaphysician, even if they differ in their words," and "If there is any nature immediate to us that is either simply rational, or at least exists for the most part rationally, it has magic in its summit, and through its participation in men can be more perfect."[2] Conclusions such as these could only have frustrated someone like Elijah Delmedigo, who had devoted much effort to convincing the count of the superiority of Peripatetic philosophy as interpreted by Averroës, and may have caused him to revise his favorable statements about Pico. His last known contact with Pico was in December of the same year, in the form of a letter with two accompanying treatises, a last-ditch effort to make Pico aware of the superiority of Aristotelian-Averroist cosmology.

However, Elijah would have felt reasonably comfortable describing himself in the way he described Pico. He considered himself very intelligent, a good philosopher, a lover of truth, and part of the intellectual elite of his time. Born in 1440 in Crete, then part of Venetian territory, he was at age twenty already composing treatises on Averroës, and was befriended by key figures in Venice and Padua such as Girolamo Donato, Domenico Grimani,

Antonino Pizzamano, Ermolao Barbaro, and the aforementioned Pico. During the decade Elijah spent in Italy, he was in great demand as a teacher and translator into Latin and expositor of Averroës. He also wrote treatises of his own on various topical philosophical issues, generally as a result of discussions held with Christian contemporaries. It was, however, only after his return to Crete in 1490 that he wrote his seminal and most important work, *Beḥinat hadat* (Examination of religion), a very personal enterprise that reflects his perplexities and works through his own beliefs. Here, Elijah makes sense of all that he had seen and heard in Italy, puts it into perspective, and comes to terms with his own religious persona. In *Beḥinat hadat*, Elijah states his opinions on the relationship between philosophy and religion, between Averroës and Jewish thought, and between Judaism and Christianity.

Much has been written about the seemingly enigmatic figure of Elijah Delmedigo, based mostly on *Beḥinat hadat*. He has been portrayed as an Averroist *par excellence*, an upholder of the double-truth doctrine, and as an extreme rationalist and therefore, an anti-kabbalist. David Geffen, like many others, thinks that Elijah adopts a version of the theory of the so-called double truth, that is, he recognizes that in different arenas there can be two different truths and therefore, where faith and reason disagree, it is possible to accept the truth of faith.[3] Aryeh Motzkin criticizes Geffen and his predecessors, suggesting that for Averroës, upon whom Elijah relies, there is no such thing as double truth. If there are two contradictory things, they cannot both be true; that would be a farce for the philosopher. Averroës believed in the supremacy of reason and accepted religion as necessary for political stability and for the governance of the masses. Motzkin claims that in *Beḥinat hadat*, essentially based on Averroës' *Decisive Treatise* (*Façl al-maqâl*), Elijah reached the same conclusions. There is not and cannot be a double truth, and where religion contradicts reason, the latter is to be followed.[4]

While Motzkin's thesis is plausible, a careful reading of *Beḥinat hadat* suggests that Elijah is just as reluctant to adopt Averroës' position as he is the double-truth theory, and in reality, he does not uphold either one. One example of this is Elijah's attitude in this work toward philosophy. Averroës (1126–98) defended the study of philosophy in his *Decisive Treatise* and *Incoherence of the Incoherence*. Although the study of philosophy is reserved only for the adept, the Koran actually mandates its study to reflect on God's design.[5] Averroës does not go along with Avicenna's emanational metaphysics and tries to return natural theology to the physics of matter and motion. This implies that God's place in Creation is only in the ordering of its elements and eternal matter. This means that on the questions of bodily resurrection, individual providence, and miracles, Averroës has to rely on authority and, in the end, his position is unclear and awkward. Elijah, who spent much of his time studying, translating, and commenting on Averroës, could not accept this apparent lack of clarity. In *Beḥinat hadat*, he does not accept the study of philosophy as mandatory and sides definitively in favor of the authority of revelation over philosophical reasoning. One is supposed to reflect upon the foundations of the faith as in the first two commandments of the Decalogue, but all the other foundational aspects of the faith have to be accepted as true because of revelation. One will not be able to prove or disprove them by philosophical reasoning.

Elijah's supposed distaste for kabbalah emerges from his Averroist leanings. Most previous scholarship, based on the polemical passages in *Beḥinat hadat*, has concluded that Elijah was one of the first real critics of kabbalah and showed overt hostility to its practitioners.[6] Kalman Bland, the most recent scholar to examine this issue, follows his predecessors in viewing Elijah as an Averroist, but takes a different stance on Elijah's attitude toward kabbalah. Bland, who bases his reading not only on sections of *Beḥinat hadat*, but on other places in his writings where kabbalah is discussed, suggests that Elijah was not really a critic, but on the whole ambivalent about the issue.[7] However, by narrowly focusing on the issue of the kabbalah, he loses sight of the broader historical context that formed Elijah's intellectual view, which is crucial for understanding his attitude toward many issues, including kabbalah, raised in the work.

There can be little doubt that by the time Elijah arrived in Italy, he already had a negative opinion of kabbalah. In 1466, there was a sharp exchange in Crete over the halakhic question of whether *yibbum*, the levirate marriage (Deut. 25:4–10), should be performed, which touched on the issue of metempsychosis.[8] The protagonists in the dispute were a native of Crete, Rabbi Michael ben Shabbtai ha-Kohen Balbo, a man learned in both philosophy and kabbalah; and a relative newcomer to the island, Rabbi Moses ha-Kohen Ashkenazi, an avid opponent of kabbalah whose son, Saul, asked Elijah to write *Beḥinat hadat*.[9] Michael Balbo defended the performance of *yibbum* because of the kabbalistic interpretation of this commandment, while Moses ha-Kohen went to great lengths to dismiss this reasoning as nonsense and heretical. Here was a clash between different halakhic traditions, the Sephardi and the Ashkenazi, and different intellectual approaches, the kabbalistic and the philosophical. Some of Elijah's comments over the years about kabbalistic teachings, such as the doctrine of the *sefirot* and metempsychosis, surely stem from this altercation, of which it is difficult to believe that he was unaware. Yet Elijah's contacts with the humanists of Florence and the intellectual trends that he tried so hard to combat clearly reinforced his opposition to kabbalah, and gave greater impetus to the existential questions troubling him.

A letter written by Marsilio Ficino to Antonio Benivieni shows that during 1485, Elijah took an active part in an interreligious polemic with Flavius Mithridates at various homes in Florence. He had a partner in these frequent debates; a man who was, quite possibly, Abraham Farissol, the author of *Magen Avraham* (Defender of Abraham).[10] It is impossible to know what exactly took place in those encounters, although the letter states that there was disagreement on the interpretation of biblical verses. However, these discussions—which surely included philosophical expositions and kabbalistic interpretations, given the presence of Flavius Mithridates—must also have influenced how Elijah perceived and understood his Judaism. Mithridates' use of Neoplatonism and kabbalah to prove the truths of Christianity must have given Elijah much food for thought and helped him clarify his position on philosophical proofs of religious truths and on kabbalah.[11] Interestingly, in his *Magen Avraham*, Farissol writes in a similar vein to Elijah's comments in *Beḥinat hadat* about philosophers and people who talk about intentions and do not actually keep the commandments.[12] In the continuation of the aforementioned letter, Ficino mentions that the Jewish interlocutors are almost irrefutable "unless the divine Plato enters the debate, the invincible defender of the holy religion."[13] For the humanists, Plato was the perfect foil for the Peripatetic, and this is an indication of the type of argument employed against Elijah in the polemical exchanges. Therefore, it is perhaps not surprising that in October 1485, while these exchanges were taking place, Elijah recorded his feelings about the study of Plato in Florence.[14] He observes that Plato, who, according to Themistius, was the most exalted of the ancients, did not complete the discussion of any topic, and in most of his dialogues said nothing of value. He adds that Plato was elliptical and often wrote in riddles. Plato's major fault was a lack of system within his arguments. This was a problem for Elijah, since he contended that without an orderly system, the acquisition and disposition of knowledge was impossible. Elijah states that there are a group of present-day thinkers, mainly men of poetry and rhetoric, who have dedicated themselves to the exposition of Platonic doctrines, and they use the demonstrations of Aristotle to explain the riddles of Plato.

Elijah explains that these thinkers do so because they believe that there is truth in every sort of wisdom. Elijah says that since this group of thinkers is getting stronger, he must clarify the doctrines of Averroës before they are lost. Given the comments of Ficino in his letter, the immediate context of interreligious polemic, the syncretistic tendencies, and the use made by this circle of Platonic philosophy, Elijah's remarks are more understandable.

Yet in a number of places in his philosophical treatises, Elijah defined his relationship to the subject he was treating in a manner that clearly exhibits the limitations of philosophy. In late January 1482, at the end of the second of his treatises on Averroës' dealing with the question of immortality, Elijah wrote: "And I will fight a *milḥemet miṣva* [obligatory war] against philosophical opinions that seemingly contradict the Torah, even though in my opinion, when Torah and Sophia are understood correctly, there is no conflict between them."[15] In the introduction to the same work, Elijah declares that he does not accept all that the philosophers teach. When they espouse doctrines opposing the Torah, he relies on revelation. Later in the work, he writes: "Let no wise man of our nation presume that I believe what I have just expounded, for my faith is truly the faith of Israel." Elijah also promises here to write a work that will explain the points of agreement and disagreement between philosophy and Torah.[16] For Elijah, philosophy was the key to the intellectual world of his time; it could, perhaps, be used to explore and confound Christianity, but could never be the criterion for examining the Jewish faith. As can be seen from his philosophical treatises, Elijah was engrossed with the subject and found in Averroës an intellectual soulmate of sorts. He saw Averroës as best explaining Aristotle and the phenomena of this world, but not as someone whose system provided all the answers to religious and existential questions.[17] Elijah was aware that philosophy is only the speculation of the human intellect and a science in which there is much disagreement, while the Torah is the revealed word of the divine. Indeed, in the explicit of his Latin commentary on Averroës' *De substantia orbis*, completed in October 1486, Elijah writes: "For I do not verify everything that has been written, but I will say that everything that I have written agrees with the opinions of the philosophers and their rules. However, that which is against the true faith, in no way do I believe or affirm, but I have spoken according to their life as it is customarily set forth."[18]

Beḥinat hadat is comprehensible only if seen in light of Elijah's Italian years and, in particular, his contacts with leading Christian intellectual figures of the time. It is first and foremost a dialogue with Christianity, and it is the latter that is consciously or subconsciously behind the work.[19] His complaints against kabbalists as well as philosophers, though perhaps dating back to Crete, can be understood only with the contemporary Christian world in mind.[20] A number of times in the work, Elijah mentions Christian doctrines and Christian thinkers, generally in a context where it is possible to see that Elijah is defining his Judaism with respect to Christianity. Thus, for example, his criteria for judging the truth of a religion come immediately after he criticizes central Christian beliefs, and these criteria are an antithesis to what has just been discussed.[21] The struggles of people such as Marcilio Ficino and Pico della Mirandola to comprehend God and Creation and see their religious beliefs and politics confirmed by the ancient sources greatly affected Elijah. The use made by these humanists of the Peripatetics, their commentators, kabbalah, and other diverse sources in the service of Christianity meant that Elijah had to look carefully at his own religious beliefs.

Elijah's frustration at what was being done by his Christian humanist contemporaries emerges from his last known contact with Pico, when he tried to turn the tables on his Christian patron. Elijah's letter of December 1486 discusses additional points not covered in his commentary *De substantia orbis*, and he tries to show Pico that Neoplatonic thinking lies at the root of kabbalah, and hence, it cannot be so ancient.[22] He does not criticize kabbalah per se, but only tries to show that the Aristotelian-Averroist concept of the universe is more valid than Neoplatonic cosmology.[23] What seems to be happening is that Elijah sought to use Aristotle and Averroës against Neoplatonism and kabbalah to convince Pico that the doctrines of Christianity could not be true. Elijah perhaps hoped that if Pico could be persuaded to follow Averroës, he would realize the implausibility of the truths of Christianity (perhaps a reverse conversion attempt). However, as *Beḥinat hadat* shows, Elijah cannot follow Aristotle and Averroës blindly himself, as this would lead to conflicts with foundational beliefs of Judaism. Thus, Elijah uses Averroës to discredit the dogmas of Christianity, but not to explain the doctrines of Judaism.[24] Pico, not surprisingly, remained unmoved, as can be seen from his *Apologia*, written in 1487. However, it may be this syncretistic trend, which Elijah saw becoming dominant even among some of his Jewish contemporaries, coupled with the attitude of other leading Jews to his philosophical leanings and attitude toward kabbalah, that eventually caused him to depart Italy and return to Crete.[25]

Yet prior to his departure, Elijah spent another couple of years in Venice with Cardinal Domenico Grimani, and five of his translations and treatises were published in 1488, three in a volume of John of Jandun's (d. 1328) works and the other two as *In meteorologica Aristotelis.* But it was only back in Crete, where he did not have to please any patron, that he dedicated himself, at the request of his student Saul ha-Kohen Ashkenazi, to serious reflection on the issue of faith. *Beḥinat hadat* opens in a pessimistic vein because Elijah thought that the state of the people was cause for all disagreement. Where peace and quiet are lacking, where there is no civil society, where there are no recognized authorities, there is disagreement, argument, intolerance, and self-hatred. It is in the latter atmosphere that he writes this book, decrying what he sees as the abysmal state of the Jewish people. The book's premise is that the only thing left for a Jew is to concentrate on the performance of the commandments, not to try to understand and rationalize the faith. There are only a few people in every generation who are truly wise and who truly understand the principles of the faith, and it is they who should explain and be responsible for the well-being of the people. As the conclusion shows, Elijah thinks that he is one of the wise men of his generation.

As mentioned previously, the beginning of *Beḥinat hadat* discusses whether there is an obligation to study philosophy. Elijah concludes that it is not an obligation, but something that is worthwhile for the wise man and not for the masses. He emphasizes that where there is a conflict between philosophy and the Torah, the latter is supreme, and one has to find a way to make the philosophical opinion agree with the Torah. Elijah writes that the usefulness of philosophy for the wise man is "that it will lead him from the knowledge of things that are caused and from there he will be able to proceed to knowledge of the Creator." However, Elijah reiterates that both the simple man and the wise man believe in the same principles of faith: "And if in the principles of faith, it seems that the Torah and philosophers are at odds, the masses and the wise men are in total agreement—in other words, both believe in these matters according to the Torah. This is [the case] unless there be an issue for which there is a special explanation for the wise man that does not contradict the principles and intentions of the Torah; yet this explanation is not fitting for the masses for certain reasons."[26]

There is no doubt that belief in miracles contradicts philosophical reasoning and conclusions, but on this point, which Elijah sees as a fundamental principle of the Jewish faith, there can be no argument. One can also use philosophical reasoning to examine the articles of faith—especially belief in God and His unity, and that there is no corporeality in God—but this is only to show that on these points, philosophical exposition and the Torah coincide. These principles, particularly the question of the nature of God, form the basis for much of his philosophical writing, from *De primo motore* to *De esse et essentia et uno*.[27] Elijah reiterates that there can be no advantage in disputing "those who wish to disagree with us" on these issues because the way one arrives at the truths of the Torah is different from the way one proceeds to philosophical truths, and the one method cannot be used for the other. And since for Jews, the truths of the Torah hold supremacy, philosophical argumentation over these issues is futile if neither side is able to find methods of proceeding toward conclusions.[28] This point is also used to emphasize that if philosophical reasoning cannot be used to prove the divine truths as revealed in the Torah, neither can it be used to ascertain the dogmas of Christianity; in other words, Christian doctrines should not be considered unimpeachable first principles.

Here Elijah faces a challenge of double standards. One can show how the doctrines of Christianity contradict reason, but one should not use reason to contradict faith, as Elijah says, regarding Judaism. In other words, Christians can also claim that there are matters in their faith that contradict reason, but this should not be a justification for not believing the truths of Christianity. In essence, if one cannot rely on reason for examining the doctrines of faith, what makes Judaism any truer than Christianity? For this question, Elijah does not find a suitable solution, although he tries in many different ways to show that unlike Christianity, Judaism is always in agreement with reason. When negating Christian doctrines, he reverts to demagogy, in that he ridicules the teachings as nonsense. He cites the parable about a man who has always lived on a mountain and has never heard of Christianity, and when told about that religion, declares that it is "impossible that any rational person believe in these teachings."[29]—clearly not a very convincing argument. These explanations are forced and not foolproof, and that is why Elijah returns to the *ṭa'amei hamiṣvot* (reasons for the commandments) and why he is so critical of the kabbalists. If kabbalah claims to be ancient and nonphilosophical and reveals hidden truths in the Torah, and if Christians can have recourse to it to prove the doctrines of their faith without the use of reason, then it must be a false teaching and contrary to the true meaning of the Torah, because it is impossible that the Torah reveal anything other than the true faith.

How can one know the true faith? Here, again, Elijah is unequivocal: "And if one finds another faith that is in agreement with our divine Torah in opinion, behold [Judaism] will differ from it in its commandments and statutes, because it is *they* that will lead man to the ultimate Good. And the truth of a religion should not be judged by opinions alone."[30] Because philosophy (and presumably, kabbalah) is not the tool to be used when examining religion and because the use of philosophy can lead to confusion and doubt as to what religion is true, it is only through the upholding and performance of the commandments that man will have knowledge of the true faith. Therefore, writes Elijah:

> in this treatise, I did not choose to argue with the philosophers on matters upon which there is no agreement between us using reason, because this cannot be achieved using philosophical reasoning, but I have chosen prophecy and true tradition as my bastion. And I am of the opinion that my predecessors who wanted to extrapolate on our faith using philosophy were mistaken in that they were using a method of learning unfit for that purpose, and they became mediators between matters that pertain to the Torah and those that do not, and they are neither Torah scholars nor philosophers. And even though they may have thought that they were increasing wisdom, they were in fact destroying it. For when people saw these quasi-scholars not following the faith properly, and they were considered men of learning, knowledge became a stain on its owner, until people concluded that these [Jewish] philosophers negate the truth of the Torah. And this is truly distant from the nature of the perfect wise man, for he is the man who will want with all his being to engage with the religion and the complete Good that is common to all its believers and who will lead them to the perfection they can achieve and to the true Good.[31]

Elijah is even critical of Maimonides for using philosophical reasoning to establish religious truth. Because Elijah admires Maimonides, his approach is apologetic, presenting reasons that the latter used philosophy in the service of religion. He explains that perhaps it was because other Jewish scholars had attempted this and arrived at negative conclusions about the truth of the Torah, and Maimonides wanted to use their methods to prove its veracity. Elijah gives two other possible reasons: that he wanted to show Muslim scholars that Judaism, like Islam, can stand the scrutiny of reason; and that he could think of no other way to distinguish the true religion from the false. However, the general impression remains that in Elijah's opinion, Maimonides should not have taken this approach from the outset: "But we have already hinted at the way the true faith can be distinguished from the false one, and I will come back to this later"—in other words, through the performance of the commandments.[32]

Elijah emphasizes the importance of explaining and understanding the meaning of the laws, which he says have their source with Moses on Mount

Sinai. Even if it seems when studying the Talmud that there is disagreement on the meaning and practice of different ordinances, this is a result of external circumstances, such as the Diaspora, which does not allow the great scholars of the nation to meet and decide together. However, regarding kabbalah, about which there is much disagreement even among those who refer to themselves as kabbalists, there can be no truth in its teachings, particularly because they cannot be proven to be ancient. Perhaps in this context, Elijah's most damning comment about kabbalah is that there is considerable parity between its doctrines and those of Plato and Neoplatonism, teachings that have been shown to be mistaken.[33] Here, the difference between the law and kabbalah becomes clear, and Elijah's resistance to kabbalah becomes understandable. The law demonstrably goes back to Moses at Sinai, and therein lies its truth; however, the affinity between kabbalah and Neoplatonism and the internal disagreement among its adherents clearly demonstrate its lack of potential for revealing the truth. Again, seen in context, this criticism must also be seen in light of the use of kabbalah to prove Christian doctrines, and if kabbalah is not inherently true, then Christianity cannot use it as a mainstay for proof of its own veracity.[34]

When dealing with the *ṭa'amei hamiṣvot*, Elijah stresses the importance of discovering their true meaning: "Just as the perfect knowledge of something that has a cause is through knowing its cause, the performance of something that has purpose will be closer to perfection if we know its end and reason."[35] Discovering the reason for the commandment is permitted above all because the performance of the commandments is the foundation of faith and the way to the ultimate Good. Elijah writes:

> However, the manner used to discover the meanings of the commandments is not in itself clear and needs further elaboration. And, therefore, we will say that this manner be taken from the general intention of the Torah, which is to lead people to the real Good, inasmuch as they can attain it, and this is either through knowledge or deeds. My preference is for deeds, because good virtue and good deeds contain all that is needed for man to be good with himself, his household, and the community as a whole. Therefore, the purpose of the commandments is not to influence or restore the divine world, as the kabbalists claim, but to restore ourselves and change for the better, in which case we attain the divine Good.[36]

Elijah Delmedigo's conclusion, which clearly upholds the veracity of Judaism and identifies the true person of faith as one who performs and tries to understand the commandments, came as a result of personal experience and long reflection on the nature of his world and society. This outcome is surprisingly similar to that of a twentieth-century figure who also examines his faith in a very personal work, and the conclusions reached in that treatise can perhaps shed light on the enigmatic figure of Elijah Delmedigo: Rabbi Joseph Soloveitchik's *Halakhic Man*, written in 1944, can be viewed as a modern *Beḥinat hadat*. When we read that Soloveitchik found himself confronted with similar challenges to his Jewishness and faith, understanding his method and solutions can open important vistas on Elijah's composition. Rabbi Soloveitchik was, like Elijah, well educated in both religious and secular subjects, was attracted to philosophy and literature, and was on intimate terms with many of the intellectual giants of his time.[37] *Halakhic Man* deals with problems posed by philosophy and mysticism (respectively, the cognitive man and the *homo religiosus*) and with the challenges of Christianity, and it finds a solution that joins the former elements from which emerges the unique figure of the halakhic man.

In *Beḥinat hadat*, Elijah deals with philosophy, not negating its importance but trying to find within it that which is useful for pursuing the Jewish way of life, in the same manner that Soloveitchik favorably compares many of the aspects of the cognitive man with the essence of the halakhic man. Elijah, although more negative about the kabbalists (this is perhaps understandable because of the Christian appropriation of kabbalah), does not totally negate it; in the same way, Soloveitchik reveals the positive attributes of the *homo religiosus*. Both, however, find the true answers within the realms of halakhah, the performance of the commandments, and a deepening knowledge of the reasons for their performance.

The comparison of *Halakhic Man* with *Beḥinat hadat* seems to present a similar understanding of reality. When one reads Soloveitchik, one grasps the importance of the commandments as being the real foundation of this-worldly existence for the Jew rather than the philosophical or mystical search for the transcendent reality beyond the empirical and concrete of the here and now. The latter is seen as esoteric escapism, as irresponsible; the former, as immersion in reality, as a total fulfillment of the revelation at Sinai. Elijah too, not finding the solutions in philosophy or kabbalah and confounded by his intellectual milieu, finds the grounding of his faith in the commandments. As Soloveitchik, some 450 years later than Elijah writes: "When halakhic man pines for God, he does not venture to rise up to Him, but rather strives to bring down His divine presence into the midst of our concrete world. . . . Transcendence becomes embodied in man's deeds, deeds that are shaped by the lawful physical order of which man is a part. . . . Holiness, according to the outlook of Halakhah, denotes the appearance of a mysterious transcendence in the midst of our concrete world, the "descent" of God, whom no thought can grasp, onto Mount Sinai, the bending down of a hidden and concealed world and lowering it onto the face of reality.[38]

Here are two highly educated and learned men searching for the meaning of their faith, who cannot find a solution within the parameters of intellectual and mystical speculation, who grasp that the essence of truth is in the actual practice and performance of the religious ordinances. Elijah is Soloveitchik's Halakhic Man.

Beḥinat hadat reflects the confusion of one who has acquired so much knowledge, rubbed shoulders with some of the giants of his generation, both Jew and Christian, and cannot remain untouched by his intellectual experiences. Elijah is a troubled man who wants to provide the ultimate answers and truths, but finds himself perplexed by similar existential questions asked by previous generations.[39] Elijah seeks to find his own Jewish identity by defining himself against others, whether it be Christian, philosopher, or kabbalist, all of whom he finds to be lacking. His solution, as it would be much later for Rabbi Soloveitchik, in the deluge of doubts and perplexities, was to take refuge and comfort in the performance and understanding of the commandments. That is the ultimate conclusion of *Beḥinat hadat.*

Notes

1. "Et quod gocit me ad hoc est dominus nobilis Joannes de Mirandula qui se dedit in speculatione scientiarum altissimarum, homo valde intelligens, philosophus honorabilis, diligens viritatem, cui similem vere non vidi in hac aetate." Elijah Delmedigo, *Expositio Averrois de substantia orbis*, Biblioteca Apostolica Vaticana Ms Codex Vat. Lat. 4553, f. 1v, cited in E. P. Mahoney, "Giovanni Pico della Mirandola and Elia del Medigo, Nicoletto Vernia and Agostino Nifo," in *Giovanni Pico della Mirandola: Convegno internazionale di studi nel cinquecentesimo anniversario della morte (1494–1994)*, ed. G. C. Garfagnini, 2 vols. (Rome, 1997), 1; 132.

2. S. A. Farmer, *Syncretism in the West: Pico's 900 Theses (1486)* (Tempe, Ariz., 1998), 1:16, 9:15 (418 and 785, respectively, in the *editio princeps*).

3. See D. Geffen, "Faih and Reason in Elijah del Medigo's *Beḥinat ha-Dat* and the Philosophic Background of the Work" (Ph.D. diss., Columbia University, 1970), and his "Insights into the Life and Thought of Elijah Delmedigo Based on His Published and Unpublished Works," *Proceedings of the American Academy of Jewish Research* 41–42 (1975): 69–86. See also J. Guttman, "Elias del Medigos Verhältnis zu Averroës in

seinem *Bechinat ha-Dat*," in *Jewish Studies in Memory of Israel Abrahams*, ed. A. Kohut (New York, 1927), pp. 192–208; A. Hubsch, "Elia Delmedigos *Bechinat ha-Dath* und Ibn Roshd's *Façl al-maqal*," *Monatsschrift für Geschichte und Wissenschaft des Judenthums* 31 (1882): 552–63, 32 (1883): 28–48; E. Schweid, *History of Jewish Philosophy from the Late Middle Ages to Modern Times* (Hebrew) (Jerusalem, 1971), pp. 108–9; and C. Sirat, *A History of Jewish Philosophy in the Middle Ages* (Cambridge, 1985), pp. 405–7.

4. A. L. Motzkin, "Elia del Medigo, Averrroës and Averroism," *Italia* 6 (1987); 7–20. See also A. Ivry, "Remnants of Jewish Averroism in the Renaissance," in *Jewish Thought in the Sixteenth Century*, ed. B. D. Cooperman (Cambridge, Mass., 1983), pp. 243–65, who highlights differences between the two texts. Elijah, like scholars in thirteenth-century Paris wrongly accused of holding a double-truth doctrine, seems to have believed that philosophy could examine natural phenomena, but miracles, Creation, and other metaphysical issues are beyond its scope. This is not a double-truth theory, but an acceptance of the limitations of philosophy. See R. C. Dales, "The Origin of the Doctrine of the Double Truth," *Viator* 15 (1984): 169–79.

5. See also E. Tornero, "Noticia sobre la publicación de obras inéditas de Ibn Masarra," *Al-Qantara* 14 (1993): 47–64, where he suggests that in his works, Ibn Masarra (d. 931), a sufi, tries to show how the Koran and philosophy are concordant.

6. Scholars have differed on the level of hostility shown by Elijah toward kabbalah, but not on the main point of Elijah's negative criticism. See H. Graetz, *History of the Jews* (Philadelphia, 1976), 4: 290–93; U. Cassuto, *Hayehudim be-Firenze bitkufat ha-Renesans* (Jerusalem, 1967) (Hebrew translation of *Gli ebrei a Firenze nell' età del Rinascimento* [Florence, 1918]), pp. 232–33; Geffen, "Faith and Reason"; D. Ruderman, *The World of a Renaissance Jew: The Life and Thought of Abraham ben Mordecai Farissol* (Cincinnati, 1981), pp. 54–56, and his "The Italian Renaissance and Jewish Thought," in *Renaissance Humanism*, ed. A. Rabil, 3 vols. (Philadelphia, 1988), 1: 387; M. Idel, "Major Currents in Italian Kabbalah 1560–1660," in *Italia Judaica* (Rome, 1986), pp. 243–44, and his *Kabbalah: New Perspectives* (New Haven, Conn., 1988), pp. 3–4; H. Tirosh-Rothschild, *Between Worlds: The Life and Thought of Rabbi David ben Judah Messer Leon* (Albany, N.Y., 1991), pp. 41–43; J. Ross, *The Beḥinat Hadat of Rabbi Elijah Delmedigo of Candia* (Hebrew) (Tel Aviv, 1984), pp. 38–43.

7. K. P. Bland, "Elijah del Medigo's Averroist Response to the Kabbalahs of Fifteenth-Century Jewry and Pico della Mirandola," *Jewish Thought and Philosophy* 1 (1991): 23–26. This line is also taken by E. P. Mahoney, "Giovanni Pico," pp. 136–37.

8. See E. Gottlieb, "A Dispute over Metempsychosis in Crete in the Fifteenth Century" (Hebrew), in *Studies in the Kabbala Literature*, ed. J. Hacker (Tel Aviv, 1976), pp. 370–96; and A. Ravitzky, "The Soles of the Kabbalists Are on the Heads of the Philosophers: On the Fifteenth-Century Dispute of Crete" (Hebrew), *Tarbiẓ* 58 (1989): 453–82. See also M. Idel, "Abraham Abulafia's Works and Doctrines" (Hebrew) (Ph.D. diss., Hebrew University, 1976), pp. 75–76, who claims that a text dealing with the transmigration of the soul, considered by G. Scholem to have been composed by Abraham Abulafia in the thirteenth century, is, in fact, an early stage of this dispute in Crete.

9. See Saul ben Moses ha-Kohen Ashkenazi, "Letter," in I. S. Reggio, *Examin Religionis: R. Elias del* Medigo (Vienna, 1833; facs., Jerusalem, 1970), pp. 80–83, in which

he praises Elijah Delmedigo and refers to himself as his disciple. Both protagonists wrote about the exchange, and both accounts are in manuscripts in the Vatican. For bibliographical details, see Ravitzky, "The Soles of the Kabbalists," p. 453.

10. See Ruderman, *The World of a Renaissance Jew*, pp. 40–43.

11. Much has been written on Flavius Mithridates. For a select bibliography, see C. Wirszubski, ed., *Flavius Mithridates: Sermo de Passione Domini* (Jerusalem, 1963), p. 12 n. 2. See also F. Secret, "Nouvelles precisions sur Flavius Mithridates maître de Pic de la Mirandole et traducteur de commentaires de kabbale," in *L'opera e il pensiero di Giovanni Pico della Mirandola*, 2 vols. (Florence, 1965), 2: 169–87; and J. Ijsewijn, "Flavius Guillelmus Raymundus Mithridates," *Humanistica Lovaniensia* 26 (1977): 236–38. For his knowledge of kabbalah and a discussion of the translations he prepared for Pico, see C. Wirszubski, *Pico della Mirandola's Encounter with Jewish Mysticism* (Cambridge, Mass., 1989).

12. See Ruderman, *The World of a Renaissance Jew*, pp. 109–118. Without doubt, Elijah would probably have disagreed with Farissol over many issues, but probably not when facing a common adversary.

13. Cited in Cassuto, *Hayehudim be-Firenze*, p. 369, and translated in Ruderman, *The World of a Renaissance Jew*, pp. 40–41.

14. In the introduction to the Hebrew translation of his Latin commentary to Averroës' *De substantia orbis*. See Paris BN Ms. hebr. 968. f. 3v; and Geffen, "Faith and Reason," pp. 19–20.

15. Ms. Paris hebr. 968, f. 177r.

16. See BN Ms. Hebr. 968, f. 79r, 150r, respectively. See also Geffen, "Faith and Reason," pp. 14–15.

17. See K. P. Bland, "Elijah del Medigo: Unicity of Intellect and Immortality of Soul," *Proceedings of the American Academy of Jewish Research* 61 (1995): 16–17. In my opinion, Bland, in the continuation of the aforementioned article, misses the point about Elijah's views regarding reason and faith, which are clearly set out in *Beḥinat hadat.*

18. See A. Bartòla, "Eliyahu del Medigo e Giovanni Pico della Miradola: La testimonianza dei codici vaticani," *Rinascimento* 33 (1993): 272: "quod ego non verifico totum quod est scriptum, sed dico quod illud quod scripsi est conveniens opinionibus philosophorum et fundamentis eorum. Illum autem quod est contra fidem veram nullo modo credo neque affirmo, sed locutus sum secundum viam eorum sicut est consuetudo exponentium, et adeo quero veniam et iuvamen in vita humana et in felicitate."

19. Elijah is not the only one to define his Judaism in relationship to Christianity. See Y. Yuval, *"Two Nations in Your Womb": Perceptions of Jews and Christians* (Hebrew) (Jerusalem, 2000), pp. 16–45, who suggests that Christianity influenced Judaism to a large degree in the Middle Ages, even in the realms of religious symbols and ritual.

20. Michael Balbo exhibited many of the humanist characteristics that so annoyed Elijah. Balbo tried, as did people like Pico, to harmonize different types of philosophy with kabbalah. See Ravitzky, "The Soles of the Kabbalists," p. 457–62.

21. See Ross, *Beḥinat hadat*, pp. 82–83. Indeed, David Ruderman has suggested

that Elijah's critique of kabbalah in *Beḥinat hadat* was mainly directed against Pico della Mirandola's appropriation of that lore. See Ruderman, *The World of a Renaissance Jew*, pp. 52–56. In another study, Ruderman suggests that although Elijah did not hold with the veracity of kabbalah, he was prepared to explain some of its elements to Pico because, as with his philosophical teachings, Elijah did not have to accept as true the ideas he elucidated. See Ruderman, "Italian Renaissance," p. 387.

22. Elijah sent two more treatises with the letter: the *Question on Being, Essence, and Unity* and a translation of parts of Averroës' *Commentary on the Prior Analytics*. The former, along with Pico's *De ente et uno*, was written as a result of discussions between them during 1486 in Perugia. Pico's *De ente et uno* is, unlike Elijah's work, inspired also by Pseudo-Dionysius and kabbalah, both anathema for Elijah. See C. B. Schmitt and Q. Skinner, eds., *The Cambridge History of Renaissance Philosophy* (Cambridge, 1988), p. 69. See also M. Idel, "Jewish Kabbalah and Platonism in the Middle Ages and Renaissance," in *Neoplatonism and Jewish Thought*, ed. L. E. Goodman (New York, 1992), pp. 331–32.

23. Paris BN Ms. Lat. 6508, f. 75r. B. Kieszkowski, "Les Rapports entre Elie del Medigo et Pic de la Mirandole," *Rinascimento* 55 (1964): 72. See also Bland, "Elijah del Medigo's Averroist Response," pp. 37–42.

24. Reminiscent of Ramon Martini in Tunis several hundred years earlier, who was prepared to disprove Islam using philosophical reasoning, but was not prepared to prove the doctrines of Christianity using the same criteria. See H. Hames, *The Art of Conversion: Christianity and Kabbalah in the Thirteenth Centuy* (Leiden, 2000), pp. 111–12; and E. Colomer, *El pensament als països catalans durant l' Edat Mitjana i el Renaixement* (Barcelona, 1997), pp. 31–34, 216–38.

25. See Geffen, "Faith and Reason, " pp. 31–33. Although not intimately connected, the translation into Hebrew of Ramon Llull's *Ars brevis*, carried out in Senegallia in 1474, which was used by Jews in such as positive way and by such figures as Yoḥanan Alemanno, who became Pico's teacher in 1488, also indicates Jewish syncretistic attempts. Pico's connection between Abulafia and Llull sounded the death knell for Elijah's attempts to promote Averroism. See H. Hames, "Jewish Magic with a Christian Text: A Hebrew Translation of Ramon Llull's *Ars Brevis*," *Traditio* 54 (1999): 283–300.

26. Ross, *Behinat hadat*, p. 77.

27. See j. Puig Montada, "Elia del Medigo and His Physical *Quaestiones*," in *Was ist Philosophie im Mittelalter?* ed. J. A. Aerrsten and A. Speer (Berlin, 1998), pp. 929–35, who gives an example of Elijah's speculation on the first principle based on Aristotle and Averroës. See also his "Continuidad medieval en el Renacimento: El caso de Elia del Medigo," *Cuidad de Dios* 206 (1993): 47–64.

28. Compare this attitude with that of Ramon Llull (1232–1316), who also suggested that there was no point in having debates between members of the various faiths if there was no common ground and method of argumentation. See my "Approaches to Conversation in the Late 13th-Century Church," *Studia Lulliana* 35 (1995): 75–84.

29. Ross, *Beḥinat hadat*, p. 82.

30. Ibid., p. 83.

31. Ibid., pp. 83–84.

32. Ibid., p. 84. Elijah admits that he, too, is guilty of sometimes going down the same path taken by Maimonides: "And I have allocated space in other treatises to speak against the philosophers and those like them. And sometimes, I have found myself arguing according to their methods, even though I disagree with it entirely." It is quite probable that Elijah is referring here to his disputations with Christains at Pico's home, or possibly to arguments with Jewish colleagues.

33. In the other places in his *oeuvre* where Elijah discusses kabbalah, this parity, which precluded the kabbalah from being ancient, and therefore perhaps as a way to truth, is reiterated. See BN Ms. hebr. 968, f. 138v (the Hebrew version of Elijah's *Treatises on Intellect and Conjunction*, written in 1482), and 41v (in the Hebrew version of Elijah's commentary to Averroës' *De substantia orbis*). When seen in the larger context of Christian appropriation of kabbalah as *prisca theologia*, this is understandable. See also text around n. 14 above for Elijah's opinion of Plato.

34. For slightly different reasons, David Ruderman suggests that Elijah's kabbalistic critique is against the Christian use of kabbalah. See Ruderman, *The World of a Renaissance Jew*, pp. 55–56.

35. Ross, *Beḥinat hadat*, p. 97. Slightly further on, Elijah reiterates: "And it is important that you know that one of the great principles of our Torah is performance [of the commandments], not just belief and intention." Ibid., p. 100.

36. Ibid., p. 99. Compare this with Maimonides, who suggests that the commandments are for educational purposes, to remove obstacles on the path to knowledge of God; emendation of the body so that one can turn to emendation of the soul. See Maimonides, *Guide for the Perplexed*, trans. S. Pines, 2 vols. (Chicago, 1963), vol. 2, III: 26–49. See also Y. Leibowitz, *The Faith of Maimonides* (Tel Aviv, 1989), pp. 101–7; and O. Leamon, *Moses Maimonides* (London, 1990), pp. 129–61.

37. See A. Rakefet-Rotcoff, "A Biography of Rabbi Joseph Dov Soloveitchik," in *Faith in Changing Times: On the Teachings of Rabbi Joseph Dov Soloveitchik* (Hebrew), ed. A. Sagi (Jerusalem, 1996), pp. 17–41. In the same volume, see Y. Turner, "The Religious Act according to Rabbi Soloveitchik: A Divine Command or Human Creation" (Hebrew), pp. 383–402.

38. J. B. Soloveitchik, *Halakhic Man* (Philadelphia, 1983), pp. 44–46.

39. See his introduction to one of his Averroist treatises, in BN Ms. hebr. 968 f. 79r, where he deals with the issues of soul, intellect, and immortality: "Added to these are the troubles due to speaking about and debating these profound, amazing and difficult problems regarding which philosophers from the time of Plato till our own day have not ceased raising difficulties, the chief of the philosophers never having completed his investigation of them." Translated in Bland, "Elijah del Medigo: Unicity of Intellect and Immortality of Soul," p. 2.

Chapter 3

Philo *and* Sophia: *Leone Ebreo's Concept of Jewish Philosophy*

Giuseppe Veltri

Leone Ebreo is considered the most eminent Jewish thinker of the sixteenth century, well acquainted—indeed, even imbued—with Neoplatonic concepts and expressions in circulation in the Italian Renaissance. His *Dialoghi d'amore*,[1] a composition whose form was common in the humanist period, is the celebration of a cosmic love as the relation between God, the universe, and the human being as *intellectus agens* in and of the world. Julius Guttmann maintained that Leone should be regarded as the "only truly Jewish Renaissance philosopher,"[2] an opinion shared by Carl Gebhardt, who saw in him the last truly Jewish philosopher before Spinoza, even a precursor of the latter's pantheistic vision. Offering a totally different interpretation, Colette Sirat thinks Leone's thought is not at all Jewish: "[The *Dialoghi* is] not a work of Jewish philosophy, but a book of philosophy written by a Jew."[3] According to this view, the *Dialoghi* should be classified as general philosophy, as another example of a philosophical disquisition such as the *Fons vitae* of Ibn Gabirol, renowned in the medieval Christian world as a work both Christian and Muslim; or Simone Luzzatto's *Socrate*, whose Judaism appears only in the guise of an author's name on the title page.[4]

Yet that does not apply to Leone, a thinker who in his writings never denied his Judaism,[5] a fact acknowledged by his contemporaries and later readers. On the contrary, it is arguable that his consciousness of Jewish identity is the essence of the philosophy permeating his work. Guttmann was correct in stressing the aspect here of a Jewish philosophy clothed in the garment of Renaissance ideology because of the humanist premise inherent to philosophy. On the other hand, in the Christian world, Leone was not regarded as a Jewish philosopher but rather a skilled physician and a writer of courtly literature (a kind of a *letterato cortese*). In the Jewish community, by contrast, he was considered an expert on Aristotelian philosophy. Was Leone a philosopher, a Jewish philosopher, or simply a writer with a philosophical background? That is still open to debate.

The discussion about where Leone belongs on the spectrum of Renaissance philosophy already surfaces in the sixteenth-century reports on his work. Amatus Lusitanus, a Portuguese physician who met Leone's grandson, also called Judah Abravanel, in 1560 in Salonika, spoke of him as a "Platonic philosopher" (*philosophus platonicus*) "who wrote divine dialogues on love for us" (*qui nobis divinos de amore dialogos scriptos reliquit*). According to his account, a manuscript of a lost work by Leone, *De harmonia mundi*, was in his grandson's possession and was the subject of their philosophical conversations. Lusitanus maintained that this work was expressly composed for Pico della Mirandola (*divini Mirandulensis Pici precibus composuerat*).[6] It is historically unclear whether Leone actually had contact with Pico and whether he wrote a composition on the harmony of the universe, perhaps indeed as the third part of the *Dialoghi*. I have no doubt about the reliability of Lusitanus's testimony, but his account is replete with questionable points. Is the *Harmonia* an Aristotelian composition[7] or a work inspired by Platonic-Pythagorean thought? Carl Gebhardt was of the opinion that Leone mentions this work in his *Dialoghi*. The main difficulty lies in the content of the text. The alleged quotation from this lost work of Leone in his *Dialoghi* (especially III, p. 51b) deals with astrological problems. If we suppose that the *Harmonia* was really written as a separate composition, then it would have to be a tractate on the harmony of the world *opposed* to Pico's theses, for Pico did not approve of astrological speculations.[8] On the other hand, Lusitanus's annotation, "but written in a scholastic style," does suggest a separate composition, because the *Dialoghi* is not a scholastic treatise. Yet if he really was a *philosophus platonicus*, his composition in a scholastic Aristotelian style would seem quite strange.

Perhaps Lusitanus's expression needs to be interpreted differently. It is, of course, possible to postulate a kinship in thinking between Pico and Leone, hence their personal acquaintance. Both of them are concerned with the harmonization of Aristotelian and Platonic philosophies,[9] albeit in different anthropological directions. To harmonize Plato with Aristotle was a project already dreamed of in antiquity and down through the Middle Ages until the Renaissance (*philosophia perennis*). Nevertheless, Jewish philosophers, Leone among them, saw in Aristotle "the bad disciple" of Plato, the decadence of that wisdom that the ancient sages of Greece had learned from the Jews in Egypt. The harmonization of Aristotle and Plato is thus nothing but the correction of Aristotle, or *reductio ad Platonem.* To sum up Lusitanus's testimony: he indirectly accentuated the nature of Leone's philosophy, hesitating between Plato and Aristotle, or—using Leone's own definitions of these philosophers—between "the physician who was the healer of the (ancient philosophical) illness by means of excess" (i.e., Plato) and "the physician who preserves the state of health already produced by Plato, by means of temperament" (*si che Platone fu medico curatore di malattia con escesso,*[10] *& Aristotile medico curatore di sanità già prodotta da l'opera di Platone, con l'uso del temperamento).*[11] It is no accident that both Plato and Aristotle are referred to as "physician," as Leone was a distinguished member of that profession, celebrated in Naples, Rome, and Venice.

The problem of Leone's position among Renaissance intellectuals is not the Jewishness of his speculations—as some modern authors maintain[12]—but the literary and philosophical value of his writing. The reception of his work, which between 1535 and 1607 went through twenty-five editions and between 1551 and 1660 saw various translations into French, Latin, Spanish, and Hebrew,[13] is due precisely to its popular appeal, namely as an entertaining nonacademic disquisition on Platonic-Aristotelian doctrines clothed in mystical, astrological raiment. The quotations from the *Dialoghi* found in Cervantes's *Galatea* and in *Don Quijote* as well as the inclusion of the Latin version in the *Ars cabalistica* of Pistorius would suggest this interpretation. That Leone stressed the Jewish origin of philosophy in general was no obstacle to the reception of his work in Christian circles, because such accents typified Christian pansophic philosophies.

The Jewish Origin of Philosophy

Although the first and second Aldo editions (1541 and 1545) of the *Dialoghi* spread the story of his alleged conversion to Christianity (*Leone Medico, di natione hebreo, et dipoi fatto christiano*), Leone not only makes no secret of his Judaism but even locates the origin of wisdom (*sophia*) in the religion of Moses. He views Jewish scholarship and himself as belonging to the tradition of ancient wisdom whose origins were deemed Jewish.

An important element to be evaluated is Leone's citing of Jewish authors or personalities qualified with the possessive adjective "our." Among the commentators of Aristotle, he mentions "our Rabbi Moses of Egypt,"[14] that is, Maimonides; he mentions Ibn Gabirol's *Fons vitae* as a Jewish work, speaking of "our Albenzubron," a name known in Christian circles.[15] Moses and Aaron are called "our saints."[16] Finally, Leone follows the calendar of the Jewish tradition, which begins its computation from the creation of the world.[17] Nevertheless, all these confessions of his Jewishness could not become a bone of contention between Christian and Jews. No one could criticize these statements, since they are historically evident. At Christian universities and in treatises of philosophical interest, Rabbi Moses of Egypt and the *Fons vitae* were to a certain extent canonized, not least because of quotations in Thomas Aquinas. The existence of a *computum hebraicum* with a computation of years different from that of the Christian calendar and originating in the Masoretic tradition of the Bible had been known at least since the days of Augustine. Leone thus does not state anything that could provoke the criticism of his contemporaries.

Even the discussion on the creation of the world and its obvious divergence from Aristotelian philosophy was not *terra incognita*. Leone states that the idea of time as infinite follows the teachings of the ancient philosophers but contrasts with Jewish tradition.[18] The Torah proclaims the absolute beginning of the world, as most Jewish scholars interpreted Gen. 1:1: "In the beginning God created the heaven and the earth." In dealing with the theories about the world's creation, Leone explicitly refers to the historical supremacy of Mosaic theology over Greek philosophy. At the school of ancient Jewish philosophers in Egypt, Plato learned about the "hidden wisdom" (*sapientia ascosa*); it was the "second principle" dependent on the first, that is, God. Although a disciple of Plato, Aristotle denied what he could not see and made the second principle (wisdom) the first principle of the universe, that is, God.

It is in this context that Leone mentions Plato's dependence on the Jewish elders of his time.[19] Yet to acquire the highest wisdom, more was needed than Plato's affinity to Jewish literature and tradition. Leone affirms: "But Plato, who had learned from the elders in Egypt, could 'hear' [an Hebraism for 'learn'] further than others, although it was not enough to see the hidden principle of the highest wisdom."[20] The source of this statement is purely Christian, for only the Christian tradition speaks of an obstacle that Plato could not have avoided "providentially" in his Egyptian contact with Jews; he could not admit the unity of God out of fear of "ending up executed like Socrates," according to the testimony of Pseudo-Justin.[21] This tradition was known in the Renaissance. A later contemporary of Leone and member of the Florentine academy, Francesco de' Vieri (1524–91), wrote the *Compendio della dottrina di Platone in quello, che è conforme con la fede nostra* (1577) in defense of Plato's ignorance of the unity of God. Against the evidence that "Plato did not sufficiently recognize that God is one in nature and essence," he affirms: "In defense of Plato, I say that although he was wise in terms of human wisdom and although he may have read the Old Testament, where these mysteries are enfolded and adumbrated, he deserves to be pardoned [for his inaccuracies]—because the mysteries were not explained to him by any member of God's elect. The same can be said of Aristotle, who held God to be one in essence and person."[22]

It is hence not surprising that Leone introduces the discussion on the difference between Plato and Aristotle in his treatment of the creation of the world and the origin of wisdom and matter. He considers the divinity to be one in essence but Triune in the prism of human perception, in the process of knowledge: "Sophia: If there is nothing in it but pure unity, where does that Triune reverberation we are discussing come from? Philone: When its pure clarity impresses itself in an intellectual mirror, it produces that Triune reverberation you have heard."[23] A similar expression can be found in the preface to the *Theologia Platonica* of Marsilio Ficino, whose aim was "to explore in the divinity of our own created mind, as if in a mirror placed at the center of the universe, the work of the creator himself and to contemplate and worship his mind."[24]

As is evident from this text and an analysis of the third dialogue, Leone's conception of knowledge is deeply indebted to Marsilio Ficino. In explaining the process of knowledge in the context of the unity of God, he uses the example of light, the sun, and the mirror—exactly as Ficino does. In 1449, Ficino wrote a tractate entitled *Orphica comparatio solis ad deum,*[25] and later a book *De sole.*[26] The symbolic images of the sun, the mirror, and light also play a significant role in the process of knowledge and in his theodicy.[27] The *Oratio ad deum* begins with the verse *Lumen immensum sine fine lucens / Te videns in te speculunsque cuncta.* Leone dedicated several pages of the third dialogue to a comparison between the sun and God.[28] Leone refers to the theory of the unity of knowledge starting from God and reaching plurality in the human being, precisely as Ficino does. In this context, he makes use of the Triune form of knowledge,[29] again precisely as Ficino does.[30] Finally, like Ficino, he speaks of the Triune nature of God as lover, beloved, and love.

It is no surprise that Jewish writers accept, even if only epistemologically, the Triune nature of God. The first to note Jewish readiness to speak about this topic was Nicolas de Kues, or Cusanus, while preoccupied with the theory of divine names.[31] The postulate that the sensual signs of the name of God change even though the signified idea always remains the same[32] can be seen in passages such as the one from *Excitationes I*,[33] where he speaks of an *interpretatio judaica* of the Trinity. According to Cusanus, the Jews had interpreted the dogma of the Trinity in terms of a triad of divine attributes. The novelty of Leone's statement is that the doctrine of divine wisdom as a unique divinity, known in Triune form, is Jewish in origin, as is also the process of knowledge, alleged to be Christian by his contemporary academic colleagues. The fact that nowhere does Leone explicitly mention his Christian partner—although he does make tacit use of Christian doctrine and writings—underlines his quietly polemical attitude toward the academies of his time; in his view, the philosophy of love is a plagiarism of genuine Jewish traditions. But none of his scholarly contemporaries responded to his polemical stance. What opinions or principles did his polemics target?

A Lost Struggle

Leone's philosophy of Judaism was too "pale" to be noticed by a contemporary Christian audience. If we compare his work with the *Me'or 'einayim* of Azariah de' Rossi, for example, it is surprising to note how directly provocative the latter is. In numerous passages of his work, Azariah was explicit about Christian doctrine, false convictions, traditions, and superstitions, whereas nowhere in Leone's work do we find such references. What was the reason for this reticence?

Consider the following quotation from Leone's poetic biographical work *Telunah 'al hazeman* (Complaint against destiny), where he talks about his attitude toward the philosophical academies of his day:

106 It is for you to advance my teaching
for you to carry the light of my knowledge and wisdom
107 Which I inherited in part from my father and teacher,
the father of my learning, my guide and rabbi.
108 The rest I obtained with my own labors,
and conquered with my bow, my sword.
109 So that the power of my mind made the wise men of Edom no more than
locusts compared to me.
110 I visited their schools of learning
and there were none who could engage with me.

111 I vanquished all who rose in argument against me,
and forced my opponents to surrender, putting them to shame.
112 Who would dare to argue with me on the secrets of creation
and the mysteries of the chariot and its rider?
113 I have a soul which is higher and more splendid
than the souls of my worthless contemporaries
115 My form has been molded by the power of my God
and my soul is imprisoned within its cage.[34]

Our first impression from this revealing poetic text is Leone's awareness of his exceptional intelligence, as an inheritance from his father and an acquisition obtained through self-discipline and painstaking reflection. This is also attested by the testimony of his father and Barukh Uziel Ḥezketo in his introduction to *Ma'yene ha-Yeshu'a*.[35] The latter stresses the greatness of Leone's *Dialoghi* in the natural and the divine sciences.

The second element evident in his complaint is his bitter observation that no one takes him seriously as a philosopher: "none who could engage with me." Of course, we can interpret the text as a statement of victory over his adversaries who are "silent" before him, since this is also a biblical quotation about wisdom. On the other hand, it could also be a tacit comment on the impossibility of having an open and decisive confrontation with his "adversaries." If we look at the Jewish and Christian testimonies on Leone, published by Carl Gebhardt at the back of the reprint of the Aldo edition of the *Dialoghi*, we are surprised that there are no Christian writers interested specifically in Leone's philosophy. The reception of his work among the Italian, Spanish, and French authors of the sixteenth and seventeenth centuries is limited to its treatment of love rather than philosophical themes. Only Jewish authors pointed out that he was indeed a Jewish philosopher.

The reception of his work was exceptional not because it was a specifically Jewish work on love, but only because it presented Platonic philosophy in a pleasant poetic manner, functioning as a handbook of ideas in circulation throughout the Renaissance humanist world. Its handbook-like character is stressed by Alessandro Piccolomini[36] in the dedication to his *Istitutione* in 1540. Piccolomini states that he is planning to write the fourth part of the *Dialoghi* on the effects of love (*delli effetti dell'amore*). The *Dialoghi* was recommended as the best book on love composed in the genre of courtly literature. Giuseppe Betussi, Tullia d'Aragona, Benedetto Varchi, and Anton Francesco Doni were representatives of the Italian intellectual elite interested in his work.[37] His profession of Judaism posed no problem for the reception of the *Dialoghi* in Italy, Spain, Portugal, and France, even though Pierre de Ronsard wrote a scathing diatribe on the poem, with clear anti-Jewish undertones:

Jamais Leon Hebreiu des Juifs n'eust prins naissance,
Leon Hebrieu, qui donne aux Dames cognoissance
D'un amour fabuleux, la même fiction:
Faux, trompeur, mensonger, plein de fraude et d'astuce
Je croix qu'en luy coupant la peau de son prepuce
On lui coupa le coeur et tout affection.[38]

On the contrary, the French translator Seigneur du Parc, in a 1551 sonnet on the content of Leone's work, was emphatic in his laudatory recommendation:

Mais vous, humains, desquels les volontés
Tendre on ne voit qu'à la fin bien heureuse
Lisez, lisez, en c'est oeuvre amoureuse
Pour mieux cognoistre et beautez et bontez.[39]

Even as late as the turn of the eighteenth century, after two centuries of oblivion, the German poet Friedrich Schiller, in a letter to Goethe dated 7 April 1797, stresses only the entertaining and educational character of the *Dialoghi*: "The text had not only amused me very much, but also improved my astrological knowledge. The mixture between chemical, mythological, and astrological things here is superb and can be readily used as poetic material."[40]

In conclusion, the *Dialoghi* is not a tractate of philosophy but a vulgarization of philosophical ideas grounded in a distinctively Jewish point of view. This starting point could not be disputed in humanistic and Renaissance circles, for it was the alchemical *pietra filosofale*, the philosopher's stone, which enables the conversion of all philosophies into the *philosophia perennis*. In the context of this insight, Leone's writing was not a novelty; it was even welcomed for its poetic style. Leone made philosophical ideas understandable, a task at which Ficino totally failed. Cosmic love, an emanation in the world's creation, is nothing but the kiss of the lover and the beloved, a kiss that leads back to the godhead with the death of a human being—something like Moses and Aaron, who died kissing God, "morirono per bocca di Dio baciando la diuinità, cioè rapiti da l'amorosa contemplatione, et unione diuina." For this reason, the *Dialoghi* was destined to be a best-seller in the cultural world of the Renaissance, despite its Jewish origin, as Tullia d'Aragona affirms in recommending the book: "io prepongo Filone a tutti (scil. quelli che hanno scritto d'amore) se bene in alcune cose, e massimamente quando entra nelle cose della fede giudaica, piu tosto lo scuso che l'approvo."

Notes

1. All quotations from Leone Ebreo's work are from the first Blado edition of the *Dialoghi d'amore*, reprinted by C. Gebhardt, ed., *Leone Ebreo: Dialoghi d'amore, hebräische Gedichte* (Heidelberg, 1929) (Bibliotheca Spinozana, 3).

2. *Die Philosophie des Judentums* (Munich, 1933; reprint, Wiesbaden, 1985), p. 271; see also Gebhardt, ed., *Leone Ebreo*, p. 4.

3. C. Sirat, *A History of Jewish Philosophy in the Middle Ages* (Cambridge, 1985; reprint, 1996), p. 408.

4. "Socrate overo dell'humano sapere esercizio seriogiocoso di Simone Luzzatto Hebreo Venetiano opera nella quale si dimonstra quanto sia imbecile l'humano intendimento, mentre non è diretto dalla divina rivelatione." (Venice, 1651). On this book, see D. Ruderman, "Science and Skepticism: Simone Luzzatto on Perceiving the Natural World," in *Jewish Thought and Scientific Discovery in Early Modern Europe* (New Haven, Ct. 1995), pp. 161–84; A. Viterbo, "Socrate nel ghetto: Lo scetticismo mascherato di Simone Luzzatto," *Studi Veneziani* 38 (1999); 79–128.

5. See *Dialoghi* III, p. 125b: "ch'io sia Mosaico." But cf. III, p. 75b, in which he mentions the Gospel of John; on this aspect, see also D. Ruderman, "The Italian Renaissance and Jewish Thought," in *Renaissance Humanism: Foundations, Forms, and Legacy*, ed. A. Rabil, vol. 1: *Humanism in Italy* (Philadelphia, 1988), p. 411.

6. *Curationum medicinalium centuriae septem* (cent. VII, cur. 98, ed. Venice, 1566), pp. 152f., ed. Burdigala, 1620, pp. 786 f., quoted from Gebhardt, ed., *Leone Ebreo*, pp. 15–16 of his "Regesten zur Lebensgeschichte Leone Ebreos" (at the end of the volume).

7. "In quo (opere) bonis ille Leo, quantum in philosophia valebat, satis indicaverat, scholastico tamen stilo inscriptum."

8. See Pico della Mirandola, *In astrol*, III, 19, mentioned by E. Garin, *Filosofi italiani del quattrocento* (Florence, 1942), pp. 460–62; see also M. Schiavone, *Problemi filosofici in Marsilio Ficino* (Milan, 1957), pp. 197 ff.

9. Pico della Mirandola, *De concordia Platonis et Aristotelis.*

10. See *Dialoghi* III, p. 116b: "Platone trovando li primi Filosofi di Grecia che non stimauano altre essentie, ne sustantie, ne belleze che le corporee, & fuora de li corpi pensauano essere nulla, fu bisogno come uerace medico curarli col contrario, mostrandoli che li corpi da se stessi, nissuna essentia, nissuna sustantia, nissuna belleza posseggono."

11. *Dialoghi* III, p. 117a. On temperament, note there: "Aristotile . . . gli parue

tempo di temperare l'estremo in questo, qual' forse in processo uerria a escedere la meta Platonica."

12. On the Jewishness of Leone and his Jewish readership, see the position of A. M. Lesley, "The Place of the *Dialoghi d'Amore* in Contemporaneous Jewish Thought," in *Essential Papers on Jewish Culture in Renaissance and Baroque Italy*, ed. D. Ruderman (New York, 1992), pp. 170–88; and M. Idel, "Kabbalah and Ancient Theology in R. Isaac and Judah Abravanel" (Hebrew), in *The Philosophy of Love of Leone Ebreo*, ed. M. Dorman and Z. Levy (Haifa, 1985), pp. 73–112. A very careful and convincing answer to this position can be found in Ruderman, "The Italian Renaissance," passim and esp. pp. 431–32 n. 152. Lesley's argumentation for a Jewish readership of Leone is based on the assumption that the original language of Leone's work was Hebrew, a controversial point; for a different viewpoint, see B. Garvin, "The Language of Leone Ebreo's *Dialoghi d'Amore*," *Italia* 13–14 (2001): 181–201.

13. Cf. Gebhardt, ed., *Leone Ebreo*, pp. 35–37.

14. *Dialoghi* II, p. 69b: "il nostro Rabi Moise d'Egitto nel suo Morhe"; III, p. 75b.

15. *Dialoghi* III, p. 51a: "come pone il nostro Albenzubron nel suo libro de fonte uite."

16. *Dialoghi* III, p. 5b: "Tale e stata la morte de nostri beati, che contemplando con sommo desiderio la belleza diuina, convertendo tutta l'Anima in quella, abandonorno il corrpo, onde la sacra scrittura parlando della morte de dui santi pastori, Moise, et Aron, disse che morirono per bocca di Dio baciando la diuinità, cioè rapiti da l'amorosa contemplatione, et unione diuina."

17. *Dialoghi* III, p. 50b: "Et quanti hauiamo noi di queste sette milia anni. PHI. Siamo secondo la uevrità Hebraica à cinque milia duecento sessanta due del principio de la creatione, & quando saran' finiti li sei milia anni si corromperà il mondo infeiore."

18. *Dialoghi* III, p. 65b: "Il tempo secondo i Philosofi è infinito, ne hebbe principio, ne hauerà mai fine, ben' che noi fideli teniamo il contrario, ma secondo loro il tempo per essere infinito è incommensurabile di nissuna quantità di tempo finito, grande o piccola."

19. G. Veltri, "Dalla tesi giudeo-ellenistica del 'plagio' dei Greci al concetto rabbinico del veus Israel: Disputa sull'appartenenza della sofia," *Revista Catalana de Teologia* 17 (1992): 85–104; G. Veltri, "The Humanist Sense of History and the Jewish Idea of Tradition: Azaria de' Rossi's Critique of Philo Alexandrinus," *Jewish Studies Quarterly* 2 (1995): 372–93; cf. N. Roth, "The 'Theft of Philosophy' by the Greeks from the Jews," *Classical Folia* 32 (1978): 53–67.

20. *Dialoghi* III, p. 125b: "Ma Platone hauendo da li vecchi in Egitto imparato, pote' piu oltre sentire se ben' non valse à uedere l'ascoso principio de la somma sapientia."

21. *Cohortatio ad Graecos*, 20. On the Plato-Moses relationship, see the testimonies gathered by Heinrich Dörrie, *Der hellenistische Rahmen des kaiserzeitlichen Platonismus*, "Bausteine," pp. 36–72 (Stuttgart, 1990) [Der Platonismus in der Antike, 2], p. 211. See also A. S. Riginos, *Platonica: The Anecdotes Concerning the Life and Writings of Plato* (Leiden, 1976).

22. All quotations are from J. Monfasani, "Francesco de' Vieri," in *Cambridge*

Translations of Renaissance Philosophical Texts, ed. Jill Kraye, vol. 1: *Moral Philosophy* (Cambridge, 1997), pp. 173–74.

23. "SO: Se in lui non è altro che pura unità, donde uiene questa trina reuerberatione, de la quale ragioniamo? PHI: Quando la sua pura chiareza s'imprime in uno specchio intellettuale fa' quella trina reuerberatione, che hai inteso."

24. Translated by L. Deitz in *Cambridge Translations*, ed. Kraye, pp. 148–49.

25. M. Ficino, *Opera omnia*, ed. P. O. Kristeller (Basel, 1576; reprint, Turin, 1962), pp. 825–26; see P. O. Kristeller, *Il pensiero filosofico di Marsilio Ficino* (Florence, 1953), p. 93. In the *Orphica comparatio*, he writes: "Qumapropter Orphycum mysterium illud si nolumus fateri verum, saltem parumper fingamus quasi verum ut solem coelestem ita suspiciendo prospiciamus in eo supercelestem illum tamquam in speculo, qui in sole posuit tabernaculum."

26. Ficino, *Opera omnia*, pp. 965–75.

27. See Schiavone, *Problemi*, p. 196.

28. *Dialoghi* III, p. 10a: "come nel' huomo [che è picco' mondo] l'occhio fra tutte le sue parti corporee è come l'intelletto frà tutte le virtù de l'anima simulacro et seguace di quella, cosi nel grande mondo il sol fra tutti i corporali è come l'intelletto diuino fra tutti gli spirituali suo simulacro."

29. *Dialoghi* III, pp. 10b–11a.

30. Ficino writes: "Et sicut in videndo triplex est actus, motus scilicet coloris, aspectus oculi, fulgor luminis [op. lumini] connectens actus reliquos invicem, sic in intelligendo, ubi actus intelligibilium veritas a Platone vocatur, actus mentis scientia, actus utrorumque nodus apud Platonem est Deus qui (op. quin) efficit ut et mens scienter intelligat et res vere intelligatur, imo facit ut ipse intelligatur."

31. On the extent of Cusanus's fame in Italy, cf. E. Wind, *Pagan Mysteries in the Renaissance*, 2d ed. (London, 1968). Pico della Mirandola and Marsilio Ficino apparently had no direct knowledge of Cusanus's writings.

32. W. P. Klein, *Am Anfang war das Wort* (Berlin, 1992), p. 36.

33. "Verum Judaei volentes trinitatem evadere dicunt per trinitatem, quae in eorum libris exprimitur tres proprietates intelligi debere, scilicet divinam sapientiam, bonitatem et potentiam, per quas proprietates dicunt creata. Et hoc Nicolaus de Lira destruit in libello quodam contra Judaeos pluribus ostendens auctoritatibus veteris testamenti trinitatem. Ego etiam aliquando disputando deprehendi sapientes Judaeos ad credendam trinitatem inducibiles, et hoc non est eis difficile persuadere. Sed quod filius in divinis sit incarnatus, hoc est, in quo sunt indurati, nec rationes nec prophetas audire volunt." This quotation is from J. Guttmann, *Die Scholastik des dreizehnten Jahrhunderts in ihren Beziehungen zum Judenthum und zur jüdischen Literatur* (Breslau, 1902; rep., Hildesheim, 1970), p. 170 n. 1.

34. Translation by D. Almagor, B. Gavin, and D. Jacobson in *The Jewish Chronicle*, winter 1992–1993, p. 59.

35. Ferrara, 1551, fol. 3b, quoted from Gebhardt, *Leone Ebreo*, "Regeste," p. 19.

36. *Istitutione di tutta la vita dell'uomo nato nobile* (Venice, 1542), dedication (1540).

37. Tullia d'Aragona, *Della infinità di amore* (Venice, 1547), in *Trattati d'amore*, ed. G. Zonta (Bari, 1912), p. 224.

38. *Oeuvres complètes*, ed. De la Pléiade (Paris, 1950), p. 61.

39. *Philosophie d'amour de M. Leon Hébreu . . . traduite par le Seigneur du Parc* (Lyon, 1551; ed. Lyon, 1595), p. 3.

40. Cited by Gebhardt, *Leone Ebreo*, pp. 107–8; see my "Jews and Judaism in Goethe's Esthetical and Reactionary World: A Typological Study," *Revue des études juives* 161 (2002): 123–44.

Chapter 4

Joseph ha-Kohen, Paolo Giovio, and Sixteenth-Century Historiography

Martin Jacobs

There is a long-standing scholarly debate over the degree to which Renaissance historiography influenced Jewish historical writing in the sixteenth century.[1] Here I would like to point to some arguments that form the poles of the discussion. On the one hand, we have the opinion of Moses Shulvass "[T]he development of Jewish Renaissance historiography paralleled that of the Italians in scope and depth."[2] On the other hand, Robert Bonfil has suggested that "the Jewish production of the Renaissance . . . should in fact be considered as the swan song of medieval Jewish historiography."[3] A third view is represented by Yosef Hayim Yerushalmi, who considers the resurgence of Jewish historical writing in early modern times as a purely internal Jewish development, while denying its characterization as an answer to any external cultural challenge.[4] Yerushalmi sees the emergence of historiography in sixteenth-century Judaism primarily as a response to a specific event: the expulsion from the Iberian Peninsula at the end of the preceding century.[5]

This perception has not only been rightly criticized for isolating Jewish literary production from its cultural context but also for overstating the "resurgence of Jewish historical writing"[6] in terms of quantity. Yerushalmi himself states that "*no less* than ten important historical works" emerged in the span of a hundred years,[7] which is still a few in comparison with contemporary Italian historiographical output. However, if we were to define historiography more precisely, this number would have to be reduced. Among the few examples that exist, I would like to focus on one author and his literary production, Joseph ha-Kohen of Genoa, hoping to shed some light on the general relation between Jewish historical literature of that period and Renaissance historiography.

Joseph ben Joshua ha-Kohen (1496–after 1577) was born in Avignon, the son of two refugees from Spain; his father, Joshua, came from Huete in Castile, and his mother was from the Aragonese Alconstani family.[8] After the expulsion of the Jews from Provence forced his family to emigrate to Genoa, Joseph spent most of his life in the port city and its vicinities, although he had to move several times due to subsequent expulsion decrees in Genoa and its provinces.[9] He came further into conflict with the politics of the maritime republic when Andrea Doria, the imperial admiral and statesman of Genoa, seized Ottoman strongholds in the Mediterranean, thereby enslaving the local Jewish population. Joseph ha-Kohen was active in organizing large amounts of money to ransom these captives.[10]

Internal family quarrels also developed into more meaningful affairs. With his sister Clara he had an ongoing dispute concerning the will of her late husband and the marriage betrothal between his son and her daughter, which Clara had dissolved.[11] In this context, Joseph ha-Kohen asked the famous physician and philosopher Jacob Mantino of Venice (d. 1549) to appeal to Andrea Doria and the Spanish ambassador in Genoa.[12] A bitter correspondence with his brother Todros reflects the latter's conversion to Christianity—a fact that Joseph does not explicitly mention in his letters but prefers only to allude to.[13]

While earning his living as the physician of Voltaggio in the 1550s, Joseph ha-Kohen had his most fruitful period of writing. His main work is the *Sefer divre hayamim lemalkhe ṣarfat umalkhe vet Otoman ha-Togar* (Chronicle of the kings of France and the kings of the dynasty of Othman the Turk), which the author completed (in its first version) in 1553 and which was printed in Sabbioneta a year later.[14] This Franco-Turkish chronicle is certainly distinguished from most older and contemporary Hebrew historical writings since its main subject is "general,"[15] not Jewish, history.[16]

This approach of *Divre hayamim* earned its author the high esteem of Christian Hebraists, such as Bartolucci, who called Joseph ha-Kohen "chronographus magni nominis apud Hebraeos, ita ut à Iosiphon Sacerdote, qui de bello Iudaico scripsit, usque ad praesentem diem nullus alius apud Iudaeos diligentior, ac praestantior isto habeatur."[17]

Modern scholars, however, were much more reluctant in judging Joseph ha-Kohen's work. While Baer at least acknowledged that his style and method demonstrate a *schwacher Abglanz späthumanistischer Gelehrsamkeit*,[18] Cecil Roth called *Divre hayamim* a "naive chronicle" not to be compared with contemporary humanist historiography.[19] Bartolucci's special esteem for Joseph ha-Kohen, whom he compared with Josephus Flavius, reflects the preface of *Divre hayamim*, where the author himself draws the same parallel: " 'For all my fellow people know' (Ruth 3:11) that no author has arisen in Israel like Yosippon the priest [*ha-kohen*], who recorded the war of the land of Judah and of Jerusalem. The writers of memories [*kotve zikhronot*] 'ceased in Israel, they ceased,' until I, Joseph, 'did arise,' who 'arose as' a writer of memories 'in Israel' (cf. Judg. 5:7).[20]

Joseph ha-Kohen expresses a certain consciousness for the gap between antiquity and his own time and describes the *intermedia aetas* as a period of decline, characterized by the absence of historiography. Furthermore, he proclaims himself a "reborn"[21] Josephus Flavius, whom he identifies as the author of the medieval *Sefer Yosippon* (as was common in his time).[22]

Here, however, he seems to step back behind his claim of uniqueness by defining the contents of his chronicle as a "remembrance of the bulk of troubles that have been visited upon us in gentile lands, from the day that Judah was exiled from its homeland until the present day."[23] This topic would not be an innovation in relation to older Jewish chronicles, and the presentation here is inconsistent with the real contents of *Divre hayamim*; rather, it would be more consistent with his later *'Emeq habakha* (see below). As mentioned, the bulk of *Divre hayamim* deals with gentile history, in which relatively few instances of the Jewish past—mainly massacres and persecutions—are included.

Although he dedicates only two out of 328 pages to the subject, Joseph ha-Kohen claims that the French and Spanish expulsions were the main events that caused him to write his chronicle,[24] quoting from 1 Sam. 2:31: "Behold, the days will come, [when I will cut off your strength and the strength of your father's house]." His detailed record of non-Jewish history seeks to show that the Gentiles would be held to account and punished for the troubles they inflicted on the Jews. In recounting historical events as examples for the rule of divine justice, Joseph ha-Kohen certainly follows a medieval understanding of historical writing, as opposed to a humanist one. His annalistic arrangement of the material is traditional as well. The innovation of *Divre hayamim* in comparison with previous Hebrew chronicles consists mainly in the choice of subject matter and material rather than in the application of humanist ideas, which he did not adopt.

The first part of the chronicle of the French and Turkish rulers begins with the origins of the Frankish empire and ends in 1520. In this framework, it mentions the wars between the Byzantine and the Persian Empires at the outset of the seventh century, the rise of the prophet Muhammad, the conquest of Jerusalem by the caliph Umar and the expansion of Seljuk rule in the eleventh century. It deals at length with the Crusades, then turns to the rise of the Ottomans in the fourteenth century and their conquests in Asia Minor and the Balkans. Afterward the focus shifts to the wars between France and the Hapsburgs struggling for supremacy in Italy; then to the campaigns of Sultan Selim I against the Safavids in Persia and the Ottoman conquest of Egypt. The first part ends with the deaths of Selim I (22 September 1520) and the emperor Maximilian I (12 January 1519), both dated by Joseph ha-Kohen to 1520.[25] The parallel he draws between the rulers reflects his view of the Hapsburgs and the Ottomans as the two superpowers of his time.

The second part covers only a few decades—in the *editio princeps*, it ends in 1553—but is even longer than the first part (176 out of 328 folios). The emphasis of the work, therefore, is contemporary history. The second part begins with the European expansion, that is, the discovery of America and the establishment of the new sea route to India by the Portuguese. A meticulous portrait of the wars between François I and Charles V in Italy is followed by a description of the battle of Padua (1525) and the *sacco di Roma* (1527), demonstrating the author's understanding of the bitter rivalry between the king of France and the emperor. Joseph ha-Kohen also presents the struggle between the Hapsburgs and the Ottomans for hegemony, giving a detailed account of Süleiman I's campaigns in Hungary and Austria, and the sea battles between the Ottoman and Christian fleets in the Mediterranean. After the book's printing in 1554, the author revised his chronicle twice and updated it to 1575.[26]

The leitmotif of *Divre hayamim* is the wars between the Christian Occident and the Muslim Orient with emphasis on one of the characteristic conflicts of the sixteenth century—the rivalry between the Hapsburg and the Ottoman Empires. Here, the author picked up on one of the most popular topics of sixteenth-century European historiography. Not only does Joseph ha-Kohen's choice of subject matter reveal contemporary influence. By studying a number of non-Jewish sources, he implicitly admitted that knowledge could no longer be obtained solely from Hebrew texts. He thus clearly distinguishes himself from most of his Jewish contemporaries, who still restricted their reading to religious compositions in Hebrew.[27] For Ottoman history, he used mainly the works of two well-known contemporary Italian historians, Andrea Cambini and Paolo Giovio.[28] Without having ever left Italy and relying only on older, Western sources, Andrea Cambini of Florence

(1455/60–1527)[29] wrote his *Libro . . . della origine de Turchi et imperio delli Ottomani*, which describes the Ottoman dynasty from its beginnings until 1520. It was published only after the author's death (Florence, 1529).[30] In the fashion of his time, Cambini composed a history that focused on the personality of rulers and on military events and developments. Joseph ha-Kohen used Cambini's detailed accounts of several battles—for example, the Ottoman conquest of Constantinople in 1453 (see below) and the battle of Negroponte (1470).[31]

Another humanist source read by Joseph ha-Kohen was Paolo Giovio's *Commentario de le cose de' Turchi* (Venice, 1531).[32] Like Cambini, Giovio (1483–1552)[33] wrote literary portraits of the Ottoman rulers from Orkhan I (1324–1360) to Süleiman I ("the Magnificent," 1520–66). In this context, he stressed the pressure placed on each sultan to surpass his predecessors in conquests and gave a detailed evaluation of the military strength of the Ottomans. Giovio intended his tract as a report to Charles V, who aimed to overcome the political and confessional rifts of the Christians in a united crusade against the "Turks."

Like Giovio, Joseph ha-Kohen locates the origin of the Turks in Tartary,[34] and in many of his dates and other details proves to depend on the *Commentario.* Relying on Giovio, he assumes that the founder of the Ottoman dynasty, Othman I (ca. 1281–1324), was the son of a certain Zich.[35] According to Ottoman sources, the father of Othman was Ertughrul, but Giovio and other Western historians transmit the legend about a shepherd called Zich who won fame at the court of the Seljuk sultan 'Ala' al-Din I.[36]

As sixteenth-century European historiography had only meager information about the early Ottoman period, Joseph ha-Kohen repeats many of the inaccuracies and mistakes of his sources. Depending on Giovio's *Commentario*, he further maintains that the first sultan who crossed the Hellespont near Gallipoli was not Orkhan I, but his successor Murad I, postdating the event to 1363 (instead of 1354).[37] From Giovio, he also copied the statement that Murad went with sixty thousand soldiers on board two(!) Genoese ships that took them for sixty thousand gold coins to the other side.[38] That Giovio thereby accused the Genoese of having a share in the Ottoman threat to Europe seems not to have troubled Joseph ha-Kohen. On the contrary, it fit in to his general critical approach toward the politics of his country of residence.

While Giovio's *Commentario*, intended as a concise report to the emperor (see above), is characterized by a spare style, his main work, the *Histo-*

ria sui temporis (Florence, 1550–52),[39] a contemporary history of the first half of the sixteenth century, includes more elaborate chapters about the Ottomans.[40] Although the *Historia* seems not to have been known to Joseph ha-Kohen, there are certain similarities in the arrangement of the material by both authors. In the fifty-five books that constitute his voluminous work, Giovio intertwines European and Middle Eastern history in one literary unit, as does his contemporary Joseph ha-Kohen. Even the humanist historian does not completely overcome the annalistic system and mainly connects the various events chronologically. He thus shifts in his narrative from scene to scene, changing the focus between Italy, Constantinople, Persia, Egypt, Hungary, and the Mediterranean.

Joseph ha-Kohen likewise shares with Giovio's *Historia* a series of fictive speeches that he composes for the protagonists of his narrative.[41] In classical tradition, historiography was considered part of the rhetorical art. The model of Livius was especially appreciated by sixteenth-century historians when they tried to increase the persuasive power of their historical writings with rhetorical phrases. While Joseph ha-Kohen probably did not intend to imitate Livius (whose writings were likely unknown to him), by composing fictive speeches he used the common tools of contemporary historical writing.

Although the subject of his chronicle and some of its literary patterns are similar to Renaissance historiography, Joseph ha-Kohen certainly does not share the conceptions of his humanist contemporaries. Giovio and Cambini wrote rhetorical, political history as instructive examples for rulers, statesmen, and military commanders, drawing on their own experiences in politics. Joseph ha-Kohen had no such audience and quite different social experiences from those of the authors of his sources, who themselves were advisers to powerful Renaissance rulers.

Cambini served as a diplomatic agent of Lorenzo de' Medici, but due to his later siding with Savonarola, he was forced to retreat from public life and dedicated himself completely to his studies. Giovio was a close associate of Clement VII and took pride in the "intimate relations and friendship with the greatest kings, popes, and famous generals," which enabled him to offer his readers an inside view, resembling the one offered by modern political correspondents.[42] While Giovio interviewed Andrea Doria personally about the Mediterranean campaigns of the Genoese in the service of the emperor,[43] Joseph ha-Kohen was in bitter opposition to Andrea Doria due to his bad treatment of the Jewish civilians he took captive in war.[44]

Therefore, the author of *Divre hayamim* celebrates every victory of Doria's strongest opponent: the Turkish corsair and Ottoman grand admiral Khair al-Din, who was ill-famed in the West under his nickname "Barbarossa." A defeat of Doria was, for Joseph ha-Kohen, not merely a military success of the Ottoman fleet, but divinely ordained, as represented by his description of the battle of Preveza at the coast of Epirus in September 1538:

> And it arrived, the huge ship of the lords of Venice and two of Andrea Doria's. They gave the sign to attack, lit the cannons, whose smoke ascended to the sky. But the Lord drove the sea in a strong northern wind (against them). So they were at their wits' end and swaggering like drunken men. Then the wind stopped, and the big ships in which they placed their confidence could not move any more. Then Barbarossa spoke: "This is a time to laugh" (Eccles. 3:4). And he approached and shelled them the whole day. . . . Then the Lord put cowardice in the heart of the vice emperor and in the heart of Andrea Doria and the commander, and they did not offer [the Venetians] any help, but turned around and returned to Corfu in shame.[45]

The battle of Preveza was planned as a united strike of a coalition consisting of the emperor, the pope, and Venice against the Ottomans, yet it ended for them quite shamefully. Contemporary accounts agree that the Turks concentrated their attack on the biggest Venetian galleon, which was disabled by a strong breeze.[46] Joseph ha-Kohen interprets this wind as a divine intervention and describes it with metaphors reminiscent of the biblical Exodus narrative (cf. Exod. 10:13, 14:21). The fact that Andrea Doria did not support the endangered Venetians but retreated is for Joseph ha-Kohen another example of God's influence, which "put cowardice" in the heart of the attackers.

In contrast to its humanist sources, in *Divre hayamim* history is not shaped by the will of men but through heavenly guidance. To see this, one has only to compare Cambini's and ha-Kohen's treatments of the fall of Constantinople. The Florentine historian does not think in medieval terms of a *historia sacra*, but sees the lust for power as a major factor in history. The conqueror, Mehmed II, is described by Cambini as a modern ruler in Machiavellian terms. He explains Mehmed's motivation to wage war against Constantinople in a way that would have been plausible for readers of the cinquecento: "Being not content with the very ample state his father had bequeathed to him and longing for a glorious operation by which he could win a reputation not only equal to his predecessors but by far surpassing them, [Mehmed II] desired to make himself the ruler of the city of Constantinople."[47]

According to Joseph ha-Kohen, the rise of the Ottomans was part of a divine plan to punish Christianity for its ongoing oppression of the Jews. Christian historiography also characterized the Turks as the *flagellum Dei* to chastise Christianity, although for other reasons.[48] Depending on the religious denomination of the respective author, the sin that caused God to use such severe measures was defined differently. In the Roman Catholic Church, the fall of Constantinople in 1453 was interpreted as a divine condemnation of the Greek Orthodox "schismatics," implying that the Protestant "heretics" might have to face a much stronger verdict.[49]

The humanist historian Cambini does not interpret the Ottoman conquest of Constantinople in religious terms, but still reflects the horror with which the pillage of the churches was echoed in older Christian chronicles: "And the church [*il tempio*] of Saint Sophia, the work of the emperor Justinian, was spoiled of all its ornaments and richness—how magnificent silver, golden, and other beautiful vessels were to be found in it!—and it was contaminated with all the impurity one can imagine."[50]

In contrast to his source, Joseph ha-Kohen describes the same event: "They came into the churches [*bamot*] and took their booty, their silver and their gold, and broke their images [*ṣalmehem*] and idols [*maṣevotam*; cf. Exod. 34;13] and expelled the priests on that day. Then the Lord kept his word, which he had spoken through the prophet Jeremiah: '[Rejoice and be glad, daughter of Edom . . .] to you also the cup shall pass, you shall become drunk and strip yourself bare' (Lam. 4:21)."[51]

The spoiling of the churches is described as the destruction of pagan high places (*bamot*) mentioned in the Hebrew Bible. Christianity is for Joseph ha-Kohen not a monotheistic religion, but a kind of idolatry. Furthermore, Joseph ha-Kohen interprets the sack of Constantinople as a fulfillment of Jeremiah's' prophecy in Lam. 4:21, where the "daughter of Edom" is compared to a drunken prostitute stripping herself bare. As is well known, Edom was identified with Rome or Christianity in medieval Hebrew terminology.[52] By the conquest of Constantinople, the hope for the end of Christian rule seemed to have at least partly come true.[53]

Although Joseph ha-Kohen quotes Lam. 4:21 in this context, he does not go as far as attributing an eschatological meaning to the event, as Yerushalmi assumes.[54] He undoubtedly rejoices in the downfall of Byzantium, but does not call it a sign of the imminent apocalypse. Joseph ha-Kohen was writing already a century after the incident and was obviously aware that the so-called Holy Roman Empire continued, at least hypothetically, through the imperial title of Charles V. In the context of *Divre hayamim*, the conquest of Constantinople is, first of all, a punishment for the persecutions of Jews under the Byzantines.[55]

From Giovio, Joseph ha-Kohen learned about the identical names of the founder of Constantinople—Constantine the Great, and its last Christian ruler, Constantine XI (Palaeologos): "Since Constantine ben Helena was the first ruling king in that city, and Constantine ben Helena was the last. The city was in the hands of the uncircumcised kings for 1,121 years and fell at that time [in 1453] into the hands of the Turks."[56]

The somewhat inaccurate calculation of Byzantine rule (between the year 330, when the Roman capital was officially transferred to Constantinople, and the Ottoman conquest in 1453, there were 1,123 years)[57] is also taken from Giovio. In the context of *Divre hayamim*, this remark clearly seeks to mark the definite end of the Byzantine Empire. But Joseph ha-Kohen does not characterize it as the end of one of the mythic four empires mentioned in the vision of Daniel (Daniel 2), which served as the model for many other religious (Jewish and Christian) interpretations of history.[58]

As exemplified by his description of the fall of Constantinople, Joseph ha-Kohen drew heavily on Cambini and Giovio, but did not adopt their thinking. His traditional view of history, based on concepts such as prophecy and fulfillment, sin and punishment, is completely different from his sources. On the one hand, he faithfully copied names, dates, and all kinds of numbers he found in them. On the other hand, he reintroduced a religious factor, which was purposely omitted by humanist historiography. This discrepancy is also documented by other works of Joseph ha-Kohen,[59] which help to understand his intellectual horizon.

A Hebrew adaptation of Johannes Boemus's *Omnium gentium mores, leges et ritus*, which he called *Sefer maṣiv gevulot ʿammim* (The one who defines the borders of nations, cf. Deut. 32:8)[60] and completed in 1555, reflects his keen historical and geographic interest as well. Joseph ha-Kohen did not simply translate his source, but sometimes omitted passages of Boemus or added others of his own. In the preface, he justifies his transmission of the *Omnium gentium mores* into "our holy tongue" with the intention "to tell the descendants of our people matters their ears have not heard until today, so that they may know something about the deeds of God, which he did, when they were among the nations."[61]

On the one hand, the preface expresses Joseph ha-Kohen's "humanistic" intention to let his readers take part in the rapidly expanding geographic and historical knowledge of his time. On the other, it documents a medieval conception of historiography in defining the task of the historian as one of documenting divine omnipotence. This ambivalence is also reflected in Joseph ha-Kohen's additions to Boemus. In the first chapter, for example, he portrays the period before and after the Flood on the basis of the Book of Genesis, while at the end of his translation he adds the discoveries of his fellow countryman Christopher Columbus, which were still unknown to Boemus: "In our time the Genoese Columbus discovered large islands and kingdoms toward sunrise, whose names were unknown until that day. And many people from Spain followed him; and they also discovered states, which Columbus did not see, as all the countries of Peru where the gold is. They waged war against these peoples, made them tributary, and they belong to the kings of Spain until today. From there they bring gold year after year. . . . Idolaters [*'ovde haba'al*] were the inhabitants of these towns, until the Spaniards arrived there and led them from darkness to the cloud and fog [converted them to Christianity]."[62]

Besides his eagerness to inform his audience about hitherto unknown countries and their remarkable wealth, the polemical description of Christian missionary activities is quite striking.[63] Two years later, Joseph ha-Kohen translated Francisco López de Gómaras's *La historia de las Indias y conquista de México* (Saragossa, 1552), a description of the Spanish discovery of North America and the conquest of Peru and Mexico. In 1557, he added the *Sefer ha-India haḥadasha* (Book about new India) and *Sefer Fernando Cortes* (= *Sefer Megsiqo*), which he called translations, to "his" *Sefer maṣiv gevulot 'ammim.*[64] The great interest Joseph ha-Kohen took in the European expansion may be rooted in the special attention of the Genoese to international trade.[65]

In 1557/58, he completed another chronicle, under the title *'Emeq habakha* (Vale of tears, cf. Ps. 84:7),[66] which contains a Jewish martyrology from the destruction of the Second Temple until the sixteenth century.[67] This chronicle of persecutions is in large part an abridgment of those passages of his earlier *Divre hayamim* that describe events of Jewish history, while Joseph ha-Kohen shortened most references to general history.[68]

In comparison with its literary predecessors, *'Emeq habakha* is certainly no innovation. It continues a tradition of Jewish martyrologies whose most famous examples are the twelfth-century Hebrew narratives about the persecutions at the outset of the First and Second Crusades.[69] Why did Joseph ha-Kohen return in *'Emeq habakha* to the traditional model of martyrology after his *Divre hayamim* had already taken a courageous step toward general history? One reason was his reading of Samuel Usque's recently (1553) published *Consolaçam às Tribulaçoens de Israel* (Consolation for the tribulations of Israel),[70] of which Joseph ha-Kohen incorporated large passages (in Hebrew translation) in his *'Emeq habakha*. Another reason for his return to the martyrological genre emerged from his experience in writing *Divre hayamim*: by isolating the Jewish material from his *Divre hayamim* and making it a subject of its own, the author followed a certain internal logic of his Franco-Turkish chronicle. As expressed in the preface (see above), his aim in writing *Divre hayamim* was to show his readers that the gentile rulers would be punished for persecuting the Jews—not only in a far-off apocalyptic future, but already in history. The Ottomans in particular were portrayed by him as a means of God to chastise Christianity.

Joseph ha-Kohen's description of non-Jewish history had its crucial point in Jewish history, although he seems to have been so taken by his own curiosity concerning general history that the Jewish parts in *Divre hayamim* have an almost marginal character. This might be partly due to his Christian sources not providing him with much information about Jewish history. Moreover, it reflects the fact that the history of the Jewish Diaspora had little material to offer that was compatible with the genre of military and dynastic historiography. Aware of his failure to integrate Jewish and general history,[71] he later stressed in *'Emeq habakha* the Jewish dimension, which actually was the basis of his Franco-Turkish chronicle, but became somehow lost there in the detailed account of the conflicts between Christian and Muslim kings. In both works, Joseph ha-Kohen interprets history in the religious terms of sin and punishment, but while *Divre hayamim* reveals certain Renaissance influences, *'Emeq habakha* is anything but humanist historiography.

That Joseph ha-Kohen did not adopt the humanist concepts of his sources for *Divre hayamim* may partly be explained by his social status, which was in no way comparable with Giovio's and Cambini's privileged situations. Joseph ha-Kohen did not write as an adviser to statesmen and rulers, but intended to offer his Hebrew-reading audience guidance in rapidly changing times. As Jews rarely could shape their history, a humanist approach to historiography could not be very convincing. *Divre hayamim* is not merely an answer to the Spanish expulsion half a century before the composition of the book. The many expulsions witnessed by Joseph ha-Kohen and his activity in freeing Jewish captives seem to have had no less impact on his vision of history.

Joseph ha-Kohen stuck to an older religious concept of history—not because of a certain backwardness, but because of the insecure situation of the Jews in the cinquecento. The ambiguities in Joseph ha-Kohen's historical writings are an expression of the ambivalent status of a Jewish intellectual who, thanks to the invention of the printing press,[72] had access to new sources of information, but who lived under quite different social conditions from those of the well-known humanist historians. The problem of integrating Jewish and general history mirrors the fact that even in Renaissance Italy, Jews were not integrated into Christian society.

However, Joseph ha-Kohen was not the only Italian chronicler who rejected the humanist concept of history. So did the universal chronicles newly emerging in the late fifteenth and early sixteenth centuries—for example, the work of Jacopo Filippo Foresti da Bergamo (1434–1520), which was known to the author of *Divre hayamim*.[73] Because they lacked classical predecessors, these chronicles *ab urbe condita* also did not follow the categories of humanist contemporary histories. They even returned to the biblical model of four empires and, like Joseph ha-Kohen, counted the years according to the creation of the world *and* the Christian era. They, too, told miracles and legends and made no clear distinction between human and divine causes in history.[74]

By stressing the opposition between a traditional versus a secular concept of history, Joseph ha-Kohen will certainly be assessed as a "medieval" historiographer. However, he did not simply reproduce the traditional chronicle genre, but used it as a system to arrange the rapidly increasing historical and geographical knowledge of his time and to adapt it to Jewish literary patterns. By bringing together divergent forms of knowledge and reshaping them, he reveals certain characteristics of a Renaissance author. While reflecting the medieval living conditions of the Jews on the one hand, he responds to early modern fascination with history and geography on the other.

Notes

1. For a selected bibliography, see A. A. Neuman, "The *Shebet Yehuda* and Sixteenth-Century Historiography," in *L. Ginzberg Jubilee Volume*, English section (New York, 1945), pp. 253–73 (reprint in Neuman, *Landmarks and Goals* [Philadelphia, 1953], pp. 82–104); Y. Ḥ. Yerushalmi, "Clio and the Jews: Reflections on Jewish Historiography in the Sixteenth Century," *Proceedings of the American Academy for Jewish Research* 46–47 (1979–80): 607–38; idem, *Zakhor: Jewish History and Jewish Memory* (Seattle, 1982); R. Bonfil, "Esiste une storiografia ebraica medioevale?" in *As-*

petti della storiografia ebraica: Atti del convegno di studi giudaici della associazione italiana per lo studio del giudaismo (Rome, 1987), pp. 227–47; idem, "How Golden Was the Age of the Renaissance in Jewish Historiography?" in *Essays in Jewish Historiography*, ed. A. Rapoport-Albert, 2d ed. (Atlanta, 1988), pp. 78–102; idem, "Jewish Attitudes Toward History and Historical Writing in Pre-Modern Times," *Jewish History* 11 (1997): 7–40; A. Melamed, "The Perception of Jewish History in Italian Jewish Thought of the Sixteenth and Seventeenth Centuries: A Re-Examination," *Italia Judaica* (Rome, 1986): 139–70; E. Gutwirth, "The Expulsion from Spain and Jewish Historiography," in *Jewish History: Essays in Honour of Chimen Abramsky*, ed. A. Rapoport-Albert and S. J. Zipperstein (London, 1988), pp. 141–61; H. Tirosh-Rothschild, "Jewish Culture in Renaissance Italy: A Methodological Survey," *Italia* 9 (1990): 63–96; A. M. Lesley, "Jewish Adaptation of Humanist Concepts in Fifteenth- and Sisteenth-Century Italy," in *Essential Papers on Jewish Culture in Renaissance and Baroque Italy*, ed. D. Ruderman (New York, 1992), pp. 46–62; G. Veltri, "The Humanist Sense of History and the Jewish Idea of Tradition: Azariah de' Rossi's Critique of Philo Alexandrinus," *Jewish Studies Quarterly* 2 (1995): 372–93.

2. M. A. Shulvass, *The Jews in the World of the Renaissance* (Leiden, 1973), p, 296.

3. Bonfil, "How Golden Was the Age of the Renaissance," p. 90.

4. Yerushalmi, *Zakhor*, p. 60: "In general . . . the dynamics of Jewish historiography after the Spanish expulsion are immanent to itself and related to what had happened within Jewry."

5. Ibid., p. 59.

6. Ibid., p. 57; Yerushalmi, "Clio," p. 608; for a critique of Yerushalmi's approach, see Bonfil, "How Golden Was the Age of the Renaissance"; I. G. Marcus, "Beyond the Sephardic Mystique," *Orim* 1 (1985–86): 35–53; Gutwirth, "The Expulsion from Spain."

7. Yerushalmi, *Zakhor*, p. 57 (emphasis added).

8. For biographical details taken from his writings and letters, see I. Loeb, "Josef Haccohen et les chroniqueurs juifs," *Revue des études juives* 16 (1888): 28–56; the introduction of D. A. Gross to his edition of *Sefer divre hayamim lemalkhe Ṣarfat umalkhe vet ha-Togar: Ḥelek shelishi* (Jerusalem, 1955) (hereafter, DHY G), pp. 3–26 (reprinted in S. Kodesh, ed., *David A. Gross Anniversary Volume* [Jerusalem, 1983], Hebrew section, pp. 54–99; English translation without notes, ibid., English section, pp. 41–71); the intrroduction of P. Leon Tello to his Spanish translation, *'Emeq habakha de Yosef ha-Kohen: Cronica hebrea del siglo XVI* (Madrid, 1964), pp. 12–24; and the introduction of K. Almbladh to her edition, *Yosef ha-Kohen, Sefer 'Emeq ha-Bakha (the Vale of Tears) with the Chronicle of the Anonymous Corrector* (Uppsala, 1981) (hereafter EHB), pp. 11–15. For further references to Joseph ha-Kohen's life in documents from Genoa, see R. Urbani, "Indizi documentari sulla figura di Joseph Hacohen e della sua famiglia nella Genova del XVI secolo," in *E andammo dove il vento ci spinse: La cacciata degli ebrei dalla Spagna*, ed. G. N. Zazzu (Genoa, 1992), pp. 59–67.

9. For the situation of the Jews in Genoa, see C. Roth, *The History of the Jews in Italy* (Philadelphia, 1946), pp. 183 f.; R. Urbani and G. N. Zazzu, eds., *The Jews in Genoa*, 2 vols. (Leiden, 1999), 1: xxxii–lxx. For Joseph ha-Kohen and his family, see document nos. 212, 218, 294, 297, 302, 330 f.

10. See letter nos. 29–41 in A. David, ed., *The Letters of Joseph ha-Kohen, Author*

of ʻEmeq habakha (Hebrew) (Jerusalem, 1985); reprinted as "L'epistolario di Joseph ha-Kohen" (Hebrew), *Italia* 5 (1985): 7–98; and the introduction, ibid., pp. 15–22.

11. *Letters of Joseph ha-Kohen,* nos. 42–49, 50–67; cf. the preface, ibid., pp. 22–31.

12. *Letters of Joseph ha-Kohen,* nos. 53 f.

13. Ibid., no. 18. Todros ha-Kohen changed his name to Ludovico Caretto and in 1554 published in Paris his missionary *Epistola Ludouici Carreti ad Iudaeos,* influenced by the works of Reuchlin; see R. Bonfil, "Who Was the Apostate Ludovico Carreto?" (Hebrew), in *Exile and Diaspora: Studies in the History of the Jewish People Presented to Prof. H. Beinart on the Occasion of His Seventieth Birthday* (Hebrew) (Jerusalem, 1988), pp. 437–42.

14. The following quotations refer to the *editio princeps* 1554 (hereafter DHY), of which only a few copies survive. The one I used has the siglum R 36 A 1972 of the Jewish National and University Library in Jerusalem. The next, censored print followed in 1733 in Amsterdam; the third in two parts in 1859 in Lemberg (Lvov). The very problematic English translation by C. H. F. Bialloblotzky, *The Chronicles of Rabbi Joseph Ben Joshua Ben Meir, the Sephardi,* 2 vols. (London, 1835–36), follows the Amsterdam edition.

15. By using the term "general" history, I differentiate Jewish from non-Jewish, i.e., Christian or Muslim, and certainly do not imply that only Jewish history is of particular interest.

16. Preceding Joseph ha-Kohen, in 1517 Elijah Capsali wrote a short chronicle about the history of Venice and five years later the longer *Seder Eliyahu Zuta* (hereafter SEZ), whose main subject is Ottoman history. Both are published in the edition by A. Shmuelevitz, S. Simonsohn, and M. Benayahu, eds., *Seder Eliyahu Zuta by Rabbi Elijah Ben Elqana Capsali* (Hebrew), 3 vols. (Jerusalem, 1975–83); the Venetian chronicle is to be found there, 2: 215–327; for a selected bibliography, see M. Benayahu, *Rabbi Elijah Capsali of Crete* (Hebrew) (Tel Aviv, 1983); C. Berlin, "A Sixteenth-Century Hebrew Chronicle of the Ottoman Empire: The *Seder Eliyahu Zuta* of Elijah Capsali and Its Message," in *Studies in Jewish Bibliography, History, and Literature in Honor of I. Edward Kiev,* ed. C. Berlin (New York, 1971), pp. 21–44; A. Shmuelevitz, "Capsali as a Source for Ottoman History, 1450–1523," *International Journal of Middle East Studies* 9 (1978): 339–44; idem, "The Jews in Cairo at the Time of the Ottoman Conquest: The Account of Capsali," in *The Jews of Egypt: A Mediterranean Society in Modern Times,* ed. S. Shamir (Boulder, Colo., 1987), pp. 3–8; idem, "Jewish-Muslim relations in the Writings of Rabbi Elijah Capsali" (Hebrew), *Peʻamim* 61 (1994): 75–82; A. Brener, "Portrait of the Rabbi as Young Humanist: A Reading of Elijah Capsali's 'Chronicle of Venice,'" *Italia* 11 (1994): 37–60. For a study on the *Malkhut yishmaʻel* (Muslim government) as reflected in sixteenth- and seventeenth-century Jewish chronicles, in which I deal with Joseph ha-Kohen and Capsali in a comprehensive way, see now M. Jacobs, *Islamische Geschichte in Jüdischen Chroniken: Hebräische Historiographie des 16. und 17. Jahrhunderts* (Tübingen, 2004).

17. G. Bartolucci, *Bibliotheca magna rabbinica* (Rome, 1683), 3: 807, no. 749.

18. F. (Y.) Baer, *Untersuchungen über Quellen und Komposition des Schebet Jehuda* (Berlin, 1923), pp. 84 f.

19. Roth, *The Jews in the Renaissance,* p. 311.

20. DHY, 1b.

21. Whether the "rebirth" is merely an empty commonplace of Renaissance scholars that was only proclaimed a paradigm of the Renaissance by Jacob Burckhardt cannot be considered here; cf. P. O. Kristeller, *Renaissance Thought: The Classic Scholastic, and Humanist Strains*, 2d ed. (New York, 1961), 1: 92 f.

22. The critical edition by D. Flusser, *The Jossipon (Josephus Gorionides)*, 2 vols. (Jerusalem, 1978), represents a different manuscript tradition from the first print (Mantua, 1476–79), which was probably used by Joseph ha-Kohen; for the different versions of the *Yosippon*, see Flusser's edition, 2: 3–53.

23. DHY, 1b.

24. DHY, 113a: "Joseph ha-Kohen says: The expulsions from France and this expulsion (from Spain) animated me to write this book, in order that the descendants of Israel will know what they afflicted upon us in their countries, in their courts and their palaces." The sentence recurs in EHB, pp. 62, 23. In fact, he does not mention the French expulsion of 1306 at all! Joseph ha-Kohen only speaks breifly (DHY, 67a–b) of the expulsion decree under Philip II (1183).

25. DHY, 152b.

26. There is a copy of the *editio princeps* in which the author corrected certain passages and inserted about 150 handwritten pages, including an extension of the second part until 1574: Ms. British Library Or. 10387, which was once in the library of the Alliance Israélite Universelle in Paris and is described by I. Loeb; see Loeb, "Additions au Dibré hayyamim de Josef Haccohen," *Revue des études juives* 10 (1885): 248–50. Another autograph, Ms. British Library Or. 3656, dated 1577, represents a complete revision of the whole chronicle until 1575. Gross's edition, DHY G, includes only the "third part" of this manuscript and is even incomplete, since it ends with 1562 (fol. 168b).

27. Cf. R. Bonfil, "The Libraries of Italian Jewry between the Middle Ages and Modern Times" (Hebrew), *Pe'amim* 52 (1992): 4–15; according to S. Baruchson, *Books and Readers: The Reading Interests of Italian Jews at the Close of the Renaissance* (Hebrew) (Jerusalem, 1993), pp. 107, 176–90, only 2.4 percent of the books possessed by the Jews of Mantua at the turn of the sixteenth to the seventeenth century were neither written in Hebrew nor in Yiddish (for included books on general history, see Baruchson, *Books*, pp. 185 f.).

28. Certain parallels between Joseph ha-Kohen and Giovio were already recognized by H. A. Gibbons, *The Foundation of the Ottoman Empire: A History of the Ottomans up to the Death of Bayezid I 1300–1403* (London, 1916; rep., 1968), pp. 32f. n. 3 (et passim), who referred only to Bialloblotzky's English translation of *Divre hayamim*. Y. Ḥ. Yerushalmi, "Messianic Impulses in Joseph ha-Kohen," in *Jewish Thought in the Sixteenth Century*, ed. B. D. Cooperman (Cambridge, Mass., 1983), p. 487 n. 56, announced an article about the sources of *Divre hayamim* (it has not yet appeared). But see instead R. Bonfil, "Riflessioni sulla storiografia ebraica in Italia nel cinquecento," *Italia Judaica: Gli ebrei in Italia tra Rinascimento ed età barocca* (Rome, 1986), pp. 57f.; and Bonfil, "Gli ebrei d'Italia e la Riforma: Una questione da riconsiderare," *Nouvelles de la Republique des Lettres* 2 (1996): 50, who identifies a number of Joseph ha-Kohen's sources.

29. For Cambini and his works, see *Dizionario biografico degli Italiani* (Rome, 1974), 17: 132 f., s.v.; E. W. Cochrane, *Historians and Historiography in the Italian Renaissance* (Chicago, 1981), pp. 331 f.

30. The following translations are based on the reprint in M. F. Sansovino, ed., *Dell' historia universale dell' origine et imperio de Turchi,* Venice, 2d ed., 1568, 149a–189b. For Sansovino's anthology, which includes several other contemporary works about the Turks, cf. Cochrane, *Historians,* pp. 333 ff.

31. DHY, 103a; cf. Cambini, *Libro . . . della origine de Turchi,* 167b

32. The reprint I used is also included in Sansovino's *Historia,* pp. 215–34 (under the title "Informatione di Paulo Giovio Vescovo di Nocerra, A Carlo Quinto Imperadorer Augusto").

33. See the biography by T. C. P. Zimmerman, *Paolo Giovio: The Historian and the Crisis of Sixteenth-Century Italy* (Princeton, N.J., 1995); cf. V. J. Parry, "Renaissance Historical Literature in Relation to the Near and Middle East (with Special Reference to Paolo Giovio)," in *Historians of the Middle East,* ed. B. Lewis and P. M. Holt (London, 1962), pp. 227–89; Cochrane, *Historians,* pp. 366–77; M. Völkel, *Die Wahrheit zeigt viele Gesichter: De Historiker, Sammler und Satiriker Paolo Giovio (1486–1552) und sein Porträt Roms in der Hochrenaissance* (Basel, 1999).

34. DHY, 11 a; cf. Giovio, *Commentario de le cose de' Turchi,* 216a.

35. DHY, 81b.

36. Giovio, *Commentario de le cose de' Tuchi,* 216a. For this legend, cf. Gibbons, *The Foundation of the Ottoman Empire,* pp. 263 ff.; A. Pertusi, "I primi studi in Occidente sull'origine e la potenza dei Turchi," *Studi Veneziani* 12 (1970): 485.

37. DHY, 85a; cf. Giovio, *Commentario de le cose de' Turchi,* 216b.

38. For other Western descriptions of the crossing of the Hellespont, see Gibbons, *The Foundation of the Ottoman Empire,* p. 100 nn. 3–4.

39. See the new edition by D. Visconti, *Pauli Iovii Opera,* vol. 3, *Historiarum sui temporis, tomus primus* (Rome, 1957); vol. 4, *Tomi secundi pars prior* (Rome, 1964); vol. 5, *Tomi secundi pars altera,* ed. T. C. P. Zimmermann (Rome, 1985).

40. For the difference between the two literary forms, see. A. Pirnát, "Gattungen der humanistischen Geschichtsschreibung: Historia et Commentarii," in *Geschichtsbewußtsein und Geschichtsschreibung in* der *Renaissance,* ed. A. Buck, T. Klaniczai, and S. K. Németh (Budapest, 1989), pp. 57–64.

41. Joseph ha-Kohen writes addresses of Bayezid's rival sons in which they try to persuade their aging father to appoint them as successors (cf. DHY, 132b–133a), as Giovio does at the beginning of book 14 of his *Historia, tomus* I, 292 ff. But, as mentioned, Joseph ha-Kohen does not depend on the *Historia.*

42. See the preface to his *Historia, tomus* I, 6.

43. See Cochrane, *Historians,* pp. 369 f.; Parry, "Renaissance Historical Literature," pp. 286 f.

44. See above.

45. DHY, 255a.

46. See R. B. Merriman, *Suleiman the Magnificent 1520–1566* (Cambridge, Mass., 1944), pp. 222 f.; A. Clot, *Suleiman the Magnificent: The Man, His Life, His Epoch* (London, 1992), pp. 112 ff.

47. Cambini, *Libro . . . della origine de Turchi*, 157b.

48. Cf. C. A. Patrides, " 'The Bloody and Cruell Turke': The Background of a Renaissance Commonplace," *Studies in the Renaissance* 10 (1963): 126–35.

49. Cf. R. Schwoebel, *The Shadow of the Crescent: The Renaissance Image of the Turk (1453–1517)* (Nieuwkoop, 1967), pp. 17 f., 20 f.; Patrides, " 'Bloody and Cruell Turke'," pp. 129 f.

50. Cambini, *Libro . . . della origine de Turchi*, 160a.

51. DHY, 97a.

52. Cf. M. Steinschneider, *Polemische und apologetische Literatur in arabischer Sprache zwischen Muslimen, Christen und Juden* (Leipzig, 1877), pp. 256–61; G. Cohen, "Esau as a Symbol in Early Medieval Thought," in *Jewish Medieval and Renaissance Studies*, ed. A. Altmann (Cambridge, 1967), pp. 19–48.

53. For contemporary interpretations of the fall of Constantinople, cf. Capsali, SEZ, 1: 80; Abraham Zacuto, *Sefer yuḥasin hashalem*, ed. H. Filipowski and A. H. Freimann, 3d ed. (London, 1963), p. 226b; David Gans, *Zemaḥ David: A Chronicle of Jewish and World History (Prague, 1592)*, ed. M. Breuer (Jerusalem, 1983), p. 371.

54. Cf. Yerushalmi, "Messianic Impulses," p. 473.

55. Cf. DHY, 5a = EHB, pp. 7, 4f.

56. DHY, 97 a–b; cf. Giovio, *Commentario de le cose de' Turchi*, 219b.

57. But in 324 (i.e., 1,121 years before the Ottoman conquest), Constantine triumphed over Licinius and thereby established complete rule over the Roman Empire.

58. Cf. Capsali, SEZ, 1: 80, where the author interprets the fall of the "daughter of Edom" as the end of the *Malkhut yawan* ("the Greek empire"), which he unites with Rome to form the "third empire" (Dan. 2:39), while he calls the Ottomans the "fourth empire," i.e., the "iron" one (Dan. 2:40); cf. SEZ, 1: 43.

59. Cf. Loeb, "Joseph Haccohen," pp. 29–40; the introduction of Gross to DHY G, pp. 10–15; Leon Tello's introduction to *'Emeq habakha*, pp. 39–46.

60. The text is to be found in Ms. Berlin, Staatsbibliothek, Or. 4° 823, fols. 1a–62b. The manuscript, which is probably an autograph, is described by M. Steinschneider, *Die Handschriftenverzeichnisse der königlichen Bibliothek zu Berlin, Verzeichnis der hebräischen Handschriften* (Berlin, 1897; rep., Hildesheim, 1980), 2: 17–19 n. 169; cf. Steinschneider, *Die hebräischen Übersetzungen des Mittelalters und die Juden als Dolmetscher* (Berlin, 1893; rep., Graz, 1965), p. 1948, § 567; Steinschneider, *Die Geschichtsliteratur der Juden in Druckwerken und Handschriften* (Frankfurt am Main, 1905; rep., New York, 1980), p. 103; R. S. Weinberg, "Yosef b. Yehoshua ha-Kohen vesifro maṣiv gevulot 'ammim,' " *Sinai* 72 (1973): 333–64, where excerpts of Ms. New York (Columbia University, X 893 K 82) are published; additional manuscripts are Ms. Paris, Alliance, H 81 A; cf. Loeb, "Joseph Haccohen, " pp. 29 ff.; M. Schwab, "Les Manuscrits et incunables hébreux de la bibliothèque de l'Alliance Israélite," *Revue des études juives* 49 (1904): 85; and Ms. Moscow, Günzburg, p. 212.

61. Ms. Berlin, fol. 2a; Weinberg, "Yosef b. Yehoshua ha-Kohen," p. 339.

62. Ms. Berlin, fol. 61a; Weinberg, "Yosef b. Yehoshua ha-Kohen," p. 363.

63. *Inter alia*, it may reflect Joseph ha-Kohen's bitterness about his brother's conversion to Christianity; see above, n. 13.

64. They follow the *Sefer maṣiv gevulot 'ammim* in the manuscripts; e.g., Ms.

Berlin, fols. 64a–162b (part 1) and 163a–275a (part 2); cf. Steinschneider, *Die Handschriftenverzeichnisse*, 2: 18 f.; Steinschneider, *Die hebräischen Übersetzungen*, p. 949, § 567; Gross's introduction to DHY G, p. 14.

65. His only Jewish predecessor was Abraham Farissol from Ferrara, who in 1525 described the new Portuguese sea route to India in his cosmographical work *Iggeret orḥot 'olam (editio princeps*: Venice, 1586). For Farissol, see D. Ruderman, *The World of a Renaissance Jew: The Life and Thought of Abraham ben Mordecai Farissol* (Cincinnati, 1981); for his *Iggeret*, see D. Ruderman, *The World of a Renaissance Jew*, pp. 131–48, 164 ff.

66. The *editio princeps* by S. D. Luzzatto, *Emek habaca: Historia persecutionum judaeorum . . . a Josepho Hacohen* (Hebrew) (Vienna, 1852), was printed by M. Letteris; for the critical edition by Almbladh, see above, n. 8; English translation by H. S. May, *Joseph Hacohen and the Anonymous Corrector, The Vale of Tears (Emek Habacha)* (The Hague, 1971).

67. In the fourth revision by the author, it is updated to 1575.

68. In addition, he included parts of Samuel Usque's *Consolaçam* (see below, n. 70) and Solomon Ibn Verga's *Shevet̩ Yehudah*; cf. the introduction by Almbladh to EHB, pp. 21, 26 ff. For Ibn Verga's work, see the edition by A. Shohat, *Sefer Shevet̩ Yehudah le-R. Shelomo ibn Verga* (Jerusalem, 1947); and as a selected bibliography, Baer, *Untersuchungen*; Baer, "New Notes on 'Shevet̩-Yehudah' " (Hebrew), *Tarbiz̩* 6 (1935): 152–79, reprinted in idem, *Studies in the History of the Jewish People* (Hebrew) (Jerusalem, 1985), 2: 417–44; Neuman, "The *Shebet Yehuda*"; E. Gutwirth, "Italy or Spain? The Theme of Jewish Eloquence in *Shevet̩ Yehudah*," in *Daniel Carpi Jubilee Volume* (Tel Aviv, 1996), pp. 35–67; J. Dan, "*Shevet Yehuda*: Past and Future History," in Dan, *Jewish Mysticism* (Northvale, N.J., 1999), 4: 25–56.

69. See the critical edition of the four most important narratives in A. Neubauer and M. Stern, eds., *Hebräische Berichte über die Judenverfolgungen während der Kreuzzüge* (Berlin, 1892), reprinted (without *apparatus criticus*) in A. M. Habermann, ed., *Sefer gezerot Ashkenaz ve-Ṣarfat* (Jerusalem, 1945; rep., 1971), pp. 24–60, 72–82, 93–104, 115–36; for English translations, see S. Eidelberg, *The Jews and the Crusaders: The Hebrew Chronicles of the First and Second Crusades*, 2d ed. (Madison, Wisc., 1996); and R. Chazan, *European Jewry and the First Crusade* (Berkeley, Calif., 1987), pp. 225–97. For the historiographical character of these chronicles, see J. Cohen, " 'The Persecutions of 1096'—from Martydom to Martyrology: The Sociocultural Context of the Hebrew Crusade Chronicles" (Hebrew), *Zion* 59 (1994): 169–208; idem, "From History to Historiography: THe Study of the Persecutions and Constructions of Their Meaning" (Hebrew), in *Facing the Cross: The Persecutions of 1096 in History and Historiography* (Hebrew), ed. Y. T. Assis, J. Cohen, et al. (Jerusalem, 2000), pp. 16–31 (the essay collection contains related articles and bibliography).

70. See the facsimile edition *Consolação às Tribulações de Israel* (Lisbon, 1989); vol. 2 includes introductions by Y. Ḥ. Yerushalmi and J. V. de Pina Martins; cf. The edition by J. Mendes dos Remedios, *Consolaçam às Tribulaçoens de Israel*. 3 vols. (Coimbra, 1906–8); English translation by M. A. Cohen, *Consolation for the Tribulations of Israel* (Philadelphia, 1965). For Usque, see also A. A. Neuman, "Samuel Usque,

Marrano Historian of the Sixteenth Century," in idem, *Landmarks and Goals*, pp. 105–32.

71. Cf. R. Bonfil, *Jewish Life in Renaissance Italy* (Berkeley, Calif., 1994), p. 155: "Since there was no Jewish history in the usual sense of the word, it was only natural that every attempt in the direction of integration [of general and Jewish history, my addition] should fail."

72. He refers several times to the invention of book printing; see DHY, 91b, 173b, 311b.

73. See Foresti's *Supplementum chronicum* (Venice, 1483), updated in several Italian editions (e.g., Venice, 1540); cf. Bonfil, "Riflessioni," p. 58.

74. See Cochrane, *Historians*, pp. 382–89.

Chapter 5
Religious Life and Jewish Erudition in Pisa: Yeḥiel Nissim da Pisa and the Crisis of Aristotelianism

Alessandro Guetta

We know a good deal about the da Pisa family, as well as about the financial and intellectual activities of its members, thanks to the research of David Kaufmann, Umberto Cassuto, and Michele Luzzati.[1] By now we know that the da Pisa family included lenders of great importance even on a national scale, as well as rabbinical authorities who were extremely productive in the field of juridical decisions, thought (both kabbalist and philosophic), and even poetry. For at least three generations, from the late fifteenth century to the mid-sixteenth century, the da Pisas were one of the main reference points of the entire Italian Jewish community.

Much attention has been given recently to the figure of Yeḥiel (Vitale) Nissim da Pisa (1493?–before 1572), author of the important philosophical text *Minḥat kenaot* (The gift of zeal), dated 1539,[2] and two shorter works, *Discourse on the Ten sefirot* (Hebrew), written before the *Minḥat*, and *Discourse on the Righteous Man and the Purpose of the World* (Hebrew), dated 1559,[3] as well as a juridical text on loans with interest, *Discourse on Eternal Life* (Hebrew).[4] In *Rabbis and Jewish Communities in Renaissance Italy*, Robert Bonfil dedicated several dense pages to this scholar, reading his work in the context of the crisis of medieval rationalism, a crisis that interested Christians as well as Jews of the time.[5] The present study intends to develop a few parts of Bonfil's interpretation, following his general orientation. We will then try to sketch the intellectual portrait of Yeḥiel, both in reference to Jewish tradition and to the Italian culture of his time.

All of Yeḥiel's works circulated as manuscripts, even though some of them (such as *Discourse on Eternal Life*) were probably meant to be published.[6] In its scope and ambition, *Minḥat kenaot* distinguishes itself from the others. It is a punctual confutation of the *Iggeret hitnaṣelut* (Letter of justification) written by the Provençal philosopher and moralist Yedaʿyah Bedersi (known as "ha-Penini," 1270–1340) in reaction to Solomon ben Adret's decision to prohibit the study of the natural sciences and philosophy before the age of twenty-five.[7]

Bedersi's *Letter* is a brief, clear list of the advantages that religion draws from the study of philosophy; Yeḥiel examines it in detail and replies to all of Bedersi's arguments, furthering the discourse remarkably. The result is an actual treatise, in which the main problems of the philosophical tradition are analyzed according to the classical structure of the Thomistic *quaestio*: first the adversary's opinion is presented, along with a detailed analysis of the argument according to the main philosophers; then the author describes his own position, based on what he considers the authentic Jewish tradition.

It goes without saying that by philosophy, or free rational research, Yeḥiel means Aristotelianism, as it developed from Aristotle, through his Greek, Arab, and Jewish commentators, up until the more recent discussions of the Italian "university philosophy." The work's objective is clearly presented from the very introduction, which is written in a precious rhymed prose: it opposes the position of those who want to "show the great advantages to be gained from the study and knowledge of that science called philosophy, as if without it the sacred Torah did not have the right to be placed in the highest ranks and as if its beliefs . . . did not make any sense without her: in short, the maid who passes as a lady. . . . But we have the obligation to destroy and shatter these confused opinions and bad beliefs: this is what ruins our people and corrupts our patrimony. . . . The Torah deserves the primogeniture; it is the light of all other sciences."[8]

Further on, Yeḥiel nuances and clarifies his idea: "My objections do not regard the intensive study of philosophy as such, because science *qua* science makes possible the knowledge of the causes or the natural hierarchy of things, and thus can be pursued with profit; as long as it helps to know the reality of the entities, as these were created, and as to their use, but not when it claims to be the main moment and the evaluating criterion of the Torah."[9]

The book's long introduction continues, developing these fundamental points:

1) the centrality of the Torah as a source of knowledge
2) the refutation of allegory as a means by which to explain the Bible; according to the allegorists: "In the Torah there would not be teach-

ings relative to what is permitted and what is prohibited, to the guilty and the innocent, to the sacrifices and the offerings; instead, it would overflow with notions of incommensurable value, like the primary material called *hyle* that is ready to assume any form, toward which it is attracted like a man to a young woman, or the rotation of the spheres, and so forth."[10]

3) the self-sufficiency of the Torah, if accompanied by its esoteric explanations: "Everything is included in brief mentions in its letters, in its vocalization and cantillation signs, in the closed passages and in the open ones, in the marks to be added over some of the letters, just as it was delivered to the greatest of the shepherds from the mouth of the Lord. . . . Such is the kabbalah, orally transmitted unto us."[11]

All this is accompanied by an affirmation of proud particularism ("Why turn to others? . . . Why return to Egypt in search of help? Why embrace a foreign breast?")[12] in which argumentation is replaced by a peremptory affirmation, and the concatenation of rational discourse by the rhetoric of suggestion.

The Components of Yeḥiel's Thought

According to Yeḥiel, the alternative way to philosophy develops through these successive phases:

1) the anti-intellectualism of Judah Halevi (1075–1141), author of the *Kuzari* (King of the Khazars), considered the champion of the traditional attitude vis-à-vis the rational[13]
2) the interpretative attitude—it, too, profoundly anti-intellectualistic—of Moshe ben Naḥman (acrostic RaMBaN [=Naḥmanides], 1194–1270)
3) the vision of the *sefirot*, according to the Italian kabbalist tradition

The Spanish scholar and poet is cited at length by Yeḥiel, who quotes *in extenso* his strong declarations against the philosophical notion of prophecy as the highest level in the scale of intellection: one does not prophesy, according to Judah Halevi, after the union of the potential intellect with the agent intellect, but thanks to the constant application of the Torah's commandments. We will consider this argument in detail later. Yeḥiel also appropriates Halevi's declarations of the uniqueness of the Jewish people, object of a special divine love and in which alone the authentic prophecy could be realized. Yeḥiel is not the only Jewish intellectual in Italy to turn to Judah Halevi as an alternative to Aristotelian-Maimonidean rationalism. During this period, the *Kuzari* reached the great level of dignity of Maimonides' *Guide for the Perplexed.*[14] At the end of the previous century, with the typical Italian Jewish respect for Maimonides, the kabbalist Elijah Gennazano had already said that he would not insist on his critique of the Spanish philosopher, because there already existed a book that could function as a perfect counterweight to the *Guide*: the *Kuzari*, "which does not have equals in its accordance with truth and its harmony with the kabbalah," a book worthy of the constant attention "of the eyes and of the heart."[15]

Yeḥiel claims to have founded his ideas entirely on Naḥmanides,[16] whom he cites in support of the fundamental idea that the Torah is the origin of all the other sciences, as well as of several interpretations, both religious—the question of individual providence—and esoteric—the transmigration of souls.[17] One needs to remember that Naḥmanides is an uncompromising upholder of the tradition, which he naturally sees going back to Moses—and therefore to the divine revelation—and which he considers in antithesis to be the result of autonomous reflection. So does he conclude his dense introduction to the commentary on the Pentateuch: "What I write on the secrets of the Torah, they certainly do not result from individual reasoning and understanding, but were transmitted to me by a master, in like manner the student is taught to become a person who understands." Close to Naḥmanides' sensibility is also the idea of God's absolute freedom with regard to the world; His action is not limited by the separate intellects, and even less by the laws of nature.[18] Omniscience corresponds to absolute freedom. Therefore the total opposition to the Provençal philosopher Gersonides (1288–1344) is more than logical, for the latter denied to God the knowledge of man's single and freely performed acts. The freedom of man—which, as we will see, is vast, although not absolute—is not for Yeḥiel in contradiction with divine knowledge, to which are then linked providence and justice.[19]

Thanks to the studies of Moshe Idel, we can distinguish a kabbalist tradition specific to Italian Jews. This tradition, which refers back to Menaḥem Recanati (thirteenth–fourteenth century) and was developed by Yoḥanan Alemanno, is characterized by a strong philosophical bent, as well as by its relative degree of freedom from the influence of the *Zohar*'s mythical thought, typical instead of the Spanish kabbalah.[20] One of the most remarkable points of divergence concerned the nature of the *sefirot.* The problem, whose delicacy and importance become clear when considering the attributes in Spinoza's *Ethics,* is whether the *sefirot* belong to the divine substance (*'aṣmut*). Recanati, the author of an important esoteric commentary on the Torah, defines the *sefirot* as instruments or receptacles (*kelim*) of divine activity ("as instruments in the hands of an artisan . . . yet tightly united among themselves and with a single spirit for all")[21]—and, as such, knowable—thereby distinguishing them from the substance of God (the *ein sof*), which remains unknowable. In his commentary on the Song of Songs, Alemanno returns to this distinction and illustrates it through the similitude of soul and body—a comparison that can give an idea of the relationship between invisible cause and visible effects, and of the relationship between the unity of God and the multiplicity of forces ruling the world.[22] Yeḥiel's uncle, Isaac of Pisa, who certainly knew Alemanno, his contemporary and a frequent guest of the da Pisas, is the protagonist of an epistolary exchange with a rabbi of Spanish origin, Isaac Mar Ḥayyim. This correspondence reveals a position different from Alemanno's, in that the *sefirot* are not considered solely as instrumental, but also—at least for the first two or three—as essential.[23]

We will not delve into a discussion of these difficult, though fundamental, classifications. Naturally, one must wonder about the degree of philosophical awareness with which these minute distinctions were made. We take it for granted that the scholars in question did not limit themselves to a servile repetition of themes whose depth they ignored. Obviously, pedagogical traditions played an important—albeit not exclusive—role in determining their various stances; nevertheless, even beyond what may appear to be mere formulas (the status of the *sefirot*; the relationship between the *sefirot ein sof* and *keter*; the classification of the *sefirot* in subcategories), the main question is whether these authors were aware that they were treating issues of great importance, such as the relationship between God and the world, between the mystery and the knowable, the ineffable and the sayable.

After recalling that Yeḥiel seems to uphold his uncle Isaac's theory,[24] it is important to note that this debate combines philosophy's conceptual terminology with the kabbalah's: the *sefirot* are defined as "attributes"; the *ein sof* is the "primary cause." In Yeḥiel, critic of philosophy, the relationship between God and the world—a relationship of entirely kabbalist inspiration—is made to overlap with Aristotelian physics and metaphysics: "God transmits his spiritual energy [*shefa*'] and strength to His attributes, without undergoing any changes; from there, this transmission of energy descends to the world of the intellect, and thereafter to the spheres, and finally to the sublunar world."[25]

This is a real overlay, in which, according to the kabbalist, esoteric doctrine, may complete, rather than refute, the philosophical: the first begins where the second leaves off. Alemanno had been clear on the subject: "The wise of Israel speak of a world that is not that of the philosophers; the world of the *sefirot* is superior to that of the corruptible entities, as well as to the world of circular movements and that of the angels."[26]

Kabbalah and Philosophy

Isaac Mar Ḥayyim had already warned his correspondent about the relationship between tradition and autonomous reflection, inviting him to choose the first as his reference point, that is, to adapt philosophy to the kabbalah, not the contrary. "Rational research in this field is prohibited to us," Isaac Mar Ḥayyim contends elsewhere. "Instead, it is to the prophetic kabbalah that we must turn, because it is superior to reason."[27]

This testimony of a Spanish teacher confirms *a contrario* the Italian kabbalah's philosophical tendency, of which Yeḥiel is a typical representative. Yeḥiel's philosophical *forma mentis* is for the rest confirmed by the scholastic course of his juridical argument. In *Discourse on Eternal Life*, his brief text on loans with interest, declaredly written as a juridical synthesis and reference book for the numerous Jews who supported themselves on financial activities, Yeḥiel pronounces the most general principles on which the arguments are constructed; elaborates a syllogism from which to deduce the general conclusion; announces the necessity of studying each particular case; and proceeds to the definitions, which delimits the problems to be discussed and facilitates their solution.[28]

Presented only to be confuted, the abundance and precision of the philosophical arguments in the *Minḥat kenaot* illustrate Yeḥiel's deep understanding of the discipline. His culture was naturally based on the Arab Jewish Aristotelian tradition in addition to the *Zohar*. Yeḥiel had personally copied Averroës' commentary on books 3 and 4 of Aristotle's *Physics*;[29] thanks to his knowledge of Latin, he was also acquainted with the most recently published works in Italy. A precious source for him are the extensive syntheses of his contemporary Agostino Nifo, to whom Yeḥiel refers many times in his thorough analyses of particular questions.[30]

Several philosophical expositions—on the intellect, for example—are far-reaching and exemplary in terms of their order and clarity. They could have been more convincing if the author had presented a more unified and coherent thought. Robert Bonfil has argued that Yeḥiel finds himself between two cultural eras and that he masters the discourse of the older era, which he rejects, but not that of the new, which is not yet well defined. This statement, important from a historical perspective, should perhaps be nuanced with regard to Yeḥiel's specific competence not only in rabbinical tradition, but in the kabbalah itself. The Pisan scholar masters basic texts such as the *Zohar*, and establishes an exact position for himself within kabbalist thought, one that reveals technical knowledge and deliberate intellectual choices.[31]

The kabbalah is not simply a philosophy, at least not in the Aristotelian sense. Apart from its origins (traditional or rational), the kabbalah represents an intuitive attitude that would function as an alternative (or complement, as we have seen) to Aristotelian discursive reason. The relationship between unity and plurality as the kabbalists intend it (as do, ultimately, the Neoplatonists) cannot be analyzed with Aristotelian conceptual instruments. When Yeḥiel refrains from analyzing these subjects in depth,[32] it is not because of any superficiality or incompetence on his part; rather, he is aware that they can only be treated in allusive and intuitive terms, with a metaphoric or even mythical lexicon: "The question of the attributes is one of the most profound of all theology [*ḥokhma elohit*, divine science]. . . . All actions that manifest themselves in reality are potentially qualities [*middot*] through which God acts, as instruments in the hands of an artisan; however, they are not separated from God; rather, they are united in Him in a total unity *that words are not capable of describing*."[33]

Yeḥiel's adhesion to the philosophical dimension and, at the same time, the distance that he keeps from it are visible in his definition of the stars' and celestial spheres' constitution. They are of "*sefirotic* material": here the ontological character of the substance serves to define an element, be this celestial or Aristotle's "fifth element." Beyond this coincidence in terminology, however, the difference between the Aristotelians' position and Yeḥiel's is evident from the very beginning. Maimonides, who in this regard referred back to Aristotle, had defined the fifth element negatively (it is neither light nor heavy, and so forth), for the obvious reason that we do not have direct experience of it.[34] Where the philosopher had prudently stopped for lack of proof, Yeḥiel advances without any scruples. The combination of his anti-intellectual and intuitive attitudes culminates in a need for positive contents, which the schools' philosophy could not provide. This is perhaps the most historically significant aspect of Yeḥiel's work, which we will discuss in further detail.

Yeḥiel, Renaissance Man

Once again, it is to Idel's research that we owe the particular attention given to the magic—and Neoplatonic—character of a certain kabbalah. This aspect had been well known for a while, thanks in part to the Christian kabbalah and its magic-alchemic elements. However, its importance had been forgotten in the shadow of the great figure of Gershom Scholem, who, in his reconstruction of the historical development of Jewish esotericism, had not highlighted this aspect.

The magical aspect is emphasized by Idel, in the same studies mentioned above, regarding Yoḥanan Alemanno and Isaac of Pisa. This step marked considerable progress in linking Jewish historiography—for a long time the prisoner of a reductive rationalism—and European historiography, which instead had learned to see magic as an important step in the development of a "modern" consciousness. To a certain extent, Yeḥiel shares this trust in magic: clearly a Renaissance man in his behavior, he was also one in his mental attitudes.

After having reached the highest level of spirituality, man can attach his soul to the superior worlds and cause divine energies to descend onto the world, by means of his moral virtues and performance of the commandments. Thanks to this union, in a way he, too, becomes divine and is thus able to intervene in the normal course of nature, which, as we have seen, is totally dependent on divine will:

> When man ascends from one level to another, thanks to those steps that are represented by the virtues that the Torah indicates and that our teachers call *pietàs* [*ḥasidut*], and after the accomplishment of the Torah in its general rules as well as in its details, his soul strongly adheres to and unites itself with the superior worlds, attracting and propagating the divine presence [*shekhinah*]; he will therefore provide the people with true knowledge, and will conduct them along the right way. That man will then be able to accomplish prodigies and miracles, and change the course of nature.[35]

> At this level he will become entirely spiritual and divine, and while remaining in this world he will belong to the superior worlds, and these will obey him as it happened with the prophets. Thus even the teachers of Israel, when the prophecy was interrupted, by virtue of their absolute adhesion [*devequt*] to God caused the dead to resurrect and the living suddenly to die. They overturned the order and nature of the world, because they adhered to blessed God, and he "fulfills the desires of those who fear him (Ps. 145:19)."[36]

All the different components of these propositions are already in Alemanno, and many of them can be found in Florentine Neoplatonism. Alemanno speaks explicitly of the descent of spiritual energies on the world thanks to the intervention of the man who is capable of receiving and directing divine emanations and their powers.[37] And if Pico della Mirandola describes man as *et caelestium et terrestrium vinculum et nodus si in se ipso pacem et foedera sancit*,[38] Yeḥiel recalls the *Zohar*'s image of the tabernacle and the terrestrial Temple (both the historical and the future) as places in which the superior and inferior worlds have been, and will be, strongly linked, thereby fulfilling the will of God.[39] One should note, however, that despite these important references, in Yeḥiel's writing magic does not have the weight that it seems to possess in Alemanno's. Yeḥiel does not insist on the subject, and more important, he ignores all descriptions of magical practices, on which Alemanno dwells at length (for example, on how to prepare to receive the divine energy through the reading of the Torah, which is the equivalent of reading the names of God);[40] in *Minḥat kenaot*, there is a single and cursory reference to the mystical properties of the letters and of the vocalization and cantillation signs.[41]

Yeḥiel is interested, on the one hand, in establishing the privileged role of man within the universe and of the Jewish people in their relationship to God in particular, and on the other hand, in showing the inadequacy of conceptual instruments to fulfill this destiny. He therefore limits the importance of magic, inserting it within the traditional and anti-intellectual framework that we have already described. As he exalts man's calling, Yeḥiel appears to emphasize the descent of divine energies onto the world by virtue of the just man's work, while he neglects the Zoharic concept of harmony between the *sefirot* themselves as a consequence of human action. The affirmation of the absolute freedom of God is combined with the anthropocentric vision of the world created for the good and perfection of man.[42]

Moreover, to this problem Yeḥiel dedicated his whole *Discourse on the Righteous Man and the Purpose of the World*, a short treatise written in answer to the letter of a certain Jacob from Modena, which contained the following questions: Is man more important than the angels? Was the world created for man? Yeḥiel correctly links the two questions and, as in *Minḥat kenaot*, reviews the philosophical doctrines on the subject, to which he then opposes others drawn from the rabbinical-kabbalist tradition.

To understand Yeḥiel's answers, it is necessary to remember that, according to Maimonides, in this regard a faithful follower of Aristotle, man cannot be seen as the object of Creation, because every entity was created for the good of that same entity, and not for any other. Furthermore, there is a hierarchy of the purity of beings, within which man occupies an inferior position in relation to the separate and celestial intellects (identified with the angels).[43]

Yeḥiel's answer is the opposite of Maimonides': man is a microcosm, a model of all worlds. When he is just, he is superior to the angels; his soul originates on the throne of God's glory, to which it returns when it separates from the body, even before death. It is the Torah, which preceded the existence of the world, that allows corruptible man to ascend to the superior worlds and to unite himself with God, leaving the angels beneath him.[44] It seems almost superfluous to point out how close this idea is to Renaissance Neoplatonism, of which it represents the Jewish version.[45]

The Uniqueness of Israel

Speaking of Yeḥiel Nissim da Pisa, Bonfil emphasizes how his opposition to scholastic thought also implies the reevaluation of the uniqueness of the Jew—as an individual and as a people—which this same thought had somewhat disregarded.[46] We have seen not only how the Torah is an instrument of elevation, but also the privileged position of the Jewish people among men: it is like the heart among the members of the body.[47]

Yeḥiel emphasizes the uniqueness of Israel time and again. This idea is highlighted especially in the "classical" argument, bent on proving the insufficiency of philosophy in comparison with authentic prophecy: indeed, if prophecy really was a union, favored by the imaginative faculty, of the potential intellect with the agent intellect, as Avicenna and Maimonides contended, it is not clear why the philosophers were not prophets, and why among the latter only the Jews prophesied in truth and at length. In reality, it is the performance of the mitzvot and the knowledge of the Torah's secrets, both reserved to Israel, that allow one to acquire prophetic abilities.[48]

Regarding divine providence, Yeḥiel establishes a hierarchy of entities that views animals as the object of divine providence qua species, humans qua individuals and the Jews qua individuals who receive a particular attention in that "their form is particular and separated from the rest of mankind, and it is therefore right that providence be more individualized in their regard. Indeed, the more a man is close to God, thanks to his accomplishment of the precepts, the more He who provides is close to the one who enjoys this providence, and never does He abandon him with His gaze.[49]

Yeḥiel alters Maimonides' argument, whose influence he explicitly acknowledges, at the end. According to the Spanish philosopher, divine providence applies to animals as species and to men as individuals. The latter receive a particular attention from God in proportion to their degree of perfection, which is mainly of an intellectual order and which, in the *Guide*, does not seem to refer to the Jews.[50] Yeḥiel replaces this hierarchy of intelligence with an essentialist hierarchy of form and with the performance of the commandments, this an essentialist act in that, by virtue of their nature, the commandments are close to God.

Furthermore, the Pisan rabbi's argument differs from the beliefs of many of his Jewish contemporaries. As humanists, they argued for the superiority of Israel on the basis of the antiquity of their laws, a claim also informed by a cultural pride that could represent itself in the idea of an "Israel redeemer of humanity," as well as in the—however limited—practice of proselytism.[51]

The real purpose of the world is the actualization of Israel, the just people. Yeḥiel therefore rejects the Aristotelian and Maimonidean idea of the internal actualization of every created thing, and he develops this through a parable. A man owns a field perfect for planting. He performs all the necessary preparations and plants a tree. This tree grows and starts bearing fruit. But many of the fruits rot on the branches; others fall before they have ripened. There remains one single fruit, which grows and ripens as it should, and it reaches its final state. If it is true that the field was the cause of the tree, as also the tree of the fruit, the farmer's intention and objective in this work would be to obtain that one perfect fruit; indeed, he knew very well that most of his crop would be lost. In the same way, God has prepared the world for the planting of that tree—mankind—with the intention of obtaining in the end one single fruit, the people of Israel with their just men.[52]

This particularism is probably not characteristic of the Jews, as it manifests itself as well in the Christian milieu associated with traditionalism and the almost exclusive reference to the Scriptures. In his *Examen vanitatis* (1520), for example, Gianfrancesco Pico della Mirandola affirmed that he "preferred the old theologians of our faith, who contended that one should undertake some action against the pagan philosophers [*gentium philosophos*] and destroy their teachings, rather than philosophize according to their doctrines (as those who cultivated such studies in the past centuries)."[53] These affirmations clearly recast the ethnic character of Jewish particularism. The equivalence made here—of a cultural, not an ethnic, character—is therefore between an "us" and the heirs of the dogmatic tradition (to whatever camp they may belong), on the one hand, and, on the other, a "them" and the rationalists who place themselves outside this tradition.

Yeḥiel's contemporary Ovadiah Sforno (1470–1550), in his important philosophical work *Or 'ammim* (Light of the peoples; Bologna, 1537),[54] returns to the subject of man as the purpose of the universe, adapting this Renaissance idea to Aristotelian, and in particular Averroist, coordinates, to which he remains faithful. Sforno contends that, even admitting that superior entities cannot exist to ensure the perfection of inferior ones, one cannot deny that man's rational soul is superior to the heavens insofar as it is separate. Indeed, the heavens, with their circular and perfect movement, are the cause of the combinations among the elements of the corruptible world. It is precisely in this world that man happens to act in order to accomplish his two goals of getting closer to God by means of his intellect, and of resembling Him, in accordance with the divine precept.

Within this conceptual framework, the Jews occupy a privileged position, not as the executors of the Torah that God Himself has reserved for them, but because they accepted His covenant and are better disposed than any other people to recognize His sovereignty and to serve Him. Further on, we will see how Sforno believes that the superiority of the Jews is justified for reasons opposite those of Yeḥiel: in his mind, the people of Israel are the true repositories of a rational tradition.[55]

If Yeḥiel exalts the centrality of man in the universe (and, among men, the Jews), nevertheless he is not ready to grant him absolute freedom. Several years before he wrote *Minḥat kenaot*, a heated debate had developed about free will, stimulated by the Protestant reform. Yeḥiel deliberately and explicitly places himself within this debate, denying any validity to the reformist doctrine of the "servant will." Even without sufficient philosophical proofs, he argues, the mere fact that the Torah presents man with commandments implies that there is a freedom of choice: free will is therefore an indispensable element in the construction of beliefs.[56] However, Yeḥiel expresses one important reservation: "Free will is not absolute, and the help of God is necessary to perfect the inclination that permits man to develop fear and follow the good. This is one of the principles of the Torah: if and when on his part, man disposes his heart to good actions and to the mitzvot, he will receive from God help and energy, which will give him sufficient strength to accomplish them. Most worthy actions that regard the Torah and the mitzvot, and the beginning of fear, depend on man: the help he receives from God is to be considered a reward."[57]

In its basic structure (man's action completed by divine intervention), this idea is similar to the Catholic doctrine of justification, as sanctioned a few years later by the Council of Trent. According to this doctrine, faith in a "propitiatory" Christ can compensate for the weakening of freedom after the original sin. Only in this way can man be born again to grace.[58]

Modernity and Tradition

One can view Yeḥiel's work as attached to a traditionalist vision, as the expression of a spirit hostile to philosophy, which within Judaism manifested itself in a contempt of Maimonides and a return to internal sources.[59] However, we know that renewal—without loading this term with the value judgments of any philosophy of history—can easily appear as a return to tradition, at least initially. In this case the historian must discover, within traditional arguments, that accent or the few significant details that nuance them in new ways.

We have seen Yeḥiel's reservations about philosophy. Naturally, his position was far from new. Judah Halevi takes it as one of the principles informing the *Kuzari*: philosophy is conceived of as the *ancilla prophetiae*, where "prophecy" means that of Moses, preserved and passed on through the oral and written tradition.[60] What characterizes Yeḥiel's position, within this anti-intellectual vein, is his insistence on the insufficiency of the philosophical method, which rests all explanations on empirical observation and on the subsequent search for the causes of the phenomenon. This search from the posterior to the anterior is deemed inappropriate by Yeḥiel if one wants to reach truth. The inductive procedure leads one to determine the cause through its effect, attested by the senses; but both the starting point and this procedure are marred by imprecision. "Prophetic knowledge, on the contrary, captures the effect through its cause, that is, the posterior along with the anterior, and this is free from errors or confusion."[61] His opposition to Peripatetic epistemology is clear, even if there is a tendency to emphasize its empirical aspect. One should consider, for a comparison, the Aristotelian statement made by Agostino Nifo, to whose works Yeḥiel referred readers: "Scire proprissimum est scire propter quid," and knowledge is only of two kinds: "Quae sunt per se notae vel per sensum, vel seipsis."[62]

The same opposition is expressed toward logic, for according to Aristotle this is the instrument of the sciences and, as such, is external to them. According to Yeḥiel, to understand the Torah there is no need to refer to external means; the necessary interpretative rules were revealed and transmitted along with the text. The Hebraic system of knowledge is configured as unitary and is in itself complete.[63]

Yeḥiel's tradition-based certainties are very different from the torments of a Pomponazzi, for example, just as their two works differ in intellectual scope.[64] The Pisan rabbi certainly would not have been able to reach the skeptical conclusions of the philosopher from Padua. However, one should not conclude that Yeḥiel's thought was not consonant with questions addressed in Christian society. The issues he considers (including the transmigration of the soul, which would be developed after the end of the sixteenth century with the Lurianic kabbalah) were of current interest even within the philosophical debate;[65] and he faces, just as his Christian contemporaries do, a philosophical tradition and possibly a whole way of thinking that by then had become insufficient. Yeḥiel's anti-intellectual *vis* and Pomponazzi's rigorously rational knowledge ultimately reach the same conclusions: on fundamental questions, such as the soul's immortality, thought conducted according to the old rules cannot give convincing answers. The Pisan's answer is to turn to tradition; the Paduan's more prudent and perhaps more skeptical solution also seems to tend toward a religious horizon—in which, however, it is not tradition, but faith, that is highlighted.[66]

In a certain sense, the extremely traditional Yeḥiel was more "modern" than figures such as Sforno, teacher of reason, and another prominent Italian Jewish intellectual, Moses Provenzali (1503–75).

Sforno critiqued blind tradition harshly, exalting reason as the only means to distinguish truth from falsehood: "The fear and zeal for the Torah (of the pure traditionalist) are founded on a story passed on from father to child. . . . God never ordered that one believe in His existence, in His power and in His providence, because faith does not depend on will, as experience has shown and as the Philosopher has demonstrated in *De anima* II, 153 . . . but he presented true and just ideas along with their rational argumentation."[67]

Finding in Aristotle many conclusions that contradicted their beliefs, the traditionalists, Sforno contends, simply denied them, without any proof. The Jews instead are the heirs of a rational tradition, founded by 'Ever and continued by Abraham, and concerned with the existence of God, His attributes, and many other similar questions. Rational Jewish science survived on the ruins of Chaldean science.[68]

As for Moses Provenzali, rabbi in Mantua and a jurist, grammarian, and philosopher of interest, his fame is essentially linked to the extremely liberal attitude of his ritual decisions, which provoked heated debates and caused him numerous difficulties in the exercise of his functions within the Jewish community. From a philosophical point of view, however, he is a conservative, or a rationalist-conservative. In his commentary on Maimonides' *Axioms*, he tries to reestablish, within the Maimonidean alveolus, that division between substantial and accidental causality, which had radically called into question an important moment of Aristotelian metaphysics. The issue at stake here is infinity in the causal chain, as well as in time and space, which, according to Aristotelian presuppositions, was impossible. Ḥasdai Crescas had attacked these conclusions in depth and with productive results, opening the idea of an infinite space and an infinity of worlds, an idea that is rightly considered one of the main foundations of modern thought.

Provenzali overturns Crescas's argument. We recall that, as he follows Crescas in demolishing the distinctions between accidental causality (whose possible infinity had already been acknowledged) and essential causality (whose infinity had been denied), Provenzali compares accidental causality with essential causality, instead of the latter with the former, as the Spanish philosopher had done. This inverted perspective allows him to establish the non-eternity of the world and its having been created, thereby accomplishing the traditional objective of religious scholars. Thus, Provenzali tries to integrate Crescas's explosive criticism within Aristotelian-Maimonidean thought, using the new to reinforce the old—a defensive action that will not be crowned with success.[69]

The great edifice of Aristotelianism is therefore about to become the legacy of a superseded past, even for the Jews. The new is constructed through the very negation of a rational structure whose conceptual precision and internal coherence were very advanced. The interiorized experience of the Florentine Neoplatonists[70]—like Yeḥiel's turning to the kabbalah, as many others did after him—might respond to similar needs that will later emerge in the new philosophy of nature and in modern science. But before Galileo and the establishment of a new rationality, the rebellion against the old seems to present itself as a reaction against rationalism qua rationalism: modernity emerges, in a way, from within an anti-intellectual field.

With his constant reliance on suggestion, rather than on argumentation, and with his difficult elaboration of an alternative worldview to that of Maimonides—which had been able to reconcile revealed religion and rationalism—Yeḥiel moves in unison with the Italian culture of his time. An important author such as Gianfrancesco Pico della Mirandola, nephew of Giovanni, formulates a critique of Aristotelianism in exactly the same terms as the Pisan rabbi ("Aristoteli demonstrandi ars incerta, quia fundatur in indicio iudicioque sensum"),[71] and he shares his idea of an authentic prophecy—which one reaches through a free gift of God—distinct from the one that originates in evil spirits.[72]

While Gianfrancesco bemoaned the uncertainty and unreliability of philosophy's results, the object of continuous debates, Yeḥiel emphasizes their insufficiency. The practical criterion of the quantity and amplitude of the answers replaces the theoretical one of demonstrability. Philosophy's caution represents for him not only a symptom, but also a reason for its inferiority vis-à-vis traditional doctrines. He voices his opinion on the matter on many occasions with surprising candor. The conclusions that philosophers can reach on the issue of the angels (corresponding to the intellects), for example, is nothing but "a drop of water in the large sea of truths revealed to the prophets by the sacred doctors."[73]

Furthermore, philosophy cannot conceive of the attributes of God merely through a negative definition: God is *not* corporeal, and so forth. But Yeḥiel declares that he cannot be content with this: "I would like to know which one finally knows this way, given that negation does not produce knowledge."[74]

Yeḥiel takes up Crescas's famous critique of Maimonides. However, while the Spanish philosopher's observations had an epistemological starting point (the negation of an attribute is equal to the affirmation of its opposite; therefore God's attributes can be predicated as analogous to man's, but infinite and original), Yeḥiel emphasizes the entirely practical need of positive contents.[75]

The move from rational argumentation to traditional-kabbalist narrative is particularly clear with regard to prophecy, as already mentioned. Let us follow it in its development.

As a first step, Yeḥiel critiques Maimonides' semi-naturalistic framework, which granted much importance to man's imaginative faculty, as well as to his ability to capture the images created by God and sent to him by means of the active intellect.[76] The next step consists in replacing the faculty of imagination with the intellect: God, in his great goodness, causes a knowledge, similar to that of the primary cause, to pass from potentiality to actuality in the prophet's intellect. In this way, every naturalistic aspect of the prophecy is eliminated, and the accent is shifted onto the will of God and away from human disposition.[77] The third step consists in the allusion to esoteric doctrines, which concern the vision of the *merkavah* (Ezekiel's divine chariot) and include the tradition relative to the "throne of glory" and to the "celestial man." But the Rabbis had explicitly prohibited that one speak of these doctrines, the "extraordinary secrets." This does not prevent one from speaking of the divine origin of the prophecy in positive terms. This is the last step of Yeḥiel's work, after the traditional distinction between Moses and the other Jewish prophets.[78] On the basis of Recanati's commentary on the Torah, Yeḥiel distinguishes between the various *sefirot* appointed to the prophecy of Israel and of the other peoples. In his examination of the maledictions of Bilam, which transform themselves into benedictions (Numbers 22–24, Deuteronomy 22:6), he arrives at the conclusion that "the nations receive the prophecy from the energy of the attribute of *judgment* [*din*], as it had happened until then to Bilam. Thanks to the great mercy that he nourishes for His people, God caused the energy of the attribute of *mercy* [*raḥamim*] to descend upon them."[79]

In this oscillation between philosophical tradition, esotericism, and a need for positive content, the method of Yeḥiel Nissim da Pisa is well represented.

Notes

1. D. Kaufmann, "La Famille de Yehiel de Pise," *Revue des études juives* 26 (1893): 83–110; "Notes sure l'histoire de la famile 'De Pise'," in *Revue des études juives* 29 (1894): 142–47; idem "La Famille 'De Pise'," *Revue des études juives* 31 (1895): 62–73; idem, "Abraham b. Isaac De Pise," *Revue des études juives* 32 (1896): 130–34; idem "Eliézer et Hanaia da Volterra," *Revue des études juives* 34 (1897): 309–11; U. Cassuto,

"Sulla Famiglia da Pisa", *Rivista Israelitica* 5 (1908): 227–38; 7 (1910): 9–19, 72–86, 146–50; 10 (1913): 48–59; M. Luzzati, *La casa dell'ebreo* (Pisa, 1985), passim.

2. The text was published by Kaufmann in Berlin in 1898 and has since been reprinted in Jerusalem, in 1970.

3. *Discourse on the Righteous Man and the Purpose of the World* (Hebrew) was published by S. G. Rosenthal in *Koveṣ 'al yad* 8 (1975): 451–78. *Discourse on the Ten Sefirot* (Hebrew) has not yet been edited. Moshe Idel published several extracts from this work in his "The Three Versions of the Letter of Isaac da Pisa" (Hebrew), *Koveṣ 'al yad* 10 (1982): 161–214 hereafer, "Versions". For a description of the manuscripts, conserved in the library of the Jewish Theological Seminary in New York, see U. Cassuto, "Sulla Famiglia da Pisa," p. 48.

4. The text, dated 1559, was published by S. G. Rosenthal in New York in 1962 *(Banking and Finance among Jews in Renaissance Italy)* and is accompanied by an English translation and introduction. S. Schwarzfuchs published four responsa of Yeḥel's in "La valeur de la Kethubah en italie au XVIe siècle," *Revue des études juives*, n.s., 18 (1958): 116–23.

5. R. Bonfil, *Rabbis and Jewish Communities in Renaissance Italy*, trans. J. Chipman (Oxford, 1990; new ed., London, 1993) (hereafter *Rabbis*); *Harabbanut be-Italiyah bitekufat ha-Renesans* (Jerusalem; 1979). Yeḥiel Nissim da Pisa's work is considered in *Rabbis* on pp. 43, 188, 253, 255, 284–89, 292–93, and 312.

6. See *Discourse on the Righteous Man and the Purpose of the World* (hereafter, *The Righteous Man*), p. 478. As for the *Minḥat kenoat* (hereafter *Minḥat*), the generally didactic tone of the work and its address to a potentially vast public ("and here I repeat myself because the matter is not considered elsewhere . . . and here I reiterated to facilitate the reading") make it appear destined for publication. See also p. 90: "I have dwelled on the subject of the soul because since the time of Hillel of Verona [1220–95] there has not been any complete review of the philosophical positions on this matter."

7. Bedersi's apologetic writing was published in 1539, the same year of the redaction of *Minḥat*, as a premise to Solomon ben Adret's Responsa. This may not have been a coincidence. Yeḥiel may have felt the need to react to the publication of Bedersi's *Iggeret*.

8. Yeḥiel, *Minḥat*, p. 7.

9. Ibid., p. 9.

10. Ibid., p. 11.

11. Ibid., p. 12.

12. Ibid., pp. 9, 13.

13. Ibid., pp. 38–39. Cf. Judah Halevi, *Kuzari* 5:20, 2:57.

14. See A. Marx, "Glimpses of the Life of an Italian Rabbi of the First Half of the Sixteenth Century," *Hebrew Union College Annual* (1924), p. 617. This article considers the alternating teaching of the two works in the community of Naples. Cf. Bonfil, *Rabbis*, p. 148.

15. Elijah Gennazano, *Iggeret Hamudot* (The letter of delights), ed. A. W. Greenup (London, 1912), p. 7.

16. "Because we live in terms of what His mouth says." Yeḥiel, *Minḥat*, p. 16. At

issue here is the transmission of the name of God. At this point, Yeḥiel cites Naḥmanides' elliptic interpretation of Exod. 3:12 *sub fine*, maintaining its extremely prudent tone.

17. Yeḥiel, *Minḥat*, pp. 113, 148, 189. Cf. Naḥmanides, *Introduction to the Commentary on the Torah* (Hebrew), ed. C. D. Shavel (Jerusalem, 1969); Naḥmanides, *Introduction to the Commentary on Job* (Hebrew) (here Naḥmanides has harsh words for the philosophers who deny divine knowledge and providence: "May God erase the memory of them"). Cf. Also Naḥmanides, *Commentary on Genesis* 38:8.

18. Yeḥiel, *Minḥat*, p. 21 (on the movement of skies), p. 41 (on prophecy), p. 45 (the polemic with the philosopher Gersonides), p. 100 (on creation *ex nihilo*).

19. Ibid., p. 45 See Gersonides, *Commentary on Genesis* 18:21.

20. On Yoḥanan Alemanno, see U. Cassuto, *Gli ebrei a Firenze nell' età del Rinascimento* (Florence, 1918), pp. 301–16, whose writings remain for the most part unpublished. Cf. Also M. Idel, "The Curriculum of Yoḥanan Alemanno" (Hebrew), *Tarbiẓ* 48 (1980): 303–31; idem, "The Magical and Neoplatonic Interpretations of the Kabbalah in the Renaissance," in *Jewish Thought in the Sixteenth Century*, ed. B. D. Cooperman (Cambridge, Mass., 1983), pp. 186–242 (hereafter, "Magical"; M. Idel, "Vases and *Sefirot*: Substantiality and Hypersubstantial Infinity in the Kabbalist Theories of the Renaissance" (Hebrew), *Italia* 3 (1982): 89–111 (hereafter "Infinity"); C. Mopsik, *Les Grands Textes de la cabale* (Paris, 1993), pp. 305–12. Fabrizio Lelli recently published Alemanno's *Ḥay ha-'Olamin* (*L'immortale*), vol. 1, *La Retorica* (Florence, 1995), with a translation, accurate commentary, and comprehensive bibliography, followed by "L'educazione ebraica nella seconda metà del 400: Poetica e scienza naturali nel Ḥay ha-'Olamin di Yoḥanan Alemanno," *Rinascimento* 36 (1996): 75–136. In "Il richiamo agli 'antichi' nella cultura ebraica tra quattro e cinquecento," in *Storia d'Italia*, ed. C. Vivanti (Turin, 1996), pt. 1 (Annali, 11), pp. 387–409, Arthur Lesley contextualizes Alemanno's work within the period's rhetoric and education. See his " 'The Song of Solomon's Ascents' by Yoḥanan Alemanno: Love and Human Perfection according to a Jewish Colleague of Giovanni Pico della Mirandola" (Ph.D. diss., University of California, 1976).

21. Menaḥem Recanati, *Commentary on the Torah* (Venice, 1545), f. 65a (section *Vayishlakh*). For an outline of Recanati's importance in Italy, see A. Diena, *Responsa*, ed. Y. Boksenboim (Tel Aviv, 1977), 1: 133. See M. Idel, *R. Menaḥem hamekubbal* (Hebrew) (Jerusalem, 1998).

22. Other than Idel's "Versions," "Infinity," and "Magical," see also Idel, "Major Currents in Italian Kabbalah, *1560–1660*," in *Italia Judaica: Gli ebrei in Italia tra Rinascimento ed età barocca* (Rome, 1986), reprinted in *Essential Papers on Jewish Culture in Renaissance and Baroque Italy*, ed. D. Ruderman (New York, 1992), pp. 345–68.

23. Y. Nadav, "A Letter of the Kabbalist R. Isaac Mar Ḥayyim on the Doctrine of the Superior Lights" (Hebrew), *Tarbiẓ* 26 (1957): 440–58; A. W. Greenup, "A Kabbalistic Epistle by Isaac b. Ḥayyim Sepharadi," *Jewish Quarterly Review* 21 (1931): 365–75.

24. Yeḥiel, *Minḥat*, p. 23: "The first three *sefirot* belong to the essence; the remaining seven are called "attributes" because they refer to His world . . . and they are as instruments in the hands of an artisan." Gennazano explicitly upholds Recanati's theory. See Gennazano, *Iggeret ḥamudot*, p. 34.

25. Yeḥiel, *Minḥat*, p 24; idem, *The Righteous Man*, p. 470.

26. Y. Alemanno, *Ḥesheq Shelomo* (The desire of Solomon), quoted in Idel, "Versions," p. 179. In the second half of the sixteenth century, this "hierarchizing" of the worlds was an established fact in the culture of Italian Jewish schools (yeshivot). Solomon di Monte dell'Olmo, a student in Siena, describes it in twenty Hebrew tercets conserved in an Oxfort Bodleian manuscript 1989/2, ff. 172–73, which will be the subject of a future publication.

27. Nadav, "A Letter," p. 456; Greenup, "Kabbalistic Epistle," p. 370.

28. Yeḥiel, *Discourse on Eternal Life*, pp. 12–16.

29. Yeḥiel, *Minḥat*, introduction, p. ix.

30. Ibid., pp. 33, 72.

31. Bonfil, *Rabbis*, p. 286. See also Kaufmann, "La Famille de Yehiel de Pise," p. 93: "Parfois le critique se montre, dans son ouvrage, juge et connaisseur plus compétent que le panégiriste."

32. Yeḥiel, *Minḥat*, pp. 15, 23, 25.

33. Ibid., pp. 21, 23.

34. Yeḥiel, *The Righteous Man*, p. 641; Maimonides, *Guide for the Perplexed*, ed. Pines, I, chaps. 58, 72; Aristotle, *De coelo* I. 3.

35. Yeḥiel, *Minḥat*, p. 39.

36. Yeḥiel, *The Righteous Man*, pp. 465, 469–70.

37. See Idel, "Magical," pp. 211, 237. M. Shulvass, *The Jews in the World of the Renaissance* (Leiden, 1973), pp. 328–32. Yeḥiel lists proofs of the reality of magic and of the existence of demons, which he takes from the Torah and from experience. See Yeḥiel, *Minḥat*, pp. 48 ff.

38. *Heptaplus*, V exposition, chap. 7, ed. Garin (Florence, 1942), p. 304; see E. Garin, *La cultura filosofica del Rinascimento italiano* (Florence, 1961); idem, *Ermetismo del Rinascimento* (Rome, 1988), esp. p. 18, on the "miracles of Pico through natural magic and kabbalist doctrine," and p. 49, for the quotation from Pico *magiam operari non est aliud quam maritari mundum.* On Ficino and the union of the male and female parts of God, see p. 67. For these questions in general, see F. A. Yates, *Giordano Bruno and the Hermetic Tradition* (Chicago, 1964); idem, *Cabala and Occult Philosophy in the Elizabethan Age* (London, 1979). The author's wish for a vast comparative study of the Jewish and Christian kabbalah is still to be fulfilled. Chaim Wirszubski's studies, now collected in *Bein hashittim* (Jerusalem, 1996), constitute a first and fundamental step in this direction.

39. Yeḥiel, *The Righteous Man*, p. 464. See *Zohar* III ff. 244b–245a; Judah Halevi, *Kuzari* III, p. 26.

40. Idel, "Magical," p. 198.

41. Yeḥiel, *Minḥat*, p. 108.

42. Yeḥiel, *The Righteous Man*, p. 477. Thus does Yeḥiel continue his reasoning: "And to the question that can be asked: what is the end of our existence in this state of perfection? We could answer: because thus has God willed. And to investigate His will would be the equivalent of investigating his essence, in that one and the other are the same." This passage is a literal citation of Maimonides, *Guide for the Perplexed* III, chap. 13 and III, chap. 53, and it proves how strong Maimonides' prestige was, even

among the opponents of Jewish Aristotelianism. In Yeḥiel, the centrality of man in the universe touches on the theurgic perspective. A few decades later, with the diffusion of the Lurianic kabbalah, human activity will be seen to directly condition the life of God Himself, in accordance with the saying "My Torah is in your hand, and your soul is in my hand." Cf. Abraham Portaleone, *Shilṭei gibborim* (The shields of the strong) (Mantua, 1612), introduction. Regarding the limited usage among the Italian kabbalists of the Zoharic doctrines on the harmony between the *sefirot*, see Idel, "Versions," pp. 198, 248.

43. See Maimonides, *Guide* II, chap. 6 and III, chap. 13. I. Tishby, *The Teachings of the Zohar* (Hebrew) (Jerusalem, 1957), 1: 386–87, 447. Elijah Delmedigo (1458–93), the last representative of the Aristotelian-Maimonidean orthodoxy, will decidedly oppose the idea that there be any possibility for humans to modify the course of the universe. See *Beḥinat hadat*, ed. J. J. Ross (Tel Aviv, 1984), pp. 99–100.

44. Yeḥiel, *The Righteous Man*, pp. 460–69.

45. We are naturally thinking of Pico della Mirandola's oration *De hominis dignitate*, ed. Garin (Florence, 1942), p. 110: "If we will so desire, we will not in any way be inferior to the angels."

46. Bonfil, *Rabbis*, pp. 290–91. To understand this issue in the Italian rabbinical context, see Bonfil, "Expressions of the Uniqueness of the Jewish People in Italy during the Renaissance" (Heberw), *Sinai* 86 (1975): 34–46.

47. Yeḥiel, *The Righteous Man*, p. 471. Yeḥiel picks up on Judah Halevi's famous analogy in the *Kuzari* (II, 36: "Israel is among the nations as the heart among the members of the body: it is the part most sensitive to sickness, as well as the most robust"), but he attributes to the heart only vitality and not delicacy or fragility, as in the original text. One can interpret this small but significant omission, keeping in mind the difficult situation in which the Italian Jews found themselves at the moment of the writing of this text, in 1559: the Talmud had just been prohibited five years earlier, and ghettos were starting to be built in various cities. It was therefore appropriate to insist on the formula of encouragement. The similitude is instead quoted in its entirety in *Minḥat*, p. 85, written in 1539 and therefore prior to these events. For a development of the similitude, see *Zohar* III f. 221b.

48. Yeḥiel, *Minḥat*, p. 38; see Judah Halevi, *Kuzari* V, 20, fourth premise.

49. Yeḥiel, *Minḥat*, p. 47.

50. Maimonides, *Guide* III, chaps. 17, 18.

51. See Bonfil, "Expressions of the Uniqueness," pp. 36–46.

52. Yeḥiel, *The Righteous Man*, pp. 471–72. Yeḥiel modifies and explains in philosophic fashion the interpretation of the Song of Songs 2:2, "Like a rose among thorns" given by *Vayiqra Rabba* 23:3. At issue is how to save the orchard invaded by brambles thanks to the one perfumed rose therein. That rose is the Torah.

53. Quoted in C. B. Schmitt, *Gianfrancesco Pico della Mirandola (1469–1533) and His Critique of Aristotle* (The Hague, 1967), p. 48.

54. For a more extensive discussion of Sforno's philosophy, see. R. Bonfil, "The Doctrine of the Soul and of Sanctity in the Thought of Ovadiah Sforno" (Hebrew), *Eshel Beersheva* 1 (1976): 200–257.

55. Sforno, "Luce dei popoli," in *Scritti di Ovadiah Sforno*, new ed. (Jerusalem, 1985), p. 495.

56. Yeḥiel, *Minḥat*, p. 11.

57. Ibid., pp. 45–46. Yeḥiel does not present in this case the usual review of philosophical opinions, but he refers to Ḥasdai Crescas, *Or Adonai* (The light of God), pt. 2 rule 5. Yeḥiel naturally does not follow Crescas in his semi-deterministic conclusions. On this subject, see the talmudic source, Talmud Bavli, Beraḥot 33, f. 2b: "Everything is in the hands of God, except for the fear of God."

58. See L. Cristiani, "L'Eglise à l'époque du Concile de Trente," *L'Histoire de l'Eglise* 17 (1948): 233; *Enciclopedia Cattolica* (Vatican City, 1951), s.v. "Giustificazione."

59. For the consideration of Maimonides in Jewish Italy in this period, see M. Shulvass, "The Italian Jewish Study of the Torah during the Renaissance" (Hebrew) *Ḥorev* 10 (1948): 105–28; and Bonfil, *Rabbis*, pp. 251–72.

60. See, for example, Judah Halevi, *Kuzari* V, 14.

61. Yeḥiel, *Minḥat*, pp. 117–18; see also pp. 9, 82, and idem, *The Righteous Man*, p. 460.

62. *Augustini Niphi suessani philosophi in Aristotelis libros posteriorum analyticorum subtilissima commentaria* (Venice, 1558), p. 43. 1 and 61. 4. F. Cf. Aristotle, *Physics* 184 A 16.

63. Yeḥiel, *Menḥat*, p. 88. In this context, the contrast between the Torah and philosophy is forcefully expressed: "To compare the two forms of knowledge means subverting true judgment, because their relationship is that of reciprocal aversion [*ki hem ṣarot zo lezo*]."

64. See P. Pomponazzi, *De fato* 709, quoted in E. Garin, *Storia della filosofia italiana* (Turin, 1966), p. 509: "Ita sunt quae me insomnem et insanum reddunt, ut vera sit interprertatio fabulae Promethei. . . . Prometheus vero est Philosophus qui dum vult scire Dei arcana, perpetuis curis et cogitationibus roditur." See also T. Gregory, in *Grande antologia filosofica* (Turin, 1964), 6:625.

65. See Garin, *Storia della filosofia italiana*, p. 536, regarding Nifo's early adhesion to the transmigration theory.

66. "Whoever wants to persevere in [philosophy] shall always move in uncertainty and vagueness. . . . Those who proceed along the way of faith remain strong and sure": "De immortalitate animae," Gregory, *Grande antologia filosofica*, 6:717. But also "Oportet in Philosophia haereticum esse qui veritatem invenire cupit" (in Garin, *Storia della filosofia italiana*, p. 511).

67. Sforno, "Luce dei popoli," p. 418.

68. Ibid., pp. 414–15.

69. See R. Bonfil, "The Commentary of Moses Provenzali on the Twenty-Five *Axioms* of Maimonides" (Hebrew), *Kiryat Sefer* 50 (1974/75): 157–76.

70. See Garin, *La cultura filosofica del Rinascimento italiano*, p. 118.

71. *Examen veritatis doctrinae gentium et veritatis disciplinae Christianae* V, 2. Quoted in Garin, *Storia della filosofia italiana*, p. 593.

72. Yeḥiel, *Minḥat*, pp. 48–50. Isadore Twersky, in "Talmudists, Philosophers, Kabbalists: The Quest for Spirituality in the Sixteenth Century," in *Jewish Thought in*

the Sixteenth Century, ed. Cooperman, highlights Yeḥiel's aspiration to completion, or spiritual perfection, which manifests itself in an exaltation of religious practice over pure intellectual activity (p. 446). Indeed, the allusions to corporeality in his writings are not few: in *Minḥat*, p. 78, he speaks of the corporeal remains in the soul after death. The service of God is described in *Discourse on the Righteous Man and the Purpose of the World* as an activity "of feelings and of all the members of the body" (and in *Minḥat*, p. 88: "the soul's perfection is in its union with the body"). Moreover, a certain importance is granted to the sense of touch, in contrast to Aristotle's and Maimonides' devaluation of said sense (Maimonides, *Guide* II, chap. 36; Yeḥiel, *Minḥat*, p. 81). This change in sensibility also merits further study.

73. Yeḥiel, *Minḥat*, p. 36.

74. Ibid., p. 22.

75. See J. Gutmann, *Philosophies of Judaism* (Philadelphia, 1964), p. 232. Maimonides, *Guide* I, chaps. 51–54; Crescas, *Or Adonai* 1, III, 3.

76. Yeḥiel, *Minḥat* p. 43 Maimonides, *Guide* II, chap. 36. For the analogous theory of Avicenna, see S. M. Afnan, *Avicenna: His Life and Works* (London, 1958). Elijah Gennazano elaborated the same kind of critique of this idea, referring, however, not to Maimonides, but to Joseph Albo's *Book of Principles*. See Gennazano, *Iggeret ḥamudot*, p. 11.

77. Isaac Abravanel, in his commentary on this passage of Maimonides, highlights the role of the intellect as well. The philosopher and political man of Spanish origin had been in close contact with Yeḥiel da Pisa, grandfather of our Yeḥiel Nissim. See the quoted articles by Kaufmann and Cassuto, mentioned above.

78. The references to this distinction are in the Talmud, Yevamot 49b *sub fine* and *Zohar* I, 170.

79. Yeḥiel, *Minḥat*, p. 44.

Chapter 6
The Beautiful Soul: Azariah de' Rossi's Search for Truth

Joanna Weinberg

From the storm-tossed sea yea to the shore
I have come and no hurricane need fear
I laugh at the vicissitudes of false time
My God will no more be strange to me
It may be asked if my merchandise find favor
With the Prince who calls all by name
But He it is who created me, I shall not want
For He His grace does lavish on every creature.

These verses composed by Azariah de' Rossi for his own grave were inserted into his discussion of the function of funereal monuments in the final chapter of his magisterial work, the *Me'or 'einayim* (Light of the eyes).[1] De' Rossi avers—but not without a fleeting allusion to his family tradition that the Rossi were one of four noble families that were exiled to Rome by Titus—that the purpose of his self-addressed epitaph was not to flaunt his own piety or lineage. He refers to the statement of Rav Perida in the Babylonian Talmud (Menaḥot 53a), who ranks the man of learning above the person of noble birth;[2] thereby implicitly, though effectively, de' Rossi fashions a most acceptable self-image—for notwithstanding any criticism that might be leveled against him, there could be no doubting his devotion to study and learning, so patently attested on virtually every page of his magnum opus.

The epitaph does not, at least from a superficial examination, betray much biographical information. Certain conventional themes appear: the final homecoming after being buffeted by fortune and trusting submission to a beneficent deity. In fact, this seemingly unpretentious epitaph reveals de' Rossi's scholarly persona. In his own copy of his book, now housed in Oxford in the Bodleian Library, he added a marginal gloss to the epitaph. He writes that he had modeled his inscription on the text that Cardinal Gasparo Contarini had prepared for his own sepulchral monument. He then transcribes the Latin text: "Venimus ad portum, Spes et fortuna valete, nil mihi vobiscum, illudite nunc alios" (We have reached port; farewell hope and fortune/ I have nothing more to do with you; now make play with others). As I have indicated elsewhere, these couplets derive from the *Anthologia palatina*, the Byzantine collection of Greek pagan epigrams, and could therefore be adopted by de' Rossi without impinging on his own religious identity.[3] The first four lines of his epitaph mirror the sentiments of the pagan couplets that speak of *fortuna* as the fickle agent of success and failure, whereas the second set of couplets, de' Rossi's addition, lend the religious dimension apparently lacking in the cardinal's epitaph.

In miniature, then, three civilizations lie embedded in de' Rossi's epitaph: the pagan, Christian, and Jewish. More germane to our quest for the scholarly persona of de' Rossi is that the epitaph reveals that even in confessional mode, de' Rossi did not erect any barrier between the Jewish and non-Jewish domains.

It is a strange quirk of fate that little is known of the life of the man called "father of scholars" by the protagonists of the *Wissenschaft des Judentums.* For his biography of de' Rossi, Zunz necessarily had to use literary texts for the most part, and he had no access to the important material that I was in the fortunate position to discover over twenty years ago.[4] The new information relates to the last years of de' Rossi's life, when unsuccessful efforts were made by the inquisitor of Ferrara to convert the "exceptionally brilliant" Buonaiuto to Christianity. It was during this stressful period of his life (1575–1577) that he turned his scholarly attention to Christian affairs, namely, an analysis of the Aramaisms in the New Testament Vulgate in light of the recently printed Syriac text (Vienna, 1555). Moreover, he wrote this novel work in Italian rather than Hebrew, and for Christians—high church figures at that—not for Jews.[5] Thus de' Rossi's intellectual legacy is to be retrieved from two distinct contexts, both of which shaped his identity—or, to use Stephen Greenblatt's terminology,[6] brought about de' Rossi's self-fashioning—conscious as he was of living in two worlds. He had to submit himself, or rather address himself, to two authorities: the rabbinic establishment and the ecclesiastical powers. This consciousness is eloquently expressed in the opening remarks of his disquisitions on the Christian Scriptures: "I am indeed convinced that I do not deserve to be persecuted either by critical Christians or by suspicious Jews for such a work. With the wise Ecclesiastes I can say *ani pi melekh shmor* (Eccles. 8:2), which in substance means *I am observing the king's commandment* by producing something which is indeed permitted and virtuous." Thereby de' Rossi articulates the perilous nature of his endeavor: his fellow Jews might misinterpret his foray into Christian scholarship as an indication of his religious proclivities, while he risked raising the ire of Christians by suggesting that their holy Scripture, namely the Vulgate, needed some revision. (It was to be revised in 1592, but not without considerable discussions and conflicts, and, not surprisingly, the task was undertaken solely by Christians.) Artful as he undoubtedly was in plying his trade, and aware of the differing sensibilities of either authority, the self he fashions in both contexts remains consistent. As we shall see, it is as an unrepentant seeker of the truth that he portrays himself, whether addressing Christians or Jews. The truth that he seeks does not concern facile matters. Rather, de' Rossi incessantly exposes himself to criticism; for he chooses to apply his brilliant mind to notably sensitive issues for both communities: the interpretation of rabbinic texts and the chronological and calendrical problems for the Jews, and the errors or incorrect interpretation of Scripture for Christians. Despite the apologetic tone that runs through both his Jewish and Christian output—and this is what irritated the Maharal of Prague so much—de' Rossi never yields his position. He constantly goes through the motions of submission, only to realign his forces and to reiterate his arguments with even greater insistence.

The attempt to delineate an intellectual portrait of de' Rossi, despite the dearth of extant biographical material, is thus facilitated by the existence of two sets of texts written in different languages and intended for rather different readers. Is Buonaiuto the same person as Azariah? Does scholarly investigation in Hebrew differ substantially from that conducted in Italian? Are the tools and mode of explication essentially the same? The quest for the true de' Rossi requires answers to such questions.

De' Rossi's Christian audience included the cardinal Santa Severina, who was involved in the encounter between the Eastern and Western Churches, and in the Casa dei Neofiti in Rome. It was the cardinal who asked the inquisitor of Ferrara to persuade de' Rossi to convert. It was also intended for Giacomo Boncompagni, who was governor general of the Church and had apparently commissioned this work on the Syriac version of the Gospels. Despite (or perhaps because of) these powerful potential readers, de' Rossi does not allow for any ambiguity as far as his religious allegiances are concerned. He speaks in no uncertain terms of his *fratelli ebrei* (Jewish brethren) and tells his Christian readers that it was for his fellow Jews that he had written his *Oculorum lumen* the (*Light of the Eyes*).[7] De' Rossi's Jewish self is further emphasized in a prefatory note to his exposition of certain verses in the Acts of the Apostles, in which he demonstrates that the readings in the Syriac version, unlike those of the Vulgate, conform to those of the Hebrew Bible.[8] The purpose of such an analysis naturally proposes the superiority of the Syriac or Oriental transmission of the text over that of the Latin Western tradition. In introducing this topic, he writes: "And so, speaking as a sincere Jew, I must in all conscience maintain that in antiquity Christians in stock and descent [i.e., Christians of gentile origin], were not called to the Mosaic law, which was only given to the Jews. Nevertheless, whether we like it or not [*velimus, nolimus*], they did come close to it for the most part, and thus certainly deserved to be protected by God's clemency, which is in fact the case. If it were relevant to my subject I would prove this contention authoritatively."

This statement of de' Rossi begs for interpretation and elucidation. To which gentile Christians is he referring? Is it perhaps a reference to Luke, the author of Acts, who was Syrian by birth? Does it also carry an implicit reference to true Christians with no Jewish taint, in contrast to the new Christians of his own time? Would inquisitors, cardinals, and papal officials have felt somewhat patronized? A committed Jew speaks of Christians who are protected by God because they come close to the Jewish Scriptures; moreover, he is certainly expressing Jewish ambivalence, *velimus, nolimus*, about Christian use of the Hebrew Bible. What is certain is that such a statement must have dashed any hope that inquisitors may still have nurtured with regard to the conversion of the great Jewish scholar. De' Rossi knew how to adhere to the outer forms of conventional address. In the conclusion of his first letter to the cardinal of Santa Severina, he writes: "I entreat you to preserve me as the object of your divine grace. It may please the highest God that when I am restored to good health I may come and kiss the hem of your holy garment, being the most devoted servant of your most illustrious and reverend worship—may you perpetually go from strength to strength." But these kinds of token gestures of civility only serve to emphasize his fearless assertion of his own Jewish identity, as the passage about the early Christians cited above clearly demonstrates.[9]

In a famous passage in the *Guide for the Perplexed* (1, 71), Maimonides makes a sharp distinction between philosophers like himself who pursue the truth, and the Mutakallimun, whose pursuit of philosophy was motivated by the need to support religious beliefs. As he put it, the Mutakallim seeks to subject his intellect to the imagination, whereas the philosopher seeks to subject his imagination to his intellect. De' Rossi's quest for truth bears some characteristics of that of Maimonides, although it does not fit neatly into either compartment. Certainly de' Rossi was not prepared to support religious beliefs if it entailed the rejection of reason and historical truth. At the same time, he argued, not unlike Maimonides, that by understanding the rabbinic mode of exegesis he could assist the uncomprehending and perplexed reader. This may be exemplified by his novel treatment of the nonlegal parts of rabbinic texts, the aggadot, which constitute a significant part of the *Light of the Eyes.* He fully acknowledged that the weirdness of the tales was proportionate to the amazing wisdom they contained. His purpose was not to fathom the depths of rabbinic wisdom, but to demonstrate that the aggadot did not stand up to historical investigation or scientific evidence. By thus eradicating the intellectually untenable elements in the aggadot and by divesting the stories of their literal meaning, de' Rossi believed that he was thereby removing the obstacle to constructive reading of the texts. He was thus able to achieve his main objective, that is, to give the true version of the historical episodes alluded to while absolving the Rabbis of responsibility for the promulgation of erroneous information, and excusing himself from what might seem an irreverent treatment of the Rabbis of old.

In his preface to chapter 11, in which he challenges rabbinic views of cosmology and geography—and points to the recent discoveries of the New World as proof that rabbinic experience and knowledge were limited in this particular domain—he states that the Rabbis "proceeded on the basis of human wisdom and evaluation, which was the scholarly approach prevalent in their time and in those parts of the world. . . . And yet, we should not constrict them by the bonds of love and press them to make statements that we palpably know were never their intention. It would simply be a case of letting the emotions take the line of least resistance. And then we would put ourselves in the fraudulent position of Job's friends who 'did not speak the truth.'" According to de' Rossi, rabbinic pronouncements in the nonlegal realm do not carry authoritative weight and should not be accorded Sinaitic status.

Thus the search for truth (in his case, not philosophical, but historical or scientific truth) is central to all de' Rossi's investigations. Even the title of his work, *Me'or 'einayim,* which at first sight appears to be simply an adaptation of Prov. 15:30,[10] reflects this objective. At the end of the introduction to the book, he writes: "Now this entire book is the light of my eyes and the joy of my heart. With it, the Lord, my heavenly refuge, will entitle me to leave behind a blessing to posterity. Under the guidance of the blessed Lord, I have now given it the enduring name *The Light of the Eyes*."[11]

There is, in my view, a correlation between the title of the book and its purpose, which comes to the fore in his Italian work. De' Rossi takes the opportunity of addressing another audience to make good publicity for the *Light of the Eyes*, and refers to relevant sections of his Hebrew work throughout the tract. He does not translate the title into Italian; rather, he lends it a certain respectability by giving it the Latin designation *Oculorum lumen*,[12] a term frequently used in classical and patristic texts to signify both physical sight and palpable sense.[13] Of particular significance in this context is the manner in which Jerome uses *oculorum lumen* in his prologue to his commentary on Daniel. Attacking Porphyry for having interpreted Daniel's vision as a reference to Antiochus Epiphanes, Jerome asserts that he will attempt to use straightforward explanations to controvert such a subversion of the palpable *oculorum lumen*, namely, the clear truth of the matter.[14] It may be, then, that de' Rossi had such a passage in mind when selecting a Latin title for his work—after all, it was Jerome's Vulgate that he was discussing. Moreover, Jerome's views on many matters were brought by de' Rossi to bear on many issues throughout the *Light of the Eyes*, and he quotes from the Daniel commentary on five occasions.[15] More significant is that the use of this Latin phrase enhances our appreciation of de' Rossi's purpose, which is inextricably bound up with evidence that is reliable and authentic.

Thus, the *Light of the Eyes* is a work of enlightenment. As I have indicated, one of the main purposes of de' Rossi is to put the historical record right. The tools used to achieve this purpose are precise historical information or correct reading of ancient works, be it in the form of establishing authenticity through textual criticism or through interpretation that takes into account the specific hermeneutic mode in which a text was created. Throughout the work, de' Rossi draws the reader into this quest. Employing a common rhetorical ploy, de' Rossi regales the reader with a variety of designations: "dear reader," "intelligent reader," "kind reader," calling readers to his attention and exhorting them to adopt his view. In this way, a tacit understanding between author and reader is formed: the author provides the relevant information, and the reader grateful for such kindnesses rendered is duly enlightened.

But the true addressee of his historical disquisitions is accorded a particular designation. In five passages in the *Light of the Eyes* (and coincidentally, also five in his Italian work), de' Rossi speaks of the *nefesh yafah* or *bel animo* or *bei* [or *elevati*] *spiriti.* In Hebrew, the expression has little significance (it is used in the Mishnah as a euphemism for someone with good digestion).[16] There is a Neoplatonic ring to the "beautiful soul," but it is difficult to determine the scope of its meaning.[17] "Beauty of the soul" is the expression typical of Plotinus, Augustine, and Renaissance philosophers such as Marsilio Ficino and Leone Ebreo, whose works de' Rossi knew well. In each case, the writer fashions his own concept of beauty with regard to the soul. It may be, for instance, that de' Rossi was thinking of Augustine's articulation of the beauty of the soul in his diatribe against Faustus the Manichee. Commenting on the verse in Psalm 30, "Lord, by your favor you have made me firm as a mighty mountain. When you hid your face I was terrified," Augustine writes: "This proves that every soul is only beautiful by virtue of its partaking of the light of God." Or to quote one Renaissance writer, Francesco Cattani da Diacceto, heavily influenced by Marsilio Ficino: "Beauty arouses our soul and seems to draw it toward itself: our soul naturally surmises that beauty opens the gates leading toward the limitless perfection of divine goodness. . . . It is clear therefore that beauty is nothing but a ray emanating from divine goodness attracting and drawing all things that are endowed with the faculty of reason toward the good, participation in which is the ultimate perfection of everything."[18]

Something of this, however vague and unspecific, is conveyed by de' Rossi's "beautiful soul"—the *nefesh yafah* belongs to the category of higher beings. It is invoked at crucial moments in the discussion. One example of his use of this phrase occurs at the end of chapter 12, in which he has been discussing the various midrashic and talmudic accounts that attribute the massacre of the Jewish population of Alexandria variously to Tarquin, Alexander of Macedon, Hadrian, and even to Trajan, the real culprit. Amassing a large array of historians, de' Rossi demonstrates that not only the Rabbis had a somewhat muddled view of this period of history but even interpreters of a later age, such as the Tosafists and Don Isaac Abravanel. He then states: "Now the greater part of this chapter has been devoted to inconsequential investigations which one could dismiss by saying 'what happened, happened' or on the grounds that it has no bearing on any law or precept. Nevertheless, the beautiful soul yearns to know the truth of every matter and the way of man in the world even when such issues are not directly relevant to it."[19]

Such a statement, despite its concern with historical—not philosophical—truth, would have met with Maimonides' approval. Here we are given side by side two images of the historian that are constantly met throughout the book: oscillation between self-deprecation and assertion of the absolute value of scholarship. Ultimately, the attention is on the beautiful soul, whose sole aim is the acquisition of truth.

In another passage, the beautiful soul rejects uncorrected texts. In chapter 19, de' Rossi, in good Renaissance fashion, examines various rabbinic texts that, in his view, had become corrupt over the centuries. Included in the study is the text of Josippon, the tenth-century adaptation of Josephus Flavius, which was used by many medieval writers to guide them through the badly charted years of the Second Temple period. De' Rossi is suspicious of the work and had actually read a contemporary edition that claimed that the work was not a genuine text of the real Josephus.[20] Apparently, he preferred not to take this brutal road, divesting a favorite author of authenticity. He nevertheless demonstrates that it is flawed, full of anachronisms. In sum, "it is not a basic text, but the beautiful soul still desires to know the truth of every matter."[21]

De' Rossi's readers have been warned: the written text is not always trustworthy. Textual criticism and detection of forgeries are essential activities for the beautiful soul. One of the chapters that, on rabbinic orders, he had to censure regards the rabbinic use of the hyperbole. In chapter 20, he demonstrates the literary use of numbers such as 60 and 400 in rabbinic texts and, in general, the use of exaggeration to communicate the message in the most effective way possible. This leads him to a discussion of the various figures for the high priests that served in the Temples. Demonstrating a clear preference for the Palestinian tradition and Josephus, de' Rossi is able to reject a potential source of conflict, the commentary on Chronicles attributed to Rashi. The evidence could be disregarded because, as de' Rossi correctly discerned, it was not a genuine text of Rashi. He then exultantly concludes: "At this juncture I had indeed to congratulate myself; after all evidence has emerged which demonstrates that my statements in the previous chapter on the detection of forgeries have not been proved false. The thoughtful person knows and is a witness of the extent to which deceit contributes and increases the confusion in the beautiful soul whose place of rest is truth and righteousness."[22]

Numbers and figures matter, and for correct accounting the most accurate readings in authentic texts must be obtained. The beautiful soul must not be subjected to false information. The most eloquent articulation of this position is contained in an oft-cited passage from chapter 29, the opening chapter of section 3 of the book, in which de' Rossi is about to prove unequivocally the uncertainty of rabbinic chronology and the convention inherent in the structure of the Jewish fixed calendar. He approaches his task charily. In his desire to put on record the true account of events, he must necessarily expose the Rabbis' lack of expertise in the field of history. Here again, he dismisses his inquiries with the talmudic dictum *mai dehava hava* "what happened, happened"—in other words, his explorations into Jewish ancient history have no practical bearing on the life of a Jew, and are actually of supreme irrelevance. He writes:

> The fact is that from the very outset I can imagine you saying to yourself, kind reader, that this investigation is a type of halakhah suitable for Messianic times or of an even lesser significance. For what relevance does it hold for us? After all, what happened, happened thousands of years ago or seven times again. But you could answer your own objection once you take into consideration the following points: First, the truth itself, which is the quest of thousands of sages in investigations more obscure than this one, is in fact like a seal of the true God, the characteristic of the beautiful soul and the good to which all aspire.[23]

Two other advantages to such an undertaking are then described: the interpretation of Scripture, for which reward is always forthcoming *derosh vekabel sakhar*; and the eradication of current messianic speculation about the imminent year 1575—if the true date cannot be known because all computations are, to a certain extent, arbitrary—all calculation of the end of days can only be speculative.

But these two justifications of his scholarship are subordinated to one overriding goal: the truth. Here we have the good aligned with the beautiful soul, certainly Neoplatonic notions as we have seen, and combined with the idea of truth as a seal of the true God, a rabbinic dictum, which is used in a variety of contexts. In certain texts, the idea is based on a play on the three letters of the word *emet* (truth), which correspond to the first, middle, and last letters of the Hebrew alphabet. Truth is God, for in Isa. 44:6, "I am the first, and I am the last, and besides me there is no God."[24] According to other views, the seal can also denote God's endorsement.[25]

The purpose of de' Rossi's Italian work was to explain to Christians the correct meaning of some key expressions in the Gospels that had become corrupt or obscure, particularly the Aramaic words, Jesus' so-called *ipsissima verba*, which had often been described erroneously as Hebrew. He presented the ancient Syriac version of the New Testament as an authentic witness that preserved the original readings of the sacred text and therefore could be used to correct or interpret the Vulgate. This was a pious duty; as he states in his prefatory letter: "There is no doubt that in such subjects, one iota clarified is of greater value to religious Christians than the entire text of any other tract." But as I have said before, this was a delicate task, given the importance and priority attributed to the Vulgate, which, according to the conclusions of the Council of Trent, had been "written under the inspiration of the Holy Spirit." De' Rossi's enterprise therefore was meant for the *bei spiriti* who would appreciate his exposure of the errors of learned commentators—indeed, in the course of his study he was to take Cardinal Gaetano (Cajetan) and Nicholas de Lyra to task for some of their interpretations of Scripture. Thus, he writes: "Now since that Syriac text was extolled for its antiquity and authenticity, it may be used to the great pleasure of *beautiful souls* for the clarification of certain passages that do indeed deserve consideration. At the same time, some errors of certain learned commentators will (with respect) be disclosed."[26] In another example, the elucidation of an expression in the Gospels by means of the Syriac text and, in this particular case, the Aramaic of the Book of Ezra, leads him to write: "Now noble intellects [*elevati intelletti*] value the discovery of the truth of any subject or the etymology of a holy word that was unknown to their recent predecessors far above any other great joy."

In other words, the beautiful souls of his Italian work, like those of the *Light of the Eyes*, are to be identified as those—whether Jewish or Christian—who, like de' Rossi himself, are intent on reaching the highest level of truth. In such a quest, little allowance is given to any tradition if erroneous or to authoritative spokesmen of tradition if regarded as mistaken in any way.

This attempt of de' Rossi to realize the pleasure of beautiful souls is not done without considerable care and artifice. The *Light of the Eyes* is packed with quotations from rabbinic sources of which the greater number are from the Babylonian Talmud, to which de' Rossi refers by tractate and chapter. In addressing Christians in his Italian work, de' Rossi does refer to the Babylonian Talmud, but deliberately omits the term "Talmud." This is a small but telling gesture of submission to the Church authorities, who in the Tridentine Index of 1563 had stipulated that the term "Talmud" was henceforth not to be used. More complex, but no less illustrative of the way in which de' Rossi fashioned his discourse to render it palatable to Christians, is his treatment of Saint Augustine. As is well known, one of the impetuses to study and publish the Syriac (an Aramaic dialect) version of the Gospels was that the original texts of the Gospel of Matthew and Paul's Letter to the Hebrews would be recovered, for according to Jerome, they had been written in Hebrew. Repeatedly in the *Me'or 'einayim* and in his work on the Syriac New Testament, de' Rossi takes pains to explain that Aramaic was the people's vernacular after the return of the exiles under Ezra and that *maran atha* and other such expressions that had erroneously been described as Hebrew were actually Aramaic. When he discusses Jerome's position that the Gospel of Matthew had been written in Hebrew, he takes a similar position. Jerome, he claims, who had spoken of the Aramaic original of the books of Judith and Tobit, would have been sympathetic to the idea that Aramaic, not Hebrew, had been the original language of the Gospel of Matthew.

De' Rossi's assessment of the Syriac text relied greatly on the views of the editor of the first printed text of the Syriac in Vienna in 1555, namely, Albrecht Widmanstetter, who provided his own prefaces to the text. But Widmanstetter had introduced a slight complication, for he had reported Augustine's view expressed in the *De consensu evangelistarum* that the original language of those texts had been Greek. Rather than disregard this divergent view, de' Rossi set himself the task of explaining Augustine's position while steadfastly adhering to his own view. He produces an assessment of Augustine, focusing on the saint's cautious literary style, which, he claims, is particularly manifested in his exegesis of the cosmological parts of Genesis. The nondogmatic nature of the man, was, in his opinion, due to his place in the history of the Church. As one of the earliest Christian doctors whose predecessors were few, writes de' Rossi, Augustine could not afford to be too assertive, for he was not equipped with a well-established tradition on which to rely. De' Rossi then records the impressive passage in *De trinitate* in which Augustine makes a protestation with regard to his own writings: "Do not uphold that which we consider certain unless you understand it to be certain."[27] Such words, comments de' Rossi, "are certainly imbued with humanity and religiosity."

One might ask why de' Rossi felt compelled to complicate the issue by bringing Augustine into the question and why he felt so moved as to defend him. Of course, Augustine had been an idol of the early humanists such as Petrarch. But according to the subject matter and religious controversy, evaluation of Augustine could vary. As Eugene F. Rice has demonstrated, Augustine had ousted Jerome in the favors of the Protestants.[28] But in his *Annotations on the New Testament*, Erasmus wrote that Augustine was undeniably "a saint and a man of integrity endowed with a keen mind but immensely credulous and moreover lacking the equipment of languages."

De' Rossi would not use such language in relation to such a revered doctor of the Church, but manages to make a similar assessment, drawing his view from his subject's own writings. Thereby he steers a careful path, neither exonerating nor actually casting blame on Augustine.

In de' Rossi's hands, therefore, Augustine becomes sympathetic to his readers. Augustine's status in the tradition of Christian doctrine and letters is unique. It is nevertheless remarkable how de' Rossi's treatment of this unique figure is no different from the way he handles revered Jewish figures, including the sages of the Talmud when they make mistakes. Having spent an inordinate number of words explaining that their calculation of the duration of the First and Second Temples was wrong, he even goes as far as to argue that they only used those figures as conventional numbers, but were actually aware that they were incorrect. Moreover, in the 1575 revised edition of the text, de' Rossi appended a list of animadversions (*hassagot*) consisting of forty-one examples from the book (cited with page numbers), in which he criticized certain post-talmudic authorities. The list comprises references to such writers as Rashi, the Tosafists, and Maimonides.[29] The inclusion of the list in the final edition of the *Light of the Eyes* indicates that de' Rossi was not prepared to yield his ground but, on the contrary, wished to draw attention to his critical views.

What emerges is a de' Rossi who pursues his scholarly goal with no essential bias—Jews and Christians, whoever they are, may be castigated if necessary. We have seen that in addressing his Christian audience he makes no bones about his Jewish identity. Like other Italian Jews of other periods, de' Rossi manifests a pronounced allegiance to his native land. Indeed, on the opening page of a Hebrew work written for Jews, he refers to the "delightful city" of Mantua, using the expression *kirya 'aliza* (Isa. 22:2), said of Jerusalem. In another context, he makes a Hebrew wordplay on the name Mantova, stressing its *ṭovah*, its goodness. These are not simple external forms of patriotic sentiment. Like so many distinguished Jewish scholars before him, de' Rossi absorbed not only the scholarly legacy of his non-Jewish environment, but also read and made his own its literature. In discussing a favorite subject of his and one that a good philologist must necessarily treat—textual criticism and, in this case, errors in Acts—de' Rossi argues in respectable Renaissance manner:

The fact is (and I say this, if I may, both in regard to Hebrew and Latin works) that antiquity should be excused and defended as much as possible. It brings to mind the

> knowledgeable response, which according to Laertius, Timon the philosopher gave to somebody who asked him how one could get hold of a flawless copy of Homer's poem. He answered that he should read the ancient copies and not those that had recently been corrected.[30] Indeed, among the usual printing errors or mistakes of ignorant copyists and the arrogance of certain people who corrupt the text when they think they are emending it (and perhaps I belong to this category) the author often gets blamed when in fact he deserves pity as well as pardon.[31]

The last phrase reads: *quando merita trovar pietà non che perdono.* Italians worthy of their nation will certainly prick up their ears at this allusion to the first poem in Petrarch's *Canzoniere.* De' Rossi has simply adapted Petrarch's personal plea to his readers and applied it to the ancient authors, including the author of Acts. This allusion to Petrarch must have registered with de' Rossi's Italian readers.

Not only his Italian literary background, but also the classical civilization that lay at the heart of the Italian Renaissance is given prominence in de' Rossi's Italian text. A study of the *Light of the Eyes*, however, does not provide a clear impression of de' Rossi's familiarity with pagan antiquity. It contains scattered references to some of the key classical authors that he had read either in Latin or Italian—he had virtually no knowledge of Greek, and he read Greek authors in Latin or Italian translation. These citations from pagan texts are usually not crucial for his scholarly argument and do not serve as a source of essential facts. But in his Italian work, his allusions to classical authors are more polished and lend the impression of an insider's grasp of the literature. The Horatian "On occasion Homer nods" (*quandoque bonus Homerus dormitat*) and other such pithy sayings adorn his prose.

Interesting, too, is his allusion to Virgil. Having demonstrated the problems of a certain expression in the Gospels and the way certain learned commentators distorted the text in an effort to ensure its consistency, he then states: "But to recall your steps, as the poet said, this is the labor, this the task." Here the reference is to the passage from the sixth book of the *Aeneid*, in which the Cumaean Sybil informs Aeneas that it is easy to go down to see his father, Anchises, in the underworld, but that the return is fraught with pitfalls. This rhetorical flourish is indicative of the self de' Rossi wishes to fashion in this context. For when he writes for his Jewish readers, he calls David, the author of the Psalms, by the simple designation "poet," or *meshorer*, while Virgil is called *hameshorer hagadol leromiyyim.* By this simple reference to the poet, de' Rossi thus insinuates a connection with his Italian Christian readers. Both author and reader know that there is only one poet, namely, Virgil (and, of course, there is an added bonding factor, which may have been important to de' Rossi: Virgil, like himself, was a native Mantuan).

The study of the Italian de' Rossi reveals some aspects of the man that could not be inferred from reading the Jewish Azariah. He was not simply a polymath scholar who had absorbed the gentile contemporary erudition and applied it to his own Jewish tradition. The classical Italian legacy was an inherent part of his intellectual being. Obviously, the Jewish tradition remained paramount for him—he was a sincere Jew, as he says—but the secular also had a considerable role to play in fashioning the self that he truly was.

De' Rossi's antiquarian interests are particularly manifest is his discussion of the Hebrew and Samaritan scripts and their use in inscriptions on shekels, which he reproduces in his *Me'or 'einayim*. He manages to insert his reflections on this subject into his Italian text in the section in which he is discussing the *titulus crucis*, or the inscription on the cross. The verse from John (19:19, 20–22) reads: "And Pilate wrote a title and put it on the cross. And the writing was Jesus of Nazareth, the king of the Jews. . . . *And it was written in Hebrew, in Greek, and in Latin. Then the chief priests of the Jews said to Pilate: Write not, the king of the Jews, but that he had said, I am the king of the Jews. Pilate answered: What I have written, I have written.*" De' Rossi takes the opportunity here to discuss how the Hebrew inscription should have read. Once again, linguistic questions preoccupy him. As we have seen, his main thesis regarded the prevalence of Aramaic in the time of the Second Temple period. The logical conclusion was that the inscription, too, would have been in Aramaic—and he points to the Syriac version, which naturally contains an Aramaic version of those words. He also argues that the letters would have been engraved in the Assyrian, namely, Ashuri, script.

The most interesting element in his treatment of this subject, as far as the purpose of this paper is concerned, is that he speaks about the form of the *titulus*, which he has actually seen. In other words, de' Rossi is referring to images of the *titulus*, which, from the fifteenth century onward, are to be found in certain paintings of the Crucifixion, and which sometimes bore the trilingual inscription with the transcription of the Hebrew letters designed in a variety of ways, occasionally more or less accurately.[32] In 1492, the presumed piece of the *titulus crucis* was recovered in the Basilica di Santa Croce di Gerusalemme in Rome, in which the Greek and Latin texts are reversed to read from right to left, like Hebrew, and above them are some comma-like signs that are presumably meant to signify the abbreviated Hebrew words.[33] Many copies of this inscription were made;[34] sometimes the complete phrase

"Jesus Nazarenus king of the Jews" is found, and sometimes—as, for instance, in the painting of Gentile Bellini—an abbreviation is given of the Hebrew and placed beneath the Latin and Greek lines.[35] Without divulging precise information, de' Rossi speaks of the attempt of those who wish to give a semblance of antiquity and who reproduce the letters *mem he* or *mem yod* in Hebrew characters at the bottom of the *titulus.* He then argues that the letters reproduced should represent the Aramaic expression as given in the Syriac text, that is, *malka dihudaia,* and as has been written in the Ashuri script.

The details of his disquisition on the script need not detain us here. What is significant is that our portrait of the Jew de' Rossi has become more vivid. We see him in the churches gazing on images of the Crucifixion with a professional eye. From one point of view, we have no reason to be surprised. His Hebrew as well as his Italian works reveal an unusually flexible person who knew his way around Jewish and Christian circles. True, on occasion both in Hebrew and in Italian, he feels compelled to defend his people. Particularly revealing is his discussion of the term "Pharisee" in one of his appendices to his work. Such an investigation was certainly not germane to his study. In fact, he admits that the term is not Aramaic and speaks of a certain diffidence in broaching such a well-worn subject. It would appear that de' Rossi was intentionally attempting to subvert a common pejorative interpretation of the term "Pharisee," which had come to be used as a synonym for "hypocrite." On the basis of rabbinic texts, he demonstrated that the ancient sages, the opponents of the Sadducees, had themselves denounced hypocrisy; thereby in the most tactful way, he was able to correct Christian misinterpretation and abuse of the term "Pharisee."[36]

But the scope of de' Rossi's personal and scholarly quest, as I hope I have shown, extended beyond mere apologetics. Like another distinctive Rossi, his compatriot Salamone Rossi, he was able to be active in both Jewish and Christian society, follow the conventions that dictated Christian hierarchy, and act as a kind of Socratic gadfly on his fellow Jews. Don Harrán has described Rossi's Hebrew *Songs of Solomon* as neutralizing through music the difference in language and liturgy.[37] Through his scholarly quest for truth, Azariah de' Rossi wittingly transcended religious differences. This was a Jew who was not filled with qualms when looking at an image of the Crucifixion, but could reflect on it as a good Jewish scholar. This image of the man becomes reinforced on reading a particularly strong plea of his in favor of his method of reading history in chapter 50 of the *Me'or 'einayim.* Fully aware that his approach would not find favor in some quarters, he still insists: "Even those holy persons who refuse to look at a coin's effigy[38] [in case it was imprinted with an idolatrous image] will lend a listening ear to innovations in Torah studies. On seeing the crowd of foreigners cited by me, they will pronounce, like Ben Zoma on the Temple mount,[39] 'Blessed be He who has created all those to serve me.' "[40]

He clearly could not identify himself as one of those pious persons—after all, he had no compunction in gazing on Christian images—but remained convinced that the beautiful soul's quest for truth was paramount.

Notes

1. *Me'or 'einayim* (ed. pr. Mantua 1573–75), ed. Cassel (Vilna, 1866), p. 484. All subsequent references will be to *Light of the Eyes*, my annotated translation of the text published in the Yale Judaica series (New Haven, Conn., 2001).

2. B. Menaḥot 53a: "If he is learned, it is fine if he is learned and of noble birth, it is fine; but if he is neither learned nor of noble birth, may fire consume him." On this critique of the Babylonian emphasis on genealogy, see R. Kalmin, "Genealogy and Polemics in Rabbinic Literature," *Hebrew Union College Annual* 67 (1996): 77–94.

3. See *Light of the Eyes*, p. xxv.

4. See my "Azariah de' Rossi: Towards a Reappraisal of the Last Years of His Life," *Annali della scuola normale superiore di Pisa*, 3d ser., 8 (1978): 493–511.

5. The title, *Osservazioni di Buonaiuto de' Rossi Ebreo sopra diversi luoghi degli evangelisti nuovamente esposti secondo la vera lezione siriaca*, appears on the fly-leaf of the manuscript found in the Biblioteca Angelica, written by a later hand. My edition of the text with an English translation is to be published in the Warburg Institute Studies and Texts series. There are two copies of the work extant: one that he sent to Giacomo Boncompagni, son of Gregory XIII (Biblioteca Vaticana, Boncompagni, Az); and a later, amplified version with variants (Biblioteca Angelica, Ms. 1948), which he sent to Giulio Antonio Santoro, Cardinal Santa Severina.

6. S. Greenblatt, *Renaissance Self-Fashioning: From More to Shakespeare* (Chicago, 1980).

7. Interestingly, de' Rossi stresses his Jewishness with greater vigor in the second version of his work, which he wrote for Santori after having received no response from Giacomo Boncompagni.

8. He discusses Acts 7 when Stephen gives his salvation history address, in the course of which he states: "So Jacob went down into Egypt and died, he and our fathers and they were carried over into Shechem and laid in the sepulcher that Abraham bought for a sum of money of the sons of Emor, the son of Shekhem." The problems in the verse are, as de' Rossi indicates, obvious. Abraham did not buy the grave from the sons of Emor (Ḥamor), and Emor was not the son, but rather the father of Shekhem (Gen. 33:19). Moreover, the verse refers not only to Jacob but also to others who were laid in the grave. To de' Rossi's satisfaction, the Syriac translator only

refers to Jacob alone being placed in the grave and does not mention the son of Shekhem at all.

9. This eloquent plea, which is dated 21 June 1577, so it seems, fell on deaf ears. The Roman authorities never responded to de' Rossi's original contribution to New Testament scholarship, and from the little evidence at our disposal, it would appear that he died in Ferrara at the end of 1577.

10. "The light of the eyes rejoiceth the heart; and a good report maketh the bones fat."

11. *Light of the Eyes*, p. 6.

12. He refers to chap. 56 of his *Libro di varie lettioni, cognominato oculorum lumen.*

13. I am grateful to Guilio Lepschy, who drew my attention to these texts.

14. P.L. XXV, col. 491–92, Prologus: "Et tamen sicubi se occasio in explanatione eiusdem voluminis dederit, calumniae illius strictim respondere conabor, et philosophiae artibus, immo malitiae saeculari per quam subvertere nititur veritatem et quibusdam praestigiis clarum *oculorum lumen* auferre explanatione simplici contraire."

15. De' Rossi quotes from several parts of the commentary, including chap. 1.

16. M. Ḥullin 4:7.

17. The term as such does not appear in Neoplatonic Hebrew medieval texts, which do, however, speak of the beauty of the soul or adornment of the soul. See A. Tanenbaum, "The Adornment of the Soul: A Philosophical Motif in Andalusian Piyyut," *Hebrew Union College Annual* 66 (1996): 223–38, who quotes Joseph ben Judah ibn Aqnin's comment on Canticles 1:10, in which "the Intellect lauds the soul for her qualities of character and for becoming beautiful when engaged in the good works prescribed by her knowledge." *Anima bella* does appear in medieval Christian writers such as Richard of Saint Victor, in his commentary on Canticles. For a discussion of the history of the eighteenth-century use the term *Seelenschönheit*, or beauty of the soul, see the entry by R. Konersman in *Historisches Wörterbuch der Philosophie*, vol. 9. See also R. Norton, *The Beautiful Soul: Aesthetic Morality in the Eighteenth Century* (Ithaca, N.Y., 1995).

18. "Panegyric on Love," in *Cambridge Translations of Renaissance Philosophical Texts*, ed. J. Kraye (Cambridge, 1997), 1: 157.

19. *Light of the Eyes*, p. 251.

20. I.e., Sebastian Münster's edition (Basel, 1541).

21. *Light of the Eyes*, p. 332.

22. Ibid., p. 341.

23. Ibid., p. 406.

24. See *Bereshit Rabbah* 81:2 (ed. Theodor, p. 971) and parallels.

25. See B. Yoma 69b; Sanhedrin 64a.

26. "A tale ch'essendo esso testo siriaco tanto lodato d'antichità et emendatione, con gran diletto de gl'elevati spiriti si possono per lui chiarire alcuni passi, degni certamente di consideratione. Scoprendosi insiememente qualche errore (sia detto con buona gratia) d'alcuni dotti commentatori."

27. De' Rossi cites this text of Augustine from a secondary source, Johannes Lu-

cidus Samotheus's *De emendationibus temporum* (Venice, 1537),p. 192v: "Dicit enim Augustinus de scriptis suis loquens in prologo 3 *De trinitate*, Noli meis literis quasi canonicis scripturis deservire; sed in illis et quae non credebas, cum inveneris, incunctanter crede: in istis autem quod certum habemus nisi certum intellexeris noli firmum tenere." The reference is to Augustine, *De trinitate*, II, proem (P.L. 869). The reading *quod certum habemus* is not the standard reading, which is *quod certum non habebas.*

28. E. F. Rice, *Saint Jerome in the Renaissance* (Baltimore, 1985), chap. 6.

29. The writers mentioned are: Rashi, Judah Halevi, Isaac Abravanel, Elijah Mizraḥi, Maimonides, Albo, Nathan ben Yeḥiel, Abraham ibn Ezra, the Tosafists, Rabbenu Nissim, Moses Isserles, Isaaç Alfasi, Meir Abulafia of Toledo, Abraham ibn David, Naḥmanides, Rabbenu Ḥananel, Moses Alashqar, and Elijah Levita.

30. Diogenes Laertius, *Timon* 9, 12, 113.

31. "He . . . pardon," an allusion to Petrarch, *Canzoniere*, *Spero trovar pietà, nonché perdono* (1.8).

32. On the subject of Hebrew inscriptions in Renaissance art, see A. Ronen, "Iscrizioni ebraiche nell'arte ebraica del quattrocento," in *Studi di storia dell'arte sul medioevo e del Rinascimento nel centenario della nascita di Mario Salmi* (Florence, 1993), 2: 601–24.

33. The discovery is described by Stefano Infessura as a miracle in his *Diario della città di Roma*, ed. O. Tommasini (Rome, 1890), p. 270: "Et primus versus erat in hoc scriptus literis Latinis, secundus versus literis Grecis, et tertius literis Hebraicis. . . . Et est omnium aestimatione tabula illa quam Pilatus posuit, in Cruce super Caput Domini Nostri Jesu Christi, posita ibi per Sanctam Helenam matrem Constantini." Leandro de Corrieris claimed that Leonardo da Sarzana, who was given custody of the *titulus*, was encouraged to send an illustration of the *titulus* with a commentary to Lorenzo il Magnifico.

34. See A. Parrronchi, "Titulus crucis," *Antichità Viva* 5 (1966): 41–42, who discusses the reconstruction of the *titulus* by Luca Signorelli in his painting of the Crucifixion in the Galleria nazionale della Marche in Urbino with the Hebrew words written out in full. See also M. Lucco and A. Pontani, "Greek Inscriptions on Two Venetian Paintings," *Journal of the Warburg and Courtauld Institutes* 60 (1997): 110–18.

35. See Bellini's Crucifixion in *La pittura nel Veneto: Il quattrocento*, ed. M. Lucco (Milan, 1990), 2: 445, fig. 521, p. 451.

36. Unfortunately, de' Rossi's entire discussion is worthless, since it is based on a confusion between two Syriac letters.

37. Don Harrán, *Salamone Rossi: Jewish Musician in Late Renaissance Mantua* (Oxford, 1999), p. 251. See also his essay in this volume.

38. This expression is based on B. Pesaḥim 104a.

39. B. Berakhut 58a.

40. *Light of the Eyes*, p. 417.

Chapter 7

The Teaching Program of David ben Abraham and His Son Abraham Provenzali in Its Historical-Cultural Context

Gianfranco Miletto

One of the most important cultural centers in Italy in the sixteenth century was Mantua, which under the rule of the Gonzagas enjoyed an artistic and economic creativity that came to a tragic end with the sack of 1630. The Jewish community benefited from the relatively liberal politics of the Gonzagas and attained a high rank in the culture of the time. One sign of the cultural wealth and the ferment that animated the community was its publishing activity. The first Hebrew printer, the physician Abraham ben Solomon Conat, set up one of the first Hebrew presses in Italy, in Mantua around 1470.[1] Except for short intervals, the Hebrew press continued to function in Mantua until the end of the eighteenth century. Its fame, surpassed only by Venice among the Hebrew Italian presses of the day, extended beyond the borders of the small duchy of Mantua. The Hebrew press of Mantua also printed works commissioned from abroad, such as the *Zohar*, published in Mantua between 1558 and 1560 on an order by emissaries from Safed. We can gain an idea of the cultural interests of the Mantuan Jews from the lists of books presented by the Jews to the censor in 1595 and 1605.[2] The libraries of the Mantuan Jews were rich in content and scope: not only prayer books, Bibles, biblical commentaries, rabbinical and kabbalistic works, but also works in Italian and Latin on medicine, philosophy, rhetoric, astronomy, and history. These bear ample testimony to the broad educational level of Mantuan Jewry during the Renaissance.

For the general historical-cultural reconstruction of the Mantuan community, we have today the excellent volume by Shlomo Simonsohn,[3] but many of the important figures in Mantuan Jewry are little known and much research is yet to be done. One of the families that played an important role in the cultural life of the community were the Provenzali.[4] They had migrated from southern France and settled in Italy during the fifteenth century. Around 1480, R. Jacob ben David Provenzali,[5] who belonged to the yeshiva of Messer Leon, lived in Naples. R. Jacob ben David Provenzali can be considered the progenitor of the Provenzali family of Mantua. Counted among its illustrious members were Moses ben Abraham,[6] considered one of the greatest Italian talmudists of his time; his brother Judah,[7] a rabbi and scholar praised by Azariah de' Rossi[8] and Abraham Portaleone,[9] whose teacher Judah was for a time; and David,[10] a rabbi and Bible commentator, grammarian and teacher of Azariah de' Rossi, along with his son Abraham Provenzali,[11] rabbi in Mantua, Ferrara, and Casale Monferrato. Abraham was a teacher of Abraham Portaleone and graduated with him from the University of Pavia in medicine and philosophy in 1563. In the short autobiography attached to his encyclopedic work *Shilṭei hagibborim* (Mantua, 1612), Portaleone mentions his teacher and friend:

After him[12] I gathered wisdom at the side of the Gaon, the wonder of his generation, "an erudite and powerful debater,"[13] chief of the academy, the divine kabbalist, physician, and philosopher, the Rabbi Abraham son of the Gaon and chief among Italian preachers, Rabbi David Provenzali of blessed memory, whose light now shines forth in Casale Monferrato and is absent from Mantua. This Gaon, may the Lord bless him, filled me with the flesh and wine of the Talmud, pouring in as much as I could absorb. For by the Lord's mercy, where we assembled were gathered all the parts of the oral law. And he instructed me, with great assiduity, in the elements of Latin, and all of logic most thoroughly. And with his honor, after several years had passed, I went to Pavia, to hear the wisdom of the philosopher Aristotle at the gathering of physicians, and the medicine of Hippocrates and Galen, the Greeks and the other wise Arab physicians.[14]

Nevertheless I never neglected to study "the perfect Torah of the Lord,"[15] because I had this wonderful sage, who was always praiseworthy, as my teacher of justice. He taught me wisdom and fear of the Lord, he filled me with wisdom. It was he who with great loving care, "gave me a portion of his glory."[16] Three months after him, after the physicians had him crowned in philosophy and medicine,[17] I too was awarded the title of doctor in the great hall of the University of Pavia along with the other philosophers and physicians.[18]

In his praise, Portaleone points out the pedagogical skills of his teacher and his ability to combine Jewish tradition and secular sciences. Portaleone admires not only the scholar in Rabbi Abraham Provenzali but also the educator, concerned in particular with the cultural and ethical molding of his pupil.

The principles on which the teaching of Abraham Provenzali and of his father, David, were based are listed in the program for the foundation of a school in Mantua in 1564. The text, long forgotten, was rediscovered at the beginning of a book[19] that belonged in 1645 to Abraham Joseph Solomon Graziano of Modena.[20] It was transcribed from there by R. Naḥman Coronel for Halberstam, who published it in the journal *Ha-Levanon* in 1868. The text, with some omissions, was reprinted by Assaf and translated into German by Güdemann and into English by Marcus.[21] I will confine myself to a summary of the principal points of the teaching program of the Provenzali.[22]

Abraham Provenzali begins with the sad observation that the Jewish people runs the risk of losing its scholars. This cultural impoverishment will leave the Jewish nation abandoned to itself among the Christians "like a flock without shepherd," while the number of Christians expert in the sciences and technology is constantly increasing. As a remedy, he proposes the foundation of a "college"[23] for educating young men in the Torah and the sciences; then they will not have to spend so many years studying in the Christian universities, where they also inevitably learn Christian ways. David's eldest son, Abraham Provenzali, a graduate in philosophy and medicine who had acquired a basic Jewish education, will be associated with his father in the tasks of teaching. The college will be regulated according to certain rules, and, with God's help, Abraham Provenzali intends to pursue the following aims:

1. First, he will pay particular attention to the ethical and religious education of the pupils, "so as to pluck out of their hearts every root that brings forth false ideas—if such there be, God forbid!—and to plant in their souls proper beliefs and ideas, those in agreement with the Bible and the rabbinic teachings, so that their expressions and their intentions in all their actions shall be directed toward God, as is befitting for every good Jew; that they be zealous in observance of both the rational and the ceremonial commandments; that they go morning and evening to the synagogue; that they acquire good manners and commendable virtues; that they keep themselves from improprieties."
2. He is willing to house the students who come from other towns and to provide for their physical needs. During meals, students will always converse on religious as well as secular matters. The students must re-

main at the college for at least three years. The course of study is to be completed in five years.

3. The chief subject matter in instruction will be the written and oral Torah, "which is the basis of everything." If permission is granted to print the Talmud again,[24] there will be detailed study of it with all the commentaries: Halakhot, Tosafot, and responsa. If permission for printing is delayed, one will begin with Alfasi and R. Nissim. If the number of students and income from fees increase, outstanding Ashkenazic talmudists will be engaged to help train students for talmudic debate, so that halakhah becomes plain and the students accustom themselves to confrontation, logical deductions, and the formulation of objections.
4. Study of the Bible will be combined with study of the best of the old and the new commentators.
5. Occasionally, one will read chapters of the foremost Jewish philosophers "whose writings are in harmony with the teachings of the Torah and rabbinic authorities, in order to establish correct beliefs, and to remove errors, false notions, and a distorted point of view."
6. One will fix periods for the study of Hebrew grammar[25] and the Massorah, for the correct understanding of the Bible and its hidden meaning are dependent upon this.
7. The study of grammar will be linked with training in rhetoric and oratory and the reading of the best poets.
8. Students will also be trained to write the standard Hebrew script properly, as well as other Hebrew scripts.
9. Students will also learn Latin, "whose knowledge is indispensable for dealing with the officials, and write essays in Hebrew and in good Italian and Latin, graced with the niceties and elegance of style that are characteristic of each language."
10. "Those who are versed in Latin can read scientific books dealing with logic, philosophy, and medicine and thus become acquainted with them step by step. In this way, students desiring to become physicians need not waste their time in a university among Christians, in sinful neglect of Jewish studies. On the contrary, through his own reading he should inform himself gradually of all that he needs to know. Then, if he should later study in a university for a brief period, he will be able, with God's help, to obtain his degree. But even those who do

not as yet know any Latin may read such scientific books as have already been translated into Hebrew, and thus save time: for the basic thing in knowledge is not language but content."

11. Other subjects in the curriculum will be arithmetic, geometry, geography, and astrology.
12. At fixed periods, the students will engage in debates in the presence of the teacher, deliberating on matters of Jewish law and the sciences "in order to sharpen their minds. Each young man will learn more or less in accordance with his individual capacity; the principle is that they be religious in spirit. Also they will gradually be taught to speak in public and to preach before congregations."

The program closes with the declaration by the son Abraham to help his father and with an appeal for providing the necessary means for the implementation of the project and for scholarships to be granted to gifted needy students. With the support of all communities, Abraham Provenzali intended to establish

> a large college of scholars and scribes in a sacred spot where the president, who is yet to be appointed, resides. . . . Then it will be possible to secure the aid of many learned and skilled instructors, every one of whom will work in his own field—for it is manifestly impossible for one or two men, except with great difficulty and extraordinary effort, to give all the lectures we have suggested above. This will be especially true if the students—may their Rock and Redeemer guard them!—are divided into separate classes that then recite their lessons before their teachers. With the help of the Jewish communities, it may be possible to employ a number of scholars, some of whom will be engaged in teaching talmudic law, and others the respective sciences.

The Provenzali project was not novel. On 17 January 1466, King John of Aragon, in response to a petition from Sicilian Jewry, authorized the foundation of a university (*studium generale*) under his patronage in any city that the Jews of Sicily might choose, with the right to hire and fire doctors, jurists, and so forth.[26]

The foundation of a rabbinical academy in Ferrara dates back to 1556, on the concession of the duke Ercole II d'Este, who granted the petition of Solomon Riva "d'introdurre uno studio d'Hebrei"[27] in Ferrara, where Rabbi Jacob Rainer[28] would come to teach. The duke points out that "ciò non può tornare se non ad honore et ornamento di essa nostra Cittade, per il profitto che ne potranno trarre molti Hebrei et Christiani scolari sì forestieri come sudditi nostri"[29] and therefore exempts the teacher and the students from payment of any taxes.[30]

Though the idea was not new, the program of the Provenzali has intriguing features that should be examined in their cultural-historical context. The school proposed by the Provenzali cannot be considered a university or an academy—rather, it is an institution within the community. One does not need to petition the prince or the pope to obtain permission for the foundation, with all associated rights and privileges, of a university like the Sicilian *studium generale.* Nor can it be compared with an academy. At least according to the wishes of the duke, the school in Ferrara was to have been not just a yeshiva (a rabbinical academy solely for Jews), but also a meeting point for Christian scholars, similar to other academies established during the Renaissance.

The Provenzali program envisions instruction only for young Jewish males. Its aims are dual: ethical-religious and cultural (see above, point 5). The cultural aim is to provide the pupil with broad knowledge of both Jewish tradition and the secular sciences, with instruction extending over a period of three or five years. Considering the distinction made in the teaching program between students who have made progress in their studies and are able to read scientific books in Latin dealing with logic, philosophy, and medicine, and those who do not as yet know any Latin and can only read scientific books translated into Hebrew, it seems correct to infer that during the first three years of the course of study, the student received a basic grounding; the two following years were preparatory for the Christian university. Particular importance was accorded grammatical and rhetorical matters (David Provenzali himself wrote a Hebrew grammar), centered on both the Bible and classical and Italian works. Little room was given to philosophy.

The teaching framework and the importance attached to rhetoric and oratory correspond with a trend in Italian Jewish culture that was already an established tradition. Under the influence of the new humanistic spirit, as early as the beginning of the fifteenth century, the humanists sensed the need for a new educational system. That spirit, discovering the intrinsic value of the human considered in the subjectivity and complexity of his personality, turned from abstract questions of metaphysics to questions of morality and from dialectics and logic to rhetoric, regarded as the sublime art of reflection on the concrete and complex experiences of the human soul.[31] The first schools or colleges were founded by such educators as Guarino Guarini

(1374–1460), in Verona, by Vittorino da Feltre (1378–1446), in Mantua, and by Gasparino Barzizza (1360–1431), in Padua. The new teaching system fused rhetoric and dialectic on the basis of Cicero and Quintilian and combined the study of classical authors with scientific matters, mathematics, geography, and physical training (dance, hunting, and swimming).[32] The practical goal of this educational method was to provide the pupil with a basic culture: a solid grounding in rhetoric and dialectic, in order to be able to attend the courses of medicine and law at the university.

Similar innovations were carried out in the traditional system of the yeshiva. The founder of what may rightly be considered Jewish humanistic scholarship in Italy was Judah Messer Leon.[33] His system was based on the application of the principles of classical rhetoric to the Bible. Messer Leon did not explain the principles of his teaching system in theoretical works, but it is evident from his writings that he conceived the tripartite structure of his teaching method in accordance with the medieval *trivium* (grammar, rhetoric, and logic).[34] For him, the *artes sermocinales* were preparatory to the study of the "speculative" sciences.[35] In the introduction to *Nofet ṣufim*, Messer Leon claims that he was urged to compose his work at the insistence of Jewish medical students who had requested a rhetorical handbook.[36] The great merit of Messer Leon lies in having recognized the cultural-social function of rhetoric for both intracommunal relations and the external relations with the Christians. Ideally, whoever was educated at his school distinguished himself by his encyclopedic knowledge, his skill in oratory, and the stylistic elegance of his writings. Rhetoric became a means for advancing the authority of the Rabbis inside the community, and at the same time it facilitated a kind of cultural equality, putting the Rabbis on the same level as Christian scholars. In this way, it was easier to introduce specifically Jewish elements into the cultural debate.[37] Rhetoric thus became a basic element for the education of the ideal Jewish scholar, namely the *ḥakham kolel.* Only that scholar can be called "wise" who will be able to master all the categories of existence and integrate them into the tradition of the fathers.[38] From this point of view, Messer Leon can rightly be considered the founder of a "Jewish humanism," in the sense of the ideal of the ethical-cultural education of the truly wise; he saw in the prophets of Israel the perfect realization of the humanistic sage as defined by Cato, *vir bonus dicendi peritus.*[39]

Though Messer Leon did not break completely with the old scholastic framework, as appears from his commentaries on Aristotle on the basis of the Averroist interpretation and the frequent references to Averroës in *Nofet ṣufim*, this does not diminish the innovative value of his teaching program.[40] The link between Messer Leon and Averroës' writings can be explained by considering the conservative tendency within Jewish culture in general that aspired to harmonize the old with the new rather than oppose the new.[41] The instruction by Messer Leon was also preparatory for the university, particularly for the course in medicine, whose program also comprised Averroës' commentaries on Aristotle.[42] We have no information from Messer Leon about the organization and structure of his curriculum, but it probably did not differ substantially from the one proposed by one of his pupils, Yoḥanan Alemanno.[43] Like Alemanno, Messer Leon believed that education should begin with the study of the Bible, training in calligraphy and literature, and the study of grammar and arithmetic (all these subjects are also included in the curriculum of the Provenzali). Later, the pupil studied Talmud with the commentaries of Rashi and the Tosafists, and the *trivium* and *quadrivium* (arithmetic, geometry, astronomy, and astrology), with the exclusion of music.

One of the goals of Messer Leon's curriculum was to prepare pupils for the study of medicine at the university. It is noteworthy and certainly no accident that a responsum[44] dealing with the relation between profane studies and tradition, though most probably a forgery, is attributed to the circle of Messer Leon, whose curriculum attempted to integrate profane knowledge with Jewish tradition.[45] In a letter written at the end of the fifteenth century (intended, as was customary during the Renaissance, for publication), Jacob ben David Provenzali answered the question of R. David ben Judah Messer Leon concerning secular wisdom: he stated that only theoretical philosophy, namely, Aristotelianism, which is contrary to the Torah and denies the *creatio ex nihilo*, was to be censured. On the other hand, the study of the practical sciences—nature, medicine, astronomy, and the pursuit of crafts such as metalworking and agriculture—was, in his view, commendable. That study should be furthered, because the practical sciences give us knowledge about matters that are part of God's creation. And even though studies in the practical sciences are nowadays taken from the works of foreign authors, the practical sciences are present in the Torah. The Rabbis never rejected knowledge that according to experience was true, even if it was expressed in a foreign language. If one rejects these truthful sciences, which are contained in the Torah, one also rejects the Torah, because the Torah is truth and all that is true is contained in the Torah.[46]

Several years later, similar ideas were expressed in a work by R. Yeḥiel Nissim (Vitale) da Pisa, *Miḥnat kenaot.* For him, the natural sciences, such as geometry and medicine, are wisdom, whereas knowledge beyond nature (namely, metaphysics), which seeks to explain all phenomena through logical argumentation, is subject to doubt and arrives at false conclusions.[47] Important as a part of the study of medicine is the study of astrology, contained in the curriculum of Alemanno (and Provenzali) in keeping with the belief at that time that the stars influence physical matter and consequently also affect human health. Geography is also listed among teaching subjects, inspired in part by new discoveries at the time. In their works, Abraham Farissol,[48] Abraham Yagel,[49] David de' Pomis, and Abraham Portaleone display a particular interest in botany, zoology, and mineralogy of the New World, especially in the strange and wonderful aspects of nature. That is reflective of baroque mentality and the interest in the bizarre.[50]

The pedagogical project of the Provenzali also has to be examined in relation to the new cultural ferment during the Counter Reformation. At the beginning of his program, R. David Provenzali describes the decay and deteriorating conditions in the yeshivot and points to the upsurge in scholarly activity among Christians: "The peoples among whom we live are ever increasing in wisdom, understanding, and knowledge, and in all arts, but Israel alone is isolated, desolate, poor. Why should we be inferior to all other peoples who have scholarly institutions and places fit for instruction in law and sciences?"[51] The reference to "scholarly institutions" may be understood in a general sense, but if we consider the historical context, there is deeper significance. One of the first effects of the Counter Reformation was the Catholic Church's promotion of religious and cultural instruction of the clergy and believers, especially by means of new religious orders.

The Jesuits were particularly involved in this field and created a new system of teaching aimed at integrating humanistic studies into ethical-religious education. Their colleges date back to the first years of the foundation of the Society of Jesus (1540). The first college was established in Messina in 1548, and the Collegio Romano dates back to 1551. While Ignatius of Loyola (1491–1556) was still alive, colleges were set up in Palermo, Naples, Gandia, Alcalà, Salamanca, Valladolid, Lisbon, and Vienna. After his death, the Society of Jesus expanded in Central Europe: Ingolstadt, Cologne, Munich and Prague became seats of important colleges. The teaching methods of the Jesuits were later codified in the *ratio atque institutio studiorum Societatis Iesu*, published in 1599 under the direction of Claude Acquaviva and made obligatory for all Jesuit schools. In its basic features, the *ratio studiorum* follows the pedagogical ideas set forth in the *Spiritual Exercises* of Ignatius of Loyola.

Care for the moral and religious education of the pupils, as stated in the program of the Provenzali, echoes advice in the *ratio studiorum* to the pupils to combine humanistic studies with the principles of Christian morality: "Qui discendi causa Societatis Iesu gymnasia frequentant, intelligant, Deo iuvante non minus curatum iri pro viribus, ut pietate ceterisque virtutibus, quam ut ingenuis artibus imbuantur" ("They who in order to learn attend the colleges of the Society of Jesus must understand that with God's help they will also be inculcated, according to their possibility, with piety and the other virtues").[52] Just as students at the Jesuit colleges must attend church services regularly,[53] so must students at the Provenzali school attend synagogue prayers.

The division of the curriculum into two periods of three and two years and the teaching method of the Provenzali program differ from that of the traditional yeshiva. The first three years, in the course of which the pupil received a general basic education, and the two following years of the advanced course, preparatory for the Christian university, correspond to the division of the *ratio studiorum* between the three years of the grammar course, which constituted a complete study cycle,[54] and the two years of the advanced course of humanities and rhetoric.[55] Whereas in the yeshiva all members, pupils, and teachers took part together in the discussion about a talmudic question put forth by the yeshiva head, who opened the discussion,[56] the technique of study at the school of the Provenzali differed. It was based upon the division of the pupils into separate classes and the recitation of lessons before the teacher.

At the Jesuit colleges, the *praelectio* was an important aspect of the teaching technique. First the teacher read a text by a classical author to the pupils, summarized its content, and, if possible, pointed out connections with previous lectures. Then he explained and expounded individual sentences, concluding with a moral observation.[57] The following day, the pupils had to recite the *praelectio* of the previous day, which was memorized, before the *decuriones*, a fellow student appointed by the teacher. The teacher then appointed some pupils to repeat the lesson publicly.[58] The written exercises in Hebrew, Latin, and Italian, with particular attention to the stylistic elegance established in the curriculum of the Provenzali (see above, point 9), find a parallel at the Jesuit school in the *esercitium stili* in both languages,

Latin and their vernacular, consisting of the compositions of themes in the style appropriate to the topic (for example, an essay of narration, eulogy, exhortation, or edification).[59] In the Provenzali (see above, point 12) as well as the Jesuit schools,[60] special efforts were made to train pupils in the art and theory of oratory. To train pupils to speak in public and better grasp the subject, the teaching technique of the Jesuits used the *disputatio* and the *concertatio*,[61] discussion in class or between different classes.[62] By means of objections and responses in a dialectic opposition of the pupils between opponents and respondents, a text was debated or a subject matter already studied was reexplained. These discussions were organized on a weekly basis, generally on Saturday, and monthly, sometimes with the participation of foreign scholars at the college.[63] Particularly important and solemn were the *disputationes* of the students of philosophy, which were staged three or four times a year.[64] Similarly, at the proposed Provenzali school, discussion (*pilpul*) was a method not only for talmudic questions but for secular sciences.

Some years later, the Rabbi Löw, Maharal of Prague (c. 1525–1609), perceived an urgent need to reform the teaching method and cultural content. He advocated a new educational system, designed to integrate Jewish tradition with the secular sciences. The principles of his pedagogy are scattered in his commentaries in the form of the annotations.[65] Conscious of the importance of education as a means of transmission and preservation of the cultural-religious legacy of Jewish tradition, Rabbi Löw, like Rabbi David Provenzali, believed that the traditional teaching system of the yeshiva was inadequate for the needs of the modern age. He rejected the misuse of *pilpul* when it was no longer a means to explain textual interpretations and what was permitted and useful (*pilpul amiti*), but only intellectual acrobatics, an end in itself to display the dialectic skills of the scholar. This was inimical to the search for truth.[66] According to the Maharal, the goal of education is communion with God, reached through study of the Torah, which has to be studied in a progressive and systematic way, not by merely following the progression of the synagogue weekly readings (*parashiyyot*). Only afterward can one gradually begin to study the Mishnah and then the Talmud, in accordance with the intellectual and psychological growth of the child.

In his view, the teaching system has to be in correspondence with the cosmological order of Creation. It leads to virtue and perfection of the pupil by developing his rationality exercised upon the Mishnah. The pupil should aim at this perfection, namely, to study by oneself without coercion. The teacher will encourage the pupil by praising him and rewarding his diligence. The teaching technique has to involve all sensory faculties of the pupil—for example, by using pictures to facilitate memorization, and by reading aloud.[67] Study must be a real activity, not only theoretical but put into concrete form in practice, that is, the doing of precepts. Among the incentives to stimulate the pupil, Rabbi Löw avoids competition, because it appeals to the negative tendency of human nature for self-aggrandizement: to make oneself conspicuous and to seek honor and to rejoice when one's fellow fails.[68] An important role is accorded the study of grammar, which allows the pupil independent and immediate access to texts. To anchor the knowledge acquired in the pupil's memory, R. Löw advocates frequent repetition of the subject matter.

Scholars have already pointed out the similarity between the teaching system of the Maharal and that of Jan Amos Comenius (1592–1670), who was a generation younger than the Maharal. When R. Löw died in 1609, Comenius was seventeen years old; consequently, it is highly unlikely that they had any direct contact. At the most, one can surmise that Comenius had read some of the Maharal's works.[69] However, over and beyond any direct influence, some prefer to explain the similarity between the two methods on the basis of the cultural context of Prague.[70] A vital cultural center, Prague was the crossroads of new ideas streaming in from Italy, Poland, and Germany. The importance attributed by R. Löw to the study of grammar and sciences (particularly astronomy) does not imply that he knew the Provenzalis' program, but he was probably aware of some of the cultural tendencies prevalent among Italian Jews. Similarly, we can suppose that R. Löw was familiar with the pedagogical method of the Jesuits.[71] The ethical goal of education, the "active study" technique, which aims to involve all sensory faculties of the pupil, the idea of the perfectibility of the human spirit, which must not be forced in any way, but encouraged and stimulated, the importance of revision of the learned material—all these are fundamental features of the Jesuit teaching system. Consider the role played by the theater in Jesuit didactics and the custom of hanging the writings of the better pupils, maxims, emblems, and pictures on the classroom walls, in keeping with the subject matter of the lessons.[72] The appropriate gestures and intonation, which had to accompany the public recitation of texts, helped learners assimilate the texts. According to the didactic method of the *ratio studiorum*, the learning process had to engage all intellectual and sensory faculties of the pupil. Religious practice and learning are strictly correlated in both educational systems.

Löw's explicit critique and rejection of the competition system as a teaching method to stimulate the pupil indicate that he was familiar with an educational system (namely, that of the Jesuits) that employed it widely.

Why was the curricular project of the Provenzali not implemented? Since the sources are silent, we can only engage in supposition. In my opinion, it is incorrect to think that the project was not put into practice because of the repressive politics of the Catholic Church from the middle of the sixteenth century on.[73] Yet the Mantuan community enjoyed substantial administrative autonomy until the eighteenth century,[74] and the academy of Ferrara continued to function when the town came under direct control of the pope.[75] One probable cause of the failure could have been the tense relations between the Ashkenazic and Italian communities. The case of the Tamari-Venturozzo divorce, which both communities opposed and which personally involved R. Moses, brother of R. David, Provenzali, was also indicative of cultural and social contrasts between the two communities.[76] It was not a question of greater or lesser rigor in the observance and application of the halakhic precepts. The thesis of Graetz,[77] who considered Messer Leon a typical example of "Italian humanistic liberalism"—as contrasted with Ashkenazic "obscurantism" represented, for example, by R. Judah Mintz—has been refuted by recent research, which indicates that Messer Leon adhered to a stricter interpretation of the halakhic rules in line with Franco-German practice, as opposed to the local customs of the Italian Jews, which conformed chiefly with Maimonides.[78] The conflict, which found particularly sharp expression in rabbinical relations, involved a different concept of culture. The attempts by some Italian Jewish scholars during the fifteenth and sixteenth centuries to integrate secular knowledge into Jewish tradition was not understood by rabbis who were anchored in the Ashkenazic tradition. It is not true that the campaign against Azariah de' Rossi was launched by Ashkenazic rabbis, who were able to find more supporters abroad than in Italy.[79]

In Italy, the reforming trend in the traditional teaching system of the yeshiva was pursued in the seventeenth and eighteenth centuries by Isaac Cantarini and Solomon Conegliano in Padua and by Isaac Lampronti in Ferrara.[80] Outside of Italy, the efforts of the Maharal had no success and gained few proponents. On the contrary, it is hypothesized that one reason for the rejection of R. Löw's appointment to the rabbinical office of Prague was his pedagogical ideas.[81]

Yet some three centuries later, the ideas of the Provenzali and the Maharal would also be implemented by Ashkenazic communities. The goals and contents of the didactic program, as explained by Leopold Zunz in his opening address for the *Jüdisches Seminar* in Leipzig (18 November 1840), reflect the Provenzali program in many ways:

Seminaries must be established to train teachers for the school, the house, the synagogue. . . . Now the task of instruction in the schools should be to strengthen the moral powers of the student, to educate the intellect for the most diverse paths in life. . . . The duration of the full course should be three to four years, during which time the necessary subjects for the Jewish teachers and schools will be presented and practiced by staff teachers, progressing from stage to stage. The seminary students themselves shall also be required to teach. The curriculum thus comprises the following: religion, Bible studies, Talmud, German and Hebrew, arithmetic, geometry, geography and history, natural sciences, penmanship, and drawing. For advanced semesters, also logic, pedagogy, Jewish history, exercises in homiletics et al. Equal care will be given to both the intellectual and moral-religious education of the pupils.[82]

The project of the Provenzali is not an isolated example of cultural connections between Jewish and Catholic, especially Jesuit, attitudes during the Counter Reformation. Robert Bonfil has proved that the account of Joseph ha-Kohen about the Protestant Reformation is based on Catholic sources, and his statement is in accord with the Catholic position. Abraham Yagel composed his *Lekaḥ ṭov* using the model of the catechism of Peter Canisius. The ethical work *Ṣemaḥ ṣaddik* of Leon Modena also imitates the Catholic catechism *Fior di virtù*.[83] The sermons of the rabbi Judah del Bene (1615?–78) of Ferrara display many features (the fight against skepticism and libertinism, the approval for inquisitorial censorship, the effort to integrate new scientific knowledge into traditional values) that were converging with contemporary trends of thought of the Catholic establishment.[84] The effort to diffuse and popularize scientific knowledge, the interest in the physical world without claim to achieve a metaphysical certainty, the preference for practicality and eclecticism, and the avoidance of larger theoretical questions reflect Jewish trends linked to contemporary Jesuit culture.[85]

This convergence of attitudes among Jews and Catholics is explainable if we consider the cultural changes challenging both religions in this era. The sixteenth century was a period of monumental ferment and transformation. The new discoveries in geography and science led to a new worldview and profound cultural changes. The Counter Reformation attempted to integrate the values of tradition into this new cultural milieu, with the Jesuits playing a leading role in that process. Jewish culture found itself in a similar crisis. Yet to question tradition could have disastrous effects, since the very identity of Judaism was anchored in tradition. The project of the Provenzali is an attempt to reform the educational system with the conservative aim to harmonize and unite tradition with new cultural forms and institutions. The school system developed by the Jesuits provided a pedagogical model—which, *mutatis mutandis*, could also be employed in Jewish education. Although it was never put into practice, the Provenzali project points to the continuing cultural vitality of Italian Jewry in the troubled times of the Counter Reformation. The educational reforms that were to come some three centuries later in the Ashkenazic Haskalah had their precursors in the rich and variegated culture of Italian Jewry.

Notes

1. Between 1474 and 1476, the physician Abraham Conat printed seven complete books and one incomplete volume; see G. Tamani, *Tipografia ebraica a Soncino 1483–1490* (Soncino, 1988), p. 3. On Abraham Conat, see V. Colorni, "Abraham Conat primo stampatore di opere ebraiche in Mantova e la cronologia delle sue edizioni," *La bibliofilia* 83 (1981): 113–28 = V. Colorni, *Judaica Minora* (Milan, 1983), pp. 443–60.

2. See N. Porges, "Der hebräische Index expurgatorius," in *Festschrift zum siebzigsten Geburtstage A. Berliners*, ed. A. Freimann and M. Hildesheimer (Frankfurt am Main 1903), pp. 273–95; S. Simonsohn, "Books and Libraries of the Jews of Mantua, 1595" (Hebrew), *Kiryat Sefer* 37 (1962): 103–22; and the more recent and precise study by S. Baruchson, *Books and Readers: The Reading Interests of Italian Jews at the Close of the Renaissance* (Hebrew) (Ramat Gan, 1993).

3. S. Simonsohn, *History of the Jews in the Duchy of Mantua* (Jerusalem, 1977).

4. A succinct presentation of the members of this family can be found in I. Levi, "La famiglia Provenzali," *Il Vessillo Israelitico* 52 (1904): 267–69.

5. Y. Horowitz, "Provençal Jacob Ben David," in *Encyclopaedia Judaica*, vol. 13, col. 1258.

6. See A. David, "Provençal Moses Ben Abraham (1503–1576)," in *Encyclopaedia Judaica*, vol. 13, cols. 1258–59; Simonsohn, *History of the Jews*, pp. 729–30; R. Bonfil, "Perush R. Moshe Provenzalo le-25 hakdamot ha-Rambam," *Kiryat Sefer* 50 (1975): 157–76; Bonfil, "Zuṭot leparashat hageṭ Tamari-Venturozzo," in *Shlomo Simonsohn Jubilee Volume*, ed. A. Oppenheimer (Tel Aviv, 1993), pp. 19–28; U. Piperno, "Rabbi Moshe Provenzalo tra tradizione e rinnovamento," in *Scritti sull'ebraismo in memoria di Emanuele Menachem Artom*, ed. S. J. Sierra and L. Artom (Jerusalem, 1996), pp. 244–57. The following works by Moses ben Abraham Provenzali are known: *Shirim 'al ḥuqqei leshon haqodesh* (alias *beshem qadmon*) (Venice, 1597), a description in verse of the grammar rules of the Hebrew language; *Ma'amar 'al shnei qavim* (Sabbioneta,

1550), a short geometric treatise about two parallel lines; *Pesaq haget*, responsum of R. Moses Provenzali about a divorce case tried in Prague on 1551, published with the *teshuvot* of R. Moses Isserles (§ 59) (Krakow, 1640); *Pesaq be'inyan get veqiddishin* (Mantua, 1556), a decision about the Tamari-Venturozzo divorce; *Haskamah 'al hadpasat sefer hazohar*, approval of the printing of the *Zohar* published in the edition of Mantua in 1560; *Hassagot 'al derush yemei 'olam*, critical observations about the chronology upheld by Azariah de' Rossi in *Yemei 'olam*, included in *Me'or 'einayim* (Mantua, 1574) with the rebuttal of de' Rossi. One part of the responsa of R. Moses Provenzali has been recently published by A. J. Yanni (Jerusalem, 1989). R. Moses Provenzali also edited *Beḥinat 'olam*, by Yeda'yah Penini (Mantua, 1556).

7. Simonsohn, *History of the Jews*, pp. 728–29.

8. *Me'or 'einayim*, chap. 60, pp. 480–81, according to the second edition of Cassel. De' Rossi quotes Azariah as a profound expert poet and author of the apparently lost work *Nefuṣot Yehudah*.

9. Abraham ben David Portaleone, *Shilṭei hagibborim* (Manuta, 1612), p. 185b.

10. Only some works authored by David are known. He wrote a commentary to the Song of Songs; a commentary to the Pentateuch, *'Ir David*, and a commentary to the Mishnah (*Ḥasdei avot*). His linguistic and grammar interests are documented in *Migdal David*, a Hebrew grammar, and *Dor hapelaga* (quoted by Azariah de' Rossi in *Me'or 'einayim*, chap. 57, p. 456, according to the second edition of Cassel), a work about the Hebrew origin of Italian, Greek, and Latin words. R. David Provenzali also published a defense (*Magen yedidya*) for his pupil and friend Azariah de' Rossi. This work is likewise lost. Moreover, he edited *'Aqedat Yiṣḥaq* (Venice, 1565) of Isaac Arama. On David, see Simonsohn, *History of the Jews*, p. 728; D. Tamar, "Provenençal David Ben Abraham," *Encyclopaedia Judaica*, vol. 13, cols. 1257–58.

11. Abraham Provenzali composed a handbook for the censors of the Hebrew works according to the orders of Pope Giulio III. His numerous writings, among which was a commentay on the *Kuzari*, have all been lost. The sole surviving text is his short foreword to the edition of *Reshit ḥokhma* of Elijah de Vidas (Venice, 1593). See Simonsohn, *History of the Jews*, pp. 686, 727–28; Horowitz, "Provenençal Abraham Ben David," *Encyclopaedia Judaica*, vol. 13, col. 1257.

12. I.e., after having studies with Judah ben Abraham Provenzali.

13. *Sinai ve'oker harim* ("Sinai and uprooter of mountains"), words of praise for a great scholar of the Talmud.

14. Quotation, slightly amended, from the translation by Simonsohn, *History of the Jews*, p. 584.

15. See. Ps. 19:8.

16. See Num. 27:20.

17. I.e., after having taken a degree in medicine and philosophy.

18. *Shilṭei hagibborim*, p. 185b.

19. Güdemann, in the foreword to his translation, states that the text was found in an appendix to a letter. By contrast, in the publication of the Hebrew text in the journal *Levanon*, it is stated, the text was found at the beginning of a book entitled *Sefer keschet gibborim* [*sic*] with an indication of possession. I am not familiar with a *Sefer keschet gibborim*, and I suppose this is a mistaken rendering of *Sefer shilṭei ha-*

gibborim. Two different works are so entitled: a misogynist composition by Jacob Fano (Ferrara, 1556) as an objection to the treatise *Magen nashim* of Judah Sommo Portaleone; and the encyclopedic work by Abraham ben David Portaleone (Mantua, 1612).

20. From his library, we are familiar with other books with owner notations housed in libraries in the Emilia Romagna and Mantua. See G. Busi, *Edizioni ebraiche del XVI secolo nelle biblioteche dell'Emilia Romagna* (Bologna, 1987), pp. 114–15; Busi, *Libri ebraici a Mantova: Le edizioni del XVI secolo nella biblioteca della comunità ebraica* (Fiesole, 1996), pp. 101 n. 120, 120 n. 158.

21. S. Assaf, *Meqorot letoledot haḥinnuch be-Yisrael*, 4 vols. (Tel Aviv, 1926–47), 2: 115–20; M. Güdemann, "Ein Projekt zur Gründung einer jüdischen Universität aus dem 16. Jahrhundert," in *Festschrift zum siebzigsten Geburtstage A. Berliners*, ed. A. Freimann and M. Hildesheimer (Frankfurt am Main, 1903) pp. 164–75; J. R. Marcus, *The Jews in the Medieval World* (Cincinnati, 1938; repr., (New York, 974), pp. 381–88. It is worth comparing both translations, which sometimes proved a different interpretation of the original text, not always easily understandable. A more profound examination of the educational program of David Provenzali is presented in A. M. Lesley, "Il richiamo agli 'antichi' nella cultura ebraica fra quattro e cinquecento," in *Storia d'Italia: Gli ebrei in Italia*, ed. C. Vivanti, 2 vols. (Turin, 1996), 1: 385–409, esp. pp. 394–400.

22. The quotations that follow are from the slightly amended English translation of Jacob R. Marcus.

23. Literally, *beit va'ad*, "college, academy."

24. Toward the end of 1563, the Jewish community of Mantua formed a committee, on which Judah ben Abraham Provenzali also sat, in order to send a delegation to the Council of Trent. The delegation had to decide whether the printing of Jewish books was to be left solely to the pope. If the petition had not been granted, the delegation would have proposed that the council limit discussion only about the Talmud and not all Jewish works. If that petition had also been rejected, a third solution would have been proposed, namely, that the Jews be allowed to keep their books after they had been censored. The petition was partially granted: Pope Pius IV in the *Index* compiled in 1564 allowed the printing of the Talmud with the condition that the passages considered injurious toward the Christian religion were to be expurgated and the new expurgated Talmud should then have another title. But already with Pius V, the Catholic Church had turned to a more uncompromising line toward the Jews, annulling the concessions of his predecessor and reconfirming the bulls of 1553 and 1557. For papal interventions on the Talmud, see K. R. Stow, "The Burning of the Talmud in 1553, in the Light of Sixteenth-Century Catholic Attitudes Toward the Talmud," *Bibliothèque d'Humanisme et Renaissance* 34 (1972): 435–59; and especially F. Parente, "La Chiesa e il Talmud," in *Storia d'Italia*, 1: 521–643, esp. pp. 598–612 with new documents of the secret archive of the Vatican and a large bibliography. On the petition of the Mantuan community to the Council of Trent, see also Simonsohn, *History of the Jews*, pp. 415–18.

25. The study and explanation of grammar was not usual in the Ashkenazic yeshivot. See M. Güdemann, *Geschichte des Erziehungswesens und der Cultur der*

abendländischen Juden während des Mittelalters und der neueren Zeit, 3 vols. (Vienna, 1888; repr., Amsterdam, 1966), pp. 68–69. On the teaching system of the Sephardic yeshivot, see A. Gross, "Trends in the History of the Yeshivot in Castile in the 15th Century" (Hebrew), *Pe'amim* 31 (1987): 3–20. For a survey of the establishment of the yeshivot in Europe and their relations with the universities see R. Bonfil, "Accademie rabbiniche e presenza ebraica nelle università," in *Le università dell'Europa dal Rinascimento alle riforme religiose*, ed. G. P. Brizzi and J. Verger (Milan, 1991), pp. 132–51 (= *Tra due mondi: Cultura ebraica e cultura cristiana nel Medioevo* (Naples, 1996), pp. 137–54).

26. C. Roth, *The Jews in the Renaissance* (New York, 1959), p. 41; idem, *The History of the Jews of Italy* (Philadelphia, 1946), pp. 240–41; A. Milano, *Storia degli ebrei in Italia* (Turin, 1963), pp. 622–23; R. Bonfil, *Rabbis and Jewish Communities in Renaissance Italy* (London, 1993), pp. 18–19; D. Abulafia, "Le comunità di Sicilia dagli arabi all' espulsione," in *Storia d'Italia*, 1: 70. The bill of permission was published by B. Lagumina, *Codice diplomatico dei giudei di Sicilia*, 3 vols, (Palermo, 1884–1909; repr., 1990), 2: 28–29.

27. "to establish a college for Jews."

28. R. Jacob ben Joseph Rainer (also spelled Reiner) was rabbi of the Ashkenazic yeshiva in Mantua and a supporter of Tamari in the Tamari-Venturozzo divorce. See Simonsohn, *History of the Jews*, p. 730.

29. "This can only serve to enhance the honor and beauty of our city as a result of the advantage that many Jewish and Christian scholars, both foreign and our own subjects, will be able to derive from it."

30. A. Balletti, *Gli ebrei e gli estensi* (Reggio Emilia, 1930; rep., 1997), pp. 96–97; Bonfil, *Rabbis and Jewish Communities*, p. 19. The "academy" of Ferrara is also mentioned by Azariah de' Rossi in *Me'or 'einayim* (p. 457, according to the Cassel edition, 1866). De' Rossi, against the objection of a member about the use of a Greek word as a name for the new institution, supposes a possible Hebrew origin of the word from *bet 'eked ro'im*. See J. Weinberg, "Azariah de' Rossi and the Forgeries of Annius of Viterbo," in *Essential Papers on Jewish Culture in Renaissance and Baroque Italy*, ed. D. Ruderman (New York, 1992), p. 266.

31. On the rediscovery of the importance of rhetoric in the fifteenth and sixteenth centurie, see C. Vasoli, *La dialettica e la retorica dell'umanesimo: Invenzione e metodo nella cultura del XV e del XVI secolo* (Milan, 1968); and E. Garin, *Discussioni sulla retorica, in Medioevo e Rinascimento* (Bari, 1990), pp. 117–39.

32. On these first educational experiments of the humanists, see E. Garin, *Educazione umanistica in Italia* (Bari, 1975).

33. In Mantua, Messer Leon opened and ran a school from 1473 till 1475, when, as a result of a heated conflict over halakhic questions with the Ashkenazic rabbi, Joseph Colon, Messer Leon was expelled with his rival from the town by order of the marquis Ludovico Gonzaga. See I. Rabinowitz, *The Book of the Honeycomb's Flow: Sēpher Nōpheth Ṣūphīm* (Ithaca, N.Y., 1983), pp. xxii–xxiii, xvii–xix; V. Colorni, "Note per la biografia di alcuni dotti ebrei vissuti a Mantova nel secolo XV," *Annuario di Studi Ebraici* 1 (1934): 172–74.

34. Among the works of Messer Leon are a grammar, *Livnat hasappir* (1454); a treatise about the first elements of logic, *Mikhlal yofi* (1455); a treatise of logic for advanced study, *Supercommentary to the Isagoge Categories: De Interpretatione* (probably in 1470); and the rhetoric treatise *Nofet ṣufim*, printed in Mantua by Abraham Conat 1475–76. See Rabinowitz, *The Book of the Honeycomb's Flow*, pp. xliii, xlv, xvii n. 151, 1 n. 177.

35. Cf. *Nofet ṣufim* I, 2, 11; IV, 33,4.

36. Rabinowitz, *The Book of the Honeycomb's Flow*, pp. li–lii.

37. On the importance of rhetoric in the Hebrew culture of the Italian Jews in the Renaissance, see A. Altmann, "Ars Rhetorica as Reflected in Some Jewish Figures of the Italian Renaissance," in *Jewish Thought in the Sixteenth Century*, ed. B. Cooperman (Cambridge, Mass., 1983), pp. 1–22 (= *Essential Papers*, ed. Ruderman, pp. 63–84); A. Altmann, *Von der mittelalterlichen zur modernen Aufklärung: Studien zur jüdischen Geistesgeschichte* (Tübingen, 1987), pp. 155–71. For a survey of the Jewish influence on painting through the humanists, see G. Busi, *Il succo dei favi; Studi sull 'umanesimo ebraico* (Bologna, 1992); idem, "Invenzione simbolica e tradizione ebraica nel Rinascimento italiano: Alcuni esperimenti figurativi," *Henoch* 21 (1999): 165–77.

38 Lesley, "Il richiamo" pp. 398–99.

39. See Quintilian, *Institutio oratoria* 12, 1, 1; and Messer Leon, I, 2, 10.

40. R. Bonfil, introduction to *Judah Messer Leon, Nofet Ṣufim: On Hebrew Rhetoric, Mantua ca. 1475* (Jerusalem, 1981); idem, *Gli ebrei in Italia nell' età del Rinascimento* (Florence, 1991), pp. 143–44; idem, "Il libro di Judah Messer Leon: La dimensione retorica dell'umanesimo ebraico in Italia nel XV secolo," in *Tra due mondi: Cultura ebraica e cultura cristiana nel Medioevo* (Naples, 1996), pp. 273–87, where Bonfil points out the medieval aspects of the work of Messer Leon and reduces his importance in humanism. A different opinion is expressed by Busi, "Letteratura ebraico-cristiana nei secoli XV e XVI," *Henoch* 6 (1984): 373–74; idem, *Il succo dei favi*, p. 44.

41. Bonfil, *Gli ebrei in Italia*, p. 144.

42. N. G. Siraisi, *Medieval and Early Renaissance Medicine: An Introduction to Knowledge and Practice* (Chicago, 1990), pp. 12, 81, 85.

43. Messer Leon, who was granted the privilege of conferring a degree upon other Jews by Emperor Frederick III through the bill of 21 February 1469, conferred a doctorate of liberal arts and medicine upon Alemanno on 27 February 1470. See Rabinowitz, *The Book of the Honeycomb's Flow*, pp. xxiv–xxvi. The study program of Alemanno included in his *Liqquṭim* ("Notebooks") has been published and expounded by M. Idel, "The Study Program of R. Yoḥanan Alemanno" (Hebrew), *Tarbiz* 48 (1979/80): 303–31; F. Lelli, "L'educazione ebraica nella seconda metà del 400. Poetica e scienze naturali nel Ḥay ha-'Olamim di Yoḥanan Alemanno," *Rinascimento* 36 (1996): 75–136.

44. Published by E. Ashkenazi, *Divrei chakamim* (Metz, 1849) pp. 63–75. M. Steinschneider has already supposed that it is probably a forgery (*Catalogus librorum hebraeorum in Bibliotheca Bodleiana*, 2 vols. (Berlin, 1852–60; repr., Hildesheim, 1998), 1: 1247–48).

45. Both David, the son of Messer Leon and Jacob ben David Provenzali, to whom the responsum is imputed, were members of the school founded in Naples by Messer Leon. See Rabinowitz, *The Book of the Honeycomb's Flow*, pp. xliv–xlv.

46. Askenazi, *Divrei*, p. 67.

47. R. Vitale da Pisa, *Minḥat kenaot* (Berlin, 1898), pp. 110–12. See also Bonfil, *Rabbis and Jewish Communities*, p. 287.

48. On Abraham ben Mordecai Farissol and the importance of geographic discovery in the Jewish literature of the Renaissance, see D. Ruderman, *The World of a Renaissance Jew: The Life and Thought of Abraham ben Mordecai Farissol* (Cincinnati, 1981).

49. D. Ruderman, *Kabbalah, Magic, and Science: The Cultural Universe of a Sixteenth-Century Jewish Physician* (Cambridge, Mass., 1988).

50. For a survey of the exotic and fanciful interests in the Jewish literature of the fifteenth and sixteenth centuries, see A. Toaff, *Mostri giudei: L'immaginario dal Medioevo alla prima età moderna* (Bologna, 1996).

51. Marcus, *The Jews in the Medieval World*, pp. 382–83.

52. *Ratio atque institutio studiorum Societatis Iesu* (1586, 1591, 1599), in L. Lukács, *Monumenta paedagogica Societatis Iesu* (Rome, 1986), vol. 5, § 466; and A. Demoustier, D. Julia, M. M. Compère, *Ratio studiorum: Plan raisonné et institution des études dans la Compagnie de Jésus* (Paris, 1997), p. 201.

53. See *Ratio studiorum* § 468: "Singulis saltem mensibus omnes peccata confiteantur; ac missae sacrificio quotidie constituta hora, concioni vero diebus festis decenter intersint" ("At least once a month everyone must confess and conveniently hear Mass daily at a fixed hour, whereas the sermon [has to be] heard only at the holidays").

54. Ibid., § 336: "Scholae omnes in suo se gradu contineant; et de rhetorica quidem et humanitate dicetur seorsim, grammaticae vero tres scholae esse debent, quibus eiusdem quidam quasi cursus absolvatur" ("All the classes must stay at their own level. We will come to speak separately about the course of humanities and rhetoric. There must be three classes of grammar, to be completed like a study cycle").

55. Ibid., § 249.

56. See the description by Elijah Capsali of the yeshiva of R. Judah Mintz (c. 1408–1506) in Verona. See also Bonfil, *Rabbis and Jewish Communities*, pp. 21–22.

57. *Ratio studiorum*, § 351.

58. Ibid., § 343, 349.

59. Ibid., § 354.

60. Ibid., § 356.

61. The two words are synonymous. But the *disputatio* in the *ratio studiorum* is a technical term that means the discussion pursued according to the logical method about a question asked by the teacher. The argumentation was developed in the form of logical sentences, based on deductive arguments, as was customary in keeping with scholastic philosophy.

62. *Ratio studiorum*, § 282–83.

63. Ibid., § 142–44, 233.

64. Ibid., § 233.

65. The pedagogical principles of the Maharal that I have summarized are discussed in C. K. Ingall, "Reform and Redemption: The Maharal of Prague and Jan Amos Comenius," *Religious Education* 89 (1994): 358–75; and A. F. Kleinberger, "The Didactics of Rabbi Loew of Prague," *Scripta Hierosolomitana* 13 (1963): 32–55.

66. B. R. Sherwin, *Mystical Theology and Social Dissent: The Life and Works of Judah Loew of Prague* (London, 1982), pp. 177–78. Already in the fifteenth century, the exaggerations and misuse of *pilpul* were being censured. See Güdemann, *Geschichte des Erziehungswesens*, 3: 81–82. Such a censure of the disputes of the scholastics was implemented in Italy by Giovanni Pico della Mirandola (1463–94) and later by the Spaniard Juan Luis Vives (1492–1540).

67. R. Joseph ben Issakar, a pupil of the Maharal, composed *Yosef da'at* (Prague, 1609), an illustrated edition of the Torah (14 illus,) with commentary by Rashi.

68. Kleinberger, "The Didactics," p. 39.

69. H. Stransky, "Rabbi Judah Loew of Prague and Jan Amos Comenius: Two Reformers in Education," in *Comenius*, ed. V. Busek (New York, 1972), quoted in Ingall, "Reform," p. 371.

70. Kleinberger, "The Didactics," p. 34; Ingall, "Reform," pp. 55, 371; and, especially, O. D. Kulka, "The Historical Background of the National and Educational Teaching of the Maharal of Prague" (Hebrew), *Zion* 50 (1985): 277–320.

71. The first twelve Jesuits were brought to Prague by Peter Canisius in 1556. They settled in the Church of Holy Clement, where they founded the college Clementinum, which competed with the Carolinum, the oldest college of Prague University.

72. *Ratio studiorum*, § 244, 392–93. On the theatrical activities of the Jesuits in Prague, see E. Trunz, "Pansophie und Manierismus im Kreise Rudolphs II," in *Die österreichische Literatur*, ed. H. Zeman (Graz, 1986), pp. 865–983.

73. See, for example, Marcus, *The Jews in the Medieval World*, p. 381.

74. Simonsohn, *History of the Jews*, pp. 352–54.

75. Balletti, *Gli ebrei e gli estensi*, p, 97.

76. See Simonsohn, *History of the Jews*, pp. 501–4; and Bonfil, *Rabbis and Jewish Communities*, pp. 107–8.

77. H. Graetz, *Geschichte der Juden* (Leipzig, 1890).

78. Bonfil, *Rabbis and Jewish Communities*, pp. 258–62; idem, *Gli ebrei in Italia*, p. 144.

79. Simonsohn, *History of the Jews*, pp. 636–37; R. Bonfil, "Some Reflections on the Place of Azariah de' Rossi's *Me'or Einayim* in the Cultural Milieu of Italian Renaissance Jewry," in *Jewish Thought in the Sixteenth Century*, ed. Cooperman, pp. 23–48, esp. pp. 26–29. On the Maharal and his severe censure of Azariah de' Rossi, see G. Veltri, "Science and Religious Hermeneutics: The 'Philosophy' of Rabbi Loew of Prague," in *Religious Confessions and the Sciences in the Sixteenth Century*, ed. J. Helm and A. Winkelmann (Sies in European Judaism, 1) (Leiden, 2001), pp. 119–35.

80. D. Ruderman, *Jewish Thought and Scientific Discovery in Early Modern Europe* (New Haven, Conn., 1995), pp. 256–60. Bonfil is of another opinion ("Accademie rabbiniche e presenza ebraica nelle università," p. 151). He considers the Provenzali project as a failed attempt to establish a Jewish university as a counterpart to the

Christian university. According to Bonfil, the project of the Provenzali aimed to provide students with a complete education of religious and scientific knowledge, in order to make superfluous the attendance of Jewish students at the Christian university and thus to avoid dangerous cultural contacts. The project, *qua* anachronistic, was not implemented. Bonfil regards it as driving at isolation, not at integration, which was the goal of Italian Jewry at the time. Integration was, however, the goal of the education system of Solomon Conegliano that was introductory to the university study. The two systems are accordingly not linked.

81. Ingall, "Reform," p. 370.

82. L. Zunz, "Rede zur Eröffnung des jüdischen Seminars zu Berlin am 18. November 1840," in *Gesammelte Schriften*, 3 vols. (Berlin, 1875–76; repr., Hildesheim, 1976), 2: 129–31:

> Es müssen Seminarien angelegt werden, Lehrer für die Schule, für das Haus, für die Synagoge zu erziehen. . . . Jetzt soll der Schulunterricht die sittlichen Kräfte stärken, für die verschiedensten Lebensbestimmungen die Fähigkeiten des Geistes bilden. . . . Die Dauer des gesammten Lehrcursus soll drei bis vier Jahre betragen, während welcher Zeit die für jüdische Lehrer und Schulen nöthigen Fächer von angestellten Lehren vorgetragen und eingeübt, stufenweise vorgeschritten wird, und die Seminaristen selbst Unterricht ertheilen müssen. Daher umfasst der Lehrplan: Religion, Bibel, Talmud, deutsch und hebräisch, Rechnen, Geometrie, Geographie und Geschichte, Naturlehre, Schönschreiben und Zeichnen; für spätere Semester auch Logik, Pädagogik, jüdische Geschichte, homiletische Uebungen u[nter] A[nderem]. Die geistige wie die sittlechreligiöse Ausbildung der Zöglinge ist Gegenstand gleicher Sorgfalt.

83. R. Bonfil, "Gli ebrei d'Italia e la Riforma: Una questione da riconsiderare," *Nouvelles de la République des Lettres* 2 (1996): 47–60, esp. 57–60. On Yagel's catechism, see Ruderman, *Kabbalah, Magic, and Science*, p. 18.

84. R. Bonfil, "Preaching as Meditation between Elite and Popular Cultures: The Case of Judah Del Bene," in *Preachers of the Italian Ghetto*, ed. D. Ruderman (Berkeley, 1992), pp. 67–88.

85. See Ruderman, *Preachers of the Italian Ghetto*, pp. 12–13; Ruderman, *Jewish Thought and Scientific Discovery*, pp. 193–94, 196–98.

Chapter 8

Judah Moscato's Scholarly Self-Image and the Question of Jewish Humanism

Adam Shear

In 1594, four years after the death of the Mantuan rabbi Judah Moscato, his sons brought his magnum opus, a detailed line-by-line commentary on Judah Halevi's *Kuzari*, to the press of Giovanni di Gara in Venice. In that year, di Gara issued the third printed edition of the *Kuzari* and the first one printed together with a commentary.[1] Moscato's introduction (labeled *petiḥah*) begins:

I raised my eyes and saw three men standing near me,[2] and they were the three great sages, the awe-inspiring brothers Rabbi Avigdor Cividali and Rabbi Raphael Cividali, may God preserve them, and the wonderful Rabbi Judah Saravel, may his years be long and good[3]. . . . **When I saw them, I ran from the entrance of the tent to greet them—I looked and I ran after them from the opening of the tent and I bowed to the ground.**[4] And they approached me and said, "**If we find favor in your eyes, do not go past** the knowledge **of your comrades.**[5] **Let a little water be brought; bathe your** reason[6] **and recline under the tree**[7] in order to increase insight and to amaze [us with] your philosophy. **And bring some bread to refresh our hearts**[8] because we have come under the shade of your reading of the *Sefer ha-Kuzari*. And expand for us the specifics of the work's intentions and compose a commentary for us. . . . [W]**e will return to you next year, and Judah will have a son.**"[9]

And thus I had a whiff of their intention. I trembled so greatly that I broke forth and quieted them and said, "but the darkness of reason strikes me; **Judah has stopped having the way of**[10] wise men in the understanding of the words of this sealed book. Woe is me that I have dwelt for a long time without approaching the opening of its house. . . . What is this that God is doing to me in raising your pure spirits to request great things from me and in these forms? I do not have **choice flour to knead and make cakes.**[11] Do they see **a tender and choice calf**[12] for them to feast on [from] tongues with spicy, peppery[13] mustard? If so, why me? Why do they call out to me? **Shall I in truth bear a child, as old as I am?**"[14]

Then the men arose and their faces reflected anger, and they **seized the corner of**

my robe[15] as if I had asked them **to commit a sin**[16]. . . . I put my soul in the palms of their hands to do that which was good in their eyes. And I drew closer to the task and rushed to do it and to give before them a stammering tongue in mustard. . . .

For a variety of reasons, it is not clear how seriously we should take this account as a truthful or literal account of the origins of Moscato's commentary. My analysis here is based on the view that while ornamental, Moscato's adoption of the biblical idiom of Genesis 18 should nonetheless be seen as valuable evidence for how he wished to present himself to his readers.[17] Perhaps, with appropriate caution, we can use this account to learn something about Moscato's self-image.

Although Moscato expresses the appropriate modesty and questions his qualifications for the task at hand (a common literary device in introductions), ultimately he does not shirk his duty. Moscato's clever rewriting of Genesis 18 actually signals his qualifications to the reader. In the biblical story, Abraham rises to greet the three men, representatives of God. There, it is Abraham who asks the travelers to rest and refresh themselves and Abraham who hopes that he finds favor in their eyes. Here, while Moscato does rush out to greet his guests, it is they who hope to find favor in Moscato's eyes and who ask Moscato to refresh himself. Moscato also interweaves phrases from Joseph's dream to explicitly identify the three visitors with angels.[18] Finally, Moscato takes on the role not only of Abraham but that of Sarah as well. In the central metaphor of the passage, the writing of a commentary is likened to giving birth. And, as the birth in the biblical story was a gift from God, so, too, the commentary appears to be divinely inspired or requested. The preface has the overall purpose of legitimating Moscato's role as commentator on a "sealed book." Since Moscato claims not only to explain the sealed book but also to add his own dialectical discussion, he is claiming to be not only an explicator but an author as well and therefore must show that he has authority. What better way than to invoke divine messengers?

Although Moscato means to invoke a sense of the supernatural, he also provides hints of a more down-to-earth social context. The "sealed book" is not well understood by the community; a scholar is visited and is asked to expound the work—to make it understandable to his community. The scholar hesitates, disclaiming special knowledge and noting that he has not recently studied the work ("a long time without approaching the opening of its house"). In the end, the scholar agrees to teach the supplicants. The format of the rest of Moscato's introduction resembles a medieval academic prologue—suggesting the possibility that his work originated in an educational context. At the same time, Moscato reminds us of the literary standard to which he hopes to rise—the "mustard" that he provides must have *pilpel.* This makes for a nice pun in Hebrew, as *pilpel* denotes not only "pepper" but also dialectical or casuistic argument. Moscato hints here that his commentary is not going to be a simplification of the text.

The invocation of the names of the three rabbis further suggests a "real-life" context. Avigdor Cividali (d. 1601) was a rabbi in Venice and succeeded his teacher Samuel Katzenellenbogen as chief rabbi there in 1597.[19] His younger brother Raphael, the chief rabbi of Mantua from 1573, was a colleague of Moscato's.[20] Judah Saravel (d. 1617) was also a rabbi in Venice, the son of a prominent family there, and an older colleague of Leon Modena.[21] Although all three of these men were well known to their contemporaries as legal authorities, none distinguished himself in the field of religious philosophy.

There appears to have been a felt need for such explication in written form, rather than oral, in late sixteenth-century Italy. Although two editions of the *Kuzari* had already been printed before Moscato began writing his commentary, there were no printed commentaries to the work and only a limited circulation for the few commentaries in manuscript. Indeed, in a 1558 letter from Isaac de Lattes to his son-in-law Abraham de Sant'Angelo in Mantua, Lattes mentions that his cousin Solomon Norzi, a resident of that city, owns "a precious book, an excellent commentary on the *Kuzari* called *Ḥesheq Shlomo*."[22] Lattes advises Abraham "to check whether the commentary is good, [as] perhaps it will be worthwhile to print it. For the book of the *Kuzari* is all true and it is founded on the Torah of Moses to chastise the wicked who raise objections to [the Torah]. [It is] a crucible of the gold of belief and the silver of understanding; it is constructed according to the true tradition; all of it is pleasant, and it achieves refined language and depth of thought, and many profit from it especially—with a good commentary.[23]

In the end, *Ḥesheq Shlomo* was not printed, because Abraham did not take his father-in-law's advice, because he did not judge his advice worthy, or for some other reason. But we can assume that Moscato's commentary filled a felt need among the Italian Jewish elite for "a good commentary" on this work. It is entirely plausible that Moscato might have been responding to the entreaties of other scholars to compose his work.

An examination, however, of the four extant manuscripts of Moscato's *Kol Yehudah* reveals an interesting problem. In these manuscripts, the three visitors are not named.[24] The addition of the names of the Cividali brothers and Judah Saravel seems to have been carried out in di Gara's printing shop in 1594. Jacob Heilbronn, a student of Avigdor, was then employed by di Gara as an editor.[25] Raphael's son, Joshua, was the editor of the edition of the *Shulḥan arukh* also published by di Gara in 1594.[26] And the editor of *Kol Yehudah*, Solomon Shemaiah Sforno, another Venetian rabbi, was a close associate of Avigdor Cividali.[27] It is tempting to imagine one of these men—the disciple or the son or the colleague—inserting the names into the text. In all likelihood, these three rabbis were approached to offer their approbation or their patronage for the work. Rather than acknowledge them directly, their names were added to Moscato's preexisting introduction. However, in the absence of more information on the workings of di Gara's shop, on the handling of the manuscript by Moscato's sons, or on Sforno's role as editor, we cannot solve the mystery of the added names.

In any case, the absence of the names of these rabbis in Moscato's original text would not have been known to most readers of the printed book. The addition of these prominent names lent an air of authenticity to Moscato's account. Rather than a fantasy of divine inspiration (Moscato engaging in a kind of self-fashioning), the preface is turned into an account of a project commissioned by prominent leaders of the Venice and Mantua communities.[28] In the printed book, Moscato's "divine" authority is linked to Italian Jewish communal leadership—a more human version of authority—as well. Regardless of whether Moscato was indeed solicited to write the commentary by the Cividali brothers and Saravel, the image of such a solicitation would have been communicated to readers and potential readers of the book. Would such an image have made sense to this audience? The request to Moscato, a preacher, might have appeared as an appeal to a specialist in Jewish thought to explain a difficult non-halakhic text from three rabbis whose own "specialty" appears to have been halakhic rather than meta-halakhic concerns.[29]

Who was this specialist? Born in Osimo in the Papal States circa 1535, Moscato served as a rabbi in Mantua from 1569 until his death in 1590.[30] He achieved fame in his lifetime as a preacher known for his use of classical models of oratory and his development of the format that would become standard in the early modern Jewish sermon.[31] Moscato was well known to his contemporaries and to later generations of Italian Jewish scholars as part of a circle of erudite rabbis in late sixteenth-century Mantua and the vicinity, a circle that included Azariah de' Rossi, the Provenzali brothers, Abraham

Portaleone, and the young David del Bene. When Moscato died, he was the subject of extensive public mourning and a number of eulogies by leading scholars. The most famous of these eulogies was given by Samuel Judah Katzenellenbogen in Padua, included in his *Sheneim 'asar derashot* (Twelve sermons), also published by Giovanni di Gara in 1594.[32]

Other than his commentary on the *Kuzari*, Moscato's other major published work was a collection of fifty-two sermons, titled *Nefuṣot Yehudah*, also published by di Gara, in 1589. In addition, Moscato wrote a number of poems (some recently published); some prayers (one of which was published in his lifetime); a no longer extant commentary on the Song of Songs; and a few responsa, one discussing the calendar (in response to Azariah de' Rossi), and one dealing with laws of kosher slaughtering.[33] We also have evidence of his involvement in communal matters: he signed a petition in favor of Moses Provenzali's position in the famous Tamari-Venturozzi divorce case;[34] he was a member of the committee of Mantuan scholars who attempted to publish an edition of the Talmud in the late 1580s, and he apparently served as an arbitrator in a bankruptcy case in the 1570s.[35] He also seems to have played a small but important role in the debate over the publication of Azariah de' Rossi's *Me'or 'einayim*. Along with Moses Provenzali, Moscato was called on by rabbis in Ferrara and Cremona to pass judgment on the book. Moscato wrote a responsum agreeing with Provenzali's criticism of Azariah's discussion of the Jewish calendar but, like most Mantuan rabbis, did not sign the ban on the book and remained on friendly terms with Azariah.[36] His major activity as a rabbi and a scholar, then (and this portrait may change if new material is discovered, of course), seems to have been in the homiletical and philosophical/theological spheres; his halakhic output and communal involvement appear to have been minimal. When called on by the community and by other rabbis for his involvement, it was most often in the case of matters that went beyond knowledge of everyday halakhic discourse.

Moscato was not a native of Mantua, arriving there as a refugee from the Papal States in 1569, and finding refuge in the home of his brother-in-law, a banker named Samuel Minzi-Berettaro, as he tells us in the dedication to *Nefuṣot Yehudah*.[37] Although Simonsohn tells us that "Moscato was appointed rabbi in Mantua in 1587," I have not been able to determine precisely what he means by this, since the first official appointment document from Mantua dates from only 1633, according to Simonsohn's own research.[38] Moscato gave sermons in the Italian synagogue of Mantua and certainly had a very public profile there; but he should not be considered a "communal" rabbi in the usual sense of the term. Rather, Moscato should be seen as a particular type of Jewish scholar of Renaissance Italy, who existed within the rabbinic institutional framework, but who served as a kind of specialist in Jewish thought, or, in the term used by Isadore Twersky, a specialist in "meta-halakhic" rather than "halakhic" studies.[39]

Although the study of Talmud and Jewish law always represented the mainstream of Jewish scholarly activity in the premodern period, various contemporary typologies of Jewish intellectuals pointed out the existence of those who—while trained in rabbinic texts—sought their spiritual path elsewhere, most frequently, in the study of kabbalah or philosophy.[40] As Twersky pointed out, the sixteenth century saw an increasing number of statements, especially among kabbalists, that meta-halakhic pursuits were superior to halakhic pursuits in the attainment of human perfection (known by Hebrew adaptations of the Aristotelian terminology as *shlemut*, "completion," or *haṣlaḥa*, "success").[41] Moscato never makes such a claim. Indeed, his adherence to the teachings of the *Kuzari* would have made such a claim anathema. Moscato often stresses the importance of action rather than pure speculation in the attainment of perfection and, in fact, declares this to be the central thesis of the work.[42] Moscato would never have denied the importance of halakhic learning for understanding what the proper actions were. Nonetheless, Moscato's public career did not consist of teaching or ruling on the intricacies of halakhic practice. And his sermons are dominated by concerns of the meta-halakhic realm. In his eulogy for Moscato, Katzenellenbogen (who was a communal rabbi) appears to have criticized this emphasis on speculative rather than halakhic matters.[43] But the criticism was mild, and Moscato's honored position at his death suggests that his role as meta-halakhic specialist was accepted by his contemporaries. In what follows, by examining Moscato's *Kol Yehudah* in some detail, I would like to take up the question of whether this special role can be usefully called that of a "Jewish humanist."[44]

Moscato's commentary was not published until 1594, but there is considerable evidence that the work was in wide circulation earlier. In his sermons, published in 1589, Moscato often cites his commentary by the name *Kol Yehudah*, suggesting that his audience would have been familiar with a written work by that title.[45] That the four extant manuscripts do not contain the names of the three rabbis mentioned in the printed edition, as discussed above, suggests that these manuscripts circulated prior to the print publication of the work. In addition, the fact that Moscato prepared a shorter, more concise version of his commentary (which he titled *Bat kol Yehudah*, "daughter of the *Kol Yehudah*") suggests perhaps that he was responding to his lay audience's inability or unwillingness to avail themselves of the longer work.[46]

The rest of Moscato's preface offers a good description of the work itself and of his own project. He offers a thesis statement of sorts for the work: "Around this point it revolves: to understand and to teach that there is no approaching God except by God's commandments themselves."[47] Moscato then describes each of the five sections of the *Kuzari* in detail. Then he addresses the reader, saying that he will soon turn to his commentary, "after introducing these seven notes, which are appropriate to provide for you."[48] The seven notes consist of (1) description of and praise for the author, Halevi; (2) discussion of the identity of the *Ḥaver* (the Jewish representative in the book's dialogue); (3) description and praise for the book; (4) discussion of the date of the book; (5) discussion of whether the frame story is true; (6) discussion of the two Hebrew translations of the work; and (7) discussion of his choice of title for his commentary.

Another translation for *petiḥah* ("opening") could be "access," and in many ways Moscato's introduction fulfills the functions of a medieval *accessus ad auctores*, the introductory lecture to a course on a classical author in arts faculties. When such lectures were published, the introductory lecture became the introduction to the book.[49] The arrangement of the material in the introduction suggests just such a context of teaching.

Various schema existed for the organization of these academic prefaces, but they generally included such elements as the life of the author, the title of the work, the purpose of the author in writing the work, a description of the sources of the work, the "utility" of the work, the organization of the work, and the place of the work in the curriculum of study.[50] Although Moscato does not include all these elements (and adds some elements of his own), his introduction seems generally to conform to the specifications of such prefaces. One of the most important elements, introduced into Christian scholasticism and Jewish scholarship in the thirteenth century, was the use of Aristotle's four causes to describe the book.[51] At the end of his introduction, Moscato introduces this terminology:

And Judah has a third reason for calling the book according to this name [*Kol Yehudah*] which takes four causes: its material, its form, its activity, and its end [material, formal, active, and final causes]. For the material is the voice of Judah Halevi in telling of the events as they occurred. Its form is the voice of the Jew, master of the disputation in strength and in splendor, breaking the cedars of Lebanon in his winning answers. And its activity is a bright spark, the voice of Judah, every man from his [own] work on that which passes before him. For their faces and their corners are to their fours as was said.[52] And its end is the voice of Judah and of Israel in general to acknowledge the name of God in the completeness of His Torah that was given completely in the hearing of the people.[53]

Moscato was not necessarily influenced by Christian scholarly practices in the writing of his academic prologue; most likely, he drew on available Hebrew texts that made use of or discussed these elements.[54]

Thus, much of Moscato's preface harks back to academic practices of the High Middle Ages—both Jewish and non-Jewish. There is nothing "Renaissance" per se about this form. However, Moscato introduces a number of elements into his preface that may be seen as more typical of Renaissance humanist practice. For example, a discussion dating the work does not seem to have been a common element in the medieval *accessus*. Likewise, Moscato devotes a fairly extensive discussion to the question of the historicity of the frame story, sifting various textual authorities to assess claims made by Halevi at the beginning of the work. Ultimately, Moscato concludes that the dialogue most likely did take place, but his concern with evidence suggests a critical approach to sources, even to *auctores*. Perhaps most significant, Moscato signals his concern with the reliability of the text before him:

And this printing follows that of Meir Parenzo, may his memory be a blessing in Venice, [published] in the year [5]308 [1547–48]. . . . And faith in my pen allows me to deviate from this text according to [other] texts that happened to come before me. But a few corrections are made from assessment and thought, and in each case, I will acknowledge the correction. . . . I will come to you to teach the text as it seems to me, and the rest are . . . taken from another text. And there are cases that are a matter of the language of the printing being a bit confused, and it is possible to maintain [such a reading] under duress. Or readings such that the meaning is unclear and the reading in another text is improved and simpler than the first. Then you will hear both of them together.[55]

Moscato's concern with close textual study, his use of different manuscripts, and his listing of variant readings were not unprecedented within Jewish scholarship.[56] Such concerns were also, however, hallmarks of humanist practice in Italy.[57] It is important to note that Moscato does not claim to produce a critical edition in the modern sense but offers corrected or improved readings. This was in keeping with humanist practice in regard to classical texts in the sixteenth century.[58] However, in cases where he thought that more than one reading would be useful in making a point or offering interpretation of the work, Moscato does not hesitate to include both readings in his text. Moscato's "Jewish" notions of the multifaceted nature of texts intersect with his "humanist" interests in textual comparison.

Moscato's sources in his introduction are all Jewish, and much of its content, especially in describing the *Kuzari*, displays none of his wide erudition in classical sources. Already in the introduction, however, the careful reader can discern that Moscato is not solely informed by medieval Jewish tradition. In the body of Moscato's commentary, this will become quite apparent.

One important marker of Moscato's orientation toward Renaissance humanist culture is his intense interest in rhetoric.[59] Moscato's commentary offers us an excellent case study of how an interest in rhetoric on the part of a Jew in sixteenth-century Italy was put into practice.[60] An important part of Moscato's commentary is his ongoing analysis of the rhetoric of the rabbi and the king. Moscato often assumes the role of a teacher of rhetoric, using the *Kuzari* as a casebook—the dialogue between two learned interlocutors becomes a model of good rhetorical form. In one case, he suggests a rephrasing of a speech by the rabbi to make the point better.[61] Likewise, he notes the king's attempt to shift the mood within the dialogue.[62] Elsewhere, Moscato praises a passage that demonstrates good organization in writing.[63] He then notes that this passage follows the practice of "many of the great authors who related their manner of speaking to the nature of the thing being spoken about."[64] Here, Moscato adheres to a long tradition in Western rhetoric that begins with Cicero—emphasizing both the arrangement of arguments (*dispositio*) and the use of appropriate language (*elocutio*).[65]

Moscato's use of classical rhetoric can also be seen in his explanation of the rabbi's statement that oral communication is superior to writing in achieving the goal of "transmit[ting] the idea of the speaker into the soul of the listener."[66] Halevi argues that speech provides more opportunities for communication than writing through devices such as tone of voice, facial expressions, and so on. Moscato cites a number of sources for Halevi's statement about facial gestures, *remizot* and *keriṣot* in Hebrew:

> [The action of] *remizot* is in the eyes—in the language of the Bible, as in the statement of Eliphaz, "and why do thine eyes wink" (Job 15:12), that is like winking as opposed to letters.[67] And [the action of] *keriṣot* is in the eyes and the lips, as in the statement "that winketh with his eyes" (Prov. 6:13) or "He that biteth his lips" (Prov. 16:30). And Quintilian has already written in the *Book of Rhetoric*, article 11, of the greatness of the beauty of eloquent statements [which are formed] by the joining of

> the pleasantness of their words with active signals of winking, voices, fixing of the face, and movement of all the limbs of the body; [and this is done] in the appropriate measure for each word according to change in its nature. [And] even according to Marco Tullio [Cicero], who would impose upon reading this section [about] the hints of the rhetoric of the body.[68]

Moscato goes on to cite a talmudic discussion and to find the types of rhetoric outlined by Cicero there.[69] For Alexander Altmann, Moscato's application of rhetorical principles to a rabbinic source (not just a biblical source) is a crucial example of "the strong impression that classical rhetoric made upon Moscato's mind."[70] Indeed, Moscato later quoted his discussion here in one of his sermons, suggesting the importance of rhetoric to his pedagogical agenda.[71]

Moscato's source for this discussion may not have been Quintilian and Cicero directly but rather a parallel discussion in Judah Messer Leon's Hebrew rhetorical textbook, *The Book of the Honeycomb's Flow*, published in 1475.[72] In this work, the Bible is analyzed according to classical rhetoric with two aims in mind. First, Messer Leon wanted to demonstrate the superiority of the Bible to all other works by showing its perfect rhetoric; second, he wanted to show that all wisdom (including the principles of good speech and writing) can be found within it. On the subject of physical expression, Messer Leon and Moscato both refer to the same section of Quintilian.[73]

In Moscato and Messer Leon, Cicero and Quintilian are brought to bear on Jewish texts, but significantly, Jewish texts are also brought into the discussion and are made to teach rhetoric. Furthermore, the Hebrew text being commented on is held up as the exemplar of good rhetoric. In Messer Leon's case, this text is the word of God. As Altmann points out, Moscato extends the application of rhetorical principles from Bible to Talmud. But Moscato's larger innovation may have been his extension of applying rhetorical analysis to his primary text, the *Kuzari*, a work that is not a divine work, like the Bible, or a work with legal authority, like the Talmud. The Bible and the Talmud are, by definition, texts to be learned from. The work of a human author such as Halevi is not, by definition, an exemplary text. That Moscato wants his reader to learn from it suggests an attempt to give the work the status of a classic—a text to be learned from, a text with authority.[74]

In the case of Messer Leon and Moscato, the crucial assumption is the primacy of the Hebrew language.[75] This is a view, of course, that both derive from many medieval authors, Halevi first among them. According to Arthur

Lesley, Halevi's Hebraism was a major reason for the appeal of the *Kuzari* to Renaissance Jewish humanists.[76] Halevi's Hebraism asserted an original perfection of the Hebrew language while also acknowledging defects in the language.

Halevi begins his discussion with a bold claim by the *Ḥaver*: "To Hebrew, however, belongs the first place, both as regards the nature of the languages, and as to fullness of meanings" (2:66). Following this assertion, the king challenges the *Ḥaver* by noting that other languages "are more finished and comprehensive" (2:67). The *Ḥaver* responds with a lengthy explanation of the original perfection of Hebrew, its debasement over time as its speakers lost power, and the closeness of Hebrew, Aramaic, and Arabic. Especially crucial for Halevi is that the Hebrew Bible "always finds the most suitable word" (2:68).

Moscato wholeheartedly agrees with Halevi's view of Hebrew and, in fact, adds examples to make Halevi's case even stronger. He notes that not only was Hebrew the language in which God spoke to Adam and Eve (which Halevi mentions); the whole Torah was given in Hebrew, and even more important, the world was created using the Hebrew language.[77] This last point is, of course, an important one in Jewish mystical traditions that stress the power of the Hebrew language.[78] And, prompted by Halevi's discussion of the mystical work *Sefer ha-Yeṣirah* in book 4 of the *Kuzari*, Moscato returns at great length to the correspondences between Hebrew letters and words and the *sefirot*, the various aspects of the godhead.[79] Moscato also comments extensively on Halevi's account of Hebrew prosody at the end of book 2, providing many examples illustrating Halevi's discussion.[80]

Moscato's wide-ranging knowledge of both Jewish and non-Jewish sources and of such fields as music, rhetoric, natural philosophy, rabbinics, and kabbalah is on display throughout his extremely detailed work. In addition to biblical and talmudic sources, Moscato cites the biblical commentaries of Rashi, Naḥmanides, Ibn Ezra, Isaac Arama, David Kimḥi, Sforno, and Gersonides; philosophical works by Maimonides, Saadiah Gaon, Baḥya, Gersonides, Albo, Crescas, Narboni, Shem Tov ibn Shem Tov, Abraham Shalom, Samuel ibn Tibbon, Profiat Duran, Abraham Bibago, and Abravanel; a number of talmudic commentaries and halakhic works; Hebrew historical and scientific works by Josippon, Abraham bar Ḥiyya, Abraham ibn Daud, Isaac Israeli, and Ibn Ezra; mystical works including the *Zohar*, *Ma'arekhet ha-Elohut*, *heikhalot* literature, and *Sefer ha-Yeṣirah*; numerous works by

Greek and Latin authors—Plato, Aristotle, Philo, Galen, Hippocrates, Josephus, Ptolemy, Cicero, Quintilian, and Boethius; Arab philosophers Avicenna and Averroës; and Renaissance figures such as Pico and Ficino.[81]

In addition to their broad range, there is another important aspect to Moscato's use of sources—his verbosity. Halevi's description of the Hebrew language and Hebrew prosody discussed above—sections 78–81 of dialogue 2—consists of approximately twelve hundred words. Moscato's comments on this section consist of approximately nineteen thousand words—nearly sixteen times the length of the object of his study.[82] One could cite numerous other examples throughout the work. While Halevi's work contains fairly detailed descriptions of a number of topics, Moscato seeks to add on additional layers of information, primarily through additional examples and, most prominently, extensive quotation from other authorities.

Moscato, of course, does not see his extensive quotation as verbose or unnecessary—such exhaustiveness is necessary to fulfill his obligations as explicator. Indeed, he even informs us, as he cuts one quotation short, that he does so because the rest is irrelevant to the matter at hand.[83] Moscato is not showing off—rather, he is doing what he sees as expected of him. Here is Anthony Grafton's description of the humanist genre of line-by-line commentary:

> Line-by-line commentaries inevitably bulk as large or larger than the texts they treat. The commentator, in other words, was expected to fill a large amount of space. His audience expected him to turn any suitable word or phrase into an occasion for an extended digression into the etymology of a word, into the formation of compounds from it, into its shades of meaning; most often, perhaps into the justification in terms of formal rhetoric for its appearance in the passage in question. Many digressions departed even farther from the text, into mythological, geographical, antiquarian, and even scientific matters. A commentary on almost any ancient author could thus become an introduction to classical literature, history, and culture. In short, the commentary was a highly flexible instrument of instruction.[84]

Grafton could easily have been writing a description of Moscato's commentary here.[85] Moscato himself described his work in a similar (although more biblicized) manner, noting that his commentary "opens its mouth wide and lengthens its tongue in its matters and the voice expands in each detail in full."[86] Moscato writes these words in the introduction to his *Bat kol Yehudah* (Daughter of the voice of Judah), a shortened version of his commentary, which was not published. When it came time for Moscato's sons to bring his manuscripts to the printer following his death, the longer version was seen as the more worthwhile, presumably from both an intellectual and a financial viewpoint.

Moscato's project may be seen as something of an "encyclopedization" of the text before him.[87] The *Kuzari* deals with a wide array of subjects—ritual law, history and chronology, the nature of God, the transmission of the biblical text, the Hebrew language, astronomy, astrology, magic, the calendar, providence, free will, angels, the human soul, the Land of Israel, geography, and so on. Yet the *Kuzari* cannot be considered an encyclopedia in the usual medieval sense of the word. It is not arranged according to the Aristotelian classification of knowledge by which most medieval encyclopedias were organized. Halevi's presentation is unsystematic—the topics are raised in the course of conversation without an immediately apparent organizational scheme. Likewise, the purpose of the work is not the presentation for its own sake.[88] While Halevi's work does deal with a staggering number of topics, no claim is made for comprehensiveness—perhaps the most salient criteria in judging whether a work is meant as an encyclopedia.

Moscato does not claim that the *Kuzari* was meant by Halevi to be an encyclopedia. As we saw above, Moscato is quite clear about what Halevi's thesis is. Almost by definition, a work with a thesis cannot be considered an encyclopedia regardless of how much useful information is imparted to the reader. On the other hand, Halevi's discussion of so many topics gives Moscato—through exhaustive examination of the opinions of other authorities—the opportunity to present the reader with what may be considered the equivalent of encyclopedia entries on various subjects.[89] As Abraham Melamed has pointed out, the line between imparting general knowledge and advocating a specific outlook is often difficult to draw in the work of other Jewish intellectuals of Moscato's period.[90] In connection with Sebastian Münster's *Cosmography*, Gerald Strauss has suggested a number of salient features of the early modern encyclopedia.[91] First, its arrangement was not necessarily alphabetical, which "encouraged consecutive reading."[92] Obviously, Moscato in his commentary intended that the *Kuzari* be read consecutively. At the same time, however, Strauss points out the importance of the index as a reference tool in Münster's work, noting that indexes to the work grew more extensive with successive editions.[93] In Moscato's introductions to the various sections and in constant cross-references to other sections of the *Kuzari*, he attempts to impose order in a manner that allowed the work to be read in a nonconsecutive manner as well. A generation after Moscato, Leon

Modena compiled a topical index to the *Kuzari*, and a generation after that another scholar composed an index to Moscato's commentary.[94] Moscato did not go this far, but his commentary can be seen, at least in part, as an attempt to create something like an apparatus enabling the reader to use the *Kuzari* as a reference work.

The ideal of "universal knowledge" in the Renaissance was not merely a concern for making information readily available to the reader. The Renaissance encyclopedia was often intended to be, in the words of A. H. T. Levi, "an esoteric guide to hermetic truth."[95] The most extreme reading of the Renaissance ideal of the encyclopedia was given by Foucault, who famously posited that the search for universal knowledge and for correspondences between seemingly disparate elements of the universe constituted a "Renaissance episteme" governing all intellectual activity in the period.[96] As one critic of Foucault's has pointed out, his notion that *divinito* equals *eruditio* in the Renaissance—that all intellectual activity is engaged in a search for hermetic truths about the universe—is based on an overrepresentation of statements by people explicitly identified as magicians (and not the full range of intellectuals).[97] Likewise, Ian McLean has recently pointed out that Foucault draws mostly on Neoplatonic texts, to the exclusion of the still-dominant Aristotelian discourse in which resemblances or correspondences were seen within the context of specific fields and not as having meaning across different disciplines.[98] These are trenchant criticisms of Foucault, and I do not mean to suggest that Moscato's attempt to "encyclopedize" the *Kuzari* is an example of his falling lockstep into an "episteme."

Neoplatonism was an important influence on Moscato's thinking—as it was on Halevi's thinking—and Moscato often points out correspondences and "resemblances" in his commentary. In 2:26, Halevi makes an elaborate analogy between the functioning of the human body and the sacrificial system in the Temple. Moscato begins his comments with a long introduction to the concept of man as microcosm as an underpinning for Hippocratic science.[99] Such a view of man as microcosm can also be found in other sixteenth-century Jewish encyclopedists.[100]

As we saw above, Moscato's discussion of the Hebrew language displays a deep concern with the interconnectedness of language with both the natural and supernatural worlds—*divinitio* and *eruditio*, in Foucault's terms.[101]

In his work on Abraham Yagel, David Ruderman has noted a similar inclination toward this Renaissance ideal.[102] Yagel was a contemporary of Moscato's, and they moved in the same circles. Ruderman argues that Foucault "captures succinctly and coherently some of the basic epistemological assumptions of Yagel and several of his contemporaries."[103] In the case of Moscato, as well, Foucault's paradigm does seem applicable: Moscato certainly should be included in this group of Jewish "encyclopedists" of the sixteenth century.

But Moscato's encyclopedic quest for "universal knowledge" or, more precisely, for the knowledge of the universe as God's divine order, does not lose sight of another, more particularistic ideal. Moscato sees Halevi's analogy in 2:26 as presenting man as a microcosm of the overall order of the universe. After presenting a chart of correspondences that summarizes the elements of Halevi's analogy, Moscato explains that there is a correspondence between attaining knowledge and understanding God's ordered creation via reason and the attainment of human perfection via the *'inyan ha-elohi*, or divine influence.[104] He reminds the reader that the divine influence adheres in the "nation" by way of the "opportunities" presented by God.[105] Ultimately, Moscato seems to be aiming at a synthesis of an encyclopedic ideal in which the harmony of the universe can be appreciated by any human and a more particularist ideal in which God created a harmonic order with a specific people in mind.

The desire for synthesis of every sort is also evident in Moscato's use of other Jewish thinkers to elucidate Halevi. Moscato most frequently quotes similar opinions to those expressed by the *Ḥaver* or the king, thus bolstering the point made. Moscato often cites authorities, however, whose views disagree or appear to disagree with Halevi. The best example of this is Moscato's use of Maimonides. Aside from references to other sections of the *Kuzari*, Moscato's most frequently cited postbiblical, post-talmudic source is Maimonides' *Guide for the Perplexed*.[106] Often, Moscato cites a view of Maimonides that agrees with the view expressed in the *Kuzari* or states a "fact" that illustrates Halevi's point.[107] This may seem surprising to contemporary scholars of medieval Jewish thought who, under the influence of Harry Wolfson, often present Maimonides and Halevi as opposites in both style and intention.[108]

In a number of places, Moscato points out differences between Halevi's view and Maimonides' view.[109] In his introduction, Moscato appears to suggest a hermeneutical principle when faced with such cases. He quotes an obscure work, *Pirke ha-Rav Barkhiel*, that "the words of Maimonides are closer to truth than to lies, the words of Gersonides are closer to lies than to truth, and the words of R. Judah Halevi are all truth."[110] While Moscato generally favors the opinions of Halevi over those of Maimonides and Gersonides when forced to choose, he often attempts to reconcile seemingly disparate views. Moscato often cites an apparently conflicting view in the *Guide* that he then reinterprets to bring it in line with the *Kuzari* or to minimize the conflict between them.[111]

The use of Maimonides' *Guide* in explaining the classical mystical text *Sefer ha-Yeṣirah* might seem strange, but was not in the least problematic for Moscato.[112] Elsewhere Moscato attempts to bring together kabbalah and philosophy more generally.[113] Likewise, Moscato's assessment of Gersonides' work is not as negative as would appear from his approving quotation of Rav Barkhiel. Although Moscato disagrees with Gersonides on specific issues, such as the question of God's knowledge of specifics,[114] elsewhere Moscato relates to Gersonides more positively. In a discussion of various types of sciences, he relies on Gersonides for a definition of "heuristic science."[115] He also cites Gersonides to support Halevi's view of the human soul.[116] Moscato's major hermeneutical assumption appears to be the basic agreement of the major works of medieval Jewish thought.

Various historiographical views of Moscato have seen him as a second-rate medieval thinker with a touch of the Renaissance here and there; a sort of Italian Halevi, broadly learned but ultimately a Jewish chauvinist; or as someone for whom Renaissance culture has had an overwhelming influence, distorting his understanding of Judaism and confirming Robert Bonfil's view of the weakness of Jewish culture at the end of the sixteenth century. For Herbert Davidson, Moscato was a medieval thinker—and not a very deep one, either: "[H]is handling of [medieval philosophic sources] is more superficial and more eclectic [than that of Leone Ebreo]."[117] Although he credits Moscato with the reintroduction of Plato (as opposed to Neoplatonism) into Jewish philosophy, Davidson does not assign much originality to Moscato: "Moscato's picture of the universe would, in fine, seem to consist of a loose harmonization of three cosmologies, with most, though not all, of the elements being available from medieval Jewish philosophy."[118] Davidson notes Moscato's use of both ancient and Renaissance sources,[119] but for him Moscato is part of a larger trend in fifteenth- and sixteenth-century Jewish philosophy—a continuation of medieval views and a corresponding lack of originality.[120]

For Isaac Barzilay, Moscato exemplifies "the unique character anti-rationalism assumed in Italy."[121] That is, Moscato was able to see value in secular learning and to gain a high degree of knowledge in secular learning. Yet

Moscato was an anti-rationalist for the same reason as Halevi: Jewish revelation represents the ultimate truth while every other source of knowledge comes up short. Joseph Dan's view, somewhat echoing that of Barzilay, is that Moscato was outwardly influenced by Renaissance humanism, especially its emphasis on classical rhetoric, but at the same time should be seen as a Jewish particularist in most respects.[122] For Dan, as for Barzilay, the crucial axis is not medieval versus nonmedieval but Jewish versus non-Jewish.

In his study of Moscato, Moshe Idel places his view of Moscato in opposition to these views.[123] Idel's view, in contrast, is quite simply that Moscato "was deeply affected by Renaissance thought and it left a noticeable imprint on the essential character of his thought."[124] In this view, his thought was neither medieval nor particularly "Jewish," in Dan's terms.

In many respects, all four of these scholars are correct. Moscato was deeply influenced by his reading of Renaissance and classical (non-Jewish) sources, but at the same time most of his categories of thought derived from rabbinic and medieval (Jewish) sources. Moscato's commentary on the *Kuzari* displays all these trends: medievalism, humanism, Jewish particularism, and Renaissance universalism. For Moscato, these categories were not mutually exclusive. Moscato was a Jewish chauvinist, but his version of chauvinism allowed him to engage with secular culture, since he strongly believed that all that was worthwhile in secular culture ultimately derived from Jewish culture. In defending his use of non-Jewish sources, Moscato tells his listeners to "not be surprised from my frequent drawing of water from the wells of foreigners, for in my hands, they come from our wells."[125] He then cites a number of Jewish authorities on the theft of philosophy and sciences from the Jews, reaffirming a Jewish version of the *prisca sapientia.*

Significantly, Moscato does not reach into a distant past to uncover a classic worthy of reverence and commentary. Rather, he turns to a twelfth-century work that is well known (if not well understood) by contemporary Jews. In many ways, Renaissance Jewish culture in general and Moscato's work in particular display clear continuities with the Jewish cultures of medieval Italy and Spain. However, Moscato's judgment that a text from this (relatively) recent past requires commentary suggests a sense of discontinuity. Moscato's choice of a medieval rather than a biblical or rabbinic text suggests an expanded notion of what constitutes a classic, that is, of what is eligible for commentary, in the Jewish Renaissance. Not only does Moscato make clear that a work such as the *Kuzari* is of high status because it is commented upon, but the printing of Moscato's work leading to its wide dissemination ensured that the *Kuzari* would, in fact, achieve the status of a classic. It is worth exploring the hypothesis that the canon of classics of Jewish thought became fixed precisely as a result of commentaries such as Moscato's and especially by those commentaries being printed.

Moscato's commentary, then, is of particular significance within the history of the reception of the *Kuzari* specifically and the reception of medieval Jewish philosophy more generally. At the same time, Moscato's deep engagement with Renaissance culture, both in its humanist and its Platonic/Hermetic manifestations, produces what is in many ways a new work. This "Renaissance *Kuzari*" has the same basic aims as Halevi's *Kuzari* and makes much the same argument, but it also takes on additional functions (such as teaching rhetoric or pointing toward universal knowledge) that reflect Moscato's interests and conceptions.

Idel reads Moscato's remarks regarding his use of "foreign" sources as indicating a defensive or apologetic posture. Of course, Moscato would have had reason to justify his use of non-Jewish sources, and his doing so places him in a long line of others who crafted a similar defense. Such a defensiveness might have been needed: a decade after the publication of *Nefuṣot Yehudah*, Moscato's student David del Bene was severely criticized for his use of Greek and Roman mythology in his sermons.[126] David's son Judah later credited (or discredited, depending on one's perspective) Moscato with having provided the teaching in secular sources that ultimately led his father astray.[127]

Ultimately, however, where Katzenellenbogen and others may have found reason to criticize Moscato for neglecting halakhah for philosophical or other such pursuits, Moscato turns his "specialization" into a strength—it is a result of his knowledge in the non-halakhic sphere that Moscato is able to explicate the "sealed book" to a community that needs to hear its message. It is possible that the addition of the names of the three rabbis at the print shop was meant to blunt criticism of Moscato by invoking a kind of sanction for his non-halakhic pursuits by communal authorities. In Moscato's original version, however, there does not seem to be any defensiveness.

Moscato's choice of the *Kuzari* was not random. Robert Bonfil and Arthur Lesley have pointed to a revival of interest in the *Kuzari* in Renaissance Italy, and the research of the present author has confirmed and elaborated on this interest.[128] In the hands of Moscato, the *Kuzari* is a vehicle for the presentation of a wide-ranging eclectic worldview that displays a number of the attributes associated with the encounter between Jewish culture and

Renaissance Italian thought: an interest in humanist concerns of rhetoric and language, an interest in Aristotelian/scholastic dialectics, and Neoplatonic encyclopedic thinking.[129]

Paul O. Kristeller has pointed out that scholastics and humanists shared the commentary form; he suggests, however, that the humanist commentary can be distinguished because of its emphasis on grammar and history rather than dialectical concerns.[130] To a certain extent, then, the question of whether Moscato is a humanist is an ill-posed one—his commentary on the *Kuzari*, at least, displays both medieval/scholastic as well as Renaissance/humanist elements. With this in mind, Moscato's status within the framework of Jewish intellectual and cultural life becomes somewhat clearer. Not only can his work be read as a version of "Jewish humanism," but he himself ought to be seen as a representative of a kind of specialization among Jewish intellectuals and scholars during the Renaissance. Moscato appears to have carved out for himself—for the most part, with the blessing of his colleagues—a professional niche that allows him to pursue a Jewish version of Renaissance humanism.

As our knowledge and understanding of Jewish life in this period grows deeper, we need not rely on the typologies enunciated by contemporaries who saw only halakhists and non-halakhists or halakhists, kabbalists, and philosophers. Instead we may offer a different typology in which one of the types consists of the "Jewish humanist" whose role in the Jewish community was to offer a synthesis between different cultural traditions necessary for forming a robust Jewish subculture in early modern Italy.[131] Charles Trinkaus has suggested that various humanists, such as Piaggio Bracciolini and Leonardo Bruni, should be looked at in a context not usually applied to them—as medieval Christian scholars who saw the classical tradition and Christianity as having basically compatible moralities although Christianity expressed a fuller truth.[132] Perhaps, then, we should put the emphasis on the "Jewish" side of the "Jewish humanist" label for someone like Moscato. His commentary on the *Kuzari* demonstrates that he has taken much from the "toolkit" of humanist scholarship.[133] At the same time, the conclusions he reaches and the text that he chooses suggest that his is a humanism tempered by a particularistic context. Although his commentary on the *Kuzari* offers something of a reconciliation between Aristotelian science and Ciceronian rhetoric on one hand, and biblical and talmudic tradition on the other, it is clear where the priority lies.

Notes

This essay represents a modified version of a paper presented at the Wolfenbüttel Conference on Jewish Scholarship and Philosophy in the Renaissance, September 2000. An earlier version was printed to the Sixteenth-Century Studies Conference in Toronto in October 1998. I am grateful to the participants in both conferences for their useful comments and suggestions. My research on Moscato was done in the context of the writing of a dissertation completed at the University of Pennsylvania in 2003 entitled "The Later History of a Medieval Hebrew Book: Studies in the Reception of Judah Halevi's *Sefer ha-Kuzari*." A more detailed analysis of Moscato's *Kol Yehudah* and more complete references to secondary sources can be found there.

1. *Sefer ha-Kuzari im perush kol Yehudah* (Venice, 1594). Unless otherwise noted, however, page references to the *Kuzari* and *Kol Yehudah* below are to the Vilna 1880 edition.

2. I have set the biblical phrases in boldface. Gen. 18:2 (Abraham is visited by three angels). My translation is rather literal in order to give the flavor of this language and to make the biblical verse allusions clearer.

3. For identification of these individuals, see the discussion below.

4. Gen. 18:2.

5. That is, do not continue on your way without stopping to teach your comrades. Gen. 18:3: "My lords, if I find favor in your eyes, do not go on past your servant."

6. An odd phrase, but the meaning presumably is something like our colloquial "clear your mind" as preparation for intense intellectual activity.

7. Gen. 18:2.

8. Ibid.

9. Gen. 18:10, "I will return to you next year, and your wife Sarah shall have a son." Judah's son will be his commentary.

10. Gen. 18:11: "Sarah had stopped having the periods of women."

11. Gen. 18:6–7: "Abraham hastened into the tent to Sarah, and said, 'Quick, three seahs of choice flour! Knead and make cakes!' Then Abraham ran to the herd, took a calf, tender and choice, and gave it to a servant boy, who hastened to prepare it."

12. *ben bakar*, "calf"; but the root *bkr* also refers to criticism or examination.

13. *plpli*, an adjective referring either to "pepper" (*pilpel*) or "dialectics" (*pilpul*).

14. Gen. 18:13.

15. 1 Sam. 15:27.

16. After Ezek. 14:13.

17. For a defense of taking seriously the biblical allusions contained in this style of writing, which takes account of contemporary theory regarding intertextuality as well as the cultural context of the late Middle Ages, see E. Gutwirth, "History and Intertextuality in Late Medieval Spain," in *Christians, Muslims, and Jews in Medieval and Early Modern Spain: Interaction and Cultural Change*, ed. M. Meyerson and E. English (Notre Dame, Ind., 1999), pp. 162–63. However, it is clear that using Genesis 18 to con-

jure up a situation needing his scholarly intervention was a favorite literary trope for Moscato. Cf. *Nefuṣot Yehudah*, sermon 18 (Bene Brak, 2000), p. 251; Cf. M. T. Weiss in *Ha-Eshkol* 7 (1913): 203.

18. In doing so, he creates a literary parallel between his own project and the frame story of the *Kuzari*, in which the origins of that work are traced to a visit from a divine messenger to the Khazar king.

19. See M. Ghirondi, *Toledot gedole Yisrael* (Trieste, 1853), p. 17; L. Blau, ed., *Leo Modenas Briefe und Schriftstücke* (Budapest, 1905), pp. 110–12. Some of his responsa were published in *Naḥalat Ya'akov* (Padua, 1628) by his student Jacob Heilbronn.

20. M. Mortara, *Indice alfabetico dei rabbini e scrittori israeliti di cose guidache in Italia* (Padua, 1886), p. 13; Blau, *Leo Modenas Briefe*, p. 110; S. Simonsohn, *History of the Jews in the Duchy of Mantua* (Jerusalem, 1977), p. 702.

21. See Blau, *Leo Modenas Briefe*, pp. 114–16; Mortara, *Indice*, p. 59.

22. The commentary of Judah of Lunel, fifteenth-century Provence.

23. Y. Boksenboim, ed., *Iggerot melamdim* (Tel Aviv, 1985), pp. 270–72. On de Lattes, see Somonsohn, *History of the Jews*, p. 717; I. Tishby, "The Controversy about the *Zohar* in the Sixteenth Century in Italy" (Hebrew), *Perakim: Yearbook of the Schocken Institute for Jewish Research* 1 (1967/68): 131–82 and the references cited there. On Abraham de Sant'Angelo, see E. Horowitz, "Speaking of the Dead: The Emergence of the Eulogy among Italian Jewry of the Sixteenth Century," in *Preachers of the Italian Ghetto*, ed. D. Ruderman (Berkeley, Calif., 1992), pp. 135–44.

24. All these manuscripts are sixteenth century: MSS Livorno Talmud Torah 5 (formerly 38) (Institute for Microfilmed Hebrew Manuscripts Film 12518), p. 1b; Moscow-Guenzburg 1666 (IMHM 48680), p. 2a; Paris-BN Heb. 679 (IMHM 11557), p. 2a; Budapest-Kaufmann 268.1 (IMHM 12652), p. 4a. The last three share the same layout and nearly identical concluding material.

25. A. M. Habermann, *Giovanni di Gara: Printer Venice, 1564–1610* (Hebrew) (Jerusalem, 1982), nos. 186, 196, 213. On Heilbronn's connection to the di Gara printing house, see J. Baumgarten, "Giovanni di Gara: Imprimeur de livres yiddish a Venise (milieu du XVe—début du XVIe siècle) et la culture juive de la Renaissance," *Revue des études juives* 159 (2000): 587–98.

26. Blau, *Leo Modenas Briefe*, p. 191 n. 3.

27. On Sforno, see *Encyclopaedia Judaica* (Jerusalem, 1971) 14: 1211, and Leon Modena, *The Autobiography of a Seventeenth-Century Venetian Rabbi*, ed. M. Cohen (Princeton, N.J., 1988), p. 92. Sforno also had responsa published in Heilbronn's *Naḥalat Ya'akov.*

28. There remains the possibility that the incident did occur in some form and that Moscato, for some reason, left out the names of the rabbis who solicited the commentary from him. In this scenario, someone "in the know," one of Moscato's sons or someone else involved with the publication, would have added the names that Moscato had left out. This scenario seems less likely.

29. For an explanation of the term "meta-halakhic," see I. Twersky, "Talmudists, Philosophers, and Kabbalists: The Quest for Spirituality in the Sixteenth Century," in *Jewish Thought in the Sixteenth Century*, ed. B. Cooperman (Cambridge Mass., 1983), p. 450.

30. The most extensive description of Moscato's life and work is found in A. Apfelbaum, *Toledot hagaon Rabbi Yehudah Moscato* (Drogobych, Ukraine, 1900). For a brief account, see Joseph Dan's entry in the *Encyclopaedia Judaica*, vol. 12, cols. 357–58.

31. Moscato's sermons were printed in *Nefuṣot Yehudah* (Venice, 1589; repr., Lvov, 1859, Warsaw, 1871, and Bene Brak, 2000). In the course of the research on which this essay is based, I have referred to various editions. Unless otherwise specified, however, references below will be to the Bene Brak edition. On Moscato's preaching, see I. Bettan, "The Sermons of Judah Moscato," *Hebrew Union College Annual* 6 (1929): 297–326 (reprinted in his *Studies in Jewish Preaching* [Cincinnati, 1939], pp 192–228); J. Dan, "The Sermon Tifilah ve-Dim'a of R. Judah Moscato" (Hebrew), *Sinai* 76 (1975): 209–32; M. Saperstein, *Jewish Preaching, 1200–1800: An Anthology* (New Haven, Conn., 1989), pp. 253–69; and M. Idel, "Judah Moscato: A Late Renaissance Jewish Preacher," in *Preachers of the Italian Ghetto*, ed. Ruderman, pp. 41–66.

32. Unfortunately, as Marc Saperstein has pointed out, Katzenellenbogen edited all of his specific "praises of the deceased" out of the written version of the sermon ("Italian Jewish Preaching: An Overview," in *Preachers of the Italian Ghetto*, ed. Ruderman, p. 22). We are left with a rather oblique description of the ideal scholar and the assumption that Katzenellenbogen viewed Moscato as a good example of this ideal (*Sheneim 'asar derashot* [Lemberg, 1811], 9a–10b).

33. For Moscato's poetry, see D. Bregman, *A Bundle of Gold: Hebrew Sonnets from the Renaissance and the Baroque* (Hebrew) (Jerusalem, 1997), pp. 86–93, and in addition to the material published there, MSS Oxford-Bodl. 2317, a poem for a wedding; Budapest-Kaufmann A492 (p. 59), London BL-Or. 10222, London BL-Or. 10471/6, London-BL Add. 27078 (306b-307a), copies of his prayer for rain. The responsa on *sheḥita* can be found in MS Frankfurt Stadt-und U. Bibliothek Oct. 135, pp. 71v–73v.

34. See Simonsohn, *History of the Jews*, pp. 423, 501–8.

35. Ibid., p. 253.

36. See R. Bonfil, "Some Reflections on the Place of Azariah de' Rossi's *Me'or 'Einayim* in the Cultural Milieu of Italian Renaissance Jewry," in Cooperman, *Jewish Thought in the Sixteenth Century* pp. 23–48; Simonsohn, *History of the Jews*, p. 637; and, most recently, J. Weinberg, translator's introduction to *Light of the Eyes* (New Haven, Conn., 2001), pp. xlii–xliii. His responsum can be found in a collection of Moses Provenzali's responsa, MS London-Montefiore 114/3, p. 51.

37. *Nefuṣot Yehudah* (Venice, 1589), p. 1v. Cf. Simonsohn, *History of the Jews*, p. 722.

38. Simonsohn, *History of the Jews*; on the 1633 appointment, p. 579.

39. Twersky, "Talmudists, Philosophers, and Kabbalists," pp. 431–59. The institutional framework has been carefully delineated by R. Bonfil, *Harabanut be-Italyah bitequfat ha-Renesans* (Jerusalem, 1979); Eng. trans. by J. Chipman, *Rabbis and Jewish Communities in Renaissance Italy* (London, 1993).

40. The most famous of these typologies is that of Profiat Duran, writing in the early fifteenth century, in the introduction to his *sefer ma'ase efod* (Vienna, 1865), pp. 4–17. For discussion, see Twersky, "Talmudists," p. 432; and, especially as it applied to

sixteenth-century Italy, R. Bonfil, "A Cultural Profile," in *The Jews of Early Modern Venice*, ed. R. Davis and B. Ravid (Baltimore, 2001), pp. 169–90, esp. 170–72. Twersky offers a long list of similar typologies in late medieval and early modern Jewish literature (p. 432).

41. Twersky, "Talmudists," pp. 436, 440.

42. See below; and see *Nefuṣot Yehudah*, sermon 18, pp. 151, 157–58; sermon 20, p. 174; sermon 44, p. 385; sermon 48, p. 400; and *Kol Yehudah* on *Kuzari* 1:98, 3:23.

43. See Idel, "Judah Moscato," p. 58, referring to Katzenellenbogen, p. 10a.

44. The overall debate over the existence of a "Jewish humanism" in Renaissance Italy—and on how Jewish culture in this period should be categorized more generally—will only be engaged here indirectly. For a full account of that debate, see D. Ruderman, introduction to *Essential Papers on Jewish Culture in Renaissance and Baroque Italy*, ed. D. Ruderman (New York, 1992), pp. 1–39; and cf. H. Tirosh-Rothschild, "Jewish Culture in Renaissance Italy: A Methodological Survey," *Italia* 9 (1990): 63–96.

45. *Nefuṣot Yehudah*, sermon 28, p. 226. See also Y. T. Porges, introduction to *Nefuṣot Yehudah*, (Bene Brak, 2000), p. 16.

46. The work is extant in one manuscript, MS Livorno-Talmud Torah 5, which also contains a copy of *Kol Yehudah*.

47. 1594 edition, p. 2b.

48. Ibid., p. 3b.

49. For a summary of this genre, see E. A. Quain, "The Medieval '*Accessus ad Auctores*,'" *Traditio* 3 (1945): 215–64; R. W. Hunt, "The Introduction to the 'Artes' in the Twelfth Century," in *Studia mediaevalia in honorum admodum Reverendi Patis Raymundi Josephi Martin* (Bruges, 1948), pp. 85–112; and A. J. Minnis and A. B. Scott, eds., *Medieval Literary Theory and Criticism c. 1100–c. 1375: The Commentary Tradition* (Oxford, 1988), esp. sec. 1, "An Anthology of Literary Prefaces."

50. Quain, "Medieval," p. 215; Hunt, "Introduction," pp. 94–100.

51. Hunt, "Introduction," p. 100.

52. The meaning of this last section is a bit obscure. Moscato seems to be referring to the activity of the four Judah's—Halevi, Ibn Tibbon, Ben Kardinal, and himself, each of whom has been involved with the work in some manner as active causes. Ben Kardinal was the author of the second translation of the *Kuzari*, dating from the early twentieth century.

53. 1594 edition, p. 4b.

54. For other examples of Jewish use of the *accessus* genre, see D. Schechterman, "The Philosophy of Immanuel of Rome in Light of His Commentary on the Book of Genesis" (Hebrew) (Ph.D. diss., Hebrew University, 1984), p. 52; S. Harvey, "The Hebrew Translation of Averroës' Proemium to His Long Commentary on Aristotle's Physics," *Proceedings of the American Academy for Jewish Research* 52 (1985): 55–84, esp. 55, 65, and 72; D. Ruderman, "An Exemplary Sermon from the Classroom of a Jewish Teacher in Renaissance Italy," *Italia* 1 (1978): 7–38; 21 n. 41.

55. 1594 edition, 4a–4b.

56. See M. Beit-Arié, "Publication and Republication of Literary Texts in Medieval Jewish Civilization: Jewish Scribality and Its Impact on the Texts Transmitted,"

in *Transmitting Jewish Traditions: Orality, Textuality, and Cultural Diffusion*, ed. Y. Elman and I. Gershoni (New Haven, Conn., 2000), esp. pp. 234–36.

57. For a case study of such practices by one humanist, see A. Grafton, "The Scholarship of Poliziano and Its Context," in his *Defenders of the Text: The Traditions of Scholarship in an Age of Science* (Cambridge, Mass., 1991), pp. 62–64.

58. See E. J. Kenney, *The Classical Text: Aspects of Editing in the Age of the Printed Book* (Berkeley, Calif., 1974), p. 25: "Their task as they saw it was to *improve* the texts by correction: *emendare, corrigere, emaculare.* In this task the critic had two resources, the manuscripts and his own brains."

59. For a brief survey of the importance of rhetoric in the Renaissance, see J. Monfasani, "Humanism and Rhetoric," in *Renaissance Humanism: Foundations, Forms, and Legacy*, ed. A. Rabil (Philadelphia, 1988), 3: 171–235.

60. For a general view on rhetoric in Italian Jewish culture, see A. Lesley, "Jewish Adaptation of Humanist Concepts in Fifteenth- and Sixteenth-Century Italy," in *Renaissance Rereadings: Intertext and Context*, ed. M. C. Horowitz et al. (Urbana, Ill., 1988), pp. 56 f. (reprinted in *Essential Papers on Jewish Culture in Renaissance and Baroque Italy*, ed. Ruderman).

61. 1:72, p. 129. The context here is a discussion of the golden calf; Moscato would place greater emphasis on the proper intentions of the Israelites in contrast to their sinful actions—thus relating the point here to the opening theme in the work.

62. 1:49, p. 67. Here Moscato notes the shift from the king's combative stance in 1:25 to his taking a more conciliatory approach.

63. 2:38, p. 103. The comment is on the rabbi's explanation of the diseases to which the heart is vulnerable, as part of a clarification of the comment in 2:36 that "Israel among the nations is like the heart among the organs of the body; it is at the same time the sickest and the healthiest of them."

64. Ibid., p. 104.

65. These are two of Cicero's five parts to rhetoric, defined in bk. 1, sec. 7 of *De inventione*: "Arrangement is the distribution of arguments thus discovered in the proper order. Expression is the fitting of the proper language to the invented matter" (trans. H. Hubbell [Cambridge, Mass., 1949], pp. 19–21). For a useful summary of Cicero's basic approach, see J. J. Murphy, *Rhetoric in the Middle Ages: A History of Rhetorical Theory from Saint Augustine to the Renaissance* (Berkeley, Calif., 1974), pp. 9 f.

66. 2:72, p. 161.

67. The meaning here is a bit obscure. Moscato has *otiyot* (with a *yud*), which generally means "letters"; but he may mean "signs," *otot* (generally without the *yud*).

68. Ibid. Cf. Quintilian, *Institutio oratoria*, bk. 11, chap. 3, trans. H. E. Butler (Cambridge, Mass., 1922), 4:243 f. For the Bible translations here, I have used the "old" JPS translation because it better expresses the meaning that Moscato intends here.

69. Moscato cites the discussion of the phrase *ve'aleihu literufah* ("and the leaf is for medicine") in BT Sanhedrin 100a, where the debate is over whether the medicine is meant to enable the dumb to speak or to open up a barren womb. Moscato's text differs from the text found in the printed edition there. This is one of a number of examples of lack of agreement between Moscato and printed editions of the Tal-

mud that bear further study. See the discussion of this passage in Moscato in A. Altmann, "Ars Rhetorica as Reflected in Some Jewish Figures of the Italian Renaissance," in *Jewish Thought in the Sixteenth Century*, ed. Cooperman, pp. 17–18.

70. Ibid., pp. 77–78.

71. *Nefuṣot Yehudah*, sermon 17, p. 145.

72. *Nofet ṣufim* (Mantua, 1475); ed. and trans. Isaac Rabinowitz, *The Book of the Honeycomb's Flow* (Ithaca, N.Y., 1983).

73. Ibid., p. 127.

74. This seems to be the sort of authority associated with "exemplary canons" as elaborated recently by Moshe Halbertal: "paradigmatic examples of aesthetic value and achievement: models for imitation which set the criteria for what is regarded as a higher form of art" (*People of the Book: Canon, Meaning, and Authority* [Cambridge, Mass., 1997], p. 3).

75. Moscato, of course, never makes the claim that the *Kuzari* is an example of this perfection, since he knows that the work is originally composed in Arabic. He does, however, think very highly of the quality of Ibn Tibbon's translation. And since Ibn Tibbon is responsible for the Hebrew version of the work, he is one of the authorities/authors of the work. For Moscato, he is one of the four "causes" of the work (see above, n. 52).

76. Lesley, "Jewish Adaptation," in *Essential Papers*, ed. Ruderman, p. 48.

77. 1, p. 153.

78. See G. Scholem, *Major Trends in Jewish Mysticism* (New York, 1961), p. 17; A. S. Halkin, "The Medieval Jewish Attitude toward Hebrew," in *Biblical and Other Studies*, ed. A. Altmann (Cambridge, Mass., 1963), pp. 233–50; M. Idel, *Language, Torah, and Hermeneutics in Abraham Abulafia* (Albany, N.Y., 1989), esp. pp. 13, 137.

79. 4, p. 94.

80. 2, 166–72. See below on the length of this section.

81. In addition to the sources he cites by name, Moscato refers to a number of sources anonymously. I. Sonne makes a case that Moscato's reference to "allegorists" in *Kol Yehudah* in 2:50 (p. 101a of the 1594 edition) is a reference to an interpretation of Judah Abravanel (Leone Ebreo). ("The Traces of the *Dialoghi d'Amore* in Hebrew Literature and the Printed Hebrew Translation" [Hebrew], *Tarbiẓ* 3 [1932]: 304–5.)

82. These estimates are based on line counts from the 1880 edition.

83. Moscato on 2:64, p. 143.

84. A. Grafton, "Quattrocentro Humanism and Classical Scholarship," in *Renaissance Humanism*, ed. Rabil, 3: 27.

85. It should be pointed out, however, that Grafton is discussing primarily mid-fifteenth-century scholarship and that such overly detailed, erudite commentaries were already seen as passé nearly a century before Moscato wrote (pp. 28–29).

86. MS Livorno TT 5 (IMHM 12518), introduction to *Bat kol Yehudah*, p. 5a.

87. Indeed, Charles Touati refers to the *Kuzari* as *une véritable encyclopédie* in the introduction to his recent French translation (*Le Kuzari: Apologie de la religion méprisée* [Louvain, 1994], p. xiii). Here, I hope to flesh out the meaning of Touati's off-hand reference, placing Moscato's work into the context of encyclopedias of the time.

88. For a summary of how the medieval encyclopedia is usually defined, see A.

Melamed, "Hebrew Italian Renaissance and Early Modern Encyclopedias," *Rivista di storia della filosofia* 40 (1985): 91–112, esp. 92.

89. I am grateful to Warren Zev Harvey of the Hebrew University of Jerusalem for a stimulating conversation that we had on this subject some years ago. Professor Harvey suggested that portions of Moscato's commentary resemble discrete essays on selected topics. Although Moscato sometimes expresses his own opinion, he is often content to serve as a compiler of the opinions of others (and sometimes to act as a reconciler of differing opinions, as I discuss below).

90. Melamed, "Hebrew Italian Renaissance," pp. 92–93. I might also point out that previous scholars have often stretched the notion on encyclopedia to refer simply to a work that covers a large number of subjects or that covers one subject in a particularly comprehensive manner. See. e.g., two articles in the volume of the *Rivista di storia della filosofia* cited above, by Bonfil, "Una 'enciclopedia' di sapere sociale: L'epistolario ebraico quattrocentesco di Josef Sark," pp. 113–30; and by G. B. Sermoneta, "La enciclopedie nel mondo ebraico mediavale: Tre trattati neo-platonizanti a carattere enciclopedico," pp. 7–50. I am trying here to distinguish between the concept of "encyclopedia" and a notion that some authors can be "encyclopedic" or, in Moscato's case, engage in a process of "encyclopedization." For more on the definition and scope of Jewish encyclopedic writing in the Middle Ages and Renaissance, see S. Harvey, ed., *The Medieval Hebrew Encyclopedias of Science and Philosophy: Proceedings of the Bar-Ilan University Conference* (Dordrecht, 2000).

91. G. Strauss, "A Sixteenth-Century Encyclopedia: Sebastian Münster's *Cosmography* and Its Editions," in *From the Renaissance to the Counter-Reformation: Essays in Honor of Garett Mattingly*, ed. C. Carter (New York, 1965), pp. 145–63. See also A. H. T. Levi, "Ethics and the Encyclopedia in the Sixteenth Century," in *French Renaissance Studies, 1540–1570*, ed. P. Sharatt (Edinburgh, 1976), pp. 170–84; F. Simone, "La Notion d'encyclopédie: Elément caractéristique de la Renaissance française," in ibid., pp. 234–62.

92. Strauss, "Sixteenth-Century Encyclopedia," pp. 148–49.

93. Ibid., p. 149.

94. Both indexes can be found in MS Budapest-Kaufman N 269 (IMHM 14558). The index to *Kol Yehudah* is by Samson ha-Kohen Modon, who lived in Mantua at the beginning of the eighteenth century. Additional copies of Modena's index are found in MS JTS 2285 and MS Moscow-Guenzburg 361.

95. Levi, "Ethics and the Encyclopedia," p. 179.

96. M. Foucault, *The Order of Things: An Archaeology of the Human Sciences* (New York, 1970), chap. 2, "The Prose of the World," esp. pp. 17–32.

97. G. Huppert, "*Divinitio et Eruditio*: Thoughts on Foucault," *History and Theory* 13 (1974): 191–207. I agree with the basic thrust of Huppert's criticism, but I would take issue with his generally dismissive attitude toward the "magicians." Even if not all were mainstream intellectuals and even if many academics of the day disdained astrology or like disciplines, many in the mainstream did take these disciplines quite seriously. In Huppert's eagerness to overturn Foucault's view, he sometimes comes close to taking an equally totalizing position that all serious or important intellectu-

als held the same views regarding Neoplatonism, Hermetism, and so forth. What is interesting about the early modern period is precisely the wide range of views held.

98. I. McLean, "Foucault's Renaissance Episteme Reassessed: An Aristotelian Counterblast," *Journal of the History of Ideas* 59 (1998): 153.

99. 2, p. 82.

100. See Melamed, "Hebrew Italian Renaissance," on Portaleone's *Shilṭei hagibborim.*

101. Another example would be his views on music, which he discusses in *Kol Yehudah* on 4:25 (1880, p. 85). Cf. *Nefuṣot Yehudah,* sermon 1, where Moscato cites the *Kuzari* 4:25 to support the view of music as representing the harmony and order of the universe (pp. 1–2). His discussion in both places relies on the same biblical prooftexts. The *Kol Yehudah* discussion appears to have been the first draft for the more extensive discussion in *Nefuṣot Yehudah.*

102. D. Ruderman, *Kabbalah, Magic, and Science: The Cultural Universe of a Sixteenth-Century Jewish Physician* (Cambridge, Mass., 1988), esp. pp. 69–73.

103. Ibid., p. 193.

104. *Kol Yehudah* on 2:26, p. 83.

105. Ibid.

106. The nearest rivals to the *Guide* seem to be the biblical commentaries of Naḥmanides and Ibn Ezra.

107. See, for example, 4, p. 142. In addition, Maimonides' *Mishneh Torah* is often cited anachronistically as a "source" for halakhic statements found in the *Kuzari.*

108. Most important in this regard is Wolfson's seminal early article "Maimonides and Halevi: A Study in Typical Jewish Attitudes toward Greek Philosophy in the Middle Ages," *Jewish Quarterly Review,* n.s., 2 (1912): 297–337 (reprinted in his *Studies in the History of Philosophy and Religion,* ed. I. Twersky and G. Williams [Cambridge, Mass., 1977], 2: 120–60). This view has been somewhat revised recently; see H. Kreisel, "Judah Halevi's Influence on Maimonides: A Preliminary Appraisal," in *Maimonidean Studies,* ed. A. Hyman (New York, 1991), 2: 95–121.

109. See, for example, 1:87, p. 104; 3:7, pp. 22–23; 4:3, pp. 47–48; 5:20, p. 89. There were certainly Jewish scholars in Italy who viewed Halevi and Maimonides as arguing in opposition to each other. See Elijah Gennazano, *Iggeret ḥamudot,* ed. A. W. Greenup (London, 1912), p. 7. "There has already been a work composed against the *Guide* and that is the *Kuzari.*" This work was known to Moscato. See his introduction, sec. *gimmel.*

110. 1594, p. 4a. Moscato quotes this work a number of times in his commentary. This is most likely a reference to the sixteenth-century Italian kabbalist Berakhiel Kaufmann. See H. J. Michael, *Or ha-Ḥayyim* (Frankfort am Main, 1891), p. 298, no. 644; E. Gottlieb, *Meḥkarim besifrut hakabbalah* (Tel Aviv, 1976), p. 423; Bonfil, *Rabbis,* p. 289. Moshe Idel has pointed to Berakhiel as one of a group of philosophically oriented kabbalists in sixteenth-century Mantua who argued for the study of philosophy as a propaedeutic to the study of kabbalah. See his "Divine Attributes and *Sefirot* in Jewish Theology" (Hebrew), in *Meḥkarim behagut yehudit,* ed. S. O. Heller Willensky and M. Idel (Jerusalem, 1989), p. 108, n. 79. Berakhiel's views on philosophy are found

in his *Sefer Lev Adam*, published in *Hame'asef* (Saint Petersburg, 1902), pp. 1–48. For his view of Aristotle, which echoes that of the *Kuzari*, see *Lev Adam*, p. 10, and the discussion (and English translation of this passage) in Bonfil.

111. See *Kol Yehudah* 1:67, pp. 80–81; 3:11, pp. 38 and 47; 3:5, p. 14; 3:53, p. 127; 3:25, pp. 86–87.

112. 4:25, pp. 86–87.

113. 4:1, p. 10.

114. M. Kellner, "Gersonides and His Cultured Despisers: Arama and Abravanel," *Jouranl of Medieval and Renaissance Studies* 6 (1976): 272.

115. 2:64, p. 141.

116. 4, p. 50. Kellner does not cite these last two examples in his survey of the negative reception of Gersonides. Moreover, in *Nefuṣot Yehudah*, sermon 49, Moscato cites Gersonides' discussion of the uniqueness of the Jewish people in his commentary on Balak (Numbers 23) and then says, "and his words agree with what the *Ḥaver* said about the superiority of this people separating its members from all other peoples in an essential way like the distinction between plants and inorganic matter and the distinction between humans and animals" (paraphrasing *Kuzari* 1:39; *Nefuṣot Yehudah*, 212). *Nefuṣot Yehudah* contains a number of other references to Gersonides, mostly positive. In the end, Moscato cannot be included as a "cultured despiser" of Gersonides. Rather, I would suggest that his synthetic impulse allows him to incorporate Gersonides (tendentiously, to be sure) into his group of medieval Jewish authorities.

117. H. Davidson, "Medieval Jewish Philosophy in the Sixteenth Century," in *Jewish Thought in the Sixteenth Century*, ed. Cooperman, p. 130.

118. Ibid., p. 132.

119. Ibid., p. 139.

120. Ibid., p. 125. Davidson concludes his study of the fifteenth-century Spanish Jewish philosopher Abraham Shalom by arguing that medieval Jewish philosophy died an "unnatural death" as a result of the expulsion of the Jews from Spain. If not for the expulsion, he assumes that Jews would have participated in the "revival of scholastic philosophy in Spain and Portugal." This view, however, ignores or downplays developments in Jewish philosophy that took place in the sixteenth century outside of Spain and Portugal (*The Philosophy of Abraham Shalom: A Fifteenth-Century Exposition and Defense of Maimonides* [Berkeley, Calif., 1964], p. 103).

121. I. Barzilay, *Between Reason and Faith* (The Hague, 1967), p. 167.

122. J. Dan, "Hebrew Homiletical Literature in Renaissance Italy" (Hebrew), *Proceedings of the Sixth World Congress of Jewish Studies* (Jerusalem, 1977), division 3, pp. 105–10. See also idem, "The Sermon Tifilah."

123. Idel, "Judah Moscato," pp. 47–48.

124. Ibid., p. 48.

125. *Nefuṣot Yehudah*, sermon 5, p. 54. Cf. Idel, "Judah Moscato," p. 52.

126. See D. Kaufmann, "The Dispute about the Sermons of David del Bene of Mantua," *Jewish Quartely Review* 8 (1896): 513–25.

127. *Kissot leveit David* (Verona, 1649), sec. 12, 34b. See Kaufmann's discussion, p. 516. On Judah del Bene, see R. Bonfil, "Preaching as Meditation Between Elite and

Popular Cultures: The Case of Judah del Bene," in *Preachers of the Italian Ghetto*, ed. Ruderman, pp. 67–88.

128. Full details are available in chap. 3 of my dissertation.

129. For a description of this encounter, outlining these categories, see D. Ruderman, "The Italian Renaissance in Jewish Thought," in *Renaissance Humanism*, ed. Rabil, 1: 382–433.

130. P. Kristeller, "The Scholar and His Public in the Late Middle Ages and the Renaissance," in idem, *Medieval Aspects of Renaissance Learning* (Durham, N.C., 1974), pp. 6–10. In this sense, Moscato's commentary is not, strictly speaking, a humanist one. But it seems to me that we ought not make too much of this distinction between humanism and scholasticism, since it refers to categories developed for Christian and not for Jewish thinkers, operating in a distinct intellectual and cultural context.

131. On the notion of a Jewish subculture as a meaningful category for discussing Italian Jewry in this period, see K. Stow, *Theater of Acculturation: The Roman Ghetto in the Sixteenth Century* (Seattle, 2001), p. 49. In creating such a typology, we do not need to go so far as Leopold Zunz, who offered an implicit typology containing a dozen or more highly specific "types" in his listing of Jewish intellectuals in Renaissance Italy. Moscato was a *theologischer Philosoph*; Azariah de' Rossi a *Kritiker*; Abraham Portaleone, an *Antiquar*; etc. (*Gesammelte Schriften* [Berlin, 1875], 1: 109).

132. C. Trinkaus, "Italian Humanism and Scholastic Theology," in *Renaissance Humanism*, ed. Rabil, 3: 327–48.

133. I borrow the notion of a humanist "toolkit" from the essay by Howard Goodman and Anthony Grafton on Matteo Ricci, "Ricci, the Chinese, and the Toolkits of the Textualists," *Asia Major*, 3d series, 3 (1990–91): 95–148.

Chapter 9

As Framed, So Perceived: Salamone Rossi Ebreo, *Late Renaissance Musician*

Don Harrán

Put your discourse into some frame.
—Shakespeare, *Hamlet,* III.ii. 325
But let the frame of things disjoint, both the worlds suffer.
—Shakespeare, *Macbeth,* III.ii. 13

The title of this essay features two components: a subject, "Salamone Rossi," and a perspective, "as framed," that is, in one or another context. Each component harbors a contradiction: a Jew, yet a Renaissance musician; a point of view, yet its mutability. Hence the two contradictory epigraphs at the head of this essay: they are meant to illustrate the conceptual extremities in the argumentation for "Salamone Rossi as framed" in the essay proper. One wonders, then, why discuss the subject? What is meant by "contextual"? Wherein lies the contradiction?

Salamone Rossi, or, in Hebrew, Shelomo min ha'adumim, warrants consideration for being the first known Jewish composer of art music—music devised according to the rules and conventions of learned composition—to have left his imprint on music history in both its Jewish and its European dimensions.[1] True, he was preceded by a handful of other rather obscure Jewish composers, among them the thirteenth-century trouvère Mahieu le Juif and the sixteenth-century loan banker and part-time musician David Sacerdote. Some of them converted to Christianity, as did Mahieu, of whom no more than two melodies are known.[2] Others left behind works so incomplete that not a single composition can be reconstructed in its entirety: Sacerdote's eighteen madrigals, for example, were written for six voices, yet of the six only one is extant.[3] With Rossi we have a composer with a somewhat fuller biography and a large, fairly complete, and qualitatively significant repertory of secular and sacred works.

Were we to write Salamone Rossi's curriculum vitae, it might read as follows:[4]

1) Born around 1570, probably in Mantua; died around 1628, in Mantua or possibly in Venice.[5]
2) Served the Mantuan court, from 1589 until presumably 1628, as an instrumentalist, more specifically a violinist; a conductor of one or more instrumental ensembles; and a composer.[6]
3) Was active in the Jewish theater, for the productions of which he probably supervised the musical portions, or *intermedi*, variously at the beginning and end of comedies and between their acts: in this capacity, he would have composed and rehearsed the same *intermedi*, even taking part in their performance as a violinist and possibly singer.[7]
4) Provided music, occasionally, for productions of the non-Jewish theater—for instance, a vocal-instrumental *balletto* for the sacred play *La Maddalena*, performed in 1617 as part of the celebrations for Duke Ferdinando's marriage to Caterina de' Medici.[8]
5) Directed, as stated, one or possibly two instrumental ensembles at the Mantuan court. At some stage, even formed his own ensemble, or *concerto*, of two or more instruments and perhaps voices, with which he appeared at the Mantuan and occasionally other courts and in private houses of the nobility.[9]
6) Participated in activities of the Mantuan Jewish community, preparing music for use in the synagogue and doubtless for private entertainments. His sponsor in the Jewish community, and the one who may to a certain degree have defrayed the expenses of his publications, was the banker Moses Sullam.[10]
7) Composed 313 or more works, of which 307 are preserved in thirteen collections printed between 1589 and 1628. Some of the collections were issued in reprints or later editions, making a total of twenty-five publications.[11]
8) Assembled, for his collections, three kinds of compositions:
   a) Italian vocal works, mainly madrigals for five voices or, in one collection, four, yet sometimes lighter types (*madrigaletti, canzonette*)

for two or three voices. Many of them are set to verses by leading poets of the day (Battista Guarini, Gabriello Chiabrera, Ottavio Rinuccini, Giovan Battista Marino). Eight collections, with 150 works altogether.[12]

b) Instrumental works, mainly in three parts (two violins and a *chitarrone*, or bass lute), yet sometimes in four or five. They range from *sinfonie*, or short works that may have introduced vocal or other instrumental compositions, to dances (*gagliarde, correnti, brandi*), executed alone or in pairs or larger groupings, and extended, autonomous *sonate*. Four collections, with 130 works altogether.[13]

c) Hebrew works, for three to eight voices, to be performed in the synagogue on Sabbaths and festivals and, where suitable, in confraternities or for private and communal events. One collection, entitled *Songs of Solomon*, with thirty-three works.[14]

9) Collaborated, for the Hebrew works, with the Venetian rabbi and cantor Leon Modena: it was Modena who, on his own testimony, strengthened and supported the composer in their preparation and oversaw the printing of the Hebrew script and its proofreading.[15]

10) Dedicated his collections to various "patrons" in Mantua (Duke Vincenzo I Gonzaga; his son Prince Vincenzo, later to become Duke Vincenzo II; and other members of the Gonzaga family, among them Felicita Gonzaga, marchioness of Pallazuolo, and Ferrante Gonzaga, prince of Guastalla) and its Jewish community (Moses Sullam), Mirandola (Prince Alessandro Pico), and Modena (Duke Cesare d'Este, his son Prince Alfonso).[16]

11) Traveled to the court of Mirandola at least once.[17] Visits to other courts, including Modena and possibly Vienna, may be conjectured.[18] Was in Venice on three occasions, if not more, to supervise the printing of his collections[19] and possibly to try out his Hebrew works, in various synagogues, before and after their publication (1623). There he would have met with Leon Modena and members of the Venetian Jewish community, including the poet and literary patroness Sara Copio Sullam, whose husband, Jacob, was, moreover, the son of Rossi's protector Moses Sullam.[20]

12) "Rediscovered" in the nineteenth century by, among others, the Viennese cantor Solomon Sulzer, known to have owned one or possibly more part books of the composer's *Songs of Solomon*,[21] and the

> Parisian cantor Samuel Naumbourg, who prepared the first modern edition of the *Songs*.[22] His style of writing seems to have been influential in shaping their works, becoming a model, more broadly, for music in the Reform Jewish liturgy.

The leading question is: "Who are you, Salamone Rossi *ebreo*?" To answer it is, naturally, to deal with the usual matters concerning his biography and works, of which the main items were summarized in the thumbnail sketch above. Clearly, a consideration of Rossi, the man, his *oeuvre*, his influence, is relative to any one of various points of reference, hence the inevitability of a selective, compartmentalized approach. Our perceptions of Rossi, as, needless to say, of everything else, are functions, ontologically, of the different ways persons, events, and ideas aggregate into composites. The same composites serve as frames, or contexts, for collocating and interpreting data. More fundamentally, contexts are surface realizations of basic epistemic categories, which, for Ernst Cassirer, are space, time, and number.[23] The construction of categories is a rational imperative. Interpretive statements, engendered by the categories, set individuals, acts, and events in patterns of causal or conceptual reciprocity.

Information theory has enlightened us on the different ways knowledge is collected and processed. Explanations are delimited by contexts, yet contexts shift from within, with the addition of new data to the old, and from without, with the reshaping of the data into other contexts: changes in collocation force changes in explanation. To return to Rossi, within each context he can be judged for how he viewed himself in relation to others or, from the opposite end, for how others viewed him in relation to themselves. The double perspective engenders an active intersubjective dialogue, on at least two planes: between Rossi and "others"; between both of them and ourselves. It coordinates, homologically, with the double perspective for viewing the connections between Judaism and Christianity: How does Rossi perceive himself in association with Jews and Christians? How do Christians perceive him in association with themselves and the Jewish community he represents? How do we, at the interpretive distance of some four centuries, perceive the *dramatis personae* as they act out their roles within the Jewish and Christian interchanges of late sixteenth- and early seventeenth-century Mantuan and, more widely, European history?

Limiting the discussion for the moment to Rossi's repertory, one might suppose that Rossi would have defined art music, as he practiced it in his Hebrew works, more broadly than Christians did. His definition is likely to have encompassed at least three components: remnants, more ideational than material, of art music in the ancient Temple; certain kinds of melodies, be they for reciting portions of Scripture, or for prayers and *piyyuṭim*, heard in the synagogue, and if not the melodies themselves then the principles behind them, namely, simplicity and intelligibility, as characteristic of a logogenic approach (music as a function of the tonic and syntactic organization of speech); and art music cultivated by Christians, in later Renaissance Italy, for performance in courts, churches, academies, and private residences. Christians, by contrast, would probably have apprehended Rossi's Hebrew works as a simulation of their own, with one exception: the substitution of Hebrew for Latin or Italian. The expanded Jewish context for Rossi's apperception of art music results from its incorporation of the one element absent from its Christian counterpart: the Jewish "experience" and "heritage," a mixture of history, religion, and custom with which Rossi identified on various levels of consciousness and sensibility.[24]

The perceptions of art music alter, however, when "Jewish art music" is exchanged for "art music by Jews"—more specifically, when Rossi's Hebrew songs are exchanged for his secular works, namely, Italian madrigals and instrumental compositions. Here, too, Rossi would probably have projected his secular works, as an appendage to his sacred ones, on the background of the rich musical practice known from biblical times, with its sacred and secular components—for example, music in the Temple ritual, music as a therapeutic aid (David playing his lyre to lift Saul's spirits), or for celebrating a wedding (Psalm 45, designated a *shir yedidot*, or "song of loves," and to all appearances an epithalamium) or a victory ("when David returned from slaying the Philistine . . . the women, from all cities of Israel, came out to sing and dance, greeting King Saul, with timbrels, with joy and with triangles"; 1 Sam. 18:6). But by the same token, his view of his secular works would not have included their affiliation with music as traditionally sung in the synagogue, the melodies and performance of which he firmly demarcated from those of art music. Christian composers are, for their part, unlikely to have sensed Hebrew or Jewish elements in the Italian or instrumental works of Rossi *ebreo*; rather, they would have related to them as an example, once again, of what they knew from their own practice or even as a presumptuous attempt by a Jewish composer to appropriate music they considered their own.

But the views of Rossi's sacred and secular music shift, again, when either kind is judged by arbiters of halakhic propriety, who, as guardians of a tradition, felt threatened by changes. The notion that Israel should not rejoice while in exile underlies their usually negative opinion of art music, particularly when performed in the synagogue. Being a concession to the *ḥukat ha-goy*, or gentile customs, it was considered anathema. Thus, when in 1604 an attempt was made by Leon Modena to introduce art music into the synagogue in Ferrara, an irate objector, Moses Coimbran, protested in these words, as reported by Modena:[25] "Outside and on the streets he spoke out, saying we sinned to our Lord God, and how is it possible for scholars whose task it is to guide others in preserving tradition to commit this offense openly and publicly. 'How can we sing the song of the Lord in a foreign land?' the scriptural passage goes [Ps. 137:4], and in the writings of our learned sages one finds a prohibition against doing so ever since the Destruction [of the Temple]. These are the things he goes around saying until he turned against us some of the unknowing: they speak of us arrogantly and believe we have transgressed customs and changed laws."

The ineluctably broader frame that the Jew Rossi would have conceived of for his conceptions of art music can be explained by his repeated encounters with Christians in the courts and private residences; by the continual pressure to which he was subjected, in performing his duties for his Christian patrons, to comply with "gentile customs," if not outwardly to convert to Christianity; by his participation, along with his fellow Jews, in performances of the Jewish theater, which forcibly brought the Jewish community into contact with Italian literary and theatrical fashions; and within the Jewish community, by his attempt to reconcile outside influences with "Jewish customs" by drawing them, syncretistically, into an amalgam, be it in his modus vivendi or in the character of his works. As a minority among the Christians, the Jewish community drew doubly from Jewish tradition and Italo-Christian modes of thought for an expanded conception of its own identity: Jews they were indeed, yet often familiar with the ways and cultural artifacts of their neighbors and versed in their sciences.[26]

The contexts are as many as the breadth and depth of the subject, here Salamone Rossi in his various sociocultural projections. They may be reduced, for present purposes, by associating them with key words in the title, each of which implies a countertype: thus, *ebreo*, in contrast to non-*ebreo*, namely, Gentile; a "Renaissance musician," and the "Renaissance" music he practices, in contrast to a medieval or baroque musician and his specifically medieval or baroque music; a "late" Renaissance musician, in contrast to an early one; a "Jewish musician," in contrast to a gentile one, or within the Jewish sphere, in contrast to a Jewish poet, actor, or dancer; and since the term *ebreo* obviously points to geographical provenance, namely, Jews in Italy, Jewish and non-Jewish Renaissance musicians and their music in Italy, in contrast to Jewish and non-Jewish Renaissance musicians and their music elsewhere (France, Holland, Germany). Thus formulated, the contexts embody the various elements, already signaled, of "space," "time," and "number." Yet as clear from their nature as composites, they are riddled with discrepancies and inconsistencies. Michel Foucault speaks of "discontinuities, ruptures, gaps" in the transmission of knowledge within defined categories. Consequently, the contexts are permeable and impermanent, and the data they comprehend are liable to varied interpretation, as would be expected from the labile conceptions that underlie the "human sciences."[27] Contradiction is of their essence.

Rather than clarify the lineaments of Rossi's biography and works, I have chosen in the present report to problematize them. I could have drawn up a fixed number of categories for reviewing the material. My original intention was, in fact, to define three such categories, namely, social, artistic, and receptive, with at least three subsets for each: for social, the collocation of Rossi within his family, his community, and non-Jewish circles; for artistic, the discussion of his vocal music, his instrumental works, and his Hebrew *Songs*; for receptive, the diffusion of his works over Italy, their appearance in transalpine anthologies, and the image of Rossi and his music drawn in later times. But it soon became apparent that none of the categories could be sustained in its integrality; in effect, their status was as arbitrary constructs that form the upper stories, as it were, of an edifice with a rather fractured infrastructure.

Uncertainty prevails within any of the categories precisely because they are ad hoc constructs. The conflicting epitaphs were meant to demonstrate the necessity "to frame the discourse" as a didactic expedient for structuring and elucidating content, yet, at the same time, to modify the explication once the "frame of things" became "disjointed." Any retracing of frames can only have adverse effects on the delineation of a "world," or unitive view. "Both the worlds" can be regarded as a metonym for the dichotomy that subtends Rossi's biography and works: in pondering his activities and his music, the observer clearly fluctuates between the way Rossi, as a Jew, sees himself and the way the Christian must have seen him. Not single, but split, or "disjoined" contexts seem to provide the framework for a more realistic depiction of how

Rossi functioned as a Jewish, yet, contrarily, Renaissance musician. The discussion centers, accordingly, on Rossi in his peregrinations within and between worlds.

Rossi as a Jew among Jews

Nothing is known of Rossi's father beyond his name, Bonaiuto (Azariah),[28] not to be confused with that of the renowned scholar Azariah de' Rossi (d. 1578). His sister Europa and brother Emanuele (Menaḥem) are recorded in a sparse number of documents. Like Salamone, Europa engaged in music, at least in her early years. She is listed, along with him, on court rolls from 1589 and 1592, and seems to have performed as the eponymous Europa in the *intermedio* by Chiabrera, *Il ratto di Europa*, staged as part of the festivities for the nuptials of Francesco Gonzaga and Margherita of Savoy in 1608. The chronicler Federico Follino raved over her performance, describing it as that of "a woman understanding music to perfection" and "singing, to the listeners' great delight and their greater wonder, in a most delicate and sweet-sounding voice . . . So delightfully did she modulate her mournful tones that the listeners shed tears of compassion."[29] What happened to Europa in subsequent years is uncertain: after marrying her cousin David, son of Elisha de' Rossi, to whom she bore at least two sons, one of whom (Angelo, or Mordecai) was hired as a musician at the court of Savoy, she probably settled into the routine of wife- and motherhood, under pressure of her family, or the community, to conduct herself, as a Jewish woman was usually expected, with greater propriety. One can only speculate on this and other matters, such as how the two Rossi musicians were regarded by parents and relatives: pride in them must have alternated with occasional embarrassment over their flamboyant lifestyle.

Rossi appears to have used his connections at court to improve his family's situation. Emanuele, whose name figures along with his brother's in 1605 on two lists of participants in the Jewish theater,[30] received certain privileges after Salamone's intervention with the authorities. In 1602, for example, Salamone asked Duke Vincenzo to grant Emanuele the right to exact income on registering, for the ducal records, the formation or dissolution of commercial partnerships. Until then, the task had been rather indifferently discharged by Lazzaro d'Italia, and Salamone sought to wrest it from him to his brother's advantage. We read, in a decree concerning the "exaction, by Emanuele Rossi, of moneys for partnerships," that inasmuch as the duke wished "to show Salamone Rossi *ebreo* some sign of gratitude for services that he, with utmost diligence, rendered over many years and continues to render us, we have resolved to confer the duties once assigned to Lazzaro d'Italia, likewise *ebreo*, who, because of his delinquencies, has proved unworthy of their execution, on the person of Emanuele, the said Salamone's brother, in whose faith and diligence we place our confidence."[31]

It is not clear whether Salamone acted out of filial instinct or was motivated by self-interest. He himself was involved in some of Emanuele's business affairs; and any improvement in Emanuele's pecuniary state would obviously reflect in his own. In 1606, Salamone renewed his appeal in a second letter to the duke, for Lazzaro appears, in the meantime, to have schemed to regain his privileges, which prevented the brothers from "the fulfillment of *our* office." Emanuele was sent to the duke, we are told, to "bring to his attention that the service [Salamone] rendered over the course of so many years does not include having such an office removed from *us* for the benefit of a Lazzaro d'Italia whose character is so well known to everyone."[32]

Rossi as "businessman": that is a new side to his biography. Until now, it has been thought that Rossi earned his livelihood from his salary at the Mantuan court, and since the salary was, by comparison with that of other musicians in its ranks, rather small, Rossi emerged as a "poor" musician, "poor" in the double sense of penniless and pitiable.[33] Such a view corresponds to the "lachrymose" conception of Jewish history, in most accounts, as a series of trials and tribulations—Joseph ha-Kohen (d. 1578) established an early precedent in his *'Emeq habakha.*[34] But there is nothing in Rossi's biography to support such a view, except perhaps for his sometimes pathetic attempt, as will be seen below, to win the attention or sympathy of his Christian patrons or to ward off the criticism of his detractors.

In addition to profits from business ventures with his brother, Rossi earned money on the side from a small tax-collecting franchise: in 1621, the dancer and apostate Giovanni Battista Perfetti leased him the right to proceeds from the sale of pledges, that is, items pawned in exchange for loans from Jewish banks.[35] The terms of the agreement stipulated that, in return, Rossi would, for each of the next six years, pay Perfetti an annuity of two hundred scudi and sell him twelve fat geese. Since the scudo came to about six times the lira,[36] Rossi, from 1622 on, was paying Perfetti some 1,200 lire a year.

Twelve hundred lire is a considerable sum of money for a musician whose annual wages were set at 156 and, starting around 1622, at 383.[37] The revenues on the privilege must have been sufficient to leave him enough, after compensating Perfetti, to score a profit. Rossi needed money to cover the cost, in part or in full, of his own publications. He needed it to support a family, assuming he had one—there is no information on his wife or children beyond a vague reference to his "heirs," who were to enjoy the income, after his death, on the sale of his Hebrew collection.[38] All in all, Rossi's financial state is indeterminate, and we do not know the degree to which he was remunerated for his efforts by the dedicatees of his thirteen collections. Rossi could have been "poor," but it is more likely that he was often just strapped for funds.

Rossi's situation within the community can only be conjectured. By "community," we are talking about some 2,325 Jews living in the city of Mantua out of a total population of fifty thousand, according to a census taken in 1612.[39] True, Rossi was its most distinguished musician, and his service for the court vicariously brought honor on his Jewish brethren. But just as the Jewish community differed from the Christian majority, so Rossi, because of his non-Jewish connections, differed from the Jewish majority. To the general socioeconomic plight of the community,[40] one might add further restrictions on clothing and movement, which, in the case of Rossi, seem to have been removed. In short, Rossi enjoyed privileges denied his coreligionists.

In a pragmatic published by the Jewish community in 1619, Rossi and the physician David Portaleone were released from observing the regulations on clothing;[41] and for his many years of service, he was exempted, by ducal decree, from wearing a badge. He might have requested an exemption in the 1590s, but the first notice of his having received one comes in a ducal decree from 1606. There Duke Vincenzo, in recognition of Rossi's faithful attendance "over many years" and his "musical talents and playing," conceded the composer "the free and unrestricted privilege to move about the city and its outer precincts without wearing the customary yellow (or orange) badge around his hat or beret."[42] In renewing the dispensation in 1612, Duke Francesco added that he does so for Rossi's years of service not only to his father, but "at the same time to us."[43] The badge was shameful to those Jews who, in their activities, were in close touch with Christians, as were Rossi and others attending them as musicians, actors, physicians, middlemen, and loan bankers. At the same time, it created a distinction between the privileged and underprivileged; and Rossi must have been viewed with a jaundiced eye by those among the Jews who coveted his gains.

Like other "privileged" Jews, Rossi occupied the unenviable position of being considered a Jew by his Christian employers, yet probably being suspected of a contaminated, that is, overly liberal, Judaism by his fellows. He could choose from two alternatives: convert to Christianity, so as to remove the blight of his Jewish identity in consorting with Christians; or stay and solidify his position within the Jewish fold. By choosing not to escape, but to emphasize his Judaism, he made his life no easier outside or inside the community: in the courts, he was subject to the usual backbiting reserved for Jews, but he held his ground; in the community, he must have been tested, by some, for his sincerity. To remove any doubts that he was "slipping," he probably lent the community his services by representing its interests, whenever he could, before the authorities, and by providing compositions and overseeing their performance whenever art music was requested: for weddings, circumcisions, the inauguration of Torah scrolls, Purim festivities, special celebrations within confraternities. We know nothing about his participation in such activities, but it may be inferred from the little we know of the activities themselves. We are better, though still meagerly, informed about his participation in the Jewish theater, which, upon ducal command, annually prepared one or two plays with musical *intermedi*;[44] unfortunately, none of the relevant documents indicates what Rossi precisely did.[45] Since the Jews were expected to act, sing, and play, it may be assumed that their leading musician, Salamone Rossi, contributed by writing vocal and instrumental works, rehearsing them, and, together with others, playing or even singing them.

It was in his Hebrew collection that Rossi, most demonstratively, signaled his allegiance to his people. His intentions were good: after having devoted his energies for so many years to secular vocal music and instrumental works, the composer decided, probably after 1612, to try his hand at writing Hebrew songs. He describes them, in his own dedication to their collection, as "new songs [*zemirot*] that I devised through 'counterpoint' [*seder*]." Though attempts were made at introducing art music into the synagogue, in various communities, from the early seventeenth century on, they seem to have been sporadic: the reports on them are too vague to give us an idea of their content, and no particular works have survived.[46] Rossi's thirty-three *Songs*, for diverse ensembles, are not only the earliest of their kind, but they constitute the first collection of Hebrew polyphonic songs to be printed.

Good intentions are one thing; the status of art music in the synagogue is another. The prayer services made no accommodation for art music as a supplement to or replacement of the traditional melodies for reading Scripture, reciting prayers, and chanting *piyyuṭim*. Rossi's aim was indeed to have his works "for thanking God and singing [*lezammer*] to His exalted name on all sacred occasions" performed in prayer services, particularly on Sabbaths and festivals,[47] yet by introducing art music into the synagogue, the composer was asking for trouble. In matters of ritual, pressure was brought to stay within the bounds of accepted tradition; and by infiltrating Christian-style works into Jewish ceremonial functions, Rossi not only exceeded the bounds, but seemed to be acting against his own interests, which were, to repeat, to demonstrate an untainted Judaism. He is said, by Leon Modena, to have "worked and labored to add from his secular to his sacred works,"[48] "secular" betokening the influence of "gentile [musical] customs." As happened previously in Ferrara, when art music met with opposition from the traditionalists, it was to be expected that Rossi's sacred, though secular, ergo Christian-sounding Hebrew works would renew their hostility. Modena anticipated as much, recalling the earlier episode in his foreword to the collection. To answer prospective objections, he appended the same responsum he wrote, at the time, on the viability of art music in the synagogue. Thus he reports:

> It could be that among the exiled there is one of those sanctimonious persons who eliminate anything new or any example of learning in which they have no part and that he may wish to prohibit this [new] work [of Rossi's *Songs*] because of what he learned, though inexactly. In order to remove any resentment from a stubborn heart, I decided to reproduce here in print what I wrote in an answer to a question eighteen years ago—I was then a teacher of Torah in the holy community of Ferrara (may God protect it!)—with the intent of sealing the mouth of someone speaking nonsense about this matter, and all the learned men of Venice at that time signed it.[49]

To palliate the protests of those same "sanctimonious persons," Rossi was clearly in need of a patron. He found him in Moses Sullam, a "courageous, versatile man, in whom learning and greatness are contained,"[50] a leader of the Jewish community, respected by all. Sullam encouraged the composer to overcome the obstacles in the way of contriving Hebrew songs, "obstacles" because it was no easy task to write effectively to Hebrew words, with their accentual and syntactic peculiarities, after having worked for so long with Italian. "How many times did I toil, at your command," so Rossi declares, "until I was satisfied, ordering my songs with joyful lips."[51] Sullam had his own private synagogue,[52] and it was there that Rossi probably first tried out the songs, to gauge the reaction of singers and listeners to their content before proceeding to their publication. His efforts in composing them were favorably received. "When people sang them," Modena reports, "they were delighted with their many good qualities. The listeners, too, were radiant, each of them finding it pleasant to hear them and wishing to hear the remainder."[53] Rossi must have taken heart from these, and other "friends," to whom vague reference is made in the prefatory matter, and at their behest he pushed his efforts through to their conclusion, or so one might deduce from Modena's report: "I, too, from the time I numbered among his *friends*, entreated him earnestly and pleaded with him until the enterprise succeeded, thanks to the Creator of all, and he reached that crucial stage I hoped he would with *us* here: he came and consented to discharge his vow to print as he had promised" (emphasis added).[54]

But it was not enough to have the influential Sullam, "highly successful and well known in Mantua,"[55] behind him. Rossi needed rabbinical support, and here Modena, who appears to have followed the progress of the collection from its inception, rushed to his defense. The idea of such a collection might even have originated with Modena, who turned to Rossi as the man most capable of bringing it to fruition. For Modena, the collection marked the resuscitation of Hebrew art music after its demise during the Exile. Modena exalted the composer, ascertaining his historical importance in what he described as a Jewish musical renascence. He wrote that "the events of our foreign dwellings and of our restless runnings are dispersed over the lands, and the vicissitudes of life abroad were enough to make [the Hebrews] forget all knowledge and lose all intellect."[56] Yet what was lost has now been recovered. "Let them praise the name of the Lord, for Solomon [= Salamone] alone is exalted nowadays in this wisdom. He not only is wiser than any man of our nation, but may be likened and compared to many famous persons, in yesteryear, among the families of the earth."[57] Rossi thus restored the once glorious music heard in the Temple. With one modification, however, and this to comply with synagogue practice: no instruments were specified.[58] Or at least none were used when the *Songs* were performed in prayer services (whether they were excluded from their performance under non-liturgical circumstances is another matter).

Modena was entrusted with preparing the works for the printer and with their proofreading, as least as far as the Hebrew is concerned (Rossi asked him "to prevent any mishap from coming to the composition, to prepare it [for typesetting], embellish it, proofread it and look out for typographical errors and defects");[59] he composed a foreword and one or possibly all three of the dedicatory poems in the introductory matter; he included, as mentioned, the responsum from 1605, together with its statements of approval by five Venetian rabbis.[60] Other signatories figure at the end of the copyright privilege, issued in 1622.[61] The collection went out into the world, then, with as much conceptual defense and rabbinical sanction as any composer could ever hope to receive.

The major problem for Rossi and Modena was to bridge the gap between contemporary art music and music as practiced in the synagogue. Its solution was to force an equation of art music with Hebrew music in the Temple. To this end, Modena resorted to a clever remark of Immanuel Haromi (d. 1335), who, after a scriptural verse, wrote: "What will the science of music [*niggun*] say to others? 'I was stolen, yes stolen from the land of the Hebrews' [Gen. 40:15]."[62] If the Christians "stole" their music from the Hebrews, who, during their medieval wanderings, forgot their erstwhile musical knowledge, then by cultivating art music in the early seventeenth century, the Jews in a sense recuperated what was theirs to start with. In short, the only thing that separates art music of the Jews from that of the Christians is, it would seem, its language: Hebrew. In *Shilṭei hagibborim* (1612), a massive treatise on the architecture and ritual of the ancient Temple, the author, Abraham Portaleone, took off from the premise that present-day art music was equivalent to music in the Temple; he then proceeded to describe the forms and instruments of music in the Temple by analogy to current practice.[63]

True, there were other things, beyond Hebrew, that distinguished the Hebrew art music of Rossi from the Italian or Latin art music of the Gentiles. The texts themselves, be they Hebrew prayers or *piyyuṭim*; their place in the synagogue services or in the ritual of the confraternities; particular themes in them running as a leitmotif through Hebrew literature, from the yearning for return and redemption to the steadfast belief in God's justice and mercy. Rossi could have strengthened the idiosyncrasy of Hebrew art music by drawing on melodies or prayer formulas used in the synagogue, but, as far as can be determined, he did not. His sacred music was both old, in the sense that it connected, in his mind, with an ancient tradition, and new, in the sense that it represented a form of composition that, for his Jewish contemporaries, was *ḥadasha ba'arets* ("something new in the Land"; Jer. 31:22), as his Hebrew collection was advertised in its title. Those who rejected the "new" were insufficiently informed about its links with the old. That is what Modena meant when he spoke about "those sanctimonious persons who eliminate anything new," though they could not fall back on rabbinic tradition, as he demonstrated in his responsum, to warrant a prohibition of art music in the synagogue. What each of them learned, therefore, was "inexact." These same persons failed to realize that after art music had fallen into oblivion among the Jews, Rossi, to their greater glory, "restored its crown to its original state as in the days of Levi's sons on the platforms."[64]

But Rossi might have had other things in mind when he composed his Hebrew art music. Christians were familiar with Jewish music from their visits to the synagogues. They were shocked by what they heard, as we learn from a report of Gregorio Leti on Jewish prayer services in Rome: "No sooner do [the Jews] enter their sanctuary than they begin to shout with angry voices, shaking their heads back and forth to one another, making certain terribly ridiculous gestures, only to continue, sitting down, with these same shouts, which 'beautiful' music lasts until their rabbi begins his sermon in Italian, though reciting the portions from Scripture in Hebrew."[65]

Even Leon Modena, who himself officiated as cantor at the Scuola Italiana in Venice, had little positive to say about the performance of music in the synagogue. He rebuked the cantors for being so negligent as to "bray like asses" or "shout to the God of our fathers as a dog and a crow."[66] Oh, how the Jews are fallen, for "we were once masters of music in our prayers and our praises, now only to become a laughingstock to the nations, for them to say that no longer is science in our midst."[67] Modena seems to be describing synagogue song as he feared it would be perceived by a Christian. There is little difference, in substance, between his and Leti's remarks.

Both Modena and Rossi were concerned over how Christians would respond to Jewish music. They wanted to prove that whatever the Christians do, the Jews can do equally well. They may not be physically strong, Modena explains, but, in the "sciences" they are outstanding:

> No more will bitter words about the Hebrew people
> be uttered, in a voice of scorn, by the haughty.
> They will see that full understanding is as much a portion
> of theirs [the people's] as of others who flaunt it.
> Though weak in [dealing] blows, in sciences
> they [the people] are a hero, as strong as oaks.[68]

Rossi's *Songs of Solomon* might have been contrived not only to further the cause of Jewish music but also to revise its negative appraisal by Christians. The double motivation is latent in the introductory matter to the collection and in the music of the *Songs* proper. It was important to maintain, in composition as in performance, the kind of decorum to which the Christians were accustomed; to demonstrate competency—how to write properly, how to sing properly; to show the Jews and Christians alike that the Jews, in composing art music, could look back to and take pride in a venerable early tradition. Jews and Christians were equally familiar with the wonders of music in the ancient Temple from their readings of Scripture; but what they did not realize, and the *Songs* were meant to demonstrate, was that there was a "new" Solomon, no less wise, musically, than his legendary forebear. His works erected a bridge, in their conception and realization, between past and present; between the ancient Hebrews and the modern Jews; between Jews and Italians; between Jews and Gentiles. Once the connections were sensed, a new consciousness of the contingencies within the Judeo-Christian tradition would arise, with repercussions, so Modena augured, on the habitually pejorative opinion, among Christians, of the Jews and their abilities. In the meantime, it was important, one might say, "to open the eyes of the blind and unstop the ears of the deaf" (Isa. 35:5).

Rossi as a Jew among Gentiles

As a Jewish musician working for the Mantuan court, and competing for the favors its other musicians, all of them Christian, hoped to gain, it was only inevitable for Rossi to have been considered, by some, an intruder. His talents as composer and instrumentalist must have been so remarkable that the duke's decision to include and retain him in his employ, over the course of some forty years, from 1589 to (probably) 1628, overrode any objections to his Judaism. In his publications he was designated an *ebreo*, but the very fact that he published so widely, as already noted, shows that to a certain degree the quality of the music was more important than the identity of its composer; or perhaps it was the heteroclite identity of the composer that, from an economic standpoint, sold his music—there is always something fascinating about a pariah.

Still, in Rossi's dealings with the authorities, his Judaism must have been a bone of contention. For one thing, Rossi was not always available when needed. For another, he could not be expected, or would not have consented, to write music to texts with Christian content. We know from a letter of Claudio Monteverdi that the Sala degli Specchi in the ducal palace held concerts of chamber music on Friday evenings, although Rossi, who observed the Sabbath, would not have been present.[69] We know also that of the various composers to write music for *La Maddalena*, a "sacred representation," by Giovanni Battista Andreini, about the sins and penitence of Mary Magdalen, Rossi was the only one to be assigned, no doubt at his request, a secular poem.[70]

Rossi appears to have had cordial relations with Duke Vincenzo I, to whom he dedicated, moreover, two publications. In the first of them, from 1589, he refers to the duke as his "most revered patron" and to himself as the duke's "most humble and devoted servant";[71] in the second, from 1600, he supplemented the phrase "most revered patron" with "my natural lord," to whom he was indebted, he admits, for everything he knows.[72] Vincenzo was described by one contemporary Jewish annalist as a person "who favored the Jews and spoke kindly to them."[73] He probably encouraged Rossi as a fledgling composer, giving him commissions, or letting his works be heard, or providing him with teachers; not to speak of the services he expected of him, and probably appreciated for their quality, as an instrumentalist. While Vincenzo was liberal and prone to arranging splendid court festivities, with his death in 1612 his successors Francesco, Vincenzo's eldest son, and Ferdinando, his second son, were less sympathetic toward Jews and, operating under a worsening economy, tightened the purse strings. The years after 1612 were difficult ones for the Jewish community, and it is then that Rossi may have turned to composing his Hebrew works, perhaps to compensate for what he hoped to achieve, but did not, in courtly circles.

Francesco himself fanned the flames of animosity. Before entering office, he was known as a Jew hater—even the pope said so—and as likely to drive the Jews out of Mantua.[74] The prediction was partly accurate, for his first actions, upon becoming duke, were directed to imposing a more restrictive legislation on his Jewish subjects.[75] He was responsible for accelerating and completing the arrangements, begun by Vincenzo under order of the pope, though he dillydallied in their execution, for confining the Jews to a ghetto. Francesco is said to have been grave and reserved whereas Vincenzo was open and affable.[76] It is uncertain what Rossi's relations were with Francesco or Ferdinando. That Rossi dedicated none of his publications to them speaks for itself.

Jews were not liked, to say the obvious, and try as he might to disguise his Judaism, by special clothing permits or exemptions from displaying the yellow (or orange) badge, Rossi was subject to criticism, if not outward slander. He appeals to his dedicatees for their help. All in all, what he wanted, or so he implies, was for them to accept and approve his collections. He asks Duke Vincenzo to keep him "safe from the hands of detractors" by lending his "felicitous name" to book 1 of his madrigals (1600), which, "without such great support, would either soon fall into oblivion or, among the hands of such persons, be torn and wasted as if by raging dogs."[77] Felicita Gonzaga is entreated to "protect and defend" the madrigals in book 2 (1602), for "no slanderer or detractor would ever dare to censure something that is protected and favored by a lady of such great distinction."[78] Dedicating his fourth book of madrigals (1610) to Federico Rossi, the composer hoped that his name would be "an impenetrable shield for resisting the fierce darts of malevolent detractors," thus preventing the book's being "lacerated by a furious tooth."[79] The tide of criticism did not wane, for in his third book of instrumental works (1613) he petitions Don Ferrante Gonzaga "to defend" him from "slanderous and deprecating tongues."[80] It was imperative to demonstrate fidelity to his patrons, and Rossi craved signs of their esteem to show that he enjoyed their "favor and name"; or "to prove to the world his desire" to serve them; or "to become illustrious" by having their illustrious name apposed to his collections; or "to acquire greater fame and greater renown" by flaunting their support.[81]

Rossi was determined to make a name for himself in a non-Jewish environment. From his dedications it is clear that he tried, time and again, to supplement his courtly income by securing individual commissions. His situation seems to have been so hopeless, in fact, that he grabbed at every opportunity to win a new patron. In choosing his dedicatees, his first consideration was to remember some positive aspect of his dealings with them; his second one, to capitalize on a previous favor, thinking that by expressing his appreciation to the person who granted it other favors would be forthcoming. The extent of these so-called favors appears to have been no more, at times, than a friendly glance, a word of commendation or the mere physical presence of the would-be patron at a performance. Thus Rossi thanks Paolo Guglielmo Andreasi, count of Rhodes, for his benevolence, saying: "May Your Eminent Lordship accept these works [book 1 of his *sinfonie*, 1607] with the same affection you showed, at other times, by not despising them."[82] Here affection means only that the count condescended to listen to Rossi's works, on one or another occasion, without condemning them. The same may be said of other collections, such as the second book of *sinfonie* (1608), dedicated to the duke of Modena (in acknowledgment of "your usual kindness, with which I, at other times, have been favored beyond all my merits . . . for you showed that you were pleased, in days gone by, with my compositions"),[83] or the third book of his *sinfonie* (1613), dedicated, as noted, to Don Ferrante Gonzaga ("because, in days past, Your Excellency favored me, much to my pleasure, by listening to some of my compositions, and because it appeared to me at the time, so far as I could perceive, that you were somewhat satisfied with them").[84] At other times, the erstwhile favors bestowed on Rossi seem to have amounted to little more than having heard his music. We learn, from the dedication of his third book of madrigals (1603), that Don Alessandro Pico, Prince of Mirandola, "was so kind as to amuse himself, over the last few months, by hearing some of [Rossi's] rough madrigals."[85]

Whatever Rossi received from his patrons put him in their debt, or so at least the composer would have us believe ("Your Excellency bound me with such a bond of obligation," "your unusual kindness and infinite solicitude . . . for which I find myself, for a long time, obliged to you").[86] His bonds of obligation served him as a pretext for dedicating one or another collection to them. By so doing, he rendered thanks for favors received and, indirectly, though no less conspicuously, requested further assistance. Flattery, praise, gratitude: these were the means by which Rossi hoped to improve his situation, to win the goodwill and protection of his benefactors, to secure their bounty. Only once did Rossi actually come out and ask point-blank for employment: in his first book of *sinfonie* (1607), he urged Paolo Guglielmo Andreasi to keep in mind his declaration of being a "devoted servant" as reason enough for "employing [him] in [his] service."[87] Otherwise, the composer proceeded more discreetly, hoping that the presentation of his collections together with their effusive dedications would be adequate to fulfill his wishes. For Rossi, then, the appellation *patrono* designated persons who, having once granted favors, were being solicited for new ones. Whether or not they acceded to his petition does not seem to have changed their status as patrons, which for Rossi meant potential benefactors.

It is difficult to know how many of the dedications are sincere and how many are engineered. In his Hebrew collection, Rossi tells us how he chose Moses Sullam as the dedicatee. "I searched in my heart for the one ruler to whom I would turn, to place on his altar the offering of this thanksgiving. Then I lifted my eyes and saw that it would be better for me to show my affection to you, honored and important in Israel, than to anyone else,"[88] a decision that the composer justifies by citing the many favors he received, and continues to receive, from Sullam and his family.[89] Despite the rhetorical veneer, the tone is genuine. Yet when Rossi dedicates his four-voice madrigals to Prince Alfonso d'Este, he speaks in another language, long-winded, cloying, and sycophantic:

> My mind, particularly disposed to serving Your Highness forever, and your infinite kindness and sublimity have given me the courage not only to dedicate to you these few efforts of mine but also to make me hope, at the same time, to be able to see them, by means of your most felicitous name, consecrated to the immortality of your fame, resting assured that you will not disapprove of my receiving this favor of your kindness, which is to reveal to the world, with my meager demonstrations, the most ardent signs of my reverent devotion to Your Highness, whom I, in all humility, beseech, with deepest affection, to accept these trifling notes of mine, assuring that every wearisome undertaking is bound to become the lightest load for me, inasmuch as I am stirred by an immense desire to serve Your Highness.[90]

While in the previous dedication the composer thanks for what he received, now he begs for what he did not, but would like to, receive. He couches the dedication in the language customary in appeals of subordinates to superiors. This is not Rossi talking as he normally would—the contents are too cunningly fabricated.[91] Rather it is Rossi framing his thoughts after the conventions of panegyric rhetoric. Or it is Rossi the Jew going out of his way to conceal his Judaism by adopting the forms of speech on the tongue of cultivated Christians; or Rossi the Jew, because of his Judaism, pleading inordinate gratitude to his Christian patrons, in so obsequious a tone as to acknowledge, as Jews were expected to, his inferiority or mediocrity. We are grateful for the dedications, yet can only be irked by them: the true story of Rossi's relations with his "patrons" lies hidden behind their veil.

As said, Rossi did not do the one thing he could have done to solve his problems: apostatize. The pressure to do so must have been tremendous. One wonders, though, whether it really would have improved his lot. Mahieu le Juif, the thirteenth-century trouvère to whom reference was already made as an early Jewish art music composer, tells us that the reason for his conversion was to please a particular lady, for whose love he "abandoned his religion and his faith in God." Little did it help him, however, for she did not "requite" him for his "woes"; her heart was like "steel"; she "betrayed" him; she "made a fool" of him.[92] The minnesinger Süsskind of Trimberg (d. c. 1250) composed various lyrics in Middle High German, preserved, without music, in a fourteenth-century manuscript from Heidelberg.[93] He, too, seems to have converted, though he suffered from chronic poverty ("the rich man has flour, the poor one has ashes instead").[94] In the end, his patrons "separated him from their estate," whence he "fled the courts," only perhaps to return to his faith, though now "with a beard," "gray hair," after the "lifestyle of an old Jew,"[95] as he is depicted, in fact, in an illustration.[96] The convert Giovanni Maria *ebreo* achieved fame as a lutenist in Rome, where, until 1523, he was active under the popes Leo X, Adrian VI, and Clement VII. His fortunes eventually dwindled, and, according to Baldassare Castiglione, "the poor man did not even have enough for his evening meal."[97]

Closer to Rossi's time, and working at the Mantuan court, is the harpist Abramino dall'Arpa. His story is interesting because it illustrates the unrelenting pressure brought on him to convert and, at the same time, his apparent refusal to surrender to it. The documentation is sparse, yet revealing. In 1582 he and his son (Malachi?) were convened to meet with a "master of theology," but they did not show up; it turned out, after searching for them, that they were in Ferrara.[98] The authorities intensified their efforts. In June 1587 the singer Giovanni Andrea Robbiato, on the way back by coach to Mantua together with Abramino as his travel companion, is reported to have explained to him that the "Christian religion . . . was the best and the only one to be practiced, superseding what Jews profess," but Abramino "did not agree, even though he appeared to listen."[99] After arriving in Mantua, Robbiato took Abramino to the church of Santa Barbara to witness, from the organ loft, the baptism of the duke's grandson, and "Abramino appeared to be pleased with the ceremonies."[100] A monk clarified to him "the substance of the said sacrament of the Holy Baptism, explaining it by comparison with circumcision," yet Abramino remained silent.[101] Rumors of the incident immediately spread to the Jewish community, and in the evening Abramino's uncle [Sansone] together with the rabbi Judah Moscato came to talk sense into him[102] (Robbiato "approached to hear what they were saying, but they spoke Hebrew to keep him from understanding them").[103] On the following day, Abramino was asked whether "he would become a Christian, to which he answered that he did not know, though believed he was more inclined to than not."[104]

The Christians kept up their coercive endeavor, while at the same time the Jews urged Abramino to "continue in the Hebrew faith and not give ear to words spoken to him about becoming a Christian."[105] Infuriated, Duke Guglielmo ordered Abramino and the interfering Jews to be arrested and separately examined to determine once and for all what the musician's intentions were.[106] Did Abramino yield to the pressure? Apparently not, for five years later (1593, the last date we have for him) he is addressed as *ebreo*.[107]

It seems likely that similar pressure was brought on Rossi. Obviously, he resisted. Yet he did not resist the more insidious effects wrought by the secularization of his musical art—"insidious" by halakhic standards, and innocuous, to be sure, by others: his Italian vocal and his instrumental works follow the conventions of late Renaissance composition, as practiced by Christians. Or do they? Is there anything about his works that, despite their otherwise Renaissance patina, might be described as "Jewish"? A difficult question, because it begs the question "what is musically Jewish?" Some observations, or perhaps speculations, might be entertained nevertheless.

Italian vocal music as a locus for Jewishness? Perhaps it may be detected in the way Rossi fits his music to the words. For Rossi, music is ever subservient to the structural and affective demands of the text. In this, he is both traditional and advanced: traditional, in that the text had always seemed to dominate in humanistic musical thought;[108] advanced, in that the text, as Monteverdi emphasized by word and example,[109] was to play a major role in shaping music in the inchoate baroque era. But Rossi's way of having the text dominate the music is for the music not to simulate words by "madrigalisms," whereby words are portrayed by seemingly analogous music (ascent by rising figures, flight by quick rhythms, and so forth), but rather to highlight words through a fairly plain, unobtrusive setting. Such an approach might parallel that familiar from synagogue chant, in particular the cantillation of Scriptures, where melodies did not compete with the text, but were generally molded to their accents and syntax. Similarly, the unpretentious melodies employed in reciting prayers served largely for textual inflection and articulation. So what is Italian? What is Jewish? Other composers of Rossi's time, such as Giovanni Giacomo Gastoldi, in his secular and sacred vocal works, or again Monteverdi, in his earlier books of madrigals, demonstrated an equally conservative approach to handling text. Yet, with Rossi, one wonders whether the tendency to model the music after the prosodic rather than semantic features of the words might not have been reinforced by what he knew of synagogue chant. Only once, toward the end of his career, did he allow the music to "compete" with the text in importance and thereby undermine its hegemony. I am referring to his *Madrigaletti* for two voices and basso continuo, from 1628. But in this final collection, Rossi may have been influenced by certain liberties he took in his instrumental music or could have been under strain to adapt to current fashions. It is to his instrumental works and to these so-called fashions that I now turn.

As a parallel question to the one raised about Rossi's Italian music, one might ask: Is there anything particularly Jewish about his instrumental works? Instrumental music did not win the approval of the Rabbis, for it escaped the control of words and was susceptible to being indecorously used in banqueting and carousing. Moreover, with the destruction of the Temple it was patently wrong, so the Rabbis maintained, to play instruments until such time as they could be reinstated with the return to Zion.[110] Yet instrumental music did undergo a renovation, as it were, in later Jewish writings, after the example of its designation, in Scriptures, as an expedient for spiritual elevation (Elisha is said to have requested a minstrel, "and when the minstrel played the power of the Lord came upon him"; 2 Kings. 3:15). Judah Moscato, one of Mantua's outstanding rabbis, considered music an "intervallic" science: he says nothing of words; rather, his concern is with the pneumatic implications of sounds per se, as, for example the octave, which for him represented perfection, or the godhead (the numerical ratio of the octave is 2:1).[111]

Instrumental music, for Rossi, seems to have been a natural vehicle of expression. He was not hampered by the semantic restrictions of words, hence did not have to fear the animadversions of those who evaluated his works by the measuring rod of their verbal "intelligibility"; he could give free rein to his talents as composer and performer, forging his works as he so desired. Not only that, but through instrumental music Rossi seems to have established his reputation at the court. He may have taken advantage of his special status as practically the only composer of instrumental music in Mantua—none of the leading figures on the court rolls published instrumental music collections, but Rossi did four—to emphasize his own individuality.

Instrumental music thus played a major role in Rossi's individuation as both a person and a composer. It was a medium in which he did not have to compete with others for being favored. Though instrumental music was not part of the Jewish synagogue tradition, it could be countenanced, hence justified, by Rossi precisely because he practiced it "outside" the synagogue. It allowed him to underscore the "primacy" of music without being subject to textual considerations in its formation; to compose without having to fret over secular or pagan words; to ply his materials according to the logic inherent in organizing music as purely an *art sonore* (intervals, chords, cadences, the melodic and rhythmic shaping of motives, sectional articulation, rhythmic accents, contrapuntal coherence); to give vent to his own ideas and inclinations; and to identify in his imagination, should he want to, with David playing his lyre or with the Levite instrumentalists in the Temple.

It was in his third collection of instrumental music, from 1613, that Rossi developed a more demanding—indeed, virtuoso—mode of expression. Does the change in style have anything to do with his status at the court? Was his music considered old-fashioned, and did he attempt to refurbish it to win greater favor? The year 1612 marked a turning point in the fortunes of the Jews in Mantua. With the death of Vincenzo, Francesco came to power, and there was a hardening of policy toward his Jewish subjects: they were confined to the ghetto; anti-Jewish sentiments increased and with them, greater oppression and even physical violence. There are telling signs of a "crisis" in Rossi's development: from 1611 to 1622, the composer ceased to publish vocal music, perhaps because his Italian works might have been regarded as overly conservative by comparison with those of others;[112] and when he did renew his vocal publications in 1622, with a fifth, and last book of five-voice madrigals, of which only the basso continuo part is extant, it is clear from the same part that the missing voices must have been written in a novel style, more dramatic and technically more challenging than the music of his previous collections.

Rossi opened his third book of instrumental works with a sonata in a "modern" vein (*sonata prima alla moderna*), which he follows up with similarly contrived works. His new approach to instrumental writing might have directed him, as mentioned above, to essay a new approach to vocal writing: the change is particularly noticeable in his last collection, the *madrigaletti*, which, in their concertato style, are truly modern. Whether these novel instrumental and vocal works improved Rossi's image at the court cannot be said. Perhaps they did, though as evidence to the contrary it might be recalled that in the years after 1613 Rossi turned his attention to composing Hebrew works. There he was under no pressure to be "modern"; rather, the very notion of writing music to Hebrew according to the conventions of art music was, for a Jewish audience, itself modern. Perhaps the Hebrew works were a way of counterbalancing his dwindling popularity at the court; perhaps they were an excuse for keeping busy musically until rehabilitating himself, in courtly circles, as a composer to be reckoned with in writing in an advanced Italian vocal style; perhaps they helped him consolidate his position within the Jewish community, dispelling any suspicion of an equivocal Judaism; or perhaps they served as a panacea for whatever ills he suffered, as a Jew, in his dealings with Christians. Each of these depends on the particular way Rossi's situation is framed.

Conclusions

Like consciously Jewish musicians in later times (for example, Ernest Bloch, Darius Milhaud, Leonard Bernstein), Rossi confronted the problems, in his own way, of preserving his Jewish identity in a non-Jewish ambience and of communicating, as a Jew, with Jews and Christians in such a manner as to be understood and esteemed by both. His solutions, biographically and artistically, were individual, but by illustrating the *paradoxe juif* they exemplify the dynamic and complexity of Judeo-Christian relations at large. There is a broad sociocultural lesson to be learned from the way Rossi, doubtless more by instinct than by intent, accommodated to his surroundings.

Rossi, the man and musician, had his Jewish and Hebrew sides, as is evident from his connections with his family and with Jews and their institutions in Mantua and Venice, to which one should add his spiritual commitment to the Hebrew tradition as a catalyst for his Hebrew works. He participated in productions of the Jewish theatrical troupe and was probably called upon to prepare or perform music for celebrations within the Jewish community; he might have been affiliated with one or more synagogues and perhaps confraternities in and even beyond Mantua.

At the same time, Rossi had his Mantuan and Italian sides. He was heavily involved in music-making for the Gonzagas and was occasionally invited to entertain guests at other courts (Mirandola, possibly Modena). He came into contact with the greater and lesser non-Jewish musicians who worked in or passed through Mantua, joining or even collaborating with them in composing, rehearsing, and often performing vocal and instrumental music for courtly or private entertainments. He met with dukes, princes, and other worthies, sometimes receiving, though probably more often soliciting, commissions from them.

The outward dichotomy between Jewish and non-Jewish influences and motivations cuts through his production. Rossi supplied Hebrew compositions for services in the synagogue and possibly events in the community; he related to these compositions, so he intimated in the dedication to the published collection, as different from his Italian ones ("the Lord has been a support for me and He put new songs in my mouth");[113] he expended special efforts, as reported above, in their elaboration. He knew of an ancient Hebrew musical practice that flourished in the Temple, only to decline thereafter in the Exile; and he perceived himself, or at least was perceived by others, as playing a major role in its revival. Leon Modena opined that by writing Hebrew music, Rossi linked with an indigenous, though distant, tradition and perpetuated it into the future. "I am convinced," he wrote, "that from the day this collection is published, those who learn [the science of music] will multiply in Israel in order to sing to the magnificence of our God by using [the *Songs*] and others like them."[114] But before, during, and after pursuing his Hebrew inclinations, Rossi operated, with no less enthusiasm, within the constraints of an ongoing Italian musical tradition.

Rossi's Hebrew *Songs* thus form the obverse side of a repertory that otherwise consists of works having historically and culturally different origins. His *canzonette* and madrigals are firmly rooted in Italian practice, as are his instrumental *canzoni*, dances, *sinfonie*, and sonatas. Here and there, Rossi innovated within this practice, especially in his *sinfonie* and sonatas. Yet in the main, he shaped the ideas of his non-Jewish works according to an inherently Italian, non-Jewish tradition of vocal and instrumental music.

What the Jewish and non-Jewish sides of Rossi's repertory have in common resides perhaps in their underlying differentiation into *antico* and *moderno*. It is with the *antico* and *moderno* as two contrasting, yet complementary frames for the placement and assessment of his works that I shall conclude this discussion. The frames will first be focused, then blurred by shifting their content according to changing perspectives.

The *antico* in Jewish music is represented by its practice in the ancient Temple and, from the Middle Ages on, by the cantillation of Scriptures and intonation of prayers in the synagogue. In effect, there was no *moderno* in Jewish music until Salamone Rossi composed his *Songs*, following the example possibly, though not necessarily, of others who, from the early seventeenth century, strove with limited success to introduce part music into prayer services. I say "part music" because as a term it is less committal than "polyphony": part music is basically any music in parts, that is, different voices, whereas polyphony conjures up an image of learned counterpoint. The Jews might have practiced some kind of "part music" in the early seventeenth century, but whether it complied with the rules of counterpoint cannot be determined: "part music" has the advantage of suggesting such a possibility without imposing it. Be that as it may, Rossi's *Songs*—regarded, by reason of their artful composition, as different from anything known among the Jews until their time, so Modena insisted—were perceived by some, it would seem, not as modern, but as foreign; with Rossi, then, "part music" denotes "polyphony" proper. To justify their novelty, they were explained, again by Modena, as effecting a reconstitution of the mythically glorious Hebrew music that thrived in the Temple; the biblical *antico* thus became a conceptual source for Rossi's *moderno.*

The same split into *antico* and *moderno* may be detected in Rossi's non-Jewish works. Stylistically, his *canzonette* and four- and five-voice madrigals, as well as his dances, *canzoni,* and certain *sinfonie,* seem to exemplify a *prima pratica,* while his *madrigaletti* and sonatas, along with other *sinfonie,* do a *seconda.* It was Monteverdi who distinguished between works of the *prima pratica* as "old" and those of the *seconda* as "new."[115] Monteverdi's views may be questioned, but there is no denying that Rossi's repertory displays markedly contrasting stylistic tendencies, of ostensibly "older" and "newer" origin.

The division into *antico* and *moderno* might apply, more generally, to the division of Rossi's *oeuvre* into vocal and instrumental works. The madrigals, thereby, are "old"; many *sinfonie* and the sonatas, "new." Yet on another level, the same distinction can be reversed: the madrigals are "new" because they are written to lyrics of the latest poets and, historically, because madrigals that form the mainstay of Italian secular music in the sixteenth century continue to be cultivated well into the second decade of the seventeenth; and *sinfonie* and sonatas are "old" because they can be traced to earlier forms of composition, among them sixteenth-century *canzoni.*

On still another level, it is difficult to sustain the differentiation between Italian and Jewish sides of the repertory as illustrated by secular vocal and instrumental compositions versus Hebrew ones. Other principles might be invoked as causal explanations for Rossi's non-Jewish works. His Italian vocal ones seem to be posited on "the word" as the determining factor of their composition. Words, of course, can be observed in widely contrasting ways, and Monteverdi's often highly dramatic madrigals from his later books are musically no less indebted to their verbal component than the much simpler, sometimes narrative, madrigals of his earlier ones. The same holds for Rossi's later *madrigaletti,* so different from his madrigals, yet no less verbally conditioned in their music.

Regard for the text usually translates, in his Italian works, into a relatively restrained melodic and rhythmic style, with emphasis on clear delivery and articulation of words and their syntactic units. Rossi might, in composition, have been bound to "the word" by the force of the Hebrew *verbum sacrum*. But he could equally have been word-conscious from humanistic currents in sixteenth- and seventeenth-century musical thought. The preeminence of the word, at any rate, narrows the distinction between whatever might be schematized as Hebrew and Italian forms of composition: they are at one in Rossi's conceptions and their realization.

Rossi's instrumental works may be posited on an opposite principle, the absence of words, with its implications for an inevitably distinctive mode of writing. Here the composer was freer to indulge his own preferences. Rossi was doubtless a virtuoso violinist, and in his instrumental music he did eventually give vent to his soloist inclinations. The result, all in all, was something quite different from his vocal music. Released from the constraints of words, Rossi was at liberty to impose his own ideas, as determined by his stylistic biases and performing capacities. While Rossi drew from verbal stimuli for his vocal works, he drew from himself for many of his instrumental ones: he is the measure of their form and content. In this, however, he is a man of his times, which, as we know, witnessed the gradual rise of the soloist in vocal and instrumental music. If Rossi did not follow through in his vocal works, it is because he worked in genres that were not particularly susceptible to soloistic penetration; the *canzonetta* and choral madrigal are not the habitat of the emerging soloist, whereas monody and dramatic music, which Rossi neglected, very much are.

Rossi could, in his mind, invoke the precedent of instrumental music among the ancient Hebrews; its wonders were common knowledge. Judah Moscato, as said, epitomized instrumental music as an ideal vehicle for transmitting divine content (consonance, proportion, joy). At root, then, instrumental music is very much part of an indigenous Hebrew tradition. For Rossi, there was no problem in accepting it, unlike many of the Rabbis who warned against it as unsuited to a people in mourning over the destruction of the Temple.

Yet there are forces tugging in the opposite direction, not toward the separation of the old and new, of the Hebrew and the Italian, but toward their unification. In daily life, Rossi moved between two cultures, combining, if not fusing them within his activities.[116] In this he seems to illustrate the possibility of breaking down civic and religious barriers, despite the increasing segregation of Jews from Christians in later sixteenth- and early seventeenth-century Mantua. After all, the Lord God who ruled His people was the same God who ruled mankind. In writing to Duke Vincenzo on his brother's behalf in 1606, Rossi terminates with the words "I pray *our* Lord for your every happiness and content";[117] and in the dedication of his four-voice madrigals to Alfonso d'Este, he addresses him as "Your Highness to whom I pay my humblest respects by entreating the Lord God that, in His benignity, He rain all favors upon you and Your Most Serene Household."[118] One wonders whether "*our* God" and the "Lord God" was the Jews' God Almighty as against Christ or the Triune; and whether Rossi was not saying, as an innuendo, that, after all, it was the Jewish God who formed the world and the nations and that it was for the Jewish God, who had chosen the Jews for His people, to dispense His benevolence to Gentiles; and whether he was not forcing the conclusion, therefore, that it was for the nations rightfully to recognize His primacy and the primacy of His chosen people. "Blessed is the nation whose God is the Lord and the people whom He chose for His inheritance," Ps. 33:12; and elsewhere in the same psalm, "Let all the earth fear the Lord" (v. 8) and "The Lord looks down from heaven; He beholds all the sons of men" (v. 13). Either way, the result is unification, be it through continuities within the Judeo-Christian tradition or through notions of Hebrew culture, intellectually, artistically, as the *fons et origo* of later developments.

These and other interpretations depend on the way one reviews Rossi's biography and his works. They form the chapters of a still "open book," whose contents can be variously organized according to the particular point of view selected for their narration. *Vivat S. R.*, to quote the acrostic in the table of contents to his first collection:[119] in "living on," Rossi's story can be told and retold, in different contexts, as a parable for the shifting associations of Jews and their music within European culture at large.

Notes

1. The most recent monograph on Salamone Rossi is D. Harrán, *Salamone Rossi: Jewish Musician in Late Renaissance Mantua* (Oxford, 1999) (hereafter *SRJM*); bibliography, 281–95. For Rossi's works, see D. Harrán, ed., *Salamone Rossi: Complete Works* [Corpus Mensurabilis Musicae 100], 13 vols. (vols. 1–12, Neuhausen-Stuttgart, 1995; vols. 13a and 13b, Middleton, Wis., with the composer's Hebrew songs, 2003 [hereafter, *CW*]).

2. Cf. H. Tischler, ed., *Trouvère Lyrics with Melodies: Complete Comparative Edition* [Corpus Mensurabilis Musicae 107], 15 vols. (Neuhausen-Stuttgart, 1997), nos. 184 (in vol. 3), 457 (in vol. 6).

3. For Sacerdote, see, for example, S. Foa, *Gli ebrei nel Monferrato nei secoli XVI e XVII* (Alessandria, 1914; repr., Bologna, 1965), pp. 48, 73, 75. His music collection,

though designated his "first," appears to be his only one: *Il primo libro di madrigali a sei voci novamente da lui composti et dati in luce* (Venice, 1575). Its single remaining voice, the quinto, along with its eighteen lyrics, will be available as vol. 1 in D. Harrán, ed., *Fragmenta polyphonica judaica (sec. 16–17)*, 6 vols. (Jerusalem, in preparation).

4. The sources of information on Rossi and his works are Mantua, Archivio di Stato, Archivio Gonzaga (hereafter ASAG), with its various Libri dei Decreti, collections of letters, and three folders on *ebrei*; and Mantua, Jewish Community Archive (hereafter JCA), with its three hundred portfolios and sixty bound volumes, including the community's minute books from 1522 to 1810; the dedications to the Italian vocal and instrumental collections; the inscriptions (altogether, twenty-seven) to certain instrumental works, with references to persons or events in courtly or Jewish circles; the composite introductory matter to the Hebrew collection; and, last but not least, the works of music themselves, where the composer can be studied and appraised for his craftsmanship. S. Simonsohn reviews the archival documents in his *History of the Jews in the Duchy of Mantua* (Jerusalem, 1977; originally *Toledot hayyehudim bedukasut mantova*), 2 vols. (Jerusalem, 1962–64) (hereafter *HJDM*). For the dedications, see D. Harrán, "Salamone Rossi, Jewish Musician in Renaissance Italy," *Acta Musicologica* 59 (1987): 46–64, and for their full quotation, the introductory matter to the various volumes in *CW*. On lacunae in the composer's life story, see idem, "Salamone Rossi, the Mystery Man of Jewish Art Composers," *Notes from Zamir* 2 (2003). 5–7.

5. Rossi signed his last collection (*Madrigaletti*) thus: "Di Venetia li 3. di Genaro 1628," after which date nothing is known of him.

6. He appears on three payrolls (from 1589, 1592, 1622) and was probably inscribed on four others no longer extant, yet reconstructed, with Rossi's name on them, by S. Parisi, "Musicians at the Court of Mantua during Monteverdi's Time: Evidence from the Payrolls," in *Musicologia Humana: Studies in Honor of Warren and Ursula Kirkendale*, ed. S. Gmeinwieser et al. (Florence, 1994), pp. 183–208. For information on his instrumental ensembles, cf. *SRJM*, esp. pp. 19–24.

7. See D. Harrán, "Salamone Rossi as a Composer of Theater Music," *Studi musicali* 16 (1987): 91–131.

8. See there also *SRJM*, pp. 179–84.

9. The mention of Rossi's own *concerto* appears in a letter to Duke Vincenzo's counselor Annibale Chieppio (ASAG 1337; 29 Sept. 1612), there as *sua compagnia, o suo concerto*; and in Hebrew, as *heḥakham min ha'adumim vesi'ato*," i.e., "the learned Rossi and his company" (*si'a = compagnia, concerto*), in a rabbinical responsum, by Netan'el Trabotto, from 1645. On the latter, see I. Adler, "The Rise of Art Music in the Italian Ghetto," in *Jewish Medieval and Renaissance Studies*, ed. A. Altmann (Cambridge, Mass., 1967), pp. 321–64, esp. p. 357.

10. On Rossi's music for the synagogue and its possible use in community events and confraternities, see *SRJM*, pp. 201–41; also D. Harrán, "Tradition and Innovation in Jewish Music of the Later Renaissance," *Journal of Musicology* 7 (1989): 107–30, repr. in *Essential Papers on Jewish Culture in Renaissance and Baroque Italy*, ed. D. Ruderman (New York, 1992), pp. 474–501. On Moses Sullam, see, for example, *HJDM*, passim (cf. index); also below.

11. For a complete listing of the collections and their works, see *SRJM*, pp. 256–68.

12. First editions only: *Canzonette* (1589) for three voices; five books of madrigals for five voices (1600, 1602, 1603, 1610, 1622); one book of madrigals for four voices (1614); *Madrigaletti* (1628) for, mainly, two voices plus basso continuo. See *CW*, vols. 1–8.

13. First editions only: book 1 (1607) for three to five voices; book 2 (1607) for same; book 3 (1613) for three voices; book 4 (1622) for same. See *CW*, vols. 9–12.

14. *Hashirim asher lishlomo* (The songs of Solomon), Venice, 1622/23. Available in two editions, one (lacking three pieces) by S. Naumbourg (Paris, 1877; repr., New York, 1954); another, more reliable in its contents, though still mared by inaccuracies, by F. Rikko, 3 vols. (New York, 1967–73). As mentioned above (n. 1), a third edition, with full commentary, will appear as vols. 13a–13b in *CW*.

15. For Modena in connection with music, including his contribution to the *Songs of Solomon*, see D. Harrán, " 'Dum Recordaremur Sion': Music in the Life and Thought of the Venetian Rabbi Leon Modena (1571–1648)," *Association for Jewish Studies Review* 23 (1998): 17–61; idem, "Jewish Musical Culture in Early Modern Venice," in *The Jews of Early Modern Venice*, ed. R. C. Davis and B. Ravid (Baltimore, 2001), pp. 211–30, 289–95; and idem, "Was Rabbi Leon Modena a Composer?" in *"The Lion Shall Roar": Leon Modena and His World*, ed. D. Malkiel (Jerusalem, 2003), pp. 195–248. See also idem, "Marriage and Music as Metaphor: The Wedding Odes of Leon Modena and Salamone Rossi," *Musica Judaica* 17 (2002–3, forthcoming).

16. Other collections are dedicated to the worthies Paolo Guglielmo Andreasi, count of Rodi, and Federico Rossi, count of San Secondo.

17. The only visit recorded is the one, at the request of its ruler, Prince Alessando Pico, for 1612. See ASAG 1337 (29 Sept. 1612).

18. Modena, on the basis of Rossi's dedications to its rulers (see below); Vienna, on the basis of a *sonata detta la Viena* in his third book of instrumental works. Rossi might have traveled to Vienna as part of the festivities for the marriage, in 1622, of Eleonora Gonzaga, daughter of Duke Vincenzo I, and Emperor Ferdinand II. Other ties to Vienna are mentioned in D. Harrán, "From Mantua to Vienna: A New Look at the Early Seventeenth-Century Dance Suite," *Journal of the Royal Musical Association* 129/1 (2004, forthcoming).

19. Three collections carry the term "Venice" in the composer's signature to their dedications: the first book of five-voice madrigals (1600); the fourth book of instrumental works (1622); and, as mentioned, the *Madrigaletti* (1628).

20. Of the various writings on Sara, see, for example, C. Boccato, "Sara Copio Sullam, la poetessa del ghetto di Venezia: Episodi della sua vita in un manoscritto del secolo XVII," *Italia* 6 (1987): 104–218. For Sara in connection with music, see D. Harrán, "Doubly Tainted, Doubly Talented: The Jewish Poet Sara Copio (d. 1641) as a Heroic Singer," in *Musica Franca: Essas in Honor of Frank A. D'Accone*, ed. I. Alm et al. (Stuyvesant, N.Y., 1996), pp. 367–422.

21. Vienna, Österreichische Nationalbibliothek: alto (signature: S.A. 78. B.73); the handwritten card, in the alphabetical catalog, identifies the part as Sulzer's gift to the library (*Geschenk des israelitischen Cantors Sl. Sulzer*).

22. Preceded by a glowing introduction: *Essai sur la vie et les oeuvres de Salomon Rossi*, pp. [3]–20 (for details of the edition, see above, n. 14).

23. E. Cassirer, *The Philosophy of Symbolic Forms* (originally *Die Philosophie der symbolischen Formen*, 3 vols. [Berlin, 1923–29]), 4 vols. (repr., New Haven, Conn., 1953–56), esp. vol. 3 (*The Phenomenology of Language*).

24. On Rossi's "Hebrew" inclinations as they reflect in his music, see D. Harrán, "Salamone Rossi as a Composer of 'Hebrew' Music," in *Studies in Honour of Israel Adler (Yuval: Studies of the Jewish Music Research Centre*, vol. 7), ed. E. Schleifer and E. Seroussi (Jerusalem, 2002), pp. 171–200.

25. From a letter that Modena wrote to Judah Saltaro da Fano: cf. Y. Boksenboim, ed., *Iggerot rabbi Yehudah Arie mi-Modena* (Tel Aviv, 1984), p. 110.

26. On Italo-Jewish tensions and interchanges, see, for example, R. Bonfil, "Change in the Cultural Patterns of a Jewish Society in Crisis: Italian Jewry at the Close of the Sixteenth Century," *Jewish History* 3 (1988): 11–30; and variously in idem, *Jewish Life in Renaissance Italy* (Berkeley, Calif., 1994); originally *Gli ebrei in Italia nell'epoca del Rinascimento* (Florence, 1991).

27. Cf. M. Foucault, *The Order of Things: An Archaeology of the Human Sciences* (New York, 1970), p. 75; originally *Les Mots et les choses: Une Archéologie des sciences humaines* (Paris, 1966).

28. In a document from 1621 ("Domino Salomoni fili Domini Bonaiuti de Rossis hebreo Mantua"): ASAG 3391.

29. F. Follino, *Compendio delle sontuose feste fatte l'anno M.DC.VIII nella città di Mantova per le reali nozze del serenissimo principe D. Francesco Gonzaga con la serenissima infanta Margherita di Savoia* (Mantua, 1608), with an account of this and other *intermedi* on pp. 72–99. On Europa, see D. Harrán, "Madama Europa, Jewish Singer in Late Renaissance Mantua," in *Festa Musicologica: Essays in Honor of George J. Buelow*, ed. X. Stuyvesant (New York, 1995), pp. 197–231.

30. JCA, file 9, doc. 1:10 (17 Feb. 1605); file 10, doc. 1:164 (31 Mar. 1605).

31. ASAG, Decreti 52, fols. 245v–246v (the document is signed by the duke's counselor Annibale Chieppio): "Per dimonstrare a Salamone Rossi hebreo qualche segno di gratitudine per la servitù fattaci da lui molt'anni, et che tuttavia ci fa con ogni assiduità habbiamo risoluto di conferire gli carichi che havevamo dati a Lazarino d'Italia parimente hebreo quale per suoi demeriti se n'è reso indegno nella persona di Emanuele fratello d'esso Salamone così confidati nella fede, et diligentia sua."

32. ASAG 2705 (21 Feb. 1606): "Mando da Vostra Altezza Serenissima mio frattello [sic] al qual Vostra Altezza restarà servita farmi gratia favorirlo appresso Sua Altezza Serenissima nel negotio del nostro Uffitio che Lazzaro d'Italia procura di levarlo a noi et inplicarlo in lui senza niuna Causa come meglio da mio frattello [sic] ne sarà informato facendoli sapere che la mia servitù fatta tanti anni sono non comporta che ci sia levato un tal Uffitio senza Caggione per benefetiare un Lazzarino d'Italia tanto noto al mondo della qualità sua."

33. Samuel Naumbourg set the tone in the introduction to his edition (see above, nn. 14, 22): "Qui donc à *cette époque néfaste pour les Juifs*, surtout en Italie, alors que l'Inquisition était encore toute puissante; qui donc se serrait intéressé à *un pauvre*

musicien israélite? N'est-ce pas déjà une chose assez étonnante qu'un enfant d'Israël, *un fils de cette race infortunée et persécutée,* ait pu, en plein XVIe siècle, tout en demeurant fidèle à sa croyance et à son culte, arriver à posséder un talent musical assez grand pour se faire un nom dans l'art?" p. [3] (emphasis added).

34. *'Emeq habakha: Seferr haqorot vehatela'ot asher 'averu 'al beit Yisra'el* (Vale of tears: Book of the happenings and hardships that befell the Jewish people), ed. M. Letteris (Krakow, 1895). Cf. B. Ravid, "Between the Myth of Venice and the Lachrymose Conception of Jewish History: The Experience of the Jews of Venice," in *The Jews of Italy: Memory and Identity,* ed. B. Garvin and B. Cooperman (College Park, MD., 2000), pp. 151–92.

35. For relevant documents, see ASAG, Filze ebrei 3010 (1 Dec. 1621, date of agreement), 5 Dec. 1621 (date of duke's approval); also 3391, fols. 172–177v.

36. See, for example, "Exchange Rates in Mantua," in *HJDM,* pp. 742–44; and more generally, C. Cipolla, *Money, Prices and Civilization in the Mediterranean World* (Princeton, N.J., 1956).

37. For Rossi's earnings, see I. Fenlon, *Music and Patronage in Sixteenth-Century Mantua,* 2 vols. (Cambridge, 1980–82), 1: 193–95; also Parisi, "Musicians at the Court of Mantua during Monteverdi's Time."

38. The copyright stipulates that "for the period of fifteen years from today [1623] nobody may print the composer's Hebrew songs without his permission or that of his heirs [*yorshav*]."

39. After *HJDM,* p. 192.

40. On the worsening situation of the Jews in the later sixteenth century, see A. Milano, *Storia degli ebrei in Italia* (Turin, 1963), pp. 244–85; Bonfil, *Jewish Life in Renaissance Italy,* pp. 63–77; and for Mantua, *HJDM,* pp. 113–43.

41. JCA, file 15, docs. 21–22. On this and an earlier pragmatic from 1599, cf. *HJDM,* pp. 530–35; for the Italian tr. submitted to the authorities, see ASAG, Mandati 100, fols. 46v–48 (22 June 1619).

42. ASAG, Mandati 97, fol. 62 (2 Aug. 1606): "Volendo Noi mostrare quanto ci sia cara la servitù che con la virtù sua di Musica, et del sonare ci va facendo da molt'anni in qua Salamone di Rossi hebreo. In virtù delle presenti che saranno firmate di nostra mano, concediamo a nostro beneplacito ampia, et libera facoltà al medesimo Salamone di poter caminare per questa nostra Città et suo Dominio senza portar il solito segno ranzo intorno a Capello o beretta."

43. ASAG, Mandati 98, fol. 2 (27 Feb. 1612): "al Signor duca nostro Padre che sia in gloria, et nell'istesso tempo anco a noi."

44. On the Jewish theater, see, for example, A. D'Ancona, *Origini del teatro italiano,* 2d ed., 2 vols. (Turin, 1891), 2: 398–429; S. Parisi, "The Jewish Community and Canival Entertainment at the Mantuan Court in the Early Baroque," in *Music in Renaissance Cities and Courts: Studies in Honor of Lewis Lockwood,* ed. J. A. Owens and A. M. Cummings (Warren, Mich., 1997), pp. 297–305; and, most recently, C. Burattelli, *Spettacoli di corte a Mantova tra cinque e seicento* (Florence, 1999), pt. 4 ("Gli ebrei di Mantova e il teatro di corte"), pp. 141–80.

45. For a review of the documents, see Harrán, "Salamone Rossi as a Composer of Theater Music"; also *SRJM,* pp. 174–200.

46. They are surveyed in Adler, "The Rise of Art Music in the Italian Ghetto."

47. As stated in the title, while more specific references to the uses and purposes of the collection are found elsewhere in its prefatory matter.

48. From Modena's foreword to the collection, after Lev. 10:10; Ezek. 22:26, 42:20, etc.

49. From Modena's foreword to the collection.

50. From the composer's dedication.

51. Ibid.

52. As is clear from its mention in a permit granted to the Sullam family, in 1611, to reside, and carry out its banking affairs, outside the walls of what was shortly to become the Mantuan ghetto: cf. ASAG, Decreti 53, fols. 261v–262 (*tenendo la loro Sinagoga*).

53. From Modena's foreword.

54. Ibid.

55. From Rossi's dedication.

56. From Modena's foreword.

57. Ibid.

58. Unlike his Italian vocal collections, which call for a basso continuo, sometimes to be played on "foundation instruments" (*strumenti da corpo*), i.e., such instruments as were suitable for providing a firm support for the voices.

59. From Modena's foreword.

60. The original responsum, along with its rabbinical confirmations (by Ben-Zion Ẓarfati, Lev Saraval, Barukh ben Samuel, Ezra da Fano, and Judah ben Moses [Saltaro] da Fano), is contained in London, British Library, MS Add. 27148, fols. 9r–10v: see L. Modena, *She'elot uteshuvot ziknei Yehudah*, ed. S. Simonsohn (Jerusalem, 1955), pp. 15–20.

61. Hebrew date: Heshvan [5]383, i.e., Oct. or early Nov. 1622. Signatories: Isaac Gershon; Moses Cohen Porto; Leon Modena; Simḥa [Simone] Luzzatto.

62. From Modena's foreword. Cf. D. Yarden, ed., *Immanuel Haromi: Maḥbarot* (Jerusalem, 1957), p. 341, where the wording was not "to others," but "to the Christians" (*el hanoṣerim*), which, in Modena's time, came under the censor's knife.

63. A. Portaleone, *Shilṭei hagibborim* (Mantua, 1612); portions relevant to music reprinted in I. Adler, ed., *Hebrew Writings Concerning Music in Manuscripts and Printed Books from Geonic Times up to 1800* (Munich, 1975), pp. 246–83.

64. From the third dedicatory poem in the Hebrew collection; also in Oxford, Bodleian Library, MS Mich. 528, *olim* 759 (fol. 63r), after which it was edited by S. Bernstein as no. 37 in Modena, *Divan lerabbi Yehudah Arye mi-Modena* (Philadelphia, 1932), pp. 82–83.

65. Gregorio Leti (d. 1701), *L'Italia regnante, o vero nova descritione dello stato presente di tutti prencipati, e republiche d'Italia*, 2 vols. (Geneva, 1675–76), 1: 162: "Subito entrati in Chiesa cominciano a gridar con voci arrabbiate, tornandosi la testa gli uni contro gli altri, facendo certi gesti ridicolissimi, e così si mettono a sedere con gli stessi gridi, la qual bella musica dura sino che il loro Rabbino comincia la predica in lingua Italiana, ma li passi della Scrittura gli recita in lingua Hebrea."

66. From the early responsum of 1605 and its repring in Rossi's *Songs*.

67. Ibid.

68. From the third dedicatory poem.

69. After *The Letters of Claudio Monteverdi*, rev. ed., trans. D. Stevens, (Oxford, 1995), pp. 83–86 (letter from 1611).

70. *spazziam pronte, o vecchiarelle*: cf. *CW*, 8: lvi–lix (for commentary), 64–68 (for music).

71. *patron mio colendissimo . . . humilissimo et devotissimo servitore.*

72. *patron mio colendissimo . . . mio Signor naturale, al quale io son tenuto di quel molto, o puoco ch'io so, et posso, come anco perchè sotto la felice ombra della sua servitù ho imparato il tutto.*

73. Joseph ha-Kohen, *'Emeq habakha*, as extended, until 1605, by an unknown editor; see the edition by Letteris(cited above, n. 34), p. 176.

74. From two letters (1612) of the Mantuan ambassador to Rome (Aurelio Recordati); after S. Parisi, "Ducal Patronage of Music in Mantua, 1587–1627: An Archival Study" (Ph.D. diss., University of Illinois, 1989), pp. 227, 257–58.

75. According to the Venetian ambassador to Mantua (Pietro Gritti): see A. Segarizzi, ed., *Relazioni degli ambasciatori veneti al senato*, 4 vols. (Bari, 1912–16), 1: 120.

76. On Vincenzo's temperament, see again the report (now by Franscesco Morosini) in Segarizzi, ed., *Relazioni degli ambasciatori veneti*, 1: 88.

77. Book 1: "io ne la supplico, azziò co'l suo felice nome possa sicuro dalle mani de detrattori dar spirito, e vita a questi miei Madrigali, i quali senza un tanto appoggio, overo traboccarebbono tosto nell'oblio, o fra le mani di questi tali, come da cani arrabbiati sariano lacerati, e guasti."

78. Book 2: "questi miei Madrigali . . . ella gli protega, e defenda, com'ella deve fare di tutte le cose sue più care, ben ch'io mi creda che niuno già mai calunniatore o detrattore, ardisa di biasmar cosa che sia da Dama di tanto valore protetta e favorita."

79. Book 4: "Questo Libro de Madrigali . . . viene in luce honorato del nome di Vostra Signoria Illustrissima non già per far di quello un'impenetrabile scudo da poter resistere ai fieri dardi de malevoli detrattori, giovandomi di credere, ch'egli sia tale, che non possa essere da rabbioso dente lacerato."

80. Book 3: "ma ch'anzi . . . che la difenderà da qual si voglia maledica, e detratrice lingua."

81. "in grazia sua, e sotto il nome di lei" (book 1); "dar saggio al mondo dell'affetto con ch'io vivo di non monstrarmi indegno servidore di tanta Altezza" (ibid.); "et illustrarsi almeno col nome suo" (Book 2); "ma sì bene per maggior fama, et maggior grido acquistare" (book 4). For a complete transcription of the dedications (along with their translation), see respective volumes in *CW*. On the dedications as a source of biographical information, see Harrán, "Salamone Rossi, Jewish Musician in Renaissance Italy," esp. pp. 48–53 (for the Italian ones).

82. Book 1 of *sinfonie*: "Gradiscale Vostra Signoria Illustrissima con quell'affetto, col quale altre volte, ha mostrato di non sprezzarle."

83. Book 2 of *sinfonie*: "Hora che l'istessa benignità (di cui mi trovo oltre ogni mio merito altre volte favorito) . . . per have ella mostrato di compiacersi alli giorni passati delle mie compositioni."

84. Book 3 of *sinfonie*: "Perchè alli giorni passati fui (con molto mio gusto) gratiato dall'Eccellenza sua nel ascoltar alcune mie compositioni, e perchè mi parve all'hora (per quanto potei comprendere) ch'ella ne restasse alquanto sodisfatta."

85. Book 3 of madrigals: "Con tanta benignità si compiacque l'Eccellenza Vostra di udire questi mesi passati alcuni miei rozi Madrigali."

86. From, respectively, book 3 ("Vostra Eccellenza mi legò con sì fatto legame di obligatione"); and book 4 ("la singolar bontà, et infinita amorevolezza di Vostra Signoria Illustrissima da me in diverse occasioni molto bene conosciuta, alla quale trovandomi di lunga mano obligato").

87. Book 1 of *sinfonie*: "et a se stesso mi ricordi per quel divoto servitore che lo professo, che con tal memoria haverrà occasione d'impiegarmi in servigio suo."

88. From Rossi's dedication.

89. Ibid.

90. Book of madrigals for four voices: "L'animo mio inclinatissimo a servir sempre Vostra Altezza et l'infinita bontà, et grandezza di lei, m'hanno dato non solo ardire di dedicarle queste mie poche fatiche, ma mi fanno insieme sperar di doverle veder col mezo del suo felicissimo nome, consecrate all'immortalità della fama, vivendo sicuro, ch'ella non sdegnerà, ch'io riceva questa gratia dalla sua benignità, di palesar al mondo con picciole dimonstrationi segni ardentissimi dell'osservante divotion mia verso l'Altezza Vostra la quale con ogni humiltà supplico a gradire queste mie lievi note, col vivacissimo affetto mio, sicura ch'ogni faticosa impresa debba essermi leggerissimo peso, rispetto all'immenso desiderio, che ho di servir a Vostra Altezza."

91. Whether Rossi wrote them, and then had them styled, is another question. He could have used an epistolarian handbook. Cf. A. Quondam, *Le "carte messaggiere": Retorica e modelli di comunicazione epistolare* (Rome, 1981); also E. J. Polak, *Medieval and Renaissance Letter Treatises and Form Letters*, 2 vols. (Leiden, 1993–94).

92. H. Tischler, ed., *Trouvère Lyrics with Melodies*, no. 457, beginning "Par grant franchise" (in vol. 6): "por vostre amor ai je guerpi ma loi / et croi en Deu maugré toz mes amis"; "qui ne me vuet mes maus guierredoner"; "froiz glaives"; "Trahi m'avez, douce dame, et por quoi?"; "que longuement en gabessiez de moi,"; also "Et si faites de moi touz voz bofoiz."

93. *Die grosse Heidelberger manessische Liederhandschrift*, facs. Ed. U. Müller (Göppingen, 1971).

94. "Der reiche Mann hat Mehl, der Arme dafür Aschen hat": from poetry as orthographically "modernized" in J. Kastein, *Süsskind von Trimberg oder die Tragödie der Heimatlosigkeit* (Jerusalem, 1934), p. 134.

95. "seit mich die Herren schieden von dem Gute / . . . Die Herren geben mir nichts mehr / Die Höfe will ich fliehen. / Ich will mir einen langen Bart / lahn wachsen grieser Haare. / Nach alter Juden Lebensart.": from ibid., pp. 157–58.

96. In the original manuscript, fol. 355r. See also R. Manesse, *Minnesänger: Vierundzwanzig farbige Wiedergaben aus der manessischen Liederhandschrift*, 3 vols., with intro. by K. Martin (Aachen, 1971–74), vol. 3, plate no. 21.

97. Letter dated 10 Nov. 1522; after C. Slim, "Gian and Gian Maria, Some Fifteenth- and Sixteenth-Century Namesakes," *The Musical Quarterly* 57 (1971): 562–74, esp. 566.

98. "Ho mandato a circar Abram dall'Arpa et suo figliuolo acciò venissero co'l signor Theologo costì, ma si è ritrovato che sono a Ferrara" (letter to the duke by his agent Luigi Olivo, signed 29 July 1582; ASAG 2617). On Malachi dall'Arpa, see, for evidence in the Mantuan Jewish archive, *HJDM*, 671n.

99. "Messer Giovanni Andrea Robbiato Milanese cantore di Sua Altezza ha detto che la mattina di San Giovanni Battista andando a Mantova in Carroccia era con lui Abramino abiatico del già Abramo dall'Arpa, et essendo entrato a palar seco della religione nostra Christiana, con sforzarsi di mostrargli che quella era ottima, et da esser osservata, non più quella che tengono gli hebrei, detto Abramino non consentì, ma però mostrò di ascoltare il ragionamento.": ASAG 2639 (letter, six pages long, by Tullio Petrozani, dated 28 June 1587).

100. "dopo arrivati a Mantova detto Robbiato condusse l'istesso Abramino su l'organo in santa Barbara mentre che si faceva il santo Battesimo del secondo signor Nipote di Sua Altezza et mostrò che a lui Abramino piacessero quelle ceremonie" (ibid.).

101. "un frate . . . ragionò co'l medesimo Abramino, dechiarandogli la sostanza di detto sacramento del santo Battesimo a comparatione della circoncisione, ma Abramino non ripose al detto Padre risposta alcuna a proposito" (ibid.).

102. "venne un zio di esso Abramino, come lui stesso disse . . . accompagnato da Leone Moscato rabì . . . et s'accostarono ad Abramino . . . et ragionando con lui" (ibid.).

103. "et detto messer Giovanni Andrea se gli accostò per intendere che discessero, ma parlavano hebraico che non li intese" (ibid.).

104. "se si sarebbe fatto Christiano, a che rispondendo che non lo sapeva, ma che credeva più de si, che di no" (ibid.).

105. "essortandolo a continouare nella fede hebraica, et non dar orecchie a parole che gli venissero dette di farsi Christiano" (ibid.).

106. As reported in a second letter by Pertozani, dated 29 June 1987 (ASAG 2639).

107. Letter written by Annibale Chieppio (ASAG 1259, 22 Nov. 1593; *ho ritrovato Abramino hebreo*). The various episodes reported above, as well as others about members of the Levi family, are treated at length in a study, by the author, "The Levi Clan: Three Generations of Jewish 'Levites' in Mantua" (in preparation).

108. Cf. D. Harrán, *In Search of Harmony: Hebrew and Humanist Elements in Sixteenth-Century Musical Thought* [Musicological Studies & Documents 42] (Neuhausen-Stuttgart, 1988).

109. Monteverdi's arguments can be found in the preface to his fifth book of madrigals (1605), and as commented by his brother, Giulio Cesare, in the Preface to his *Scherzi musicali* (1607); see G. Malipiero, ed., *Monteverdi: Tutte le opere*, 16 vols. (Vienna, 1926–48), respectively vols. 5, 10. His works in book 5 and later books were meant to illustrate his intentions.

110. See, for example, Maimonides, "Laws of Fasts" (*Mishneh torah, hilkhot ta'aniyyot*, chap. 5, law 14).

111. Judah Moscato published an impressive sermon on music entitled "Higgayon bekhinnor" (Strummings [*also* contemplations] on the lyre), in his *Sefer*

nefuṣot Yehudah (Book of the dispersed of Judah) (Venice, 1588/89), fols. 1r–84; available in *Hebrew Writings Concerning Music*, ed. Adler, pp. 223–39, and in an annotated Ger. trans. by H. Shmueli, *Higgajon bechinnor: Betrachtungen zum Leierspiel des Jehudah . . . Moscato* (Tel Aviv, 1953).

112. True, he published a collection of four-voice madrigals in 1614; but they seem to have been composed much earlier, possibly around 1600 (as argues in *SRJM*, pp. 68–70).

113. From the composer's dedication to his Hebrew *Songs*.

114. From Modena's foreword to the *Songs*.

115. In his two prefaces, mentioned above (n. 109).

116. On processes of conceptual and stylistic consolidation, see D. Harrán, "Cultural Fusions in Jewish Musical Thought of the Later Renaissance," in *In Cantu et in Sermone: For Nono Pirrotta on His 80th Birthday*, ed. F. Della Seta and F. Piperno (Florence, 1989), pp. 141–54; and Harrán, "Tradition and Innovation in Jewish Music of the Later Renaissance."

117. "pregando nostro signore per ogni sua felicità et contento."

118. "Vostra Altezza a cui fo humilissima riverenza, con pregar il Signor Iddio che benigno sopra di lei, et della Serenizzima sua Casa piova tutte le gioie."

119. Of the nineteen madrigals, the first seven are those that, in their initial letters, form the acrostic.

Chapter 10
Amatus Lusitanus and the Location of Sixteenth-Century Cultures

Eleazar Gutwirth

New perspectives on the Renaissance, humanism, and sixteenth-century culture are helping to modify previous views. Among those earlier approaches, older narratives of sixteenth-century Jewish histories and cultures tended to postpone modernity until the seventeenth and even into the eighteenth century, thereby assuming there was no early modern Jewish history. At times, the rise of the communities in the East, in the Ottoman Empire, was seen in strong contrast to the West. The Eastern communities were "isolated," far from the centers of culture. If the Renaissance affected the Jews, it was a phenomenon generally associated with the West, with Italy first and foremost and northwestern Europe at a later stage.

In recent years, various research projects have provided evidence for constructing a more diverse profile of the period. Some of this research corroborates the strong interests of certain Ottoman Jewish reading communities (such as Cairo) in a variety of cultural phenomena (the theater, the classics, the emerging national languages and literatures of Iberia and various other cultures) formerly associated with the "West."[1] In the 1560s in another Ottoman Jewish community, Salonika, an Iberian exile was exhibiting clear and strong cultural affinities with the trends associated with the beginnings of modernity at the time. Interacting with this Jewish community no less intensely than he had with the Jews and conversos of Italy since the 1540s, Amatus Lusitanus (João Rodrigues de Castelo) can be seen as a well-documented example of the human and cultural resources within Ottoman Jewish communities in the sixteenth century. Moreover, if viewed from the perspective of Jewish history and culture, he can help change our perspectives, antedating trends we tend to associate with later decades.

At first glance, Amatus Lusitanus would seem to be an obvious case of

Ottoman Jewish humanism. His "Jewishness" in the Salonikan phase has never been doubted. The Jewish textual passages (or "passages of Jewish interest") in his published works have long since been noted by scholarship, though not exhaustively. In the sixteenth century, the work of identifying such passages was carried out by expurgators and censors.[2] Ironically, their inky erasure marks on these passages drew the attention of subsequent owners of these copies directly to the censored (Jewish, converso) passages. In the twentieth century, Harry Friedenwald published a study of what he termed Amatus's "Jewish interests."[3] In Amatus's case, the question arises of the location of culture. Part of the problematics of scholarship on him can be explained in terms of its fragmentation.

Today that sense of fragmentation in scholarship on Amatus seems to be stronger than ever. Although there appears to be no attempt to raise a *status questionis* on one of the most famous and influential of sixteenth-century writers, in the field of Jewish studies the latest work would seem to be a study debating how well informed Amatus was on whether Pico or his nephew was the recipient of Leone Ebreo's lost work.[4] However important this bibliographic question may be from other points of view, it is based on a single paragraph from one of his seven hundred cures. A similar example is Dov Front's work on the expurgation of the books of Amatus Lusitanus, where the emphasis is on censorship and the individual book, that is, the individual copy, or at least edition, of the printed book.[5] Similarly, Renata Segre's valuable discovery of the inventory of his possessions in his rooms in Ancona at the time of the persecution of the conversos there in 1555 contributes to one aspect of his biography, since the confiscators left us no accurate description or inventory of his library.[6] George Hugo Tucker's interest in Amatus is relevant to the peculiarities of Renaissance neo-Latin exile literature written by conversos, particularly the question of his epitaph.[7]

If the fragmentation in research is clear in the humanities, it is far more pronounced in the sciences. Silvio Pampiglione's recent articles show that Amatus Lusitanus was a pioneer in the scientific description of dirophilariasis.[8] Amatus presents this in one of the seven hundred cures, where he relates the case of a woman from whose eye a worm came forth. So inquiry tends to concentrate on single contributions and individual cures. To be sure, there were such approaches in the past: in 1955, Jacob Seide pointed out Amatus's contribution to the history of diabetes mellitus.[9] Joshua Leibowitz worked on a number of mainstream contributions, discoveries, and inventions as well as scientific descriptions, such as that of (de' Rossi's) peptic ulcer in 1556[10] or sudden death due to obstruction in the heart (coronary disease) as described by Amatus in 1560.[11] Jose de Paiva Boleo's article on Amatus's invention of the palatine obdurator is a similar kind of research.[12] The trend seems to have gained impetus in the last several decades.

This mode of fragmentation, in which scholars write about one aspect independently of or uninformed by other research on Amatus, is not a new development nor is it only affected by the gulf between the sciences and the humanities. It has to do in part with the particular constructions of national origin. In the works of some writers, there is an emphasis on the region of Amatus's birth, in Castelo Branco, Portugal, in 1511 and, if not always an erasure of the Jewish and converso factors, certainly after Maximiano Lemos's efforts a reluctance to deal with them in a scholarly fashion.[13]

In the work of Harry Friedenwald and possibly Cecil Roth, the converso and Jewish aspects are more emphasized and examined than the Iberian cultural factors. In addition, there is the question of regionalism and linguistic barriers. Lavoslav Glesinger, at a conference marking the fourth centenary of Amatus's death, in 1968, complained that his own work on Amatus, written in Serbo-Croatian, had not been given the broad attention it deserved because *slavica non leguntur.*[14] Mario Santoro's recent work on Amatus Lusitanus and Ancona seems to follow this trend of localism in Amatus's studies by concentrating on Amatus's Ancona phase.[15] Samuel Kottek's 1992 paper dealt with Amatus's Salonikan period.[16]

The most decisive factor in this fragmentation is the very nature of Amatus's work and biography. Amatus Lusitanus is not amenable to a comfortable monodisciplinary, monocultural, monolinguistic approach. Even within one of the fields that he touched on decisively, anatomy, J. Caria Mendes listed nine specialized subareas (ranging from myology to phlebology and splanchnology), each of which has its own history that must be taken into account before charting Amatus's particular place within it.[17] This relatively brief and incomplete *status questionis* indicates that Amatus's texts, particularly the seven hundred case studies or cures, are seen as a vademecum or source of miscellaneous bibliographical *faits divers* on other individuals or other themes, rather than the expression of his own coherent cultural personality. While it has been known—as Harry Friedenwald, for example, emphasized (following Heinrich Graetz, Cecil Roth, and others)—that various problems in sixteenth-century literary history and biography arise from the use of his writings as evidence, the coherent profile of the writer is more elusive. Whether research is progressing because of the fragmentation and concentration on minute aspects or because of the perspectives of Lemos and his followers (Friedenwald, Roth) is uncertain at this time. It is with these questions in mind and against this background of deferral and fragmentation that I have attempted to formulate a task that is concrete enough to permit research, and yet will tell us something about the scholar himself in his context.

The introduction to (the second edition of the) fifth volume of the *Centuriae* is a text frequently cited because it refers to the events of Ancona in 1555.[18] As is well known, Lusitanus did not escape from Ancona to Salonika, but rather first to Pesaro and later Ragusa. The text is signed Salonika 5320, that is, possibly the beginning of December 1559, and is a remarkable dedication to Joseph Nasi. The style is not quite that of an encomium but is more reminiscent of the appreciation (by then perfectly traditional) for the *epistolae familiares*, a sensibility that draws on a Petrarchan model.

In this prologue or dedication, he refers to a work that Friedenwald believes does not exist.[19] The existence of lost works by Amatus will surprise no one who remembers that we do not have his commentary on Avicenna or his treatise on the Chinese root. Reading Friedenwald, one has to assume that before 1560, he had been engaged in translating the Roman history by Eutropius into an Iberian/Hispanic language, probably Spanish rather than Portuguese. He had dedicated it to João Micas (Joseph Nasi), and it had shown how devoted he was to Joseph Nasi and the illustrious Doña Gracia, his aunt, and their community. Cecil Roth, on the other hand, was far less clear about this question. His formulation was that "Amatus informed Don Joseph that he had also inscribed to him a translation of the Roman history of the Latin historian Eutropius; but this has unfortunately been lost."[20] Unlike Friedenwald, Roth does not specify the language of the translation or its author. Amatus's engagement with the Spanish language and the authorship of Amatus are thereby erased from the record. Amatus's relevant text says: "Eutropio Historico Romano, / a me in linguam Hispanicam verso." Amatus Lusitanus knew the Latin word for Portuguese, but he uses the term *linguam Hispanicam.*

Whatever the case, there can be no doubt that all three were interested in reading the text of Eutropius. Which is to say that in the Sephardi communities of the Ottoman Empire in the sixteenth century (c. 1560), there was interest in and demand for Eutropius's work on Roman history among at least three leading, influential Sephardi Jews of converso origin: Amatus Lusitanus, the translator; and the two dedicatees, Doña Gracia and Joseph, one of Louvain's alumni, later duke of Naxos. As far as one can determine, historians of Ottoman Jewry have not attributed any significance to this phenomenon. My question is, What is the context of such Ottoman Sephardi interest in Eutropius in the 1550s and 1560s?

The reconstruction of such a context in full will not be attempted here. Such a task is, in my view, threefold and concentric. Since the subject is a translation into a European national language, the first answer has to do with the reading of Eutropius against the background in early modern Europe of the tensions between learned languages and the emerging national languages, particularly Spanish. This leads me to examine elsewhere the European and particularly the Spanish reception or readings of Eutropius, particularly at the time when Amatus expresses his interest in him. As the translation of the history book is the work of a physician, the second approach (the one I present here) centers on the common features between Renaissance medicine and Renaissance historiography as practiced by Amatus, according to the evidence of his texts. The third, here omitted, has to do with the Sephardi practice or reading of historiography in that particular period.

As will be recalled, Eutropius was a fourth-century pagan historian who, in his *Breviarium ab urbe condita* in eleven volumes, provides a concise survey of Roman history, one whose brevity required of its author concision and selectivity. He writes in a straightforward readable style and offers the translator little difficulty. The narrative covers about eleven hundred years, from the foundation of the city to the emperor Valentius (364 C.E.). Eutropius was writing circa 369 C.E. He was contemporary with Constantine and had to treat the complex problem of representing the converted emperor—a problem that, as Clifford Ando remarks, was caused by his own ambivalent self-presentation.[21] Here I would like to treat the unexplained phenomenon of a botanist, anatomist, and surgeon who seems interested in history to such an extent that he devotes himself to the translation into Spanish of the eleven volumes of the *Breviarium*. What is the relation between Spanish, translation, history, and medical writing in the particular case of Amatus?[22] I will argue that there are certain habits of reading and writing that are reflected in Amatus's *Centuriae* and that these bear comparison with and do not always radically differ from those of the Sephardi intellectuals who form the overwhelming majority of writers within the so-called sudden rise of Jewish historiography in the sixteenth century. They involve a certain sense of space and distance. Geography, textual problems, openness to non-Jewish sources, reading habits, and chronology are all themes in approaches to history and historiography from Isaac Abravanel, Abraham Zacuto, Samuel Usque, Solomon ibn Verga, the alleged author of *Shevet Yehudah*, Joseph ha-Kohen, Gedaliah ibn Yaḥia and onward. They are also similar themes in Amatus's writings. It would be banal to call his work a mixture of geography, history, and medicine. Rather than a heterogeneous admixture, the interest in these areas can be shown to have intellectual links to the practice of writing case histories.

Here again, the *Centuriae* are not a mere collection of case notes. Even the most cursory reading of the seven hundred items will show the diversity of stylistic vehicles and the intensity of investment in style. Some are mere remedies for a particular ailment. The *Dedications* are a completely different type of composition, sometimes bearing the character of a prose encomium or an example of polished epistolography, in an age in which Iberian literature produced notable examples of the genre. Some are essays dealing with a particular simple, such as wine, or a medical problem (for example, the critical days or the fontanels of bloodletting). The essay, the epistle, and the encomium are joined by the composition of a fourth type: dialogues—that favorite of sixteenth-century European writers in general and Iberian authors in particular. Some general considerations regarding his style are inescapable. In the case of Iberian contemporaries such as Andrés Laguna, in his glosses to Dioscorides, the question of why in books of science there are so many personal or other digressions that appear unrelated to the discipline in question, such as botany or medicine, has been examined briefly.[23] But for readers of Amatus, this question of digression has still not been answered in an entirely satisfactory manner. Nevertheless, these digressions are numerous and serve to reconstruct something of the author's self-presentation and attitudes. I will deal with each theme or habitus separately.

Representation of Iberia

The question of self-presentation is common to historians and to Amatus. In an age of the rise of European nations, national vernaculars, and humanist national encomia and invective, the representation of Spain and Portugal could be a significant element. A reading of the seven volumes of the *Centuriae* shows this representation to be effected by a number of elements. The Iberian component in Amatus Lusitanus's self-representation expresses itself at various levels in a variety of ways. Amatus introduces reminiscences of his

Iberian youth. He praises his Iberian alma mater. Geography plays a part in medical thought. Among the Jewish patients selected for explicit mention in the writings composed in Italy, but even more in Salonika, there seems to be a preponderance of conversos and Sephardim. About fifty are mentioned in the Salonikan period. He introduces fictitious dialogues with his relatives into the text, members of his family who are evidently as Iberian as he is. The basic move or literary strategy is the attention to geography, the mention of place in the medical case histories. Writing about pleuritis, he mentions the case of Antonio Carrion, aged thirty, who came from Naples and passed through Ancona on the way to his native city, Bruges, in Flanders; Amatus uses the epithet "illustrious city" (V, 5). In another cure (V, 69), he says that he arrived in the ancient city of Pesaro, of which Catullus writes: *sedes moribunda Pisauri.* Elsewhere (II, 18) he writes about his cure for a Jew named Salafantino (probably Sarfati) who came from the famous city of Bruzia near Constantinople on his way to Ancona. For Amatus, then, we note that cities are characterized as famous, illustrious, or, conversely, old, moribund.

These are cases in which the mention of the city is accompanied by an epithet. I see the epithet as the basic unit that could in some cases be turned into or developed into a laudation of a city, region, or country. Examples may be found throughout the *Centuriae.* But from the point of view of this inquiry, the most interesting case is his reference to his own native Portuguese village, Castelo Branco in lower Beria. Rising to the challenge of writing something encomiastic about Castelo Branco, he solves the problem in an ingenious way.

In 1554 (III, 13), he was treating Alfonso de Lancaster and his household in Rome. Don Alfonso's servants and slaves had been brought by him to Rome from Portugal by ship. This is the subject that leads Amatus to a learned excursion on the comparative climates and geography of Lisbon and Rome. In all climes, there are temperate and distemperate places. This leads him to mention Castelo Branco, his *patria*, which is temperate, mentioned by Ptolemy, and is equidistant from Lisbon and Salamanca, the city with the most famous university in all of Europe. Amatus thus finds three reasons for praising his native Castelo Branco.

Is this trait merely ornamental? In general, questions of airs and waters, climate and places may not be ornamental in writings by readers of Hippocrates or Galen. It would seem that there is evidence that questions of geography, regional origins, or cities are connected with the central themes of his work. Thus, in one cure (III, 96), he writes that Hispanics are more frequently attacked by bile than Italians, who eat more vegetables; the latter are more prone to attack by worms. In another (IV, 19), he tells us about his cure of Gualter, an illustrious forty-year-old Neapolitan afflicted with gonorrhea. The commentary on the cure refers to a small book by Laguna recently published in Rome. He refers to a discovery for extirpating caruncles and to a certain Filipo. This leads to memories of Amatus's practice in Lisbon, where he claims to have preceded Filipo in the application of the lancet through the penis. He shows his admiration for Laguna and Filipo. He produces a list of illustrious Portuguese physicians (Luis Moniz of Coimbra, Jorge Henrique of Lisbon) and, as elsewhere, there is a reference to his teacher in Salamanca, Alderete. It could be argued that there is evidence that in the early 1550s, Amatus is concerned in his writings with establishing the status of the Iberian Peninsula in the world of medical scholarship.

In another case (II, 31), he criticizes Vesalius, the learned physician of the emperor, author of *De radice synarum.* The German anatomist abstained from certain discussions pertaining to the Chinese and to the Portuguese, who were in frequent touch with the Chinese. The Portuguese introduced the use of this root into Europe, and they are the ones who must be asked about the true, genuine, and characteristic manner of administering this root. That is to say, nationality affects medical expertise. History, geography, and medicine are not merely a mixture in Amatus's texts, but are intellectually interrelated. In the particular genre of the *Centuriae*, where the individual observation of a particular patient cannot be reenacted, the authority and credibility of the narrator assume a larger role. The interrelation of the different fields are part of the central epistemological problem rather than mere ornaments.

Judaism

Amatus's attitude toward Judaism is not as simple as might be inferred from the usual accounts, but neither is it completely indeterminate. We have already mentioned his cure for Salafantino from Bruzia in search of a remedy to have children. Jews are very superstitious and believe that the reciting of prayers by male progeny after the death of their parents leads to the parents' salvation. In the same cure, he tells us that everybody knows that Venus is sterilized without Ceres and Bacchus. In another cure (IV, 33), for no apparent reason, he mentions the twelve-year-old son of the mason Benedictus

(Baruch), who lives under the synagogue of the Jews. When dealing (II, 20) with the death of the daughter of Leone Ebreo, he writes (in the age of trilingualism) that Leone Ebreo used to teach many the holy language. He continues and expatiates on her natural temper. He sees her as representing a cold ailment. In connection with a patient who is Jewish, this is explained in terms of the cold humors of the Jews, a disposition dependent on their diet. The Jews eat food that is melancholic, flatulent, and has a cold-generating effect, which is why Jews have a propensity to colics. In other words, we are offered a naturalist rather than a supernatural explanation of supposedly Jewish characteristics. The attempt to explain ostensible "Jewish" character or history by appeal to naturalistic factors is familiar in the historiography of that period as well. The *Sheveṭ Yehudah* (which also contains references to items of food and a disquisition on the character of people who abstain from pork or otherwise) shows interest in social, economic, military, and other non-providential or supernatural factors in Jewish history.[24]

Conversos and Inquisition

He writes in Ancona (II, 30) about the treatment of patients of African origin who were suffering from headaches and coughing. This leads to his mentioning their origin in the equinoctial zone and the assertion that they were bought and came to Ancona from Portugal with the neophytes, who were fleeing the Inquisition. He writes that he calls them "neophytes," using the term of Saint Paul, when he refers to those who were forced against their will to renounce Judaism for Christianity. Here we have a succinct summary of one view of Jewish history, namely, that the conversos are not really Christian, because the conversions were forced rather than voluntary. This is, of course, a matter of controversy down to today. Amatus opts in favor of one view of a history that by then extended back for at least a century and a half. In the fifteenth century, a rather large and extremely well-known polemical corpus had dealt repeatedly with this question in Spain. Here again, we could find parallel Hebrew texts of historiography that show an interest in the question and interpret it in this way. But in his case, what he tells us about the neophytes is also a statement of self-presentation: he is publicizing the view that Portuguese New Christians, like himself, are leaving Portugal (like himself) because of the Inquisition. This is an impression we might gather from another Spanish text of the 1550s, the *Viaje de Turquia*.[25]

Writing about apoplexy (IV, 23), he refers to a case in Salamanca, site of the most famous university in Hispania. A physician who, since he was twenty-eight, had treated Queen Isabel, visited a patient and found the patient's pulse very weak. Nevertheless, he did not prognosticate death. In the afternoon, while returning to see the patient, he was informed that the patient had died. He found him clad in Franciscan habit surrounded by friars. Amatus writes that the physician was a noble and courageous professional who was not greatly impressed by the tricks of the inquisitors. With gravity and serenity, he requested that the shroud be removed, and found the patient still alive. The man lived on for many years. The story is narrated in a dialogue with Armelinus, who wonders whether the inquisitors were moved by avarice and showed contempt for the fear of God. The Iberian Jewish historians mentioned above also express certain positions on the questions of representing Iberia, Judaism, and conversos. Like many of them, Amatus had to confront the realities of reading books in an age that witnessed, among other trends, the transition from manuscript to print.

Humanism and Books

As the epistemological basis of medicine in this period is not only the observation of reality but also the authority of the ancients and certain contemporaries, the practice of medicine involves reading and erudition. Amatus's connections with what we might call the world of books is evident in various ways. For example, his texts always appeal to written authorities. These appeals are usually by citation of a passage from the ancients (for example, Hippocrates and Galen) but also from medieval authorities (for example, Avicenna and Avenzohar) and from his contemporaries. Such erudition hinges on access to books. But Amatus comes from and moves in cultures where the possession and reading of books is not identical for all readers and all books. These basic considerations become more directly relevant when we recall the particular associations of Jews and conversos with books in the sixteenth century. According to Pimenta Ferro, after the forced conversions in Portugal, King Manuel permitted converso physicians or surgeons who knew no Latin to own Hebrew books of medicine. Yet João Nogueira, resident of Matosinhos, lost all his moveable and immoveable goods as punishment for keeping books written in Hebrew in his home. Tome Lopes, merchant of Lisbon, had his possessions confiscated as penalty for writing books and letters in Hebrew characters. Mestre Rodrigo was imprisoned and condemned to public flogging and was to be sent to Cabo Verde for the crime of possession of books in Hebrew.[26] Caro Baroja mentions the Portuguese Cortes that were convened in 1641. According to them, the majority of physicians, surgeons, and pharmacists in Portugal were still conversos. The pharmacists wrote their prescriptions in Hebrew. If we were to believe such evidence, Hebrew was still current almost a century and a half after the expulsion, and knowledge of technical Hebrew texts and terminology was not entirely unrelated to ethnicity.[27] For Amatus, the acquisition of these books depended on booksellers. In a number of cases, he makes specific mention of booksellers, although there is little apparent medical relevance that could justify this introduction of booksellers into the scientific medical text. In a cure in Salonika (VII, 41), he refers to a man who was bitten in the leg by a dog, telling us he is a German who sells books in Salonika. The cure for the dog's bite is the same whether the patient is a bookseller or not. In another cure (III, 48), he tells us that the brother-in-law of the Venetian bookseller Marcos had a tumor in his liver. Although medical theory could be invoked to justify the relevance of a patient's profession to the ailment (because patients with different work habits need different medicines, for example), it is doubtful there is any medical reason for mentioning the profession of the patient's brother-in-law unless this is of special interest for Amatus personally.

Reading is done either in the original language or in translation, a fact that Amatus finds important. Key passages in printed books are consciously underlined. The existence of books or their loss and information about their possible survival are topics broached in the *Centuriae* and in various ways in historical writings from Zacuto through Usque to the *Shevet Yehudah* and beyond. In a dialogue with his nephew Brandão (V, 6), he refers to Dioscorides' commentaries on Hippocrates, noting that a credible person told him that they could be found in Constantinople. Why is the person left anonymous? This could be an example of belated European interest in the remnants of Hellenistic culture in former Byzantium, but is also reminiscent of the Christian European interest in Jewish books of medicine as remains of antiquity, an interest attested in sixteenth-century sources I studied on another occasion.[28] Amatus distinguishes between the original text of Galen, the translation of Avicenna, and the commentaries on Avicenna (I, 1). The corruptions are the products of the commentaries. That is why the editions must take Arabic and the history of the transmission of the text into account and why the translators into Latin have to master these skills. In various cases (I, 9), he shows the importance of translation for the practice of medicine. Speaking of Giovanni Cornario's translation of Hippocrates into Latin, he says that he wishes Cornario had left the terms for the ailments in the original Greek. It is noteworthy that he singles out a polyglot Jew, Jacob Mantino, as the first and optimal choice for such textual work. Mantino, famous for the consultation in Henry VIII's divorce, was known in medical circles for the printed translation of a section of the Canon. Amatus tells us that he encouraged Jacob to continue the partial translations that he had already produced of Avicenna, but that bad luck had prevented it, because a Venetian took Mantino with him to Damascus, in Syria, where Mantino died.[29]

Here we see Amatus as encouraging a certain kind of reading practice as well as leaving a public statement in memory of the deceased translator, a statement that would keep his memory alive as long as the *Centuriae* continued to be printed. Once again, the *Centuriae* prove to be more than a collection of case studies and become models of certain cultural habits such as the praise and encouragement of translations, of textual accuracy, and of polyglossia. Amatus shows interest in textual scholarship and projects of translation—projects facilitating European access to the main texts of medical knowledge. In other words, Amatus's mode of interaction with the society around him (and this means *inter alia* with the conversos in Antwerp, Ferrara, and Salonika) is not restricted to purely clinical treatment. Quite the contrary: the evidence shows that he was an active agent of culture.

What is clear from other passages, although silenced in this case study, is that Amatus believed that these scholarly tasks involved access to and study of manuscript codices with the Arabic text in Hebrew characters (see below on his contempt for those who are beggars from the Hebrew). That is, for him the textual progress of European medical scholarship hinged on acquiring the kind of skills characteristic (though not absolutely exclusive) of Sephardi Jewry. There is no need here to restate the facts of the medieval tradition of Iberian Jewish involvement in translations, but one point is worth stressing. Following Benjamin Richler's list of manuscripts of Avicenna's Canon[30] (which enlarges that offered by Moritz Steinschneider), Nancy Siraisi affirms that the most extensive use made of the Canon outside the universities in Western Europe during the Middle Ages was unquestionably that by Jewish physicians.[31] As late as the seventeenth century, Paolino acknowledged that he wrote a medical work relying on consultation with a "Jewish physician who owned" a Hebrew translation of the Canon.[32] According to Siraisi, "sixteenth-century Italian physicians were perhaps not much more likely to know Hebrew than they were to know Arabic but . . . they had the advantage of the presence of scholarly Jewish medical men who owned and used Hebrew medical manuscripts."[33] Siraisi, who is mainly concerned with Latin texts, nonetheless affirms that quite frequently throughout the sixteenth century, "recourse was made to the medieval Hebrew translations as a means of improving the Latin text of the Canon. . . . In Italy, this strategy was facilitated by the presence of a Jewish medical community" reinforced by recent exiles from the Iberian Peninsula.[34]

Reading

In the third volume (III, 38), Amatus constructs a dialogue with Pirro (probably Didaco Pyrrho), where Pirro states: "I read Galen in his language that is Greek and I saw it in his Book of Aphorisms where I noted it with a line in my copy/codex: there is no acute ailment without continuous fever." In another cure (IV, 42), he refers to the work of Areteu de Capadocia, which, he tells us, he had read some days earlier in the rendering of Paulo Crasso, an erudite and elegant translator. In a cure (II, 20) that I would call an essay on wine, he mentions that Galen believed in wine's curative powers. Then he mentions Angelo Poliziano, who is always named with honor and who in his Epistles proposes an emendation of a corrupt passage in Pliny where hemlock is the subject. In the cure of a naval captain (III, 31), he writes a commentary on Galen's view of bloodletting. Here he shows how he reads Galen. In one passage, Galen says that the bloodletting was conducted until the youth lost his senses. In another passage, in a completely different book, Galen says that six pounds of blood have to be let in order to extinguish the fever. This kind of bloodletting was called lipotimia by the Greeks. But Averroës understood it as syncope, a much more drastic bloodletting than lipotimia, which destroys the motor and sensitive virtues. That is to say, the difference between the original Greek and the Arabic translation and its derivatives is seen as significant from a medical point of view. It hardly needs to be emphasized that the difference between original and translation was one of the methodological cruxes of textual criticism and historiographic practice at this time. But in Amatus's writings, the implications are that the difference between a corrupt text and one that is correctly reconstructed or translated is the difference between life and death.

One section in the work (VII, 53) is entitled "A cure in which Avicenna is reconstituted based on a great error about plagues." He begins by criticizing Andreas Alpagus of Bellune and Benedictus Rinius Venetus, editor of the Venetian Giunta edition of the Canon of Avicenna.[35] They promised a great deal in their translations or reconstitutions of Avicenna into Latin and claimed to confront the Arabic original with the Latin. Yet they committed a grave error, causing Amatus and others great anguish. The question has to do with the difference between refrigerating and humectant properties of substances (or refrigerating and humectant [humidifine] substances). Amatus examined various Latin texts of Avicenna and found that they referred to substances. Then he consulted a Hebrew text and verified that the Latin derives from the Hebrew, or rather that the Hebrew terms were translated by Latinists. In the Hebrew text, Amatus read *bibdarim hakkatim* (for *badvarim hakarim) vmartibim bechoam* (for *umartivim bekoḥam*). He continued to search and used an Arabic text written in Hebrew characters, where he found the truth. And for this he gives great thanks to God Omnipotent and claims that those who are proficient in Arabic know that he is telling the truth. He calls Alpagus and Rinius beggars from a Hebrew text or from a commentary of the Hebrew text. Their reconstitutions of Arabic are not translated from an Arabic original. If they had translated from an Arabic original, they would not have committed such monumental errors.

Again, Amatus seems to be arguing about textual scholarship from a particular cultural context. The ownership, access to, and reading of Judeo-Arabic manuscript codices is well attested and was perhaps commonplace in Spain and Portugal among Jews and conversos, particularly among physicians. Research on Hispano-Jewish attitudes toward the culture of the Muslims has led to the argument that Hispano-Jewish interest in and possession of such texts did not, as was conventionally asserted, cease after the thirteenth century with the Christianization of the peninsula. It is rarer among the Christians, even in an age of Hebraists and Arabists.

The interest in the difference between the original and translation is bound up with textual criticism and the question of particular editions. This brings us to a discussion of relatively new ways of reading in the age of print. For example, when telling us about his cure (VII, 41) of the wife of Samuel da Capua, in the form of a dialogue with Stopio, Amatus cites Galen in a discussion of melancholy, mentioning a consequent abhorrence of water. Here he notes that he found the idea in Galen's *De theriaca ad pisonem*, in the folio of Trincavelio (1081, Latin translation of Johannes Winther, 1545)—which shows that books can now be quoted in a particular edition, with a precise reference to the folio or page in question.

In Amatus's dialogue with Stopio concerning rabies, they debate whether persons are stricken with rabies as the result of a dog's bite. This leads to citations from Leoniceno's work *De Plinii et aliorum medicorum erroribus* (Nicolo Leoniceno, *Opuscula*, Basel, 1532). That in turn leads to a reference to Comotius in the marginal notes that he added to Paulo Egineta, printed in the Venetian typography of Aldo in 1554 (III, 5/6). In a dialogue with Brandão, he gives a brief history of authors, including those Roman and Moorish, who dealt with a problem (V, 6) concerning a form of bloodletting from Galen and Hippocrates down to his own time. He then concludes with the book on surgery by Pietro d'Argellata printed in Venice twenty-five years earlier and containing engravings of various surgical instruments. His nephew replies that the exposition he just heard is very instructive and at the appropriate time he will be able to verify it in the writings of these illustrious authors.

We are naturally led to the topic of the lost texts of antiquity and their reconstruction. According to VI, 94, Arquigenes (the Roman physician from Syria, vol. 75, chap. 129) was a man of singular science. Amatus expresses his longing for the works, wishing they were still existent. In a few cited lines, Arquigenes taught the proper way to drink thermal waters, a practice still observed throughout Italy. Savonarola and other learned persons are in accord with him. A Venetian publisher collected the remains in one volume some years earlier and published them to aid the cause of human health, he adds.

A similar positive attitude to the publisher's role may be found in Amatus's discussion of critical days and the importance of the seventh day (I, 1). Gordon prefers the sixth to the seventh day. Some are quite critical of that interpretation, claiming that he based his reading on a corrupt text of Avicenna. Amatus refers to a recent emendation by Alpagus and Rinius that shows there was indeed a corrupt text. This last example, which conflates our evidence for his consciousness of mediations of the text (such as those of the publishing houses) with the medical question of critical days, brings us to our next topic: chronology in the works of Amatus.

Chronology

Amatus's interest in chronology is, I would argue, related to the notion that the knowledge of the past is relevant to his medical concerns. This leads to thinking about medicine in a way that includes the lessons of the past (although he also believes that everything is changing). The amalgam between history, historiography, and medicine is evident in various ways, and the evidence may be culled from various cures among the seven hundred case studies. In one case, writing about garlic and its beneficial effects on the chest, he refers to Emperor Nero, who firmly believed this and who claimed that when he sang well, it was because of the large amount of garlic he had consumed. That has been noted by Platina in his *De obsoniis* or *De honesta voluptate.* The relation between history and medicine is evident in other cures as well. He cites Thucydides (end of the sixth century, B.C.E.), whose history was published in Ragusa in 1558. Thucydides was one of the grave and illustrious Athenians who stated that history is like a treasure that should never leave one's hands. Amatus states that his *Centuriae* is to medicine what Thucydides' work is to history, a treasure. On the evidence of Amatus's own views, we can assert the presence of a conscious, explicit link between medicine and historiography. He explains the structure of the whole work, the number of the centuries by analogy to Roman history, where Scipio vanquished Sicily and Carthage through three hundred strong young men. Chronology, as is well known, is a crucial subject of sixteenth-century scholarship and historiography, both Christian and Jewish. The question thus arises as to whether it is a marginal, ornamental element in Amatus's *oeuvre* or a significant component.

Amatus's general introduction to the *Centuriae* focuses on the critical or decisive days of an illness and represents a medical work in its own right, with arguments ranging from the texts of the ancients (Hippocrates, Galen) to the more moderns. To this learned disquisition, Amatus adds, however, his own views on the causes of the quality of some days versus others. Since this is presented as a departure from the practice of listing authorities, it deserves comment. He invokes Pico della Mirandola and argues that there is something in the nature of the days, the time, and the chronology itself that causes the medical effects. The analogy is from music, octaves, seven-note scales.

One may briefly recall the general and Jewish Pythagorean tradition. In the field of philosophy of music, there had been a kind of philosophical discourse since the Pythagoreans: it conceived music as a paradigm of celestial or metaphysical truths and thus found significance in the numbers involved in music. Without in any way attempting to summarize Jewish Pythagoreanism, one should recall the Pythagoreanism of the *Sefer ha-yeṣirah*'s thirty-two paths of Creation or the Maimonidean quasi-obsession with the number four.[36] Amatus's awareness of and commitment to this Pythagorean strand lead to the argument of the superiority of the number seven. Here he invokes the *Somnium scipionis*, Virgil, but also the Bible. Seven is the day for mourning, combat, discordance. Nature cannot return to the original state of health without first battling with the enemy. That is to say, a negative, catastrophic phase precedes the ultimate return to a desired original situation. In Jewish thought, this type of thinking is common in messianic texts. The identification of Jews with Saturn, the seventh planet, also occurs in medieval texts. But in reading a text of the 1540s, one might also call attention to Philo's reverence for the number seven (compare the Armenian text, Philo's commentary on Genesis).

Accordingly, in isolation and out of context, various elements of Amatus's argument appear to have an ancient lineage. But in reality, they are not isolated only in his text. In a Hebrew composition closer to Amatus's time, a similar discussion on the properties of the number seven occurs. It was authored in the late fourteenth century or early fifteenth by Profiat Duran, an Iberian Jewish author whose significance has been argued in a number of recent studies. Our interest here is the underlying notion of the significance of chronology. That is to say, both history and medicine have to take account of chronology. In other cases, too, Lusitanus evinces this fascination with chronology.

Dealing with the death of the daughter of Leone Ebreo (II, 20), he tells us that at that time, Ancona was governed by Vicencio de Nobilis, lieutenant of Julius III. What possible medical relevance to the death of this woman could the fact of Nobilis's office be—unless there is an attempt to coordinate different chronologies? Such attempts to coordinate the chronologies of his own life, or the patients' history, with wider events of general history occur elsewhere and are sometimes present explicitly in the various volumes of the *Centuriae*. Thus, the fifth "century" is finished in Ancona in September 1553, while a civil war is raging between Charles V and Henry II and the Turks have occupied Corsica (V, 100). But perhaps the most noteworthy case is that of the explicit articulation or elaboration of a personal reason for engaging in this kind of work, a statement of intention for the *Centuriae* as a whole.

In one of the earliest cures, Amatus tells us in somewhat oblique fashion about the precise moment when he decided to engage in this large task of composing the *Centuriae.* We can take his declaration here as a statement of basic intentionality. At the beginning of the cure of the Jew Alizalain (apparently Alcalay), he says that in Ferrara, the Jew (then twenty-seven) fell ill, stricken with a mortal illness on 4 September 1546. He immediately adds that this was the moment when he proposed to write the *Centuriae.* One may observe that Amatus is by no means accustomed to give such precise dating for his other patients' case histories. After a medical exposition of the illness, he ends by telling us that it was a great comfort to his friends that the patient led a holy life and died blameless on the day in which the Jews ask God's forgiveness for all their sins. There is no medical justification for these comments, and they are unparalleled in all the cases of the death of Christian patients. If we read the whole cure, we realize that Amatus Lusitanus is telling us that the time of the decision to engage in the composition of the *Centuriae* was Yom Kippur, the day that Jews are accustomed to asking for forgiveness. What possible connection or relevance could there be for a Christian between Yom Kippur, the forgiveness of sins, the desire for atonement, and the decision to engage in a long, arduous, intellectual project of medical writings? Amatus attributes the work to the patient's death, and the death directly to the practice by this pious Jew of the customary reciting of prayers at midnight for forty days. He is obviously referring to the special liturgical period of *Seliḥot,* from Rosh Hodesh Elul to Yom Kippur. He adds that this was coupled with care for his elderly father, then eighty years of age. Amatus can thus be perceived as deciding to construct a public statement that relates his work, the *Centuriae,* to the Jewish view of atonement and appeal for forgiveness of sins. This view of the centrality of atonement has too long a history in converso practices and writings to be ignored.[37]

Conclusion

When dealing with the problem of former conversos in the Ottoman Empire with a proven interest in Eutropius and its translation into Spanish, we might proceed in the concentric fashion I suggested. As well evidenced in the sources, texts, and documents, this was a society with great attachment to the languages and hence, the cultures, of Iberia. Thus, a vantage point for understanding cultural phenomena in this society is to give proper consideration to Iberian culture in Iberian languages.

The relation to historiography is a second point. The primary step in understanding Amatus's own interest has to do with the explicit articulation of the Jewish reading principle: that what matters is the quality or truth of a text rather than whether it comes from any particular community. Amatus (I, 15) describes the case of an eighteen-year-old female patient with suppressed menstruation whose body was covered by eruptions. He discusses successive treatments, mainly purges and bloodletting. This leads to a learned disquisition on the polemics between various textual authorities who recommend different places for the bloodletting. In choosing which authority to follow, Amatus says, it is not advisable to hold on obstinately to the teachings of Galen, or to any other sect. Having made his point abundantly clear, Amatus does not stop there. He adds that those who have spoken well should be followed, irrespective of whether they are Roman, Greek, Arab, or Jewish.

This is a principle articulated or practiced in various ways in historiography written by Sephardim, and with different emphases, by Abravanel, Zacuto, Ibn Verga, the alleged author of *Sheveṭ Yehudah*, Usque, and ha-Kohen. The attention to Eutropius has some relation to this principle. I would argue that it is connected with the opening of spaces of scholarly discourse that, while by no means secular or devoid of ethnic allegiance, are nonetheless spaces of ambiguity. An example would be the conversation allegedly held in a bookshop that begins with the topic of Galatinus's work. Azariah de' Rossi enters the conversation.[38] The bookshop is emblematic of the space for such Jewish converso–Christian dialogue. The publishing houses are related spaces where Jews publish non-Jewish books and vice versa. They also enable access to texts of the past.

This is one of Amatus's worlds. Christian Hebraism becomes a factor in permitting engagement with Jewish texts without necessarily engaging in questions of religious polemic or allegiance. The classics are another such factor. But in addition, we note other trends in Amatus's writings that are closely aligned with historiographic readings. First, there were the new reading practices in printed uniform editions, the practices of glossing, underlining, of confronting the page numbers in editions published in particular places that are explicitly mentioned and allow confirmation of the steps that lead to conclusions in medicine or in history. Evaluating translations and differentiating them from originals, constantly questioning translations (word by word)—these are features that mark the author of the *Centuriae*. They substantiate his evident interest in the field of translation. This might help to understand his translation of the Roman historian Eutropius. Attention to chronology and to chronological concordances are additional characteristics of Amatus's writings that render his explicit interest in an ancient historian less puzzling.

Notes

1. E. Gutwirth, "Sephardi Culture of the Genizah People," *Michael* 14 (1997): 9–34.

2. D. Front, "The Expurgation of the Books of Amatus Lusitanus: Censorship and the Bibliography of the Individual Book," *Book Collector* 47 (1998): 520–36.

3. H. Friedenwald, "Some Jewish Interests of a Marrano Physician," in idem, *The Jews and Medicine* (Baltimore, 1944), 1: 381 ff. (first published in *Menorah Journal* 28 [1940]).

4. D. Harari, "Mihu hamelumad hayehudi shedarko noda' sefer or ha-Shem le-Pico," in *Miromi le-Yerushalayim*, ed. A. Ravitzky (Jerusalem, 1998), pp. 257–69.

5. Front, "The Expurgation."

6. R. Segre, "Nuovi documenti sui marrani d'Ancona," *Michael* 9 (1985): 130–33.

7. G. H. Tucker, "To Louvain and Antwerp and Beyond: The Contrasting Itineraries of Diogo Pires (Didacus Pyrrhus Lusitanus, 1517–1599) and João Rodrigues de Castelo Branco (Amatus Lusitanus, 1511–1568), *Medievalia Lovaniensia* 26 (1998): 83–113.

8. S. Pampiglione, "Un cas probable de dirofilariose humaine sous conjonctivale observé par Amatus Lusitanus," *Parasite* 2 (1995): 92; see also idem, "Dirofilariosi umana sottocongiuntivale," *Parasitologia* 37, no. 1 (1995): 75–78. Another example would be J. Garcia Silva, "Amatus Lusitanus on Tumors of the Skin," *American Journal of Dermatopathology* 9 (1987): 533–36.

9. J. Seide, "The Two Diabetics of Amatus Lusitanus," *Imprensa Medica* 19 (1955): 1–6.

10. J. O. Leibowitz, "A Probable Case of Peptic Ulcer as Described by Amatus Lusitanus (1556)," *Bulletin of the History of Medicine* 27, no. 3 (1953): 212–16.

11. J. O. Leibowitz, "Amatus Lusitanus on Sudden Death Due to Obstruction in the Heart (1560)," *Estudos Castelo Branco* 2 (1962): 1–18.

12. J. de Paiva Boleo, "Amatus Lusitanus: The Inventor of the Palatine Obdurator," *Estudos Castelo Branco* 8 (1968). See also J. O. Leibowitz, "Amatus Lusitanus and the Obdurator in Cleft Palates," *Journal of the History of Medicine and Allied Sciences* 13 (1958): 492–503.

13. Maximiano Lemos could be seen as the last attempt to try to integrate the various facets of Amatus. See his *Amato Lusitano* (Porto, 1907).

14. See, for example, L. Glesinger, "Lijecnik Amatus Lusitanus," in *Zbornik* (Jevrejski istorijski muzej Beograd) 1 (1971): 291–312.

15. M. Santoro, *Amatus Lusitanus ed Ancona* (Coimbra, 1991).

16. S. S. Kottek, "Amatus Lusitanus in Salonica: The Last Paragraph in an Eventful Biography," in *Actas del XXXIII Congreso Internacional de Historia de la Medicina* (Seville, 1994), pp. 409–16. See also J. O. Leibowitz, "Amatus Lusitanus a Salonique," *XXI Congresso Internazionale di Storia della Medicina* (Siena, 1968), pp. 1769–72; see also idem, "Amato Lusitano a Salonica," *Revista Mensile Israelitica* 37 (1971): 378–81.

17. See J. Caria Mendes's contribution to the memorial volume to Amatus, *Centenario de Joao Rodrigues de Castelo Branco* ed. M. Correia et al. (Castelo Branco, 1968).

18. I refer in the following to the volume of the *Centuriae* first in capital Roman numerals and then to the specific cure by number. The bibliography of the editions seems to be a subject that has not yet been exhausted. There are still apparently unrecorded items while others are recorded but were not accessible to Friedenwald. Friedenwald's bibliography of the *Centuriae*, beginning with the first edition of the first volume (i.e., *Curationum medicinalium Centuria prima multiplici variaque rerum cognitione referta. Praefixa est eiusdem auctoris commentatio in qua docetur quomodo se medicus habere debeat in introitu ad aegrotantem simulque de crisi et diebus decretoriis iis qui artem medicam exercent et quotidie pro salute aegretorum in collegium descendunt longe utilissima* [Florence, 1551]) up to the seventh (Venice, 1566) contains about sixteen items. Jose Lopes Dias mentions about nineteen editions of different volumes, formats, etc. See his "O Renascimento em Amato Lusitano e Garcia D'Orta," *Estudos Castelo Branco* 4 (1964): 29 n. 52. See also more recently the list in *Firmino Crespo Amato Lusitano* (Lisbon, 1987), to which I am greatly indebted.

19. Friedenwald, *The Jews and Medicine*, p. 361.

20. C. Roth, *The Duke of Naxos* (Philadelphia, 1948), p. 178.

21. See C. Ando's review in *Bryn Mawr Classical Review* (1993) of Eutropius, *Breviarium*, trans. H. W. Bird (Liverpool, 1993), as well as Bird's discussion of the question of the *fortuna* in the introduction and bibliography cited there.

22. This has little in common with the cases of other sixteenth-century Jewish historians, whose theory and practice of medical writing is, at least in the present state of research, little more than an anecdotal curiosity because their medical writings did not assume the importance of and never achieved the fame of those of Amatus, and they have not been comparaby preserved.

23. Castro saw this as part of the general "semitism" of Hispanic culture, where the norm was the Hispano-Arabic integralism derived from authors such as Avicenna. For Bataillon, this seems to be the norm in European scientific texts as a whole: "ces excursus ou un naturaliste invoque son experience professionelle, c'est de la science encore. . . . Dans le cas des sciences naturelles, il semble qu'il faille tenir compte d'une tradition très large et d'une exigence même de ces sciences dans lesquelles la qualité du temoin et les circonstances de son observation important à la valeur du temoignage qu'il apporte. Dans la littératuer scientifique française on pour-

rait citer des pages très pesonnelles de forme franchement autobiographique chez des entomologistes du XVIIIe ou du XIXe siècle," That is to say, Bataillon here does not provide sixteenth-century parallels to Laguna's peculiarities regarding the habit of personal digression. For Castro and Bataillon, see the latter's "Nouvelles recherches sur le *Viaje de Turquia*," *Romance Philology* 5 (1951): 77–97.

24. E. Gutwirth, "Gender, History and the Medieval Judaeo-Christian Polemic," in *Contra Iudaeos: Ancient and Medieval Polemics between Jews and* Christians, ed. O. Limor (Tübingen, 1996), pp. 257–78.

25. On the *Viaje de Turquia* and its relation to Jewish and Christian history and culture, see E. Gutwirth, "Language and Medicine in the Ottoman Empire," in *Religious Confessions and the Sciences in the Sixteenth Century*, ed. J. Helm and A. Winkelmann (Studies in European Judaism, 1) (Leiden, 2001), pp. 79–98.

26. M. J. Pimenta Fero, *Os judeus em Portugal no seculo XV* (Lisbon, 1982), p. 493.

27. J. Caro Baroja, *Los judios en la España moderna y contemporanea* (Madrid, 1978), 2: 184.

28. Gutwirth, "Language and Medicine in the Ottoman Empire," pp. 79–98.

29. On Jacob Mantino, see, for example, D. Carpi, *Between Renaissance and Ghetto* (Hebrew) (Tel Aviv, 1989), pp. 89–95; see also Carpi, "Sulla permanenza a Padova nel 1533 del medico ebreo Jacob di Shemuel Mantino," *Quaderni per la storia dell'Università di Padova* 18 (1985): 196–203.

30. B. Richler, "Manuscripts of Avicenna's Canon in Hebrew Translation: A Revised and Up-to-Date List," *Koroth* 8 (1982): 145–68.

31. N. Siraisi, *Avicenna in Renaissance Italy* (Princeton, N.J., 1987), p. 48 n. 19.

32. Ibid., p. 144.

33. Ibid., pp. 138, 135.

34. As is well known, it was believed (by Abraham Halkin, Cecil Roth, etc.) that around the time of the Almohad invasion, the Jews rejected Arabic and turned to Hebrew as the language of culture. For research on attitudes toward Arabic, see, for example, E. Gutwirth, "Hispano-Jewish Attitudes to the Moors in the Fifteenth Century," *Sefarad* 49 (1989): 237–62; idem, "Toledo, circa 1320: Los judios y el Arabe," in *Creencias y culturas*, ed. C. Carrete Parrondo (Salamanca, 1998), pp. 97–112; Gutwirth, "Oro de Ophir: El arabe y Don Shem Tov de Carrion," *Bulletin of Hispanic Studies* 77 (2000): 275–86.

35. *Liber canonis de medicinis cordialibus cantica de remouendis nocementis in regimine sanitatis de syrupo acetoso*, ed. Benedictus Rinius and Andreas Alpagus. *His acceßit vita Avicennæ ex Sorsano Arabe eius discipulo a Nicolao Masso philosopho, & medico egregio sumpta, & latine scripta.* Liber I–III (von 5) (Venice, 1562).

36. I cannot go into detail here on the persistence of Pythagoreanism in Jewish culture, a subject treated by Y. Tzvi Langermann in his May 2001 lecture at the Bar-Ilan University Medievalists Symposium, or on the issue of Philonic continuity treated by Chiesa from the age of H. A. Wolfson's predecessors down to the present. For the medieval Jewish tradition of analogy between musical, medical, and philosophical ideas, see the texts in I. Adler, *Hebrew Writings Concerning Music* (Munich, 1975). For the persistence of the identification of Jews with Saturn in late medieval Iberia, see E. Gutwirth, "The Persecution of the Jews in Mediaeval Spain," in *Judios*

entre arabes y cristianos, ed. A. Sáenz-Badillos (Córdoba, 2000), pp. 111–32. Amatus is working within the genre of critical days' literature while also subverting this authoritative tradition by attachment to the number seven. In explaining this phenomenon, one would wish to have the facts. And in a converso Hebraist from Iberia, there is no reason to exclude the kind of culture that made possible Profiat Duran's composition on the number seven. On Profiat Duran's significance, see, for example, E. Gutwirth, "History and Apologetics in XVth c. Hispano-Jewish Thought." *Helmantica* 35 (1984): 231–42; idem, "Actitudes judias hacia el cristianismo: Ideario de los traductores hispano-judios del latin," in *Actas II Congreso Internacional Encuentro de las Tres Culturas*, ed. C. Carete Parrondo (Toledo, 1985), pp. 189–96; idem, "Conversions to Christianity in Late Medieval Spain: An Alternative Explanation," in *S. Simonsohn Jubilee Volume: Studies on the History of the Jews in the Middle Ages and Renaissance Period*, ed. D. Carpi (Tel Aviv, 1993), pp. 97–122; idem, "Religion and Social Crriticism in Late Medieval Rousillon: An Aspect of Profayt Duran's Activities," *Michael* 12 (1991): pp. 135–56; idem, "Profiat Duran on Ahitofel: The Practice of Jewish History in Late Medieval Spain," *Jewish History* 41 (1989): 59–74; idem, "Italy or Spain? The Theme of Jewish Eloquence in the *Sheveṭ Yehudah*" in *Daniel Carpi Jubilee Volume*, ed. M. Rozen (Tel Aviv, 1996), pp. 35–67; idem, "The Stranger's Wisdom: Translation and Otherness in Fifteenth-Century Iberia," *Portuguese Studies* 13 (1997): 130–42. The issue of the number seven in converso cultures has been treated in some cases, but must still be seriously investigated in others, such as the texts authored by Daniel Levi de Barrios and Joseph de la Vego Penso. It would be a very curious and eccentric approach to deny the Pythagoreanism of the author of *El siglo pitagorico*. On seven in the tradition that goes from Leone Ebreo to Gomez, see the modern annotated edition by C. Rose of *Loa sacramental de los siete planetas* (Exeter, 1987); Rose, "Antonio Enriquez Gomez y el Templo de Salomon," in *Encuentros y desencuentros*, ed. A. Doron (Tel Aviv, 2000), pp. 413–29.

37. In addition, it could be argued that as a result of his writings, the printing presses of Europe acted to disseminate, communicate, and teach Jewish customs to all those who were forbidden to learn about customs connected with the calendar (such as *Seliḥot* ["penitential prayers"] in this case, or the avoidance of pork in others, as well as other customs, e.g., Kaddish), which attracted the attention of the sixteenth-century censors and were partially collected by Harry Friedenwald and Dov Front.

38. See G. Veltri, "Der Lector Prudens und die Bibliothek des (uralten) Wissens: Pietro Galatino, Amatus Lusitanus und Azaria de' Rossi," in *Christliche Kabbala: Johannes Reuchlins geistesgeschichtliche Wirkung*, ed. W. Schmidt-Biggemann (Pforzheim, forthcoming).

Chapter 11

Italy in Safed, Safed in Italy: Toward an Interactive History of Sixteenth-Century Kabbalah

Moshe Idel

Introduction

Writing good history consists, to a great extent, in resisting natural tendencies to anachronism and homogeneity. This is true of both history in general and Jewish mysticism. Any historian is a child of his time who, more often than not, attempts to recapture something in a distant past and use modern lenses to make sense of the different. If good historians, they continuously endeavor to retrieve something, frequently something quite spectacular, that differs from their ordinary present experiences, to conceptualize views that may not only be different from their own but also may even offend their sensibilities. The search for relevance, a natural propensity, is seldom more than an attempt to adapt the past to the present in order to adopt it while changing it retroactively. Anachronism is not only a matter of projecting our present concerns upon distant events in the past but of projecting more recent worldviews, now considered past, upon those more distant. The process of writing history may be negatively affected not only by imposing our belated agendas, but also by adopting points of view informed by historical developments posterior to the event that a historian wants to describe, though found long before the historian starts his investigation. An inherent determinism of historical events may unconsciously project an "effect" backward on what is deemed to be a cause. Events that become important later may put in the shadows a secondary series of events that may be misread because of the strong light shed by the posteriorly important events. This does not mean that there are no main events versus secondary ones from the point of view of greater or smaller effects, but that we should be aware that interpretation of certain early events is often determined by later, and perhaps even more important, ones. This observation can also be formulated in another way: by establishing a historical causality between two events, it is possible that we impose the importance we attribute to the effect likewise on its hypothesized cause.

Dealing again with methodology, we shall have to take into account the transformation inherent in the very process of transmission of a given lore from one center to another. Transmission entails transformation to a greater or lesser extent.[1] Homogeneity is rarely a characteristic of a vital and creative center, and a portrayal of kabbalah as a whole as homogenous is hardly a prescription for an adequate understanding of any of its main phases. We may speak about the importance of the interference intrinsic in the transition of a literary corpus from one cultural area to another, from one group of authors to another, even if they belong roughly to the same social status, or what may be called "horizontal mobility." The transition from one culture to another is particularly evident in the case of kabbalah in the sixteenth century. After the expulsion, the various types of this lore moved from Christian regions to areas under Muslim and Ottoman authority, and during the time that the Safedian center flourished, its achievements radiated to Christian cultural ambiences. This move invites more complex solutions, which will be discussed below.

In principle, the mobility of ideas and modes of thought may also create transitions from one type of life to another, or what can be called "vertical transition." Those distinctions are pertinent for the history of the dissemination of many writings produced by the kabbalistic center in Safed, outside the Land of Israel.[2] However, the question of whether a neat type of export—in our case, from Safed to the outside—is possible in principle is complicated by the quandary raised in our first observation: we look to Safed as the great spiritual center that radiates to the outside. The major question is whether this picture, true from a certain moment in history, is not in fact more complex, entailing forms of interaction that relate to Safedian kabbalah before the town acquired the reputation of the great center. It is sufficient to read the comparison that R. Judah Hallewah drew between Safed around 1545 and Fez, from which he came: Fez is perceived as better organized and superior in an ethical sense.[3] Isn't the teleological reading of scholars of Safed in the first stages of its floruit in the 1540s and 1550s colored by the status this city and its kabbalists achieved later, in the 1560s and 1570s? Two examples can illustrate how Safed has been imagined, anachronistically: according to Solomon Schechter's portrayal of the town, Safed would seem to be an anticipation of Polish Hasidism.[4] However, from G. Scholem's perspective on the nature of the Safedian kabbalah, especially Lurianic, this lore anticipated Sabbatean messianism, and its dissemination contributed substantially to the very emergence of this mass movement.[5] Both descriptions indeed contributed in varying degrees to a better understanding of later developments.

The only question is to what extent the later developments influenced scholarly retroactive understanding of the Safedian ambience and its spiritual creativity. Thus, for example, Scholem creates a unilinear history with the expulsion from Spain as the starting point, Safed as the peak, and Sabbateanism as the organic follow-up: "The development of Jewish mysticism from the time of the Spanish exodus onward has been singularly uniform and free from crosscurrents. There is only one main line. The catastrophic events of that period led directly to the rise of the new school of Safed, whose thoughts, as we have seen, centered round certain problems created and become visible through that great cataclysm."[6] Just as the expulsion shaped Safedian creativity, the latter shaped Sabbatean thought. If the expulsion was described as the trigger of certain conceptual developments in kabbalah, most eminently the Safedian current, the Sabbatean movement affected the way in which Safed has been read, namely, retroactively. To my mind, Scholem's most important historiosophical statement on kabbalah is: "Lurianic kabbalism, Sabbateanism, and Hasidism are, after all, three stages of the same process."[7]

In the following, I discuss various facts and events that problematize the assumption of a uniform, unilinear history of kabbalah, "free from crosscurrents," and for this purpose I focus on the interactions between Italian kabbalists and the kabbalistic sources written in Safed. This means that the arrival of the Cordoverian and Lurianic types of kabbalah to Italy should be understood not only as the move of a series of writings from one place to another, a technical issue dealing with copyists, disciples and emissaries, and modalities of oral transmission; what is even more central is the assimilation of one type of thought, the mythical visions of Cordovero and Luria, into an ambience impregnated by a Neoplatonic mode of thinking. Scholarship should deal much more with questions concerning the meaning of the arrival of a corpus of writings in a new cultural environment. That move is not a mechanical transportation of books and manuscripts, but of complex ideas appropriated in strong ways, informed by the rich intellectual background produced by Marsilio Ficino's translation of Greek and Hellenistic treatises. This is not a simple encounter between an active father (Lurianic kabbalah) and a passive mother (the Italian Jewish Renaissance), allegedly impregnated by the father. The reading of Safedian kabbalah by the Italian kabbalists is sometimes a very strong one, reflecting hermeneutical grids of the Italian Jewish thinkers. This understanding is clear in the interpretations offered, for example, for the Lurianic concepts of *ṣimṣum*.[8] They were not only fervent adherents of kabbalistic traditions that had been continuously radiating from Safed since the mid-sixteenth century, or simple-minded consumers who learned new religious truths transpiring from the sacrosanct center, but also active thinkers who contributed modes of looking at the material they were consuming, perspectives stemming from their being part of an intellectual world alien to that of the Safedian kabbalists. This is why the scholarly assumption that the arrival of Lurianic kabbalah in Italy, conceived as fraught with messianic valences, automatically means the transmission of such valences to the Italian kabbalists is too simplistic.[9] Scholem's assumption, as he formulated it, is that the "new kabbalism," namely, the Lurianic, "conquered Judaism."[10] He even speaks about a "movement" emanating from Safed.[11] An unqualified Safedo-centric triumphalism is strongly coupled to the claim of a messianic vision of the spiritual life in the town, an issue to which I shall return below. Let me emphasize the importance of the epithet "unqualified": it is to prevent a misunderstanding of my position, which accepts the rare creativity and deep impact of Safedian kabbalah while qualifying it by examining how the Safedian impact happened. I propose to qualify the unqualified assessment of Safedian mystical culture as influencing, without significant changes, Italian kabbalah. To a certain extent, unqualified Safedo-centrism has something to do with expressions of topocentrism related to the Land of Israel, expressed in sixteenth-century Safed by R. Solomon le-Veit ha-Turiel,[12] and later in R. Abraham Azulai's *Ḥesed le-Avraham* and R. Nathan Neta Shapira of Jerusalem's *Ṭuv ha'areṣ*.

The non-hermeneutic approach to the history of dissemination of knowledge dominant in modern scholarship is obvious: the messianic spirit of Lurianic kabbalah was portrayed as leaving the Galilean soil in a triumphant march to spread itself intact throughout the Jewish world, becoming a movement that culminated in Sabbateanism. However, what happened in reality in the Italian center is an attenuation of the theurgical, and implicitly of many of the messianic elements found in Lurianic kabbalah, due to the philosophical orientation of the active recipients. We shall return to this topic in the following discussions.[13] Ioan P. Couliano, in his *Eros and Magic*, illuminates the possible importance of hermeneutical grids in a passage dealing with this topic in the Renaissance:

> The originality of an era is not measured by the content of its ideological systems but rather by its "selective will," that is, according to the *interpretive grille* it imposes between preexisting contents and their "modern" treatment. The passing of a message through the hermeneutical filter of an era produces two results of a semantic kind: the first, aiming at the very organization of the cultural structure of the time and hence located outside it, is set forth as a complex and subtle mechanism of emphasis or, on the contrary, of suppression of certain ideological contents; the second, which operates in the very interior of the cultural structure, is set forth as a systematic distortion or even a semantic inversion of ideas which pass through the interpretive grille of the era.[14]

Thus, the specific modes of emphasis and suppression, on the one hand, and the specific semantic distortions, on the other, may be part of the selective will that contributes to the spiritual structure of a certain period. I am not interested in portraying an era but rather a number of specific developments that took place between two centers active during roughly the same period and intensely interacting between themselves. I am especially interested in pointing out the selective will of sixteenth-century and early seventeenth-century Italian kabbalists in comparison with their contemporary Safedian kabbalists.

Three features of Jewish kabbalah flowered during the Italian Renaissance, which characterize it in comparison with the Safedian variety. The Italian kabbalists are much more universalistic than their contemporaries in the Galilee. This observation has something to do with their relative indifference toward the *Zohar*, which became the most important source for Safedian kabbalah. Though printed in Italy in the mid-sixteenth century, this book was commented on time and again only in Safed. Another aspect of Italian universalism is its relative neglect of the importance of the commandments in the overall structure of their books, a topic we will return to at the end of this paper. The attitude toward Christianity is more open and welcoming in Italian Jewish kabbalah than in its Safedian counterpart, which we shall illustrate below. Finally, the Italian kabbalists had a much more positive attitude toward philosophy than the Safed kabbalists did. The different syntheses between kabbalah and philosophy contributed to a more diversified kabbalistic literature in Italy than we encounter in Safed. This diversity also reflects the basic diversity of the Italian Renaissance. It should be emphasized that the early Florentine Renaissance, from the late fifteenth century, emerged not as a purely internal development, but from the appropriation of two main corpora. These arrived in Florence: Greek-Hellenistic literatures, from the East, from Byzantium, translated and with commentary by Marsilio Ficino; and kabbalistic literature, largely from the West, from Spain, translated into Latin by Flavius Mithridates and Christianized even more by Pico della Mirandola. As I have suggested in a number of studies[15] and as has been recently irrefutably demonstrated,[16] the main topics in the early Florentine Renaissance might have been influenced by Jewish and Judeo-Arabic texts available in Florence. As pointed out by Pines, some aspects of Leone Ebreo's theory of love were influenced by Arab philosophy.[17] Thus, the beginning of the new intellectual development in Florence is quite heterogeneous; indeed, it seems that heterogeneity may well be a principal trigger of creativity in cultural centers. Safed was doubtless a heterogeneous center from the point of view of the communities that constituted its Jewish population, and this heterogeneity contributed to the creativity in the town.[18] Nevertheless, let me emphasize that by and large, Safedian kabbalah as a whole is more homogenous than its Italian counterpart.

Safedian kabbalah, the Cordoverian as well as the Lurianic schools, developed against a variety of religious backgrounds, enumerated and briefly discussed below. After the renascence of kabbalistic lore in the relatively isolated ambience of Safed, which cultivated a particular mythological attitude, those traditions arrived in Italy, where some Jews were steeped in Italian Renaissance modes of thinking. Those modes shaped, and sometimes significantly dictated the manner in which Safedian traditions were accepted and interpreted. Specific examples of selection and interpretation should be analyzed one by one. Below, I suggest the methodological question of the necessity of reading two centers of culture together. However, this more detailed examination is not a mere desideratum: more elaborate treatments of the qualified acceptance of Safedian kabbalah in Italy and thinkers shaped by Italian culture are already available, especially in the detailed analysis of Nissim Yosha of R. Abraham Kohen Herrera's thought, mentioned above, and in my study dealing with late sixteenth- and early seventeenth-century perceptions of kabbalah.[19] The following remarks take into consideration developments in two great fields of Jewish studies in the late sixteenth and early seventeenth century: the voluminous studies on Safedian kabbalah; and Jewish kabbalah in Italy. In recent generations, those fields have been given special attention in the studies by Joseph Avivi, Meir Benayahu, Robert Bonfil, Jeffrey Chayes, Yoni Garb, Ephraim Gottlieb, Yoram Jacobson, Arthur Lesley, Fabrizio Lelli, Yehudah Liebes, Abraham Melamed, Ronit Meroz, David Ruderman, Bracha Sack, Havah Tirosh-Rothschild, Nissim Yosha, and me. This work significantly alters the rather general and nebulous picture of what happened in those two centers. We now have a better picture: a more diversified and detailed understanding of their respective emergences. Thanks to Ronit Meroz's recent studies on Lurianic kabbalah, the picture of the development of this lore already in its nascent phases has become more diversified. She was able to differentiate between Sarug—whom Meroz, unlike most previous scholars, views as a direct disciple of Luria—and other trends in Luria's circle. Moreover, she posits the development of a previously unknown school to which Sarug belonged, located somewhere in the Orient contemporary with Luria and his students, which had an impact on crucial formulations of Sarug's kabbalah while he was in Italy. Scholarship has advanced even more rapidly with regard to Italy: the studies on R. Ezra of Fano and his student R. Menaḥem Azariah of Fano, Abraham Yagel, Abraham Herrera, Joseph Delmedigo of Crete, and Leon Modena have progressed in a remarkable manner.

Are these numerous studies facilitating the emergence of a picture different from that of two generations ago? The answer is not clear. To believe some scholars who belong to Scholem's school of research and who are still writing on kabbalah, nothing in his findings needs emendation, and the old picture should be faithfully reproduced, as indeed happens. Unacquainted with or unable to see the dramatic changes taking place in the work of so many scholars, they resort to a simplistic recapitulation.[20] My own answer, however, is positive. The new material discovered and analyzed over the last thirty years is immense and contributes substantial changes to the old picture of kabbalah. What is emerging from some of these studies is a more complex picture of each of the two centers. Those complexities are not only a matter of inner differentiation between members of a certain group: they may culminate in the emergence of different types of exchanges between various factions in the two centers. For example, the role played by several unknown kabbalists who sent Lurianic material to Italy may be more significant for some aspects of the history of kabbalah than the writings of a certain disciple of Luria. Indeed, we know that such an event took place, perhaps more than once, but we do not know who was instrumental in this dissemination, interdicted by both Luria and Vital. I think that the change in scholarship dealing with the history of kabbalah will emphasize the importance of perceiving complex cultural processes in lieu of the earlier unilinear progression.

The previous scholarly picture, which viewed Safed as the sole important religious center dictating most of the major developments abroad, has been modified in a number of studies, though none seems to have been aware of the implications of the specific claims for the thesis I would like to propose here. I suggest that categories such as centers, trajectories, and the reactions and interactions between them are central to an explanation of cultural processes in general and the history of kabbalah in particular. I will present another example to demonstrate the importance of interactions between the two centers in the discussion below.[21]

The Awareness of Italy and Its Culture in Safed

What created the particularly rich Safedian productivity in kabbalah? Several factors can be suggested: first, the encounter between different forms of Jewish tradition—Ashkenazi, Sefardi, and autochthonous Jewish culture in the Galilee. This culture includes visits to the tombs of holy men around Safed, such as that of the traditionally assumed author of the *Zohar*, R. Simon bar Yoḥai in Meron,[22] and the belief that the Messiah's advent will appear in the Galilee.[23] The second factor is the emergence of a critical mass, or significant kabbalistic groups that encouraged and sustained large-scale kabbalistic systems unknown earlier in the history of this lore.[24] Another factor, often ignored in modern studies of Safedian culture, especially that of kabbalah, is an awareness by the Safedian kabbalists of the developments in kabbalah taking place in Italy. From its beginning, Safedian kabbalah had significant contacts with Italy. For example, one of the first Spanish kabbalists to arrive in Safed immediately after the expulsion was R. Isaac Mor Ḥayyim. His stay in Italy is connected with a polemic against the more philosophical position of the Italian kabbalists.[25]

Events in Italy surrounding R. Solomon Molkho had various impacts on Safedian kabbalists: for R. Joseph Karo, the death of Molkho as a martyr in Mantua was an example he very much desired to imitate.[26] Yet Cordovero and Vital described Molkho's involvement in magic in quite negative terms.[27] Despite their relatively short stay in Italy, those two kabbalists reflect more the Spanish than the Italian kabbalah in their writings. Likewise, the main sources of Safedian kabbalah are of Spanish provenance, especially the *Zohar.* Nevertheless, the impact of the ecstatic kabbalah of Abulafia and his followers is also discernible in the kabbalah of Cordovero and some of his disciples. Most of the ecstatic material was composed in Italy in the late thirteenth century and the fourteenth century.[28] Later Italian developments in the kabbalah, especially the writings of Yoḥanan Alemanno and Abraham de Balmes, did not attract the attention of Safedian kabbalists. Nevertheless, at least one kabbalistic treatise written by an Italian kabbalist was available and quoted explicitly by R. Moses Cordovero: R. David Messer Leon's *Magen David.* As pointed out by Ephraim Gottlieb, Cordovero's view of the nature of the ten *sefirot* was shaped in interacting with Messer Leon's views.[29]

Beyond Cordovero's specific reference to Messer Leon, there can be no doubt that indirectly, some of his discussions on the *sefirot* were related to the dispute in Italy in the late fifteenth century, a fact corroborated by several important kabbalistic documents.[30] R. Judah Ḥayyat, like Isaac Mar Ḥayyim, was a Spanish kabbalist who encountered a different type of kabbalah when he arrived in Italy from Spain, and while disputing the Jewish Italian kabbalah because of its more philosophical inclinations, he was nevertheless influenced by it.[31] It is possible that the view of cosmic love found in Cordovero and his circle may have something to do with David Messer Leon's thinking, though it would be plausible to assume a more substantial impact of Renaissance cosmoeroticism.[32] Cordovero had an Italian kabbalist, R. Mordekhai Dato, as a student; Dato wrote an enthusiastic description of his master and of his own stay in Safed.[33] Cordovero was also in contact with the rising leader of Italian kabbalists, the young R. Menaḥem Azariah of Fano, to whom he sent as a gift a manuscript copy of his voluminous *Pardes rimmonim,* a gesture that demonstrates his great appreciation of a young kabbalist who by then was not a disciple of Safedian kabbalism.[34] It is plausible that R. Ezra of Fano, an acquaintance of both Menaḥem Azariah and Codovero, also studied in Safed with R. Abraham Galante. It should be mentioned that Galante, a major Cordoverian kabbalist, was, like his brother Moses, born in Italy, apparently in Rome.[35] R. Samuel de Uzeida, one of the main disciples of Luria and Vital, also had an Italian student, R. Gershon ben Simḥah Kitzman, who in 1583 printed in Venice his commentary on Esther. His influential *Midrash Shmuel* went through several printings there. The issue is not to point out the easily identifiable affinities between the two centers, but to determine the extent of those affinities and the possibility that there was a more interactive type of relationship rather than just the spread of contents from one center to another.

In more general terms, David Tamar and I have pointed out the linkage between sixteenth-century Italy and the Safedian center, and this linkage may account for the impact of the Italian interest in messianism on Safedian speculations on the topic.[36] We may assume that messianic impulses, widespread in Italy among Jews and non-Jews before the ascent of Safed, could have contributed to Safedian messianism. After all, both in Safed and Italy, treatises were composed that do not evince any betrayal of messianic impulses, such as R. Judah Hallewah's *Ṣafnat pa'aneaḥ*, R. Ovadiah Hamon's short treatises, most of Cordovero's and Solomon Alqabeṣ's writings, da Vidas's *Reshit ḥokhma*, Azikri's books and later, outside Safed, even R. Ḥayyim Vital's *Sha'arei kedushah*. To what extent R. Isaac Luria's books are messianic is a complex question hitherto not addressed in detail by the "messianists" in modern scholarship, who all too easily messianized the content of many Safedian kabbalistic works.[37]

The main contribution of Safedian kabbalah is not its overt or latent messianism, although undoubtedly such impulses were in Safed, as they appear in many other kabbalistic systems. However, they do not constitute the thrust of kabbalistic creativity in that city. I see Safed as the first large-scale systematization of detailed and authoritative mystical interpretations of the Jewish ritual by means of complex theosophical superstructures. It is the stabilizing or the cementing aspects of Safedian kabbalah that most attracted the attention of other Jewish thinkers, especially in the form of ethical-kabbalistic literature, rather than arcane hints at "implicit" messianism.

The awareness of Safedian kabbalists of what was happening in Italy is more pronounced with respect to new developments related to the emergence of Christian kabbalah: "Just as foxes had damaged the vineyard of God, the Lord of the Hosts, nowadays in the land of Italy the priests studied the science of kabbalah and they diverted it to heresy, because of our sins, and the Ark of the Lord's Covenant, the very science [of Kabbalah] had hidden itself. But blessed is he who gave it to us, because neither they[38] nor the Gentiles distinguish between right and left, but are similar to animals[39] because, ultimately, they did not fathom the inner [essence of the lore]."[40] This passage reflects an explicit awareness of the appropriation of kabbalah by Christians, which created a strong reaction among Lurianic kabbalists, who accordingly emphasized particular aspects of kabbalah and a strong esoteric attitude toward this lore.[41]

Attempting to establish an affinity between the prominent Safedian kabbalist Luria and the Renaissance Italian interest in kabbalah is not a simple historical task. It presupposes the possibility of documenting an acquaintance, fascination, or even an obsession on the part of kabbalists in the Land of Israel with the quandary sparked by the emergence of Christian kabbalah in Italy. That an awareness of the problems generated by this form of kabbalah was found in Jerusalem and Safed is obvious from quotations from R. Abraham ben Eliezer Halevi and, more important, from R. Moses Cordovero, Luria's acknowledged master in kabbalah. The most eminent Christian kabbalist, William Postel, visited the Land of Israel, mainly Jerusalem, in 1549–1550, the beginning of the flowering of Cordovero and Safedian kabbalists, who could have learned about this visit.[42] Cordovero was familiar with R. Moses Basola, himself an acquaintance of Postel from their Italian years.[43] There is, therefore, little doubt that Safedian kabbalists knew of this visit, though Postel himself is never mentioned by any of them.

Even in a passage by one of the closest kabbalists to Luria, his disciple R. Ḥayyim Vital—he, too, a former student of Cordovero's—we may discern interest in the transmission of secrets to Christians. In one of his dreams he committed to writing, he reported that he arrived in Rome, only to be arrested by the officials of the "Roman Caesar." He is brought by soldiers to the "Caesar" and the latter orders the hall cleared, leaving them alone. Vital reports his dream as follows: "We were left by ourselves. I said to him: 'On what grounds do you want to kill me? All of you are lost in your religions like blind men. For there is no truth but the Torah of Moses, and with it alone can exist no other truth.' He (the Roman Caesar) replied: 'I already know all this and so I sent for you. I know that you are the wisest and most skilled of men in the wisdom of truth.[44] I, the most knowledgeable, want you to reveal to me some of the secrets of the Torah and the names of your blessed Lord, for I already recognized the truth.' . . . Then I told him a bit of the wisdom [of kabbalah] and I awoke."[45]

It is likely that "Caesar of Rome" refers to the pope, with whom at least two messianic figures, Abraham Abulafia and Solomon Molkho, sought an audience. Vital was certainly an aspirant to a messianic mission. There is no doubt from the context, where Vital portrays himself as dwelling in a cave with the paupers in Rome, that a messianic background informs the dream.

According to the above passage, the pope offers total recognition of the superiority of Vital over other kabbalists, as well as his own acceptance of the truth of Judaism over Christianity. However, Vital must have ultimately associated the phrase *Keisar Romi* (Roman Caesar) with the destruction of the Second Temple by Titus. The sudden interruption of the dream reflects an unconscious resistance, even while asleep, to the teaching of kabbalistic secrets to a Gentile. Vital nevertheless started to reveal some parts of kabbalah before awakening. Thus, though only in a dream, intellectual exchange between the greatest of the kabbalists, the student of Luria who had forbidden the export of kabbalah from the Land of Israel, and the pope was imagined to have taken place. Indeed, there is historical background for this assumption. There are at least two examples of dedications of kabbalistic books to the pope prior to Vital's dream: Reuchlin dedicated his *De arte cabalistica* to Pope Leo X; and around 1575, Lazarus da Viterbo dedicated a Latin kabbalistic treatise on the Jubilee to Gregory XII.[46] Vital, a kabbalist of Italian extraction and a member of a Calabrian family, had been born in the Land of Israel, yet was still called Ḥayyim Calabrese. This dream is also interesting from another point of view: Safed is located in the Galilee, an area where Muslim and, to a certain extent, Druze cultures were dominant, not to mention the Ottoman administration. Some kabbalists active there in the sixteenth century came from Muslim countries, especially North Africa. Vital even studied occult sciences with Arab masters.[47] R. Joseph Karo visited a *tekie*, a small Sufi monastery, as he himself confessed. There is little reason to doubt that kabbalists were acquainted with Muslim thought and mystical practices.[48] Nevertheless, both the attraction and repulsion documented in the writings of Safedian kabbalists are formulated relative to cultural processes that were taking place in Italy. To recall a statement of Karo: "Someone is where his thought is." Nevertheless, it will be too simplistic to relate all the main developments in Safedian kabbalah to Italy, even less to the awareness of the dangers inherent in Christian kabbalah. As mentioned above, there were various factors behind the arrival of the kabbalists in Safed and the interaction between them there, and all of them contributed to the creativity in the town. While emphasizing these topics, I do not rule out the possibility of a substantial impact of additional sources—Muslim, Druze, or other, such as Orthodox Christianity—or the importance of other spiritual trends that flourished in the kabbalistic center in Safed. Whenever new material surfaces, its contribution will certainly help to configure an even more complex understanding of the processes that contributed to the Safedian renascence.

Awareness of the emergence of Christian kabbalah may account for a crucial turn in Isaac Luria's politics of dissemination of his type of kabbalah. According to one of the most important documents describing the study of Luria's secrets in his circle, he explicitly forbade the disclosure of those secrets to kabbalists outside his small circle and their dissemination outside the Land of Israel. Luria's students and those of Vital, themselves mature kabbalists, had to sign pledges not to disclose Lurianic secrets.[49] This is a clear-cut change that has not as yet been satisfactorily explained, given the quite exoteric propensity of his master Cordovero and his disciples. Is it connected with the danger of another "exile of the Torah"? I am not sure that the connection between the claim and a certain aspect of the ritual of *tikkun haṣot* regarding the secrets of the Torah, on the one hand, and the change in Luria's politics of esotericism, on the other, can be demonstrated in a conclusive manner. Yet such a nexus seems plausible.[50]

Finally, Lurianic kabbalah as formulated in the Galilee in its different versions is reticent toward philosophical thought.[51] This anti-philosophical bent is certainly not new in the history of kabbalah, and not the strongest. We can easily trace it to earlier sources in Spanish kabbalah, and its reverberations outside the Iberian Peninsula after the expulsion.[52] It is obvious that the powerful reliance on the *Zohar*,[53] conceived of as an inspired book, was accompanied by the rejection of intellectual speculations in matters of kabbalah.[54] An interesting portrayal of this propensity among Safedian kabbalah toward this kabbalistic canon was provided by an Italian kabbalist who studied there.[55] In the case of Luria, the centrality of the *Zohar*—a bit less evident in Cordovero—was accompanied by a certain purist approach, far less synthetic, harmonistic, or eclectic than Cordovero's books. Luria's works are more homogenous, unlike the more harmonizing and eclectic works of Cordovero, at least as regards his most influential book, *Pardes rimmonim*. To a certain degree, we may describe Luria's system as a case of counter-Renaissance, to echo Hiram Haydn's term.[56] Indeed, the more magically oriented system of Cordovero is more consonant with a Renaissance mode found in Pico and his many followers in what is termed the "occult philosophy." Moreover, Cordovero's cosmoeroticism is much closer to Renaissance theories. In a certain propensity to purism and counter-Renaissance, Luria, surprisingly, is in the same camp as the most adamant critic of kabbalah, Leon Modena.[57] On the other hand, Luria, like several of his contemporaries in Safed, lived in an ambience of adherence to an ostensibly ancient text, the *Zohar*, attempting to relive the life of the "ancient" kabbalists by returning to the place where they believed the *Zohar* had been composed. Indeed, Liebes has compared Luria to Marsilio Ficino, another figure who revived an ancient body of learning.[58]

Italian Receptions of Safedian Kabbalah

There is no doubt that Safedian authors, kabbalists and non-Kabbalists, enjoyed a special status among Italian Jews, as they did in other Jewish communities. Not only did important figures visit Safed, such as R. Mordekhai Dato[59] and R. Moses Basola. The numerous laments expressed by Italian rabbis over the death of R. Joseph Karo are clear testimony to the veneration in which he was held in Italy.[60] The economic assistance extended by Italian Jewry to the Safedian community is well known; one of the main figures in this respect was the most important kabbalist in Italy at the end of the sixteenth and the early seventeenth century, R. Menaḥem Azariah of Fano.[61] In his preface to *Pellaḥ harimmon*, his compendium of Cordovero's *Pardes rimmonim*, his reverence for Cordovero and Luria knows scarcely any limit. Thus, it is clear that almost all Italian kabbalists in the late sixteenth and early seventeenth century accepted Safed's superiority. That recognition was not only a matter of reverence, a feeling welling up from the special geographic location of Safed in the Holy Land, or the propinquity to sacred tombs. That is doubtless a fact, yet there are additional important dimensions to the veneration of the Safedians. Their intellectual achievements were impressive. Karo, Cordovero, and Luria wrote comprehensive systems, the first in halakhah and the latter two on kabbalah, exemplary achievements that are milestones in the creativity of generations of Jewish writers before and since. It is this outstanding contribution to Jewish thought that spurred recognition by Italian thinkers and Jewish authors elsewhere.

If the objective attainments are the main source of reverence, there is another factor that must have played a role in the aura of sanctity surrounding the image of the Safedians: they were not only preeminent minds in matters of Judaism but belonged to powerful groups, and their cooperation must have enhanced their achievements as individuals. By contrast, the Italian counterparts of the Safedian kabbalists were not organized in a definite grouping. There is no extant written agreement about keeping secrets with respect to any group of Italian kabbalists. In general, Italian kabbalists showed no interest in maintaining secrecy. The names of R. Isaac de Lattes,

R. Abraham ben Meshullam of San Angelo, R. Berakhiel Kaufmann, R. Mordekhai Dato, R. Abraham Yagel, and R. Moses Basola hardly constitute a group. With the exception of the family relationship between the first two, and their common sources, it is hard to document a significant common literary activity except the participation by some in the project of printing the *Zohar*. Yagel was acquainted with R. Menaḥem Azariah of Fano, but their kabbalistic positions differed, and there is no evidence for a prolonged and intimate relationship between them as kabbalists. Unlike Safedian kabbalah in both its major schools, which emerged in a small compact place and was organized in relatively coherent study groups, Italian kabbalah in the second half of the sixteenth century is marked by the presence of various individuals. Viewed from this vantage, they bore more similarity to the Spanish kabbalists immediately after the Spanish expulsion.[62] Though they may have known one another, no one ever described them as a group. They thus represent a mode of creativity that differs dramatically from the emphasis on the importance of the group found in some kabbalistic circles in Spain: Naḥmanides' circle in Catalonia, the circle of the *Zohar* in Castile,[63] and the *Sefer hameshiv* circle apparently likewise in Castile, or their reverberations in Safed. In the Galilean town, there is solid evidence that a group, the *ḥavurah*, sometimes called the *ḥavurah kedushah*, the holy fraternity, not only afforded an opportunity to pursue rabbinic and kabbalistic studies in common, but was also a fraternity that undertook peregrinations around Safed for mystical purposes.[64] Nor do the Italian Jewish kabbalists follow the pattern of the Accademia in Florence in the fifteenth century.

To an appreciable extent, kabbalistic literature of the Italian Renaissance among Jews and Christians relied on kabbalistic traditions articulated and widespread in Italy in the two centuries preceding the end of the fifteenth century, basically the writings of Abraham Abulafia and Menaḥem Recanati. They were studied without a kabbalistic master. The classic work of the Spanish kabbalah, the *Zohar*, had little impact before its first printing in the mid-sixteenth 16th century.[65] This is part of a more philosophical orientation among Renaissance Italian Jews, who differed intellectually from the far more particularistic state of mind dominant in Spain and then Safed.[66]

R. Abraham Yagel did not become a Lurianic kabbalist, notwithstanding the fact that he was aware of the existence of this sort of kabbalah. In contact with R. Menaḥem Azariah of Fano, the chief Italian kabbalist who introduced versions of Lurianism, Yagel apparently resisted the new wave of kabbalism. He writes, for example, that he heard that R. Ḥayyim Vital was a wondrous kabbalist, a student of Luria and head of the kabbalists in the Galilee.[67] Does this statement imply that Vital was indeed an important kabbalist, but only insofar as the kabbalists of Safed are concerned? Such a reading would strongly support a claim made in this study that an awareness of the difference between the two centers is not only a matter of the phenomenology of a modern scholar, but part of the awareness of the sixteenth-century kabbalist, and that such an awareness influenced his evaluation and allegiance. Yagel's reticence to adopt the system of Vital and Luria may indicate that this is the real significance behind the above formulation. In any case, it is obvious that his propensity for both kabbalah and philosophy, including that of the Renaissance, sparked a resistance toward the mythical tenor of Safedian traditions.[68]

It is important to note the long Italian tradition that identified the *sefirot* with Platonic ideas. It perhaps began in the late thirteenth century with R. Nathan ben Sa'adiah Harar, becoming explicit in R. Judah Romano,[69] R. Isaac Abravanel, R. Yeḥiel Nissim da Pisa, Mordekhai Rossilo, R. Abraham Yagel, R. Azariah de' Rossi,[70] and then in Leon Modena.[71] Thus, the association of Platonic philosophy with kabbalah, evident in Herrera and in Delmedigo, represents just another more intense phase in the history of the affinities, real or imaginary, between the two types of speculation. Nonetheless, it is still an open question whether some concepts of *sefirot* might have been connected historically and directly (or indirectly) with Platonism.[72] However, it is certain that beginning in the sixteenth century in Italy, the nexus between the two is mentioned.

After the disintegration of the center of kabbalah in Safed, Lurianic kabbalistic writings arrived in Italy as early as 1580, when R. Samson Bakki, a student of R. Joseph ibn Tabbul, sent an entire Lurianic treatise from Jerusalem to Italy, and R. Ezra of Fano copied Lurianic material, apparently in the Land of Israel, which he then brought to Italy.[73] We are concerned here with one of the changes Lurianism underwent in Italy, especially in the manner it was formulated by R. Israel Sarug.[74] Let me start the short survey of the affinities between the two types of lore with a citation from Joseph Delmedigo's *Novelot ḥokhma.* After quoting at length the descriptions of the first stages of Creation according to the *malbush* theory identified as that of R. Israel Sarug, Joseph Delmedigo writes: "As I announced beforehand, most of what I wrote here is taken almost verbatim from the books of the disciples of Luria. Therefore, let no philosopher criticize our words,[75] but if his opinion is proper,[76] he should interpret and divert them to the view of the true philosophers, and he will be blessed by God."[77]

The positive attitude toward a philosophical interpretation is conspicuous: the philosopher will be blessed for such an enterprise. What is fascinating is the manner in which this interpretation should be done: the words of Luria and his disciples should be diverted (the Hebrew is *yatteh*) so that they may become closer to, or perhaps even coincide with, the opinion of the true philosophers. This means that the latter may possess a sort of truth that kabbalistic writings, including Luria's, may perhaps approximate but do not express in clear terms.[78] To return to Couliano's passage cited earlier, Joseph Delmedigo espouses the importance of a "semantic distortion" of kabbalistic views to bring them closer to the true philosopher's thought.

It is useful to examine the manner in which an Oriental kabbalist was portrayed by Leon Modena. He describes the activity of R. Israel Sarug: "And I have heard, too, from the mouth of the kabbalist R. Israel Sarug, an outstanding pupil of Luria, blessed be his memory . . . that there is no difference between kabbalah and philosophy. And all that [Sarug] taught about kabbalah, he interpreted through philosophy."[79] I assume that this passage contains the words of two speakers: those of Sarug, to the effect that there is no difference between philosophy and kabbalah; and Modena's own statement about Sarug's interpretation of kabbalah. Though Modena mentions Plato in connection with two other kabbalists—R. Jacob Naḥamias (according to a testimony of R. Joseph Delmedigo) and his own student R. Joseph Hamiṣ[80]—the Greek philosopher is not mentioned in Sarug's own statement or in Modena's: both use the more general term "philosophy." Nevertheless, Gershom Scholem interprets this term as "certainly" referring to "Platonic philosophy."[81] Alexander Altmann has already questioned this view and pointed out that there is insufficient evidence for such an interpretation.[82] A perusal of Sarug's works reveals no quotation of Plato or any Platonic thinker. We thus have to ask ourselves whether Modena's statements about Sarug are reliable or perhaps only a weapon used by Modena in his attack on kabbalah. I think it almost inconceivable that Modena would falsify a statement of Sarug and then add his interpretation. Sarug presumably taught his version of Lurianic kabbalah without any philosophical quotations. This version was written by Sarug himself or his pupils; this is the meaning of the phrase "all he taught about kabbalah." Afterward, and apparently only orally, a philosophical interpretation was given. Yet how could Sarug offer a philosophical interpretation that had nothing to do with the original kabbalistic text, even more so in Italy, where some among the Jewish elite were engaged in exploring the philosophical culture of the Renaissance? A probable answer to this question may be that though Platonic philosophy cannot be detected in Sarug's works, traces of another philosophy could be hidden in his works and taught orally by Sarug through his kabbalistic terms, a point we return to below.

I analyzed Modena's short statement to emphasize the selective will of Jewish Italian circles: though transmitting the sacrosanct Lurianic teachings, Sarug claimed that there was no difference between kabbalah and philosophy, whatever that philosophy may be. Perhaps we have a reverberation of the Renaissance attitude toward religious knowledge known as *prisca theologia*, which assumed a correspondence between various bodies of ancient knowledge.[83] I would argue that the insistence on a correspondence between kabbalah and philosophy stands in strong opposition to the Safedian reticence toward philosophy, as mentioned above.

The above dynamics of rapid exchange between Safed and Italy is unparalleled insofar as Safed and another center are concerned, not only in Europe but throughout the entire Jewish world. Nothing similar is known regarding the arrival of Cordoverian kabbalah, or regarding the availability of Lurianic kabbalah in print and by oral teaching, paralleling the content of the aforementioned documents. In fact, as we learn from the very first lines of the introduction by R. Menaḥem Azariah of Fano to his *Pelaḥ harimmon*, he compiled at least the second version of his compendium of Cordovero's *Pardes rimmonim* at the request of R. Isaac ben Mordekhai of Poland (described as a distinguished scholar who came to study with him) and for the rabbis of Ashkenaz. This is evidence that Italy around 1600 became a center in itself, a hub from where kabbalah radiated to the North. The crucial role of Italy for printing kabbalistic books needs no elaboration, that country being the prime center for the printed dissemination of kabbalah from the beginning of printing to the end of the sixteenth century.

Jewish Renaissance: A Reassessment

One conclusion of the above discussion is the necessity to qualify the predominant unqualified Safedo-centric vision of modern scholarship of the history of kabbalah. I do not wish to criticize the Safedo-centric vision per se, because of its originality or its impact, but to reject its unqualified application for the understanding of subsequent developments in the history of Jewish mysticism. To clarify my view: from the mid-sixteenth century, Safed was the most fertile and influential center of Jewish mysticism and, to a great extent, of halakhah. I therefore do not question Safed's immense contribution to many other centers in the Jewish world. However, scholarship has described the propagation of Safedian material in too simple a manner. For Scholem and his followers, the history of subsequent Jewish mysticism is a matter of adopting and actualizing—or later, combating or neutralizing—elements of Safedian kabbalah, especially in its Lurianic form. In Scholem's historiosophy, the gist of the history of Jewish mysticism was the triumphant conquest of the Jewish world by a messianically portrayed Lurianism.[84] Tishby's important corrective, which assumes that Cordoverianism survived as a vital option even after the emergence of Lurianism—for example, in the writings of R. Abraham Azulai and R. Aharon Berakhiah of Modena—is likewise but another form of Safedo-centrism: that is, Safed exported not just one trend of kabbalah, namely, Lurianism, to the Jewish communities abroad, but two—Cordoverianism and Lurianism—and the history of Jewish mysticism can be understood as the interplay between the two.[85] In both forms of Safedo-centrism, the problematics characteristic of the future history of kabbalah had already been established in Safed alone. I have attempted elsewhere to attenuate this scholarly triumphalism by pointing out the limitations of the diffusion of Lurianism,[86] as well as the importance of other forms of pre-Safedian forms of kabbalah for the history of Jewish mysticism.[87] The above discussions serve as an additional corrective to the unilinear history of Jewish mysticism that begins with the expulsion and ends with Hasidism.

Let me attempt to place the earlier discussions in a wider context, namely, the Italian Renaissance as one of the salient backgrounds for the creative flowering of the Safedian kabbalists. Two crucial moments in kabbalistic literature are its emergence in the late twelfth century in the area designated by Jews as Provence, and the floruit in late thirteenth-century Castile. In both cases, kabbalistic literature emerged against backgrounds of creativity in non-Jewish circles: the Renaissance of the twelfth century in Western Europe, and the Alfonsine Renaissance in Castile. In the case of the emergence of kabbalah in the twelfth century, there were also other spiritual processes that triggered the articulations of the first kabbalistic documents. One is the Maimonidean controversy and, more generally the impact of

Maimonidean Aristotelianism in Western Europe, an intellectual development that triggered a structured theological response and an alternative vision of the meaning of Jewish rituals.[88] Maimonides' thought represents one of the most universalistic approaches in Judaism, and the emergence of the theosophical-theurgical kabbalah should also be understood against this background. The wide intellectual horizons at the court of Alfonso Sabio are well known, as is the contribution of Jewish translators who participated in the intellectual project of the king of Castile.[89] The need to react to Maimonidean intellectualism might also have informed some of the Castilian configurations of kabbalah, including parts of the *Zohar*.[90] Against the more universalistic trends at the Castilian court, the strong bent of particularism in Castilian kabbalah from 1275 onward can be better understood.[91] Last but not least: the attraction of the renascence at the Castilian court drew several Jewish masters interested in matters of the occult, kabbalistic and other forms, and the encounters between the different varieties of Jewish esotericism in Castile were catalytic for the Jewish Castilian Renaissance, including Zoharic literature.[92]

Thus we may propose a correlation between the floruit of strong kabbalistic centers and various renascences in the cultural environments of the nascent kabbalistic centers. The interactive dynamic I propose is not a simple dichotomy between Jewish and non-Jewish thought, but a more complex picture that assumes the absorption of elements of those cultural developments within Judaism and the feeling of some Jewish thinkers that an answer should be offered to those new spiritual challenges. Major classics of Jewish mystical thought were composed under the influence of this encounter as response to the efflorescence of new ideas and literatures in its environments.

It is a historical irony that Lurianic kabbalah, whose main founder insisted upon its esoteric nature and formulated a special interdiction regarding its dissemination, was dramatically disseminated in Christian kabbalah of the late seventeenth century, as the Latin translation of texts of R. Abraham Herrera and even texts of Luria himself in Knorr von Rosenroth's *Cabala denudata* amply demonstrate.[93] Though effective for a short while, Luria's interdiction on disseminating Lurianic kabbalah outside the Land of Israel ended as a great fiasco. His kabbalah had substantial influence upon Christian kabbalists and Christian philosophers no less than any other form of kabbalah, and perhaps even more so. This impact was achieved, at least in part, because of the allegorical and philosophical readings of Lurianism, a mode that had already been adopted before the arrival of Lurianism in Italy, even in public sermons.[94] A complementary development is the relative indifference toward the *Zohar* that, though printed first and in two parallel editions in 1558 in Italy, did not attract the attention of Italian kabbalists. Unlike Safedian kabbalists, who were immersed in its study and wrote extensive commentaries, Italian kabbalists were much less enamored of the mythical tenor of the book. Indeed, as Jean Seznec has sensitively formulated the situation in Renaissance Italy, "Mythology still plays a considerable role (even more so than in the past) but it is fatally submerged in allegory."[95] In both cases, Renaissance thinkers have appropriated mythical material in a manner keeping with their intellectual orientations, and the mythical elements were more often reduced to ahistorical speculative truths. The Spanish mythical kabbalah in its Lurianic elaborations as well as the ancient Greek myths informed Italian thought in the Renaissance by adapting them to the mindset of their recipients.

An important shift in Italian kabbalah with regards to Lurianic kabbalah is selective adoption. It is intriguing that Italian Kabbalists were interested in the concept of *ṣimṣum*. A series of concepts becomes a system only when a more cohesive structure is radiating within its components, creating a "*gestalt*-contexture."[96] Thus, in the Middle East the meaning of *ṣimṣum* was to be related to the importance of other important concepts such as *tikkun* and the general attitude toward theurgy and the performance of the commandments. Since the latter were important, then the theosophical speculations constitute a framework for understanding the meaning of ritual more than any theosophy or theogony. We may thus describe in Safed the lengthy discussions dealing with theosophy as an extended discourse on *ta'amei miṣvot* rather than a pure theological discourse that attempts to offer a raison d'être for a certain historical upheaval. If this assumption about the Middle East visions of *ṣimṣum*—which continued the realistic reading found in Spain before the expulsion—is correct, it should be better understood in the context of the concerns of other parts of the Lurianic corpus such as *Sefer hakavvanot*, and *ta'amei hamiṣvot*.

Italian versions of kabbalah not only attempt to understand a certain theosophical complex of concepts allegorically and philosophically; they constitute approaches that put greater emphasis on theosophical concepts rather than on theurgy, on philosophical interpretations of theogonies rather than on the interpretations of the raison d'être for commandments. With the exception of R. Menaḥem Azariah's writings, Italian kabbalists such as Yagel, Joseph Delmedigo, and Abraham Herrera were much less concerned with issues of ritual. *Ṣimṣum* and its allegorical interpretations are but prisms that constitute attitudes that run deeper than a local and restricted shift of the meaning of a certain important term. One of the most important aspects of Lurianism, the theory of the transmigration of souls, was not accorded special attention in Italy. I am not referring here to the general theory of transmigration, found in kabbalah long before Luria and accepted by many Italian kabbalists, including Abraham Yagel,[97] but to the specific Lurianic form, which consists of detecting the soul of a specific person in the past that has transmigrated into a concrete living person. The knowledge of prior transmigrations was regarded as one of Luria's great achievements, and Vital discusses this issue at length in his writings. According to a tradition adduced by Joseph Delmedigo, Luria taught his students how to discern the former transmigration of the soul of a human being into an animal.[98] Sarug displayed this skill in public in Venice, and he discovered the previous avatars of contemporary persons. No wonder this facet of Sarug's activity provoked a sarcastic remark on Modena's part.[99] Though this negative remark may not reflect the general attitude in Venice, it is interesting to note the more practical aspects of the dissemination of Lurianism, on the one hand, and the reticence to accept it even by accomplished kabbalists, on the other. Indeed, no interest in similar séances was ever displayed in the Italian interpretation of Lurianic kabbalah.[100]

Finally, let me address an issue broached several times over the last two decades: Was there indeed a Jewish Renaissance?[101] Some answers have been positive.[102] Other scholars are inclined to negate the existence of such a phenomenon.[103] The answer is complex, largely depending on the manner in which "Renaissance" is defined and, even more difficult to determine, the minimum necessary for establishing the existence of a Jewish Renaissance. I am in favor of a more complex answer that distinguishes between two phases: the initial phase was 1470–1550, when Jewish intellectuals were part of the Florentine group that contributed so much to the emergence of the speculative aspects of the Italian Renaissance. This period is characterized by an interactive situation in which Jewish intellectuals both consumed and influenced a type of culture emerging in the Christian environment. The second phase, from the mid-sixteenth century, brought the impact of the Italian Renaissance, now a powerful intellectual and cultural phenomenon, which became ever more visible. Italian Jews became consumers of, rather than significant contributors to, culture and intellectual views.[104] This is certainly true with regard to general culture, though the interpretations of various versions of Lurianism had an important impact on the Jewish kabbalah, and later, and only outside Italy, on European culture.[105] To a considerable extent, the filter used by Italian kabbalists in their absorption of their Safedian counterparts was not only bound up with Jewish Italian culture; it served to mediate and transmit Safedian kabbalah to various other Jewish centers, especially in Europe. The books of Delmedigo and Herrera are the two most important examples.

Regarding the attitude of Italian intellectuals to Safedian kabbalah, the admixture between consumers and contributors may be the best way to describe their activity. They consumed Safedian kabbalah while contributing their selective will in their understanding of the sources, having recourse to categories they had absorbed from their Italian Renaissance background. Or, to put it differently: like Pico before them, the late sixteenth-century Italian Jewish kabbalists were not so much original thinkers, but rather played a synthetic role, bringing together divergent forms of knowledge. As Cassirer noted, "What is characteristic of Pico is . . . not the way in which he increased the story of philosophic truth, but the way in which he made it manifest."[106] If we accept Cassirer's view of Pico—a major scholar describing a major Renaissance figure—I see no reason to negate the contribution of the Italian kabbalists discussed above as belonging to a certain intellectual trend that differs from what we find in other centers of Jewish culture in the sixteenth century. Neither in the Land of Israel nor in North Africa, neither in Central nor Eastern Europe, do we encounter such intense literary activity in speculative matters. None of these centers adopted the forms of Safedian kabbalah so rapidly; none contributed so much originality in the manner in which they adopted kabbalistic lore by adapting it to Italian Renaissance culture. By absorbing the voluminous Safedian kabbalistic works quickly and enthusiastically, their religious and intellectual identity was strengthened. This is more evident in a period when the originality of Jewish intellectual production in Italy was on the wane. Many Italian kabbalists, by dint of their philosophical proclivities and selective approach, constituted a crosscurrent that significantly qualified the way in which Safedian kabbalah was understood in Italy.

As in the case of the earlier development of Jewish Italian culture, when it drew on the sources written in the Land of Israel, and then on sources from Spain and Germany, the emergence of the Safedian centers generated another inspirational source for the Italian Jewish elite, who were immediately receptive to developments there. However, in the case of kabbalah from the mid-sixteenth century, Italian Jews sometimes also contributed elements steeped in their familiarity with a major intellectual development that was part of their intellectual environment, namely, Renaissance thought. This is the case of Azariah de' Rossi, David del Bene, Judah Moscato, Abraham Yagel, Abraham Herrera, and Joseph Delmedigo. No wonder the last two refer to one of their illustrious predecessors, Leone Ebreo.[107] R. Menaḥem Azariah did so in a much more reticent manner, and the details of his particular and creative interaction with Safedian material require elaborate analysis. To mention just one important topic, his influential interpretation of the Lurianic theory of *ṣimṣum* is at least partially inspired by a philosophical approach.

A new complex interplay between particularism and universalism emerged with the advent of Safedian material in Italy: Jewish elites celebrated new theosophical types of lore radiating from their almost sacred center, but attempted to make sense of the messages found in those texts through the prisms of their intellectual apparatus. They had grids of their own that filtered various streams of books and ideas flowing from Safed. Those grids were not always adequately understood by the modern scholarship of kabbalah, whose messianic preoccupations dramatically distorted the much more variegated trends of sixteenth-century kabbalah.

Transmission, then, is never a case of simple transportation. The arrival of Safedian kabbalah in other centers of Jewish culture engendered other forms of transformation than those described above, and they should be investigated in accordance with the prevailing hermeneutical grids of those particular centers. For example, the Ashkenazi nature of the grid of Polish kabbalists in the early seventeenth century is obvious.[108] However, unlike as in the Italian case, it is much more difficult to demonstrate the possibility of impact by an articulate Polish center of kabbalah on the nature of kabbalah in Safed.

Notes

1. On the question of transmission, see E. R. Wolfson, "Beyond the Spoken World: Oral Tradition and Written Transmission in Medieval Mysticism," in *Transmitting Jewish Traditions: Orality, Textuality, and Cultural Diffusion*, ed. Y. Elman and I. Gershoni (New Haven, Conn., 2000), pp. 166–223; and M. Idel, "Transmission in the Thirteenth-Century Kabbalah," in ibid. pp. 138–64.

2. The bibliographical aspects of the diffusion of kabbalah and of the kabbalistic ethical literature remain an issue to be addressed by future studies. For the time being, see M. Pachter, "*Sefer Reshit Ḥokhma* of Rabbi Elijah de Vidas and Its Abbreviations" (Hebrew), *Kiryat Sefer* 47 (1972): 686–710; idem, "Traces of the Influence of R.

Elijah de Vidas's *Reshit Ḥokhma* upon the Writings of R. Jacob Joseph of Polonnoye" (Hebrew), in *Studies in Jewish Mysticism, Philosophy and Ethical Literature Presented to Isaiah Tishby*, ed. J. Dan and J. Hacker (Jerusalem, 1986), pp. 569–92; B. Sack, "The Influence of Cordovero on Seventeenth-Century Jewish Thought," in *Jewish Thought in the Seventeenth Century*, ed. I. Twersky and B. Septimus (Cambridge, Mass., 1987), pp. 365–79; J. Elbaum, *Openness and Insularity: Late Sixteenth-Century Jewish Literature in Poland and Ashkenaz* (Hebrew) (Jerusalem, 1990), pp. 90–93, 146–49, 183–222, 357–66; Z. Gries, *Conduct Literature (Regimen Vitae): Its History and Place in the Life of Beshtian Hasidism* (Hebrew) (Jerusalem, 1989); M. Pachter, *From Safed's Hidden Treasures* (Hebrew) (Jerusalem, 1994); and the preface by L. Fine to his *Safed Spirituality* (New York, 1984).

3. See M. Idel, "R. Judah Hallewah and His Composition *Ṣafenat Pa'aneaḥ*" (Hebrew), *Shalem* 4 (1984): 122–23.

4. S. Schechter, "Safed in the Sixteenth Century," reprinted in his *Studies in Judaism: Essays on Persons, Concepts, and Movements of Thought in Jewish Tradition* (New York, 1970), pp. 231–97.

5. See G. Scholem, *Major Trends in Jewish Mysticism* (New York, 1974), p. 287; idem, *Sabbatai Ṣevi: The Mystical Messiah* (Princeton, N.J. 1973), pp. 49–77.

6. Scholem, *Major Trends*, p. 287.

7. Ibid. p. 327.

8. This topic will be the subject of an additional study. See, meanwhile, N. Yosha, *Myth and Metaphor: Abraham Herrera's Philosophic Interpretation of Lurianic Kabbalah* (Hebrew), (Jerusalem, 1994), pp. 178–210. More on this topic in M. Idel, "On the Concept of *Ṣimṣum* in Kabbalah and Its Research" (Hebrew), in *Lurianic Kabbalah*, ed. R. Elior and Y. Liebes (Jerusalem, 1992), pp. 59–112.

9. See Scholem, *Sabbatai Ṣevi*, p. 68.

10. Ibid., p. 51. See also Scholem, *Major Trends*, p. 251, where he speaks about the "victorious march" of this kabbalah.

11. Scholem, *Sabbatai Ṣevi*, p. 77, and see also his *Major Trends*, pp. 251, 286.

12. See G. Scholem, "The Sermon on Redemption of R. Solomon le-Veit ha-Turiel" (Hebrew), *Sefunot* 1 (1956): 62–79.

13. For questions inherent in the transition of kabbalah from one place to another, see M. Idel, "Encounters Between Spanish and Italian Kabbalists in the Generation of the Expulsion," in *Crisis and Creativity in the Sephardic World*, ed. B. R. Gampel (New York, 1997), pp. 194–97.

14. I. P. Couliano, *Eros and Magic in the Renaissance* (Chicago, 1987), p. 11. See also E. Cassirer, "Some Remarks on the Question of the Originality of the Renaissance," *Journal of the History of Ideas* 4 (1943): 49–56. On worldviews in the Renaissance, see P. Burke, *Culture and Society in Renaissance Italy, 1420–1540* (New York, 1972), pp. 170–206.

15. M. Idel, "The Anthropology of Yoḥanan Alemanno: Sources and Influences," *Topoi* 7 (1988): pp. 201–10; reprinted in *Annali di storia dell'esegesi* 7 (1990): 93–112; idem, "Jewish Mystical Thought in the Florence of Lorenzo il Magnifico," in *La cultura ebraica all'epoca di Lorenzo il Magnifico*, ed. D. Liscia Bemporad and I. Zatilli (Florence, 1998), pp. 31–32.

16. S. Toussaint, "Ficino's Orphic Magic or Jewish Astrology and Oriental Philosophy? A Note on Spiritus, the Three Books on Life, Ibn Tufayl, and Ibn Zarza," *Accademia* 2 (2000): 19–33.

17. S. Pines, "Medieval Doctrines in Renaissance Garb? Some Jewish and Arabic Sources of Leone Ebreo's Doctrines," in *Jewish Thought in the Sixteenth Century*, ed. B. Cooperman (Cambridge, Mass., 1983), pp. 365–98.

18. See M. Idel, *Studies in Ecstatic Kabbalah* (Albany, N.Y., 1988), pp. 126–40.

19. M. Idel, "Differing Conceptions of Kabbalah in the Early Seventeenth Century," in *Jewish Thought in the Seventeenth Century*, ed. Twersky and Septimus, pp. 137–200.

20. See R. J. Z. Werblowsky, "The Safed Revival," in *Jewish Spirituality*, ed. A. Green (New York, 1987), 2: 11; Werblowsky, in the recent summary of Sabbateanism in "Shabbetai Zevi," in *The Sephardi Legacy*, ed. H. Beinart (Jerusalem, 1992), 2: 207–16.

21. See Idel, "Encounters"; idem, "The Ecstatic Kabbalah of Abraham Abulafia in Sicily and Its Transmission during the Renaissance," in *Italia Judaica: Gli ebrei in Sicilia sino all'espulsione dell 1492*, (Rome, 1995), pp. 330–40; idem, "Religion, Thought and Attitudes: The Impact of the Expulsion on the Jews," in *Spain and the Jews: The Sephardi Experience, 1492 and After*, ed. E. Kedourie (London, 1992), pp. 123–39.

22. See P. Giller, "Recovering the Sanctity of the Galilee: The Veneration of Sacred Relics in Classical Kabbalah," *Journal of Jewish Thought and Philosophy* 4 (1994): 147–69; and the study of Fenton, n. 48 below.

23. See e.g., *Zohar*, vol. I fol. 119a, vol. II fols. 7b, 9a, 120a; "Hanhagot ha-Ari," printed in *Toledoth ha-Ari*, ed. M. Benayahu (Jerusalem, 1967), p. 354; Scholem, *Sabbatai Ṣevi*, p. 53.

24. See M. Idel, "On Mobility, Individuals and Groups: Prolegomenon for a Sociological Approach to Sixteenth-Century Kabbalah," *Kabbalah* 3 (1998): 145–73.

25. See J. Hacker, "A Collection of Epistles on the Expulsion of the Jews from Spain and Sicily and on the Fate of the Exiles" (Hebrew), in *Studies in the History of Jewish Society in the Middle Ages and in the Modern Period Presented to Professor Jacob Katz* (Jerusalem, 1980), pp. 64–70; Idel, "Encounters," pp. 206–7.

26. See R. J. Z. Werblowsky, *Joseph Karo, Lawyer and Mystic* (Philadelphia, 1977), pp. 97–100.

27. M. Idel, "Solomon Molkho as Magician" (Hebrew), *Sefunot*, n.s., 3 (1995): 198–202.

28. See M. Idel, "R. Nathan ben Sa'adiah Harar," in *Le porte della giustizia*, ed. M. Mottolese (Milan, 2001), pp. 13–39.

29. E. Gottlieb, *Studies in Kabbalah Literature* (Hebrew), ed. J. Hacker (Tel Aviv, 1976), pp. 402–8, 411–23, 432–33. For more on this author, see H. Tirosh-Rothschild, *Between Worlds: The Life and Thought of Rabbi David ben Judah Messer Leon* (Albany, N.Y., 1991), and her earlier "Sefirot as the Essence of God in the Writings of David Messer Leon," *Association of Jewish Studies Review* 7–8 (1982–83): 409–25.

30. See Gottlieb, *Studies in Kabbalah Literature*, pp. 397–476; M. Idel, "Between the View of *Sefirot* as Essence and Instruments in the Renaissance" (Hebrew), *Italia* 3 (1982): 89–111.

31. See Idel, "Encounters," pp. 199–206.

32. For more details on this topic, see Idel, *Kabbalah and Eros*, chap. 5 (forthcoming).

33. See Y. Jacobson, *Along the Paths of Exile and Redemption: The Doctrine of Redemption of Rabbi Mordekhai Dato* (Hebrew) (Jerusalem, 1996), p. 13.

34. On this seminal figure, see R. Bonfil, "Halakhah, Kabbalah and Society: Some Insights into Rabbi Menahem Azariah da Fano's Inner World," in *Jewish Thought in the Seventeenth Century*, ed. Twersky and Septimus, pp. 39–61: Bonfil, "New Information Concerning Rabbi Menahem Azariah of Fano and His Age" (Hebrew), in *Perakim betoldot haḥevrah hayehudit bimei habeinayim uva'et haḥadashah (Jacob Katz Festschrift)*, ed. E. Etkes and Y. Salmon (Jerusalem, 1980), pp. 103–4; J. Avivi, "Rabbi Menahem Azariah of Fano's Writings on Matters of Kabbalah" (Hebrew), *Sefunot* 19 (1989): 347–76.

35. See M. Benayahu, *Yosef beḥiri* (Hebrew) (Jerusalem, 1991), pp. 298–305.

36. See D. Tamar, "The Year 1575 and the Messianic Excitement in Italy" (Hebrew), in his book *Studies in Jewish History in Israel and Italy* (Jerusalem, 1973), pp. 11–38; see also the material collected and analyzed by Jacobson, *Along the Paths of Exile*; and M. Idel, *Messianic Mystics* (New Haven, Conn., 1998), pp. 154–61.

37. See epecially the discussions of I. Tishby, J. Dan, R. J. Z. Werblowsky, and, more recently, R. Elior, "Messianic Expectations and the Spiritualization of Religious Life in the Sixteenth Century," *Revue des études juives* 145 (1986): 35–49.

38. Apparently, the priests.

39. Cf. Ps. 49:13.

40. See B. Sack, *The Kabbalah of Rabbi Moses Cordovero* (Hebrew) (Beersheva, 1995), p. 37 n. 22, quoted from Cordovero's *Commentary on the Tiqqunei Zohar* (Jerusalem, 1975), 3: 204.

41. For more on this passage and its context, see M. Idel, "Jewish Thinkers versus Christian Kabbalah," in *Christliche Kabbalah: Reuchlins geistesgeschichtliche Wikung*, ed. W. Schmidt-Biggeman (Pforzheim, 2003) (forthcoming).

42. See F. Secret, *Les Kabbalistes chrétiens de la Renaissance* (Paris, 1964), pp. 173, 175.

43. See Jacobson, *Along the Paths of Exile*, p. 339 n. 73.

44. Namely, kabbalah.

45. A. Aescoli, ed., *Sefer haḤezyonot* (Jerusalem, 1954), p. 68; M. M. Faierstein, ed., *Jewish Mystical Autobiographies: Book of Visions and Book of Secrets* (New York, 1999), pp. 98–99; A. Berger, "Captive at the Gate of Rome: The Story of a Messianic Motif," *Proceedings of the American Academy for Jewish Research* 44 (1977): 16–17; D. Tamar, "The Messianic Dreams and Visions of R. Ḥayyim Vital" (Hebrew), *Shalem* 4 (1984): 211–29; and Idel, *Messianic Mystics*, pp. 167–68.

46. See F. Secret, "Le 'Tractatus de anno Jubilaei' de Lazaro da Viterbo, Grégoire XIII et la kabbale chrétienne," *Rinascimento*, 2d ser., 6 (1966): 305–33.

47. See G. Bos, "Ḥayyim Vital's Practical Kabbalah and Alchemy: A 17th Century Book of Secrets," *Journal of Jewish Thought and Philosophy* 4 (1994): 55–112.

48. P. B. Fenton, "Influences soufies sur le development de la qabbale a Safed: Le cas de la visitation des tombes," in *Experience et écriture mystiques dans les religions du livre*, ed. P. B. Fenton and R. Goetschel (Leiden, 2000), pp. 163–90.

49. Cf. Scholem, *Major Trends*, pp. 256–57; idem, "Bill of Obligation of Pupils of the Ari" (Hebrew), *Zion* 5 (1940): 133–60; M. Benayahu, "Documents of Connection of Safed Kabbalists with Egypt" (Hebrew), *Assufot* 9 (1995): 33–34; R. Meroz, "The Brotherhood of Rabbi Moses ben Makkir and Its Regulations" (Hebrew), *Pe'amim* 31 (1987): 40–61.

50. See Idel, *Messianic Mystics*, pp. 308–20.

51. On the attitude toward philosophy in Safed, see J. Ben-Shlomo, *The Mystical Theology of Moses Cordovero* (Hebrew) (Jerusalem, 1965), pp. 31–36; Sack, *The Kabbalah of Rabbi Moses Cordovero*, p. 49; G. Scholem, "New Information about Joseph Ashkenazi, the Tanna of Safed" (Hebrew), *Tarbiẓ* 28 (1959): 59–89, 201–35.

52. See M. Idel, "Inquiries in the Doctrine of Sefer Hameshiv" (Hebrew), *Sefunot* 17 (1983): 232–43: idem, "Encounters," pp. 206–9; Scholem, *Major Trends*, p. 249. See also Leon Modena, *Ari nohem* (first published Lipsia, 1840; Jerusalem, 1971), p. 52.

53. See Benayahu, *Toledoth ha-Ari*, pp. 319–20.

54. On the view that Safedian kabbalah is a renaissance of the *Zohar*, see Y. Liebes, "The *Zohar* as Renaissance in Castile" (Hebrew), *Da'at* 46 (2001): 11.

55. See R. Mordekhai Dato's views as discussed by R. Bonfil, *Rabbis and Jewish Communities in Renaissance Italy* (Oxford, 1993), pp. 295–96. Dato himself was much more open to philosophical interpretations. See ibid., 296–97. See also B. Huss, "Sefer ha-Zohar as a Canonical, Sacred and Holy Text: Changing Perspectives in the Book of Splendor Between the Thirteenth and Eighteenth Centuries," *Journal of Jewish Thought and Philosophy* 7 (1998): 284, 290–93.

56. See H. Haydn, *The Counter-Renaissance* (New York, 1950).

57. See Idel, "Differing Conceptions of Kabbalah," p. 174; D. Ruderman, introduction to *Preachers of the Italian Ghetto*, ed. D. Ruderman (Berkeley, Calif., 1992), pp. 14–15.

58. Y. Liebes, "*Zohar* and Eros" (Hebrew), *Alpayim* 9 (1994): 67–119.

59. See I. Tishby, *Studies in Kabbalah and Its Branches* (Hebrew) (Jerusalem, 1982), 1: 131–76; Liebes, "*Zohar* and Eros."

60. See Benayahu, *Yosef beḥiri*, pp. 523–85.

61. See, for example, E. Kupfer, "The Jewish Community of Safed and the Activity of R. Menaḥem Azariah of Fano on Behalf of the *Yishuv* in Eretz Israel" (Hebrew), *Shalem* 2 (1976): 361–64; Benayahu, *Yosef beḥiri*, p. 184.

62. See Idel, "On Mobility."

63. See Y. Liebes, *Studies in the Zohar* (Albany, N.Y., 1993).

64. See Benayahu, *Yosef beḥiri*, pp. 204–9; Meroz, "The Brotherhood."

65. The first scholar to observe that the *Zohar* was not known so much in Italy, though quotations from it were known through the intermediacy of Menaḥem Recanati's writings, by the first two important Christian kabbalists active in Italy, was F. Secret, *Le Zohar chez les kabbalistes chrétiens de la Renaissance* (Paris, 1958), p. 25. See also C. Wirszubski, *Pico della Mirandola's Encounter with Jewish Mysticism* (Cambridge, Mass., 1989), pp. 55, 253. Cf., however, I. Tishby, *The Wisdom of the Zohar: An Anthology of Texts* (London, 1991), p. 33.

66. See M. Idel, "Particularism and Universalism in Kabbalah, 1480–1650," in *Es-*

sential Papers on Jewish Culture in Renaissance and Baroque Italy, ed. D. B. Ruderman (New York, 1992), pp. 324–44.

67. See Idel, "Major Currents in Italian Kabbalah, 1560–1660," in *Italia Judaica*, ed. G. Sermoneta and S. Simonsohn (Rome, 1986), p. 253. For more on Yagel's relation to Lurianic kabbalah, see D. Ruderman, *Kabbalah, Magic, and Science in the Cultural Universe of a Jewish Physician* (Cambridge, Mass., 1988), pp. 128–29, 139–40.

68. On the different functions of kabbalah in Italy in this period, see R. Bonfil, "Changes in the Cultural Patterns of a Jewish Society in Crisis: Italian Jewry at the Close of the Sixteenth Century," *Jewish History* 3 (1988): 11–30. On the cultural situation among the Jews duing the Italian Renaissance, see D. Ruderman, "The Italian Renaissance and Jewish Thought," in *Renaissance Humanism, Foundations, Forms, and Legacy*, ed. A. Rabil (Philadelphia, 1988), 1: 382–433.

69. See G. Sermoneta, "Jehuda ben Moshe Daniel Romano: Traducteur de Saint Thomas," in *Hommage à Georges Vijda*, ed. G. Nahon and C. Touati (Louvain, 1980), p. 246; M. Idel, "Jewish Kabbalah and Platonism in the Middle Ages and Renaissance," in *Neoplatonism and Jewish Thought*, ed. L. E. Goodman (Albany, N.Y., 1993), pp. 319–51.

70. See M. Idel, "The Magical and Neoplatonic Interpretations of Kabbalah in the Renaissance," in *Jewish Thought in the Sixteenth Century*, ed. Cooperman, pp. 226–27.

71. Modena, *Ari nohem*, p. 53.

72. See H. A. Wolfson, "Extradeical and Intradeical Interpretations of Platonic Ideas," in his *Religious Philosophy* (Cambridge, Mass., 1965), pp. 27–68.

73. See M. Benayahu, "Rabbi Ezra of Fano: Sage, Kabbalist, and Leader" (Hebrew), in *Sefer hayovel lehaga'on Yosef Dov Soloveitchik* (Jerusalem, 1984), 2: 786–855. On the arrival of the Lurianic manuscripts to Italy, see J. Avivi, "The Writings of Rabbi Isaac Luria in Italy before 1620" (Hebrew), *Alei Sefer* 11 (1984): 91–134.

74. G. Scholem, "Rabbi Israel Sarug: A Student of Luria?" (Hebrew), *Zion* 5 (1940): 214–43; R. Meroz, "R. Israel Sarug: A Student of Luria?—A Reconsideration of the Question" (Hebrew), *Da'at* 28 (1992): 41–50; idem, "Faithful Transmission versus Innovation: Luria and His Disciples," in *Gershom Scholem's Major Trends in Jewish Mysticism: 50 Years After*, ed. P. Schaefer and J. Dan (Tübingen, 1993), pp. 257–75; idem, "Contrasting Opinions among the Founders of R. Israel Sarug's School," in *Experience et écriture mystiques dans les religions du livre*, ed. Fenton and Goetschel, pp. 191–202; idem, "An Anonymous Commentary on Idra Raba by a Member of the Sarug School" (Hebrew), in *Rivkah Shatz-Uffenheimer Memorial Volume*, ed. R. Elior and J. Dan (Jerusalem, 1996) 1: 307–78; and idem, "The School of Sarug: A New History" (Hebrew), *Shalem* 7 (forthcoming).

75. *Yitfos bannu filosof.*

76. *Da'ato yafah.*

77. *Novelot ḥokhma* (Basel, 1631), fol. 166b.

78. See also a somewhat more ambiguous remark by the editor of Delmedigo's book, R. Samuel ben Judah Leib Ashkenazi, ibid., fol. 17a.

79. Modena, *Ari nohem*, pp. 294–95.

80. Ibid., p. 53.

81. Scholem, *Abraham Kohen Herrera and Sefer Sha'ar Hashamayyim* (Hebrew) (Jerusalem, 1968), p. 17; idem, *Major Trends*, p. 257; idem, "Rabbi Israel Sarug," pp. 228–32.

82. A. Altmann, "Notes on the Development of R. Menaḥem Azariah of Fano's Kabbalistic Doctrine" (Hebrew), in *Studies in Jewish Mysticism, Presented to Isaiah Tishby*, ed. J. Dan (Jerusalem, 1984), pp. 255–56.

83. See D. P. Walker, *The Ancient Theology* (London, 1972); C. Schmitt, "Perennial Philosophy from Agostino Steuco to Leibniz," *Journal of the History of Ideas* 27 (1966): 505–32; idem, "Prisca theologia e filosofia perennis: Due temi del Rinascimento italiano e a loro fortuna," in *Il pensiero italiano del Rinascimento e il tempo nostro* (Florence, 1970), pp. 211–36; P. O. Kristeller, *Renaissance Thought and Its Sources*, ed. Michael Mooney (New York, 1979), pp. 196–210; C. Trinkaus, *In Our Image and Likeness: Humanity and Dignity in Italian Humanist Thought* (Notre Dame, Ind., 1995), pp. 726–42, 754–56; J. Hankins, *Plato in the Italian Renaissance* (Leiden, 1990), pp. 459–63; C. Wirszubski, *Pico della Mirandola* p. 198 n. 41; B. Tambrun, "Marsile Ficin et le 'Commentaire' de Plethon sur les 'Oracles Chaldaiques,' " *Accademia* 1 (1999): 9–48; M. Idel, "Kabbalah and Philosophy in Isaac and Judah Abravanel" (Hebrew), in *The Philosophy of Leone Ebreo*, ed. M. Dorman and Z. Levi (Tel Aviv, 1985), pp. 73–112, esp. pp. 84–86; idem, "Platonism and Prisca Theologia: The Case of Menasseh ben Israel," in *Menasseh ben Israel and His World*, ed. Y. Kaplan, H. Méchoulan, and R. H. Popkin (Leiden, 1989), pp. 207–19; Ruderman, *Kabbalah, Magic, and Science*, pp. 139–50.

84. See, for example, Scholem, *Major Trends*, p. 327, and the discussions on this topic above.

85. See Tishby, *Studies in Kabbalah and Its Branches*, 1: 177–267.

86. M. Idel, " 'One fom a Town, Two from a Clan': The Diffusion of Lurianic Kabbalah and Sabbateanism: A Reexamination" (Hebrew), *Pe'amim* 44 (1990): 5–30, and an English version, printed in *Jewish History* 7 (1993): 79–104; idem, "Saturn and Sabbatai Tzevi: A New Approach to Sabbateanism," in *Toward the Millennium: Messianic Expectations from the Bible to Waco*, ed. P. Schaefer and M. Cohen (Leiden, 1998), pp. 173–202; and additional important material adduced in J. Barnai, *Sabbateanism: Social Perspectives* (Hebrew) (Jerusalem, 2000), pp. 20–29.

87. See, for example, M. Idel, *Hasidism: Between Ecstasy and Magic* (Albany, N.Y., 1995), pp. 45–145; and idem, *Messianic Mystics*, passim.

88. See Idel, "Maimonides and Kabbalah," in *Studies in Maimonides*, ed. I. Twersky (Cambridge, Mass., 1990), pp. 31–81. See also I. Marcus, *Rituals of Childhood* (New Haven, Conn., 1996), pp. 103, 156 n. 1; M. Idel, *Kabbalah: New Perspectives* (New Haven, Conn., 1988), p. 251; idem, *Kabbalah and Eros*, chap. 1 par. 7.

89. See J. S. Gil, *La escuela de traductores de Toledo y sus colaboratores judios* (Toledo, 1985), pp. 57–87.

90. See Scholem, *Major Trends*, p. 398.

91. See Liebes, "The *Zohar* as Renaissance in Castile"; and M. Idel, "Historical Introduction" to Rabbi Joseph Gikatilla, *Gates of Light*, trans. A. Weinstein (San Francisco, 1994), pp. xxxx–xxxxi.

92. See Idel, *Kabbalah: New Perspectives*, pp. 211–12.

93. See A. P. Coudert, *The Impact of the Kabbalah in the Seventeenth Century: The Life and Thought of Francis Mercury van Helmont (1614–1698)* (Leiden, 1999); idem, *Leibniz and the Kabbalah* (Dordrecht, 1995).

94. See the debate analyzed by D. Kaufmann, "The Dispute about the Sermons of David del Bene of Mantua," *Jewish Quarterly Review*, o.s., 8 (1896): 513–24; M. Idel, "Judah Moscato: A Late Renaissance Jewish Preacher," in *Preachers of the Italian Ghetto*, ed. Ruderman, pp. 45–47, 52–53.

95. J. Seznec, *The Survival of the Pagan Gods: The Mythological Tradition and Its Place in Renaissance Humanism* (Princeton, N.J., 1972), p. 287.

96. See A. Gurwitsch, "Phenomenology of Perception: Perceptual Implications," in *An Invitation to Phenomenology*, ed. J. M. Edie (Chicago, 1965), p. 21.

97. See Ruderman, *Kabbalah, Magic, and Science*, pp. 121–38.

98. *Novelot ḥokhma*, fol. 186a.

99. Modena, *Ari nohem*, pp. 42–43.

100. See Modena's "Ben David" printed in *Ta'am zeqenim*, ed. E. Ashkenazi (Frankfurt am Main, 1854), pp. 61–64.

101. See the survey of H. Tirosh-Rothschild, "Jewish Culture in Renaissance Italy: A Metholodological Survey," *Italia* 9 (1990): 63–96.

102. See C. Roth, *The Jews in the Renaissance* (Philadelphia, 1959); D. Ruderman, "Cecil Roth: A Reassessment," in *The Jewish Past Revisited*, ed. D. N. Myers and D. B. Ruderman (New Haven, Conn., 1998), pp. 128–42; Ruderman, *Kabbalah, Magic, and Science*, pp. 139–60; idem, *A Valley of Vision: The Heavenly Journey of Abraham ben Hananiah Yagel* (Philadelphia, 1990), pp. 23–68.

103. See, for example, R. Bonfil, "Expressions of Uniqueness of the Jewish People in Italy in the Period of the Renaissance" (Hebrew), *Sinai* 76 (1975): 36–46; idem, "The Historian's Perception of the Jews in the Italian Renaissance," *Revue des études juives* 143 (1984): 59–82; J. Dan, *Hebrew Ethical and Homiletical Literature* (Hebrew) (Jerusalem, 1975), p. 183.

104. Idel, "Differing Conceptions of Kabbalah," p. 140; idem, "Judah Moscato," p. 58; Ruderman, *Kabbalah, Magic, and Science*, p. 160.

105. See Yosha, *Myth and Metaphor*.

106. E. Cassirer, "Giovanni Pico della Mirandola," *Journal of the History of Ideas* 3 (1942): 124.

107. See, for example, Delmedigo, *Novelot ḥokhma*, fols. 14b–15a, 66b.

108. See Scholem, *Sabbatai Ṣevi*, pp. 80–87, 90–93; Y. Liebes, "Jonah ben Amitai as Messiah ben Joseph" (Hebrew), in *Studies in Jewish Mysticism*, Dan, pp. 269–311; Y. Liebes, "Mysticism and Reality: Toward a Portrait of the Martyr and Kabbalist R. Samson Ostropoler," in *Jewish Thought in the Seventeenth Century*, ed. Twersky and Septimus, pp. 221–55.

Chapter 12

A Bibliography of Jewish Cultural History in the Early Modern Period

Giuseppe Veltri

The following bibliography on Jewish cultural history in the Early Modern Period is based mostly on the contributions of this volume. Some additional references to works of general interest have been included as well. A detailed bibliography on the Renaissance Jewish cultural world and philosophical thought is in preparation.

Acanfora Torrefranca, M. "Sulle musiche degli ebrei in Italia." In C. Vivanti, ed., *Storia d'Italia: Gli ebrei in Italia.* Vol. 11. Turin, 1996, pp. 475–93.

Adler, I., ed. *Hebrew Writings Concerning Music in Manuscripts and Printed Books from Geonic Times up to 1800.* Munich, 1975.

———. "The Rise of Art Music in the Italian Ghetto." In S. Gmeinwieser, ed., *Jewish Medieval and Renaissance Studies.* Cambridge, Mass., 1967, pp. 321–64.

Altmann, A. "Ars Rhetorica as Reflected in Some Jewish Figures of the Italian Renaissance." In B. Cooperman, ed., *Jewish Thought in the Sixteenth Century.* Cambridge, Mass., 1983, pp. 1–22.

———. "Notes on the Development of R. Menaḥem Azariah of Fano's Kabbalistic Doctrine" (Hebrew). In J. Dan, ed., *Studies in Jewish Mysticism, Presented to Isaiah Tishby.* Jerusalem, 1984, pp. 255–56.

———. *Von der mittelalterlichen zur modernen Aufklärung: Studien zur jüdischen Geistesgeschichte.* Tübingen, 1987.

Apfelbaum, A. *Toledot hagaon Rabbi Yehuda Moscato.* Drogobych, Ukraine, 1900.

Avivi, J. "The Writings of Rabbi Isaac Luria in Italy before 1620" (Hebrew). *Alei Sefer* 11 (1984): 91–134.

———. "Rabbi Menaḥem Azariah of Fano's Writings on Matters of Kabbalah" (Hebrew). *Sefunot* 19 (1989): 347–76.

Baer, F.(Y.). *Untersuchungen über Quellen und Komposition des Schebet Jehuda.* Berlin, 1923.

———. "New Notes on 'Shebet Jehuda' " (Hebrew). *Tarbiẓ* 6 (1935); 152–79.

Barnai, J. *Sabbateanism: Social Perspectives* (Hebrew). Jerusalem, 2000.

Bartòla, A. "Eliyahu Delmedigo e Giovanni Pico della Mirandola: La testimonianza dei codici vaticani." *Rinascimento* 33 (1993): 253–78.
Baruchson, S. *Books and Readers: The Reading Interests of Italian Jews at the Close of the Renaissance* (Hebrew). Ramat Gan, 1993.
Barzilay, I. *Between Reason and Faith.* The Hague, 1967.
Baumgarten, J. "Giovanni di Gara: Imprimeur de livres yiddish a Venise (milieu du XVe–début du XVIe siècle) et la culture juive de la Renaissance." *Revue des études juives* 159 (2000): 587–98.
Benayahu, M. *Rabbi Elijah Capsali of Crete* (Hebrew). Tel Aviv, 1983.
———, ed. "Rabbi Ezra of Fano: Sage, Kabbalist, and Leader" (Hebrew). In *Sefer hay-ovel lehaga'on Yosef Dov Soloveitchik.* Vol. 2. Jerusalem, 1984, pp. 786–855.
———. *Yosef beḥiri* (Hebrew). Jerusalem, 1991.
Ben-Shlomo, J. *The Mystical Theology of Moses Cordovero* (Hebrew). Jerusalem, 1965.
Berger, A. "Captive at the Gate of Rome: The Story of a Messianic Motif." *Proceedings of the American Academy for Jewish Research* 44 (1977): 16–17.
Berlin, C., ed. "A Sixteenth-Century Hebrew Chronicle of the Ottoman Empire: The *Seder Eliyahu Zuta* of Elijah Capsali and Its Message." In Berlin, ed., *Studies in Jewish Bibliography, History, and Literature in Honor of I. Edward Kiev.* New York, 1971, pp. 21–44.
Berti, E. "Il concetto rinascimentale di philosophia perennis e le origini della storiografia tedesca." *Verifiche* 6 (1977): 3–11.
Bettan, I. "The Sermons of Judah Moscato." *Hebrew Union College Annual* 6 (1929): 297–326.
Bialloblotzky, C. H. F., ed. *The Chronicles of Rabbi Joseph Ben Joshua Ben Meir, the Sephardi.* 2 vols. London, 1835–36.
Bland, Kalman P. "Elijah Delmedigo's Averroist Response to the Kabbalahs of Fifteenth-Century Jewry and Pico della Mirandola." *Journal of Jewish Thought and Philosophy* 1 (1991): 23–53.
———. "Elijah del Medigo: Unicity of Intellect and Immortality." *Proceedings of the American Academy of Jewish Research* 61 (1995): 1–22.
Boccato, C. "Sara Copio Sullam, la poetessa del ghetto di Venezia: Episodi della sua vita in un manoscritto del secolo XVII." *Italia* 6 (1987): 104–218.
Boksenboim, Y., ed. *Iggerot melamdim.* Tel Aviv, 1985.
Bonfil, Robert. "Expressions in Italy of the Uniqueness of the Jewish People during the Renaissance" (Hebrew). *Sinai* 76 (1975): 36–46.
———. "Perush R. Moshe Provenzali le-25 hakdamot ha-Rambam." *Kiryat Sefer* 50 (1975): 157–76.
———. "The Doctrine of the Soul and of Sanctity in the Thought of Ovadiah Sforno" (Hebrew). *Eshel Beersheva* 1 (1976): 200–257.
———. "Introduction," in *Judah Messer Leon: Sefer nofet ẓufim.* Jerusalem, 1981, pp. 7–53.
———. "Some Reflections on the Place of Azariah de' Rossi's *Meor Enayim* in the Cultural Milieu of Italian Renaissance Jewry." In B. Cooperman, ed., *Jewish Thought in the Sixteenth Century.* Cambridge, Mass., 1983, pp. 23–48.
———. "Halakhah, Kabbalah and Society: Some Insights into Rabbi Menaḥem

Azariah da Fano's Inner World." In I. Twersky and B. Septimus, eds., *Jewish Thought in the Seventeenth Century.* Cambridge, Mass., 1987, pp. 39–61.

———. "Esiste une storiografia ebraica medioevale?" In *Aspetti della storiografia ebraica: Atti del convegno di studi giudaici della associazione italiana per lo studio del giudaismo.* Rome, 1987, pp. 227–47.

———. "Changes in the Cultural Patterns of a Jewish Society in Crisis: Italian Jewry at the Close of the Sixteenth Century." *Jewish History* 3 (1988): 11–30.

———. "How Golden Was the Age of the Renaissance in Jewish Historiography?." In A. Rapoport-Albert, ed., *Essays in Jewish Historiography.* 2d edition. Atlanta, 1988, pp. 78–102.

———. "Who Was the Apostate Ludovico Carreto?" (Hebrew). In *Exile and Diaspora: Studies in the History of the Jewish People Presented to Prof. H. Beinart on the Occasion of His Seventieth Birthday.* Jerusalem, 1988, pp. 437–42.

———. *Rabbis and Jewish Communities in Renaissance Italy.* (Oxford, 1990).

———. "Accademie rabbiniche e presenza ebraica nelle università." In G. P. Brizzi and J. Verger, eds., *Le università dell'Europa dal Rinascimento alle riforme religiose.* Milan, 1991, pp. 132–51.

———. *Gli ebrei in Italia nell'età del Rinascimento.* Florence, 1991.

———. "The Book of the Honeycomb's Flow by Judah Messer Leon: The Rhetorical Dimension of Jewish Humanism in Fifteenth-Century Italy." *Jewish History* 6 (1992): 21–33.

———. "Preaching as Meditation between Elite and Popular Cultures: The Case of Judah del Bene." In D. Ruderman, ed., *Preachers of the Italian Ghetto.* Berkeley, Calif., 1992, pp. 67–88.

———. "The Libraries of Italian Jewry between the Middle Ages and Modern Times" (Hebrew). *Pe'amim* 52 (1992): 4–15.

———. *Rabbis and Jewish Communities in Renaissance Italy.* London, 1993.

———. "Zuṭot leparashat hageṭ Tamari-Venturozzo." In A. Oppenheimer, ed., *Shlomo Simonsohn Jubilee Volume.* Tel Aviv, 1993, pp. 19–28.

———. *Jewish Life in Renaissance Italy.* Berkeley, Calif., 1994.

———. "Lo spazio culturale degli ebrei d'Italia fra Rinascimento ed età barocca." In C. Vivanti, ed., *Storia d'Italia: Gli ebrei in Italia.* Vol. 11. Turin, 1996, pp. 411–73.

———. "Gli ebrei d'Italia e la Riforma: Una questione da riconsiderare." *Nouvelles de la Republique des Lettres* 2 (1996): 47–60.

———. *Tra due mondi: Cultura ebraica e cultura cristiana nel Medioevo.* Naples, 1996.

———. "Jewish Attitudes Toward History and Historical Writing in Pre-Modern Times." *Jewish History* 11 (1997): 7–40.

———. "A Cultural Profile." In R. Davis and B. Ravid, eds., *The Jews of Early Modern Venice.* Baltimore, 2001, pp. 169–90.

Bos, G. "Ḥayyim Vital's Practical Kabbalah and Alchemy: A 17th-Century Book of Secrets." *Journal of Jewish Thought and Philosophy* 4 (1994): 55–112.

Bregman, D. *A Bundle of Gold: Hebrew Sonnets from the Renaissance and the Baroque* (Hebrew). Jerusalem, 1997.

Brener, A. "Portrait of the Rabbi as Young Humanist: A Reading of Elijah Capsali's 'Chronicle of Venice' " (Hebrew). *Italia* 11 (1994): 37–60.

Burke, P. *Culture and Society in Renaissance Italy: 1420–1540*. New York, 1972.
Busi, G. "Letteratura ebraico-cristiana nei secoli XV e XVI." *Henoch* 6 (1984): 369–78.
———. *Il succo dei favi: Studi sull'umanesimo ebraico*. Bologna, 1992.
———. "Invenzione simbolica e tradizione ebraica nel Rinascimento italiano: Alcuni esperimenti figurativi." *Henoch* 21 (1999): 165–77.
Carpi, D. "Notes on the Life of Rabbi Judah Messer Leon." In *Studi sull' ebraismo italiano in memoria di Cecil Roth*. Rome, 1974, pp. 37–62.
Cassirer, E. "Some Remarks on the Question of the Originality of the Renaissance." *Journal of the History of Ideas* 4 (1943): 49–56.
Cassuto, D. "La sinagoga in Italia." In C. Vivanti, ed., *Storia d'Italia: Gli ebrei in Italia*. Vol. 11. Turin, 1996, pp. 319–38.
Cassuto, U. *Gli ebrei a Firenze nell'età del Rinascimento*. Florence, 1918.
Cochrane, E. W. *Historians and Historiography in the Italian Renaissance*. Chicago, 1981.
Cohen, M., ed. *The Autobiography of a Seventeenth-Century Venetian Rabbi: Leon Modena's Life of Judah* Princeton, N.J., 1988.
Colomer, E. *El pensament als països catalans durant l'Edat Mitjana i el Renaixement*. Barcelona, 1997.
Colorni, V. "Note per la biografia di alcuni dotti ebrei vissuti a Mantova nel secolo XV." *Annuario di Studi Ebraici* 1 (1934): 169–82.
Coudert, A. P. *The Impact of the Kabbalah in the Seventeenth Century: The Life and Thought of Francis Mercury van Helmont* (1614–1698). Leiden, 1999.
———. *Leibniz and the Kabbalah*. Dordrecht, 1995.
Couliano, I. P. *Eros and Magic in the Renaissance*. Chicago, 1987.
Dales, R. C. "The Origin of the Doctrine of the Double Truth." *Viator* 15 (1984): 169–79.
Dan, J. "The Sermon *Tefilah ve-Dim'a* of R. Judah Moscato" (Hebrew). *Sinai* 76 (1975): 209–22.
———. "La cultura ebraica nell'Italia medievale: Filosofia, etica, misticismo." In C. Vivanti, ed., *Storia d'Italia: Gli ebrei in Italia*. Vol. 11 Turin, 1996, pp. 339–58.
———. "Shevet Yehuda: Past and Future History." In J. Dan, ed., *Jewish Mysticism*. Vol. 3. Northvale, N.J., 1999, pp. 25–56.
David, A. "L'epistolario di Joseph ha-Kohen" (Hebrew). *Italia* 5 (1985): 7–98.
———. ed. *From Italy to Jerusalem: The Letters of Rabbi Obadiah of Bertinoro from the Land of Israel*. Ramat Gan, 1997.
Davidson, H. "Medieval Jewish Philosophy in the Sixteenth Century." In B. Cooperman, ed., *Jewish Thought in the Sixteenth Century*. Cambridge, Mass., 1983, pp. 126–45.
———. *The Philosophy of Abraham Shalom: A Fifteenth-Century Exposition and Defense of Maimonides*. Berkeley, Calif., 1964.
Ebert, H. "Augustinus Steuchus und seine Philosophia perennis: Ein kritischer Beitrag zur Geschichte der Philosophie." *Philosophisches Jahrbuch* 42 (1929): 342–56, 510–26; 43 (1930): 92–100.
Edwards, J. *The Jews in Christian Europe 1400–1700*. London, 1988.

Elbaum, J. *Openness and Insularity: Late Sixteenth-Century Jewish Literature in Poland and Ashkenaz* (Hebrew). Jerusalem, 1990.
Elior, R. "Messianic Expectations and the Spiritualization of Religious Life in the Sixteenth Century." *Revue des études juives* 145 (1986): 35–49.
Faierstein, M. M., ed. *Jewish Mystical Autobiographies: Book of Visions and Book of Secrets.* New York, 1999.
Fenlon, I. *Music and Patronage in Sixteenth-Century Mantua.* 2 vols. Cambridge, 1980–82.
Fenton, P. B. "Influences soufies sur le development de la qabbale a Safed: Le cas de la visitation des tombes." In P. B. Fenton and R. Goetschel, eds., *Experience et écriture mystiques dans les religions du livre.* Leiden, 2000, pp. 163–90.
Fishman, T. *Shaking the Pillars of Exile: "Voice of a Fool," An Early Modern Jewish Critique of Rabbinic Culture.* Stanford, Calif., 1997.
Foa, A. *The Jews of Europe After the Black Death.* Berkeley, Calif., 2000.
Freudenberger, T. *Augustinus Steuchus aus Gubbio: Augustinerchorherr und päpstlicher Bibliothekar.* Münster, 1935.
Front, D. "The Expurgation of the Books of Amatus Lusitanus: Censorship and the Bibliography of the Individual Book." *Book Collector* 47 (1998): 520–36.
Garin, E. *Ritratti di umanisti italiani.* Florence, 1967.
———. *Educazione umanistica in Italia.* Bari, 1975.
———. *Discussioni sulla retorica, in Medioevo e Rinascimento.* Bari, 1990.
———. "L'umanesimo in Italia e la cultura ebraica." In C. Vivanti, ed., *Storia d'Italia: Gli ebrei in Italia.* Vol. 11. Turin, 1996, pp. 359–83.
Garvin, B. "The Language of Leone Ebreo's *Dialoghi d'Amore.*" *Italia* 13–14 (2001): 181–201.
Gebhardt, C., ed. *Leone Ebreo, Dialoghi d'amore: Hebräische Gedichte.* Heidelberg, 1929 (Bibliotheca Spinozana, 3).
Geffen, D. "Faith and Reason in Elijah Delmedigo's *Beḥinat ha-Dat.*" Ph.D. diss., Columbia University, 1970.
———. "Insights into the Life and Thought of Elijah Delmedigo Based on His Published and Unpublished Works." *Proceedings of the American Academy of Jewish Research* 41–42 (1975): 69–86.
Ghirondi, M. *Toledot gedole Yisrael.* Trieste, 1853.
Gil, J. S. *La escuela de traductores de Toledo y sus colaboratores judios.* Toledo, 1985.
Giller, P. "Recovering the Sanctity of the Galilee: The Veneration of Sacred Relics in Classical Kabbalah." *Journal of Jewish Thought and Philosophy* 4 (1994): 147–69.
Gottlieb, E. "A Dispute over Metempsychosis in Crete in the Fifteenth Century" (Hebrew). In his work *Studies in Kabbalah Literature.* Ed. J. Hacker, Tel Aviv, 1976, pp. 370–96.
Graetz, H. "Elijah del Medigo; Ein jüdischer Popularphilosoph." *Monatsschrift zur Geschichte und Wissenschaft des Judenthums* 20 (1871): 481–94.
Gries, Z. *Conduct Literature (Regimen Vitae): Its History and Place in the Life of Beshtian Hasidism* (Hebrew). Jerusalem, 1989.
Gross, A. "Lines of the History of the Yeshivot in Castile in the Fifteenth Century" (Hebrew). *Pe'amim* 31 (1987): 3–20.

Guttman, J. "Elijahs Delmedigos Verhältnis zu Averroës in seinem *Bechinat ha-Dat.*" In A. Kohut, ed., *Jewish Studies in Memory of Israel Abrahams.* New York, 1927, pp. 192–208.

Gutwirth, E. "History and Apologetics in XVth c. Hispano-Jewish Thought." *Helmantica* 35 (1984): 231–42.

———. "The Expulsion from Spain and Jewish Historiography." In A. Rapoport-Albert and S. J. Zipperstein, eds., *Jewish History: Essays in Honour of Chimen Abramsky.* London, 1988, pp. 141–61.

———. "Hispano-Jewish Attitudes to the Moors in the Fifteenth Century." *Sefarad* 49 (1989): 237–62.

———. "Profiat Duran on Ahitofel: The Practice of Jewish History in Late Medieval Spain." *Jewish History* 41 (1989): 59–74.

———. "Religion and Social Criticism in Late Medieval Rousillon: An Aspect of Profiat Duran's Activities." *Michael* 12 (1991): 135–56.

———. "Gender, History and the Medieval Judaeo-Christian Polemic." In O. Limor, ed., *Contra Iudaeos: Ancient and Medieval Polemics between Jews and Christians.* Tübingen, 1996, pp. 257–78.

———. "Italy or Spain? The Theme of Jewish Eloquence in *Shevet Yehudah.*" In M. Rozen, ed., *Daniel Carpi Jubilee Volume.* Tel Aviv, 1996, pp. 35–67.

———. "Sephardi Culture of the Genizah People." *Michael* 14 (1997): 9–34.

———. "The Stranger's Wisdom: Translation and Otherness in Fifteenth-Century Iberia." *Portuguese Studies* 13 (1997): 130–42.

———. "History and Intertextuality in Late Medieval Spain." In M. Meyerson and E. English, eds., *Christians, Muslims, and Jews in Medieval and Early Modern Spain: Interaction and Cultural Change.* Notre Dame, Ind., 1999, pp. 162–63.

———. "Language and Medicine in the Ottoman Empire." In J. Helm and A. Winkelmann, eds., *Religious Confessions and the Sciences in the Sixteenth Century.* Leiden, 2001 , pp. 79–98.

Habermann, A. M., *Giovanni di Gara: Printer, Venice, 1564–1610* (Hebrew). Jerusalem, 1982.

Hames, H. "Approaches to Conversion in the Late 13th-Century Church." *Studia Lulliana* 35 (1995): 75–84.

———. "Jewish Magic with a Christian Text: A Hebrew Translation of Ramon Llull's Ars Brevis." *Traditio* 54 (1999): 283–300.

———. *The Art of Conversion: Christianity and Kabbalah in the Thirteenth Century.* Leiden, 2000.

Hankins, J. *Plato in the Italian Renaissance.* Leiden, 1990.

Harari, D. "Mihu hamelumad hayehudi shedarko noda' sefer Or ha-Shem le-Pico." In A. Ravitzky, ed., *Mi-Romi le-Yerushalayim.* Jerusalem, 1998, pp. 257–69.

Harrán, D. "Salamone Rossi: Jewish Musician in Renaissance Italy." *Acta Musicologica* 59 (1987): 46–64.

———. "Salamone Rossi as a Composer of Theater Music." *Studi musicali* 16 (1987): 91–131.

———. "Tradition and Innovation in Jewish Music of the Later Renaissance." *Journal of Musicology* 7 (1989): 107–30.

———. ed. *Salamone Rossi: Complete Works.* 13 vols. Neuhausen-Stuttgart, 1995. vols. 1–12; vols. 13a and 13b, (Middleton, Wis., 2003) (Corpus Mensurabilis Musicae, 100).

———. "Madama Europa: Jewish Singer in Late Renaissance Mantua." In X. Stuyvesant, ed., *Festa Musicologica: Essays in Honor of George J. Buelow.* New York, 1995, pp. 197–231.

———. " 'Dum Recordaremur Sion': Music in the Life and Thought of the Venetian Rabbi Leon Modena (1571–1648)." *Association for Jewish Studies Review* 23 (1998): 17–61.

———. *Salamone Rossi: Jewish Musician in Late Renaissance Mantua.* Oxford, 1999.

———. "Jewish Musical Culture in Early Modern Venice." In R. C. Davis and B. Ravid, eds., *The Jews of Early Modern Venice.* Baltimore, 2001.

Harvey, S., ed. *The Medieval Hebrew Encyclopaedias of Science and Philosophy.* Dordrecht, 2000.

Hayoun, M. "Judentum und Averroismus im Zeitalter der Renaissance: Der Fall Eliya Delmedigo." *Aschkenas* 4 (1995): 201–45; 417–24.

Horowitz, E. "Speaking of the Dead: The Emergence of the Eulogy among Italian Jewry of the Sixteenth Century." In D. Ruderman, ed., *Preachers of the Italian Ghetto.* Berkeley, Calif., 1992, pp. 135–44.

Hubsch, A. "Elijah Delmedigos *Bechinat ha-Dath* und Ibn Roschd's *Façl ul-maqal.*" *Monatsschrift für Geschichte und Wissenschaft des Judenthums* 31 (1882): 552–63; 32 (1883): 28–48.

Huss, B. "Sefer ha-Zohar as a Canonical, Sacred and Holy Text: Changing Perspectives in the Book of Splendor Between the Thirteenth and Eighteenth Centuries." *Journal of Jewish Thought and Philosophy* 7 (1998): pp. 257–307.

Idel, M. "Between the View of *Sefirot* as Essence and Instruments in the Renaissance" (Hebrew). *Italia* 3 (1982): 89–111.

———. "Inquiries in the Doctrine of Sefer Hameshiv" (Hebrew). *Sefunot* 17 (1983): 232–43.

———. "The Magical and Neoplatonic Interpretations of Kabbalah in the Renaissance." In B. Cooperman, ed., *Jewish Thought in the Sixteenth Century.* Cambridge, Mass. 1983, pp. 226–27.

———. "R. Judah Hallewah and His Composition *Ṣafenat Pa'aneaḥ*" (Hebrew). *Shalem* 4 (1984): 122–23.

———. "Kabbalah and Philosophy in Isaac and Judah Abravanel" (Hebrew). In M. Dorman and Z. Levi, eds., *The Philosophy of Leone Ebreo.* Tel Aviv, 1985, pp. 73–112.

———. "Major Currents in Italian Kabbalah, 1560–1660." In G. Sermoneta and S. Simonsohn, eds., *Italia Judaica.* Rome, 1986, pp. 243–62.

———. "Particularism and Universalism in Kabbalah, 1480–1650." In D. Ruderman, ed., *Essential Papers on Jewish Culture in Renaissance and Baroque Italy.* New York, 1992, pp. 324–344.

———. The Study Program of R. Yoḥanan Alemanno" (Hebrew). *Tarbiẓ* 48 (1979–1980): 303–31.

———. "The Anthropology of Yoḥanan Alemanno: Sources and Influences." *Topoi* 7 (1988): 201–10.

———. *Studies in Ecstatic Kabbalah.* Albany, N.Y., 1988.

———. "Platonism and Prisca Theologia: The Case of Menasseh ben Israel." In Y. Kaplan, H. Méchoulan, and R. H. Popkin, eds., *Menasseh ben Israel and His World.* Leiden, 1989, pp. 207–19.

———. "The Magical and Neoplatonic Interpretations of the Kabbalah in the Renaissance." In D. Ruderman, *Essential Papers on Jewish Culture in Renaissance and Baroque Italy.* New York, 1992, pp. 107–69.

———. "Judah Moscato: A Late Renaissance Jewish Preacher." In D. Ruderman, ed., *Preachers of the Italian Ghetto.* Berkeley, Calif., 1992, pp. 41–66.

———. "On the Concept of *Ṣimṣum* in Kabbalah and Its Research" (Hebrew). In R. Elior and Y. Liebes, eds., *Lurianic Kabbalah.* Jerusalem, 1992, pp. 59–112.

———. "Religion, Thought and Attitudes: The Impact of the Expulsion on the Jews." In E. Kedourie, ed., *Spain and the Jews: The Sephardi Experience, 1492 and After.* London, 1992, pp. 123–39.

———. "Jewish Kabbalah and Platonism in the Middle Ages and Renaissance." In L. E. Goodman, ed., *Neoplatonism and Jewish Thought.* Albany, N.Y., 1993, pp. 319–51.

———. " 'One from a Town, Two from a Clan': The Diffusion of Lurianic Kabbala and Sabbateanism: A Re-examination." *Jewish History* 7 (1993): 79–104.

———. "The Ecstatic Kabbalah of Abraham Abulafia in Sicily and Its Transmission during the Renaissance." In *Italia Judaica: Gli ebrei in Sicilia sino all'espulsione del 1492.* Rome, 1995, pp. 330–40.

———. "Solomon Molkho as Magician" (Hebrew). *Sefunot,* r.s., 3 (1995): 198–202.

———. "Encounters Between Spanish and Italian Kabbalists in the Generation of the Expulsion." In B. R. Gampel, ed., *Crisis and Creativity in the Sephardic World.* New York, 1997, pp. 194–97.

———. "On Mobility, Individuals and Groups: Prolegomenon for a Sociological Approach to Sixteenth-Century Kabbalah." *Kabbalah: Journal for the Study of Jewish Mystical Texts* 3 (1998): 145–73.

———. "Jewish Mystical Thought in the Florence of Lorenzo il Magnifico." In D. Liscia Bemporad and I. Zatelli, eds., *La cultura ebraica all'epoca di Lorenzo il Magnifico.* Florence, 1998, pp. 17–42.

———. "R. Nathan ben Sa'adia Harar." In M. Mottolese, ed., *Le porte della giustizia. Milan,* 2001, pp. 13–39.

Ijsewijn, J. "Flavius Guillelmus Raymundus Mithridates." *Humanistica Lovaniensia* 26 (1977): 236–38.

Ingall, C. K. "Reform and Redemption: The Maharal of Prague and Jan Amos Comenius." *Religious Education* 89 (1994): 358–75.

Israel, J. *European Jewry in the Age of Mercantilism 1550–1750.* 3d edition. London, 1998.

Ivry, A. L. "Remnants of Jewish Averroism in the Renaissance." In B. Cooperman, ed., *Jewish Thought in the Sixteenth Century.* Cambridge, Mass., 1983, pp. 243–65.

Jacobson, Y. *Along the Paths of Exile and Redemption: The Doctrine of Redemption of Rabbi Mordekhai Dato* (Hebrew). Jerusalem, 1996.

Kaufmann, D. "The Dispute about the Sermons of David del Bene of Mantua." *Jewish Quarterly Review* o.s. 8 (1896): 513–24.

Kieszkowski, B. "Les Rapports entre Elie Delmedigo et Pic de la Mirandole." *Rinascimento* 55 (1964): 41–49.

Kleinberger, A. F. "The Didactics of Rabbi Loew of Prague." *Scripta Hierosolomitana* 13 (1963): 32–55.

Kreisel, H. "Judah Halevi's Influence on Maimonides: A Preliminary Appraisal." In A. Hyman, ed., *Maimonidean Studies.* Vol. 2. New York, 1991, pp. 95–121.

Kristeller, P. O. *Renaissance Thought: The Classic, Scholastic, and Humanist Strains.* 2d edition. New York, 1961.

———. *Medieval Aspects of Renaissance Learning.* Durham, N.C., 1974.

———. *Renaissance Thought and Its Sources.* New York, 1979.

Kulka, O. D. "The Historical Background of the National and Educational Teaching of the Maharal of Prague" (Hebrew). *Zion* 50 (1985): 277–320.

Kupfer, E. "The Jewish Community of Safed and the Activity of R. Menaḥem Azariah of Fano on Behalf of the Yishuv in Erets Israel" (Hebrew). *Shalem* 2 (1976); 361–64.

Lelli, F. "Retorica, poetica e linguistica nel *Ḥay ha-'Olamim* (L'Immortale) di Yoḥanan Alemanno." Ph.D. diss., University of Turin, 1992.

———. "Un collaboratore ebreo di Giovanni Pico della Mirandola: Yoḥanan Alemanno." *Vivens Homo* 5 (1994): 401–30.

———. ed. *Yoḥanan Alemanno: Ḥay ha-'Olamim (L'Immortale).* Vol. 1: *La Retorica.* Florence, 1995.

———. "L'educazione ebraica nella seconda metà del 400: Poetica e scienze naturali nel Ḥay ha-'Olamim di Yoḥanan Alemanno." *Rinascimento* 36 (1996): 75–136.

———. "Umanesimo laurenziano nell'opera di Yoḥanan Alemanno." In D. Liscia Bemporad and I. Zatelli, eds., *La cultura ebraica all'epoca di Lorenzo il Magnifico.* Florence, 1998, pp. 49–67.

Lesley, A. M. " 'The Song of Solomon's Ascents' by Yoḥanan Alemanno: Love and Human Perfection according to a Jewish Colleague of Giovanni Pico della Mirandola." Ph.D. diss., University of California, 1976.

———. "The Place of the *Dialoghi d'Amore* in Contemporaneous Jewish Thought." In D. Ruderman, ed., *Essential Papers on Jewish Culture in Renaissance and Baroque Italy.* New York, 1992, pp. 170–88.

———. "Jewish Adaptation of Humanist Concepts in Fifteenth- and Sixteenth-Century Italy." In D. Ruderman, ed., *Essential Papers on Jewish Culture in Renaissance and Baroque Italy.* New York, 1992, pp. 46–62.

———. "Il richiamo agli 'antichi' nella cultura ebraica tra quattro e cinquecento." In C. Vivanti, ed., *Storia d'Italia: Gli ebrei in Italia.* Vol. 11. Turin, 1996, pp. 385–409.

Levi, T. "Ethics and the Encyclopedia in the Sixteenth Century." In P. Sharatt, ed., *French Renaissance Studies, 1540–1570.* Edinburgh, 1976, pp. 170–84.

Liebes, Y. "Mysticism and Reality: Toward a Portrait of the Martyr and Kabbalist R.

Samson Ostropoler." In I. Twersky and B. D. Septimus, eds., *Jewish Thought in the Seventeenth Century*. Cambridge, Mass., 1987, pp. 221–55.

———. "Zohar and Eros" (Hebrew). *Alpayim* 9 (1994): 67–119, 523–85.

Loeb, I. "Additions au Dibré Hayyamim de Josef Haccohen." *Revue des études juives* 10 (1885): 248–250.

———. "Joseph Haccohen et les chroniqueurs juifs." *Revue des études juives* 16 (1888): 28–56.

Mahoney, E. P. "Giovanni Pico della Mirandola and Elijah Delmedigo, Nicoletto Vernia and Agostino Nifo." In G. C. Garfagnini, ed., *Giovanni Pico della Mirandola: Convegno internazionale di studi nel cinquecentesimo anniversario della morte (1494–1994)*. Vol. 2. Rome, 1997, pp. 127–56.

Marcus, I. G. "Beyond the Sephardic Mystique." *Orim* 1 (1985–86): 35–53.

Marx, A. "Glimpses of the Life of an Italian Rabbi of the First Half of the Sixteenth Century (David Ibn Yaḥya)." HUCA 1 (1924): 605–24.

May, H. S. *Joseph Hacohen and the Anonymous Corrector: The Vale of Tears (Emek Habakha)*. The Hague, 1971.

Mayer, T. F. "Biography and Autobiography." In P. F. Grendler, ed., *Encyclopedia of the Renaissance*. Vol. 1. New York, 1999, pp. 226–29.

Melamed, A. "Rhetoric and Philosophy in *Nofet Ṣufim* by R. Judah Messer Leon." *Italia* (1978): 7–39.

———. "Hebrew Italian Renaissance and Early Modern Encyclopedias." *Rivista di storia della filosofia* 40 (1985): 91–112.

———. "The Perception of Jewish History in Italian Jewish Thought of the Sixteenth and Seventeenth Centuries: A Re-Examination." *Italia Judaica*. Rome, 1986, pp. 139–70.

———. "The Hebrew 'Laudatio' of Yoḥanan Alemanno in Praise of Lorenzo il Magnifico and the Florentine Constitution." In H. Beinart, ed., *Jews in Italy: Studies Dedicated to the Memory of U. Cassuto on the 100th anniversary of His Birth*. Jerusalem 1988, pp. 1–34.

———. "Elijah Delmedigo and the Platonic Political Tradition in the Renaissance" (Hebrew). *Italia* 11 (1994): 57–76.

Meroz, R. "R. Israel Sarug, a Student of Luria?: A Reconsideration of the Question" (Hebrew). *Da'at* 28 (1992): 41–50.

———. "Faithful Transmission versus Innovation: Luria and His Disciples." In P. Schäfer and J. Dan, eds., *Gershom Scholem's Major Trends in Jewish Mysticism: 50 Years After*. Tübingen, 1993, pp. 257–75.

———. "An Anonymous Commentary on Idra Raba by a Member of the Sarug School" (Hebrew). In R. Elior and J. Dan, eds., *Rivkah Shatz-Uffenheimer Memorial Volume*. Vol. 1. Jerusalem, 1996, pp. 307–78.

Milano, A. *Storia degli ebrei in Italia*. Turin, 1963.

Mortara, M. *Indice alfabetico dei rabbini e scrittori israeliti di cose giudache in Italia*. Padua, 1886.

Motzkin, A. L. "Elijah Delmedigo, Averroës and Averroism." *Italia* 6, nos. 1–2 (1987): 7–19.

Nadav, Y. "A Letter of the Kabbalist R. Isaac mar Ḥayyim on the Doctrine of the Superior Lights" (Hebrew). *Tarbiẓ* 26 (1957): 440–58.

Neuman, A. A. "The Shebet Yehuda and Sixteenth-Century Historiography." In *L. Ginzberg Jubilee Volume*. English section. New York, 1945, pp. 253–73.

Pachter, M. "*Sefer Reshit Ḥokhma* of Rabbi Elijah de Vidas and Its Abbreviations" (Hebrew). *Kiryat Sefer* 47 (1972): 686–710.

———. "Traces of the Influence of R. Elijah de Vidas's *Reshit Ḥokhma* upon the Writings of R. Jacob Joseph of Polonnoye" (Hebrew). In J. Dan and J. Hacker, eds., *Studies in Jewish Mysticism, Philosophy and Ethical Literature Presented to Isaiah Tishby*. Jerusalem, 1986, pp. 569–92.

———. *From Safed's Hidden Treasures* (Hebrew). Jerusalem, 1994.

Parente, F. "La Chiesa e il 'Talmud': L'atteggiamento della Chiesa e del mondo cristiano nei confronti del 'Talmud' e degli altri scritti rabbinici, con particolare riguardo all'Italia tra XV e XVI secolo." In C. Vivanti, ed., *Storia d'Italia: Gli ebrei in Italia*. Vol. 11. Turin, 1996, pp. 521–643.

Parisi, S. "Musicians at the Court of Mantua during Monteverdi's Time: Evidence from the Payrolls." In S. Gmeinwieser et al., eds., *Musicologia Humana: Studies in Honor of Warren and Ursula Kirkendale*. Florence, 1994, pp. 183–208.

———. "The Jewish Community and Carnival Entertainment at the Mantuan Court in the Early Baroque." In J. A. Owens and A. M. Cummings, eds., *Music in Renaissance Cities and Courts: Studies in Honor of Lewis Lockwood*. Warren, Mich., 1997, pp. 297–305.

Pimenta Ferro, M.J., *Os judeus em Portugal no seculo XV*. Lisbon, 1982.

Pines, S. "Medieval Doctrines in Renaissance Garb? Some Jewish and Arabic Sources of Leone Ebreo's Doctrines." In B. Cooperman, ed., *Jewish Thought in the Sixteenth Century*. Cambridge, Mass., 1983, pp. 365–98.

Piperno, U. "Rabbi Moshe Provenzalo tra tradizione e rinnovamento." In *Scritti sull'ebraismo in memoria di Emanuele Menachem Artom*. Jerusalem, 1996, pp. 244–57.

Prosperi, A. "Incontri rituali: Il papa e gli ebrei." In C. Vivanti, ed., *Storia d'Italia: Gli ebrei in Italia*. Vol. 11. Turin, 1996, pp. 495–520.

Puig Montada, J. "Continuidad medieval en el Renacimiento: El caso de Elijah del Medigo." *Ciudad de Dios* 206 (1993): 47–64.

———. "Elijah Delmedigo and His Physical 'Quaestiones.' " In J. A. Aertsen and A. Speer, eds., *Was ist Philosophie im Mittelalter?* Berlin, 1998, pp. 929–36.

Rabinowitz, I. "A Rectification of the Date of Judah Messer Leon's Death." In C. Berlin, ed., *Studies in Jewish Bibliography, History and Literature in Honor of I. Edward Kiev*. New York, 1971, pp. 399–406.

———. *The Book of the Honeycomb's Flow. Sefer Nōpheth Ṣūphīm*. Ithaca, N.Y., 1983.

Ravid, B. "Between the Myth of Venice and the Lachrymose Conception of Jewish History: The Experience of the Jews of Venice." In B. Garvin and B. Cooperman, eds., *The Jews of Italy: Memory and Identity*. College Park, Md., 2000, pp. 151–92.

Ravitzky, A. "The Soles of the Kabbalists Are on the Heads of the Philosophers: On the Fifteenth-Century Dispute of Crete" (Hebrew). *Tarbiẓ* 58 (1989): 453–82.

Rice, E. F. *Saint Jerome in the Renaissance*. Baltimore, 1985.

Richler, B. "Manuscripts of Avicenna's Canon in Hebrew Translation: A Revised and Up-to-Date List." *Koroth* 8 (1982): 145–68.

Ronen, A. "Iscrizioni ebraiche nell'arte ebraica del quattrocento." In *Studi di storia dell'arte sul Medioevo e del Rinascimento nel centenario della nascita di Mario Salmi.* Vol. 2. Florence, 1993, pp. 601–24.

Rose, C. "Antonio Enriquez Gomez y el Templo de Salomon." In A. Doron, ed., *Encuentros y desencuentros.* Tel Aviv, 2000, pp. 413–29.

Rosenthal, G. S. *Banking and Finance among Jews in Renaissance Italy.* New York, 1962.

Ross, J. *The Beḥinat ha-Dat of Rabbi Elijah Delmedigo of Candia* (Hebrew). Tel Aviv, 1984.

Roth, C. *The History of the Jews of Italy. Philadelphia,* 1946.

———. *The Duke of Naxos.* Philadelphia, 1948.

———. *The Jews in the Renaissance.* New York, 1959.

Roth, N. "The 'Theft of Philosophy' by the Greeks from the Jews." *Classical Folia* 32 (1978): 53–67.

Ruderman, D. "An Exemplary Sermon from the Classroom of a Jewish Teacher in Renaissance Italy." *Italia* 1 (1978): 7–38.

———. *The World of a Renaissance Jew: The Life and Thought of Abraham ben Mordecai Farissol.* Cincinnati, 1981.

———. "The Italian Renaissance and Jewish Thought." In A. Rabil, ed., *Renaissance Humanism: Foundations and Forms.* Vol. 1. Philadelphia, 1988, pp. 382–433.

———. *Kabbalah, Magic, and Science: The Cultural Universe of a Sixteenth-Century Jewish Physician.* Cambridge, Mass., 1988.

———. ed. *A Valley of Vision: The Heavenly Journey of Abraham ben Hananiah Yagel.* Philadelphia, 1990.

———. "Contemporary Science and Jewish Law in the Eyes of Isaac Lampronti of Ferrara and Some of His Contemporaries." *Jewish History* 6 (1992): 211–24.

———. "Jewish Thought in Newtonian England: The Career and Writings of David Nieto." *Proceedings of the American Academy for Jewish Research* 58 (1992): 193–219.

———. ed. *Essential Papers on Jewish Culture in Renaissance and Baroque Italy.* New York, 1992.

———. *Jewish Thought and Scientific Discovery in Early Modern Europe.* New Haven, Conn., 1995.

———. "Medieval and Modern Jewish History." In *American Historical Association Guide to Historical Literature.* New York, 1995.

———. "Cecil Roth: A Reassessment." In D. N. Myers and D. B. Ruderman, eds., *The Jewish Past Revisited.* New Haven, Conn., 1998, pp. 128–42.

Sack, B. "The Influence of Cordovero on Seventeenth-Century Jewish Thought." In I. Twersky and B. Septimus, eds., *Jewish Thought in the Seventeenth Century.* Cambridge, Mass., 1987, pp. 365–79.

———. *The Kabbalah of Rabbi Moshe Cordovero* (Hebrew). Beersheva, 1995.

Santoro, M. *Amatus Lusitanus ed Ancona.* Coimbra, 1991.

Schechter, S. "Notes sur Messer David Leon, tirées de manuscripts." *Revue des études juives* 24 (1892): 118–37.

———. "Safed in the Sixteenth Century." In S. Schechter, ed., *Studies in Judaism: Essays on Persons, Concepts, and Movements of Thought in Jewish Tradition.* New York, 1970, pp. 231–97.

Schmitt, C. B. *Gianfrancesco Pico della Mirandola (1469–1533) and His Critique of Aristotle.* The Hague, 1967.

———. "Perennial Philosophy: From Agostino Steuco to Leibniz." *Journal for the History of Ideas* 27 (1966): 505–32.

———. "*Prisca theologia e philosophia perennis:* Due temi del Rinascimento italiano e la loro fortuna." In G. Tarugi, ed., *Il pensiero italiano del Rinascimento e il tempo nostro.* Florence, 1970, pp. 211–36.

———. *Studies in Renaissance Philosophy and Science.* London, 1981.

———. And Q. Skinner, eds. *The Cambridge History of Renaissance Philosophy.* Cambridge, 1988.

Scholem, G. "Rabbi Israel Sarug, Student of Luria?" (Hebrew). *Zion* 5 (1940): 214–43.

———. "The Sermon on Redemption of R. Solomon le-Veit ha-Turiel" (Hebrew). *Sefunot* 1 (1956): 62–79.

———. "New Information about Joseph Ashkenazi, the Tanna of Safed" (Hebrew). *Tarbiẓ* 28 (1959): 59–89, 201–35.

———. *Major Trends in Jewish Mysticism.* New York, 1946.

Schweid, E. *History of Jewish Philosophy from the Late Middle Ages to Modern Times* (Hebrew). Jerusalem, 1971.

Secret, F. *Le Zohar chez les kabbalistes chrétiens de la Renaissance.* Paris, 1958.

———. *Les Kabbalistes chrétiens de la Renaissance.* Paris, 1964.

———. "Nouvelles precisions sur Flavius Mithridates maître de Pic de la Mirandole et traducteur de commentaires de kabbale." In *L'opera e il pensiero di Giovanni Pico della Mirandola.* Vol. 2. Florence, 1965, pp. 169–87.

———. "Le 'Tractatus de anno Jubilaei' de Lazaro da Viterbo, Grégoire XIII et la kabbale chrétienne'." *Rinascimento,* 2d ser., 6 (1966): 305–33.

Segal, L. A. *Historical Consciousness and Religious Tradition in Azariah de' Rossi's Me'or 'Einayim.* Philadelphia, 1989.

Segre, R. "Nuovi documenti sui marrani d'Ancona." *Michael* 9 (1985): 130–33.

———. "La Controriforma: Espulsioni, conversioni, isolamento." In C. Vivanti, ed., *Storia d'Italia: Gli ebrei in Italia.* Vol. 11. Turin, 1996, pp. 707–78.

———. "La formazione di una comunità marrana: I portoghesi di Ferrara." in C. Vivanti, ed., *Storia d'Italia: Gli ebrei in Italia.* Vol. 11. Turin, 1996, pp. 779–841.

Sermoneta, G. "Aspetti del pensiero moderno nell'ebraismo italiano tra Rinascimento ed età barocca." In *Italia Judaica: Gli ebrei in Italia tra Rinascimento ed età barocca.* Rome, 1986, pp. 55–66.

Seznec, J., ed. *The Survival of the Pagan Gods: The Mythological Tradition and Its Place in Renaissance Humanism.* Princeton, N.J., 1972.

Shechterman, D. "The Philosophy of Immanuel of Rome in Light of His Commentary on the Book of Genesis" (Hebrew). Ph.d. diss., Hebrew University, 1984.

Sherwin, B. R. *Mystical Theology and Social Dissent: The Life and Works of Judah Loew of Prague.* London, 1982.

Shmuelevitz, A. "Capsali as a Source for Ottoman History, 1450–1523." *International Journal of Middle East Studies* 9 (1978): 339–44.

———. "Jewish-Muslim Relations in the Writings of Rabbi Elijah Capsali" (Hebrew). *Pe'amim* 61 (1994): 75–82.

Shohat, A., ed. *Sefer Shevet Yehudah le-R. Shelomo ibn Verga.* Jerusalem, 1947.

Shulvass, M. A. "The Disputes of Messer Leon and His Attempt to Exert His Authority on the Jews of Italy" (Hebrew). *Zion* 12 (1947): 17–23.

———. *The Jews in the World of the Renaissance.* Leiden, 1973.

Siegmund, S. "La vita nei ghetti." In C. Vivanti, ed., *Storia d'Italia: Gli ebrei in Italia.* Vol. 11. Turin, 1996) pp. 843–92.

Simonsohn, S. "Books and Libraries of the Jews of Mantua, 1595" (Hebrew). *Kiryat Sefer* 37 (1962): 103–22.

———. *History of the Jews in the Duchy of Mantua.* Jerusalem, 1977.

———. "A condizione degli ebrei nell'Italia centrale e settentrionale." In C. Vivanti, ed., *Storia d'Italia: Gli ebrei in Italia.* Vol. 11. Turin, 1996, pp. 95–120.

Siraisi, N. G. *Avicenna in Renaissance Italy.* Princeton, N.J., 1987.

———. *Medieval and Early Renaissance Medicine: An Introduction to Knowledge and Practice.* Chicago, 1990.

Stow, K. *Theater of Acculturation: The Roman Ghetto in the Sixteenth Century.* Seattle, 2001.

———. "The Burning of the Talmud in 1553, in the Light of Sixteenth-Century Catholic Attitudes Toward the Talmud." *Bibliothèque d'Humanisme et Renaissance* 34 (1972): 435–59.

Strauss, G. "A Sixteenth-Century Encyclopedia: Sebastian Münster's Cosmography and Its Editions." In C. Carter, ed., *From the Renaissance to the Counter-Reformation: Essays in Honor of Garett Mattingly.* New York, 1965, pp. 145–63.

Tamani, G. *Tipografia ebraica a Soncino 1483–1490.* Soncino, 1988.

Tamar, D. "About *Kevod Ḥakhamim* by David ben Judah Messer Leon." *Kiryat Sefer* 26 (1950): 96–100.

———. "The Year 1575 and the Messianic Excitement in Italy" (Hebrew). In D. Tamar, ed., *Studies in Jewish History in Israel and Italy.* Jerusalem, 1973, pp. 11–38.

———. "The Messianic Dreams and Visions of R. Ḥayyim Vital" (Hebrew). *Shalem* 4 (1984): 211–29.

Tambrun, B. "Marsile Ficin et le 'Commentaire' de Plethon sur les 'Oracles Chaldaiques.'" *Accademia* 1 (1999): 9–48.

Tirosh-Rothschild, H. *Between Worlds: The Life and Thought of Rabbi David ben Judah Messer Leon.* Albany, N.Y., 1991.

———. "The Concept of Torah in the Works of David ben Judah Messer Leon." *Jerusalem Studies in Jewish Thought* 2 (1982): 94–117.

———. "In Defense of Jewish Humanism." *Jewish History* 3 (1988): 32–57.

———. "Jewish Culture in Renaissance Italy: A Methodological Survey." *Italia* 9 (1990): 63–96.

———. "Sefirot as the Essence of God in the Writings of David Messer Leon." *AJS Review* 7–8 (1982–83): 409–25.

Tishby, I. "The Controversy about the *Zohar* in the Sixteenth Century in Italy" (Hebrew). *Perakim: Yearbook of the Schocken Institute for Jewish Research* 1 (1967–68): 131–182.

Toaff, A. "Gli ebrei a Roma." In C. Vivanti, ed., *Storia d'Italia: Gli ebrei in Italia.* Vol. 11. Turin, 1996, pp. 121–52.

———. "Gli insediamenti askenaziti nell'Italia settentrionale." In C. Vivanti, ed., *Storia d'Italia: Gli ebrei in Italia.* Vol. 11. Turin, 1996, pp. 153–71.

———. "La vita materiale." In C. Vivanti, ed., *Storia d'Italia: Gli ebrei in Italia.* Vol. 11. Turin, 1996, pp. 237–63.

———. " 'Banchieri' cristiani e 'prestatori' ebrei?" in C. Vivanti, ed., *Storia d'Italia: Gli ebrei in Italia.* Vol. 11. Turin, 1996, pp. 265–87.

———. *Mostri giudei: L'immaginario dal Medioevo alla prima età moderna.* Bologna, 1996.

———. *Love, Work, and Death: Jewish Life in Medieval Umbria.* London 1998.

Toussaint, S. "Ficino's Orphic Magic or Jewish Astrology and Oriental Philosophy? A Note on Spiritus, the Three Books on Life, Ibn Tufayl and Ibn Zarza." *Accademia* 2 (2000): 19–33.

Trinkaus, C. *In Our Image and Likeness: Humanity and Divinity in Italian Humanist Thought.* Notre Dame, Ind., 1995.

Tucker, H. "To Louvain and Antwerp and Beyond: The Contrasting Itineraries of Diogo Pires (Didacus Pyrrhus Lusitanus, 1517–1599) and João Rodrigues de Castelo Branco (Amatus Lusitanus, 1511–1568)." *Medievalia Lovaniensia* 26 (1998): 83–113.

Twersky, I. "Talmudists, Philosophers, and Kabbalists: The Quest for Spirituality in the Sixteenth Century." In B. Cooperman, ed., *Jewish Thought in the Sixteenth Century.* Cambridge, Mass., 1983, pp. 431–59.

Urbani, R. "Indizi documentari sulla figura di Joseph Hacohen e della sua famiglia nella Genova del XVI secolo." In G. N. Zazzu, ed., *E andammo dove il vento ci spinse: La cacciata degli ebrei dalla Spagna.* Genoa, 1992, pp. 59–67.

Vasoli, C. *La dialettica e la retorica dell'umanesimo: Invenzione e metodo nella cultura del XV e del XVI secolo.* Milan, 1968.

Veltri, G. "The Humanist Sense of History and the Jewish Idea of Tradition: Azaria de' Rossi's Critique of Philo Alexandrinus." *Jewish Studies Quarterly* 2 (1995): 372–93.

———. "Die humanistischen Wurzeln der 'jüdischen' Philosophie: Zur Konzeption einer konfessionellen Ontologie und Genealogie des Wissens." In W. Stegmaier, ed., *Die philosophische Aktualität der jüdischen Tradition.* Frankfurt am Main, 2000, pp. 249–78.

———. "Science and Religious Hermeneutics: The 'Philosophy' of Rabbi Loew of Prague." In J. Helm and A. Winkelmann, eds., *Religious Confessions and the Sciences in the Sixteenth Century.* Leiden, 2001, pp. 119–35.

———. "Der Lector Prudens und die Bibliothek des (uralten) Wissens: Pietro Galatino, Amatus Lusitanus und Azaria de' Rossi." In W. Schmidt-Biggemann, ed., *Christliche Kabbala: Johannes Reuchlins geistesgeschichtliche Wirkung.* Pforzheim, 2003.

Veronese, A. "Il viaggio di Meshullam ben Menaḥem da Volterra." In G. Busi, ed., *Vi-*

aggiatori ebrei: Berichte jüdischer Reisender vom Mittelalter bis in die Gegenwart. Bologna, 1992, pp. 45–66.

Viterbo, A. "Socrate nel ghetto: Lo scetticismo mascherato di Simone Luzzatto." *Studi Veneziani* 38 (1999): 79–128.

Vivanti, C., ed. *Storia d'Italia: Gli ebrei in Italia.* Vol. 11: *Dall'alto Medievo all'età dei ghetti.* Turin, 1996.

Walker, D. P. *The Ancient Theology.* London, 1972 vesifro.

Weinberg, J. "Azariah de' Rossi: Towards a Reappraisal of the Last Years of his Life." *Annali della Scuola Normale di Pisa* ser. 3, 8 (1978): 493–511.

———. "Azariah de' Rossi and Septuagint Traditions." *Italia* 5 (1985): 7–35.

———. "The Quest for Philo in Sixteenth-Century Jewish Historiography." In A. Rapoport-Albert and S. J. Zipperstein, eds., *Jewish History: Essays in Honour of Chimen Abramsky.* London, 1988, pp. 163–87.

———. " 'The Voice of God': Jewish and Christian Responses to the Ferrara Earthquake of November 1570." *Italian Studies* 46 (1991): 69–81.

———. "Azaria de' Rossi and the Forgeries of Annius of Viterbo." In D. B. Ruderman, ed., *Essential Papers on Jewish Culture in Renaissance and Baroque Italy.* New York, 1992, pp. 252–279.

———. "An Apocryphal Source in the *Me'or 'Enayim* of Azaria de' Rossi." *Journal of the Warburg and Courtauld Institutes* 56 (1993): 280–284.

———. "Invention and Convention: Jewish and Christian Critique of the Jewish Fixed Calendar." *Jewish History* 14 (2000): 317–30.

———. ed. *Azariah de' Rossi: The Light of the Eyes.* Translated from the Hebrew with an introduction and annotations. New Haven, Conn., 2001.

Weinberg, S. R. "Yosef b. Yehoshua ha-Kohen vesifro maṣiv gevulot 'amim.' " *Sinai* 72 (1973): 333–64.

Werblowsky, R. J. Z., *Joseph Karo, Lawyer and Mystic.* Philadelphia, 1977.

Wirszubski, C., ed. *Flavius Mithridates: Sermo de Passione Domini.* Jerusalem, 1963.

———. *Pico della Mirandola's Encounter with Jewish Mysticism.* Cambridge, Mass., 1989.

Wolfson, E. R. "Beyond the Spoken Word: Oral Tradition and Written Transmission in Medieval Mysticism." In Y. Elman and I. Gershoni, eds., *Transmitting Jewish Traditions: Orality, Textuality, and Cultural Diffusion.* New Haven, Conn., 2000, pp. 166–223.

Yarden, D., ed. *Immanuel Haromi: Maḥbarot.* Jerusalem, 1957.

Yates, A. F. *Giordano Bruno and the Hermetic Tradition.* Chicago, 1964.

———. *Cabala and Occult Philosophy in the Elizabethan Age.* London, 1979.

Yerushalmi, Y. H., ed. "Exile and Expulsion in Jewish History." In B. Gampel, ed., *Crisis and Creativity in the Sefardi World 1391–1648.* New York, 1997, pp. 3–22.

———. "Clio and the Jews: Reflections on Jewish Historiography in the Sixteenth Century." *Proceedings of the American Academy for Jewish Research* 46–47 (1979–1980): 607–38.

———. *Zakhor: Jewish History and Jewish Memory.* Seattle, 1982.

———. "Messianic Impulses in Joseph ha-Kohen." In B. Cooperman, ed., *Jewish Thought in the Sixteenth Century.* Cambridge, Mass., 1983, pp. 460–87.

Yosha, N. *Myth and Metaphor: Abraham Herrera's Philosophic Interpretation of Lurianic Kabbalah* (Hebrew). Jerusalem, 1994.

Yuval, Y. *"Two Nations in Your Womb": Perceptions of Jews and Christians* (Hebrew). Jerusalem, 2000.

Zunz, Leopold. "Toledot le-R. Azariah min ha'adumim." *Kerem Ḥemed* 5 (1841): 131–58; 7 (1843): 119–24.

Contributors

ALESSANDRO GUETTA is professor of Hebrew literature at the Institut National des Langues et Civilisations Orientales, Paris. He is the author of numerous works on the history and literature of the Jews of Italy, including *Philosophie et cabbale: Essai sur la pensée d'Elie Benamozegh* (1998).

ELEAZAR GUTWIRTH is professor of Jewish history at Tel Aviv University. He has published numerous essays on the history of Jewish culture and society in medieval and early modern Spain. He is the author of a forthcoming book on Doña Gracia, Amatus Lusitanus, and their circle in the sixteenth century.

HARVEY HAMES is senior lecturer in the Department of History of Ben-Gurion University of the Negev. He is the author of numerous publications in the field of Christian-Jewish relations, magic, mysticism, and medieval thought. He recently published *The Art of Conversion: Christianity and Kabbalah in the Thirteenth Century* (2000).

DON HARRÁN is the Arthur Rubinstein Professor of Musicology at the Hebrew University of Jerusalem. His many books and articles on the history of Renaissance Jewish musicology include *In Search of Harmony: Hebrew and Humanist Elements in Sixteenth-Century Musical Thought* (1988) and *Salamone Rossi: Jewish Musician in Late Renaissance Mantua* (1999). He is the editor of the *Complete Works* of Salamone Rossi, in thirteen volumes.

MOSHE IDEL is the Max Cooper Professor of Jewish Thought at the Hebrew University of Jerusalem. He is one of the leading authorities on the history of the kabbalah. Among his books in English are *Kabbalah: New Perspectives* (1988), *Messianic Mystics* (1998), and *Absorbing Perfections: Kabbalah and Interpretation* (2002). In 1999, Professor Idel received the prestigious Israel Prize for his scholarly work.

MARTIN JACOBS is assistant professor in Jewish, Islamic, and Near Eastern studies at Washington University in St. Louis. His writings focus on ancient and medieval Jewish history and include *Die Institution des jüdischen Patriarchen: Eine quellen- und traditionskritische Studie zur Geschichte der Juden in der Spätantike* (1995) and *Malkhut Yishma'el: Die Herrschaft des Islam im Bild jüdischer Chroniken des 16. und 17. Jahrhunderts* (2003).

FABRIZIO LELLI is lecturer in Hebrew language and literature at the University of Lecce, Italy. Among his publications on Renaissance Judaism are his editions of Yoḥanan Alemanno's *Hay ha'Olamim (L'Immortale)*. Vol. 1: *La Retorica* (1995) and Elijah Ḥayyim Gennazano's *La lettera preziosa (Iggeret ḥamudot)* (2002).

GIANFRANCO MILETTO is research assistant at Martin Luther University of Halle-Wittenberg, Germany. His published work on the history of the biblical text and Italian Jewish thought includes *L'Antico Testamento ebraico nella tradizione babilonese: I frammenti della Genizah* (1992). He is editor and translator of *Die Heldenschilde*, the German-language edition of Abraham Ben David Portaleone's *Shilte ha-Gibborim.*

DAVID B. RUDERMAN is the Joseph Meyerhoff Professor of Modern Jewish History and director of the Center for Advanced Judaic Studies at the University of Pennsylvania. He is the author of many works on Jewish history and thought in early modern Europe, including *Kabbalah, Magic, and Science: The Cultural Universe of a Sixteenth-Century Jewish Physician* (1988), *Jewish Thought and Scientific Discovery in Early Modern Europe* (1995), and *Jewish Enlightenment in an English Key: Anglo-Jewry's Construction of Modern Jewish Thought* (2000).

ADAM SHEAR is assistant professor of medieval and early modern Judaism in the Department of Religious Studies at the University of Pittsburgh and has recently completed a dissertation on Judah Halevi's classic text, the *Kuzari*, in early modern and modern Jewish culture.

GIUSEPPE VELTRI is professor of Jewish studies at Martin Luther University of Halle-Wittenberg, Germany, and director of the university's Leopold Zunz Center for the Study of European Judaism. His extensive publications on ancient, medieval, and Renaissance Judaism include *Eine Tora für den König*

Talmai: Untersuchungen zum übersetzungenverständnis in der jüdisch-hellenistischen und rabbinischen Literatur (1994), *Magie und Halakha: Ansätze zu einem empirischen Wissenschaftsbegriff im spätantiken und frühmittelalterchen Judentum* (1997), and *Gegenwart der Tradition: Studien zur jüdischen Literatur und Kulturgeschichte* (2002).

JOANNA WEINBERG is the Catherine Lewis Fellow in Rabbinics at Oxford University and reader in rabbinics at Leo Baeck College, London. She is the author of many essays on the history and culture of Judaism in the Renaissance and has translated and edited the massive *Light of the Eyes* of Azariah de' Rossi (2001).

Index

Acknowledgments

This book originated at a conference held at the famous Herzog August Bibliothek of Wolfenbüttel, Germany, through the special initiative of Professors Friedrich Niewohner and Herbert Smolinsky. The conference itself received generous financial support from both the library and the Leopold Zunz Zentrum of the Leucorea Foundation in Wittenburg, Germany. The book was also supported by a generous grant from the Herbert Katz Publication Fund of the Center for Advanced Judaic Studies at the University of Pennsylvania, a fund newly created to honor the past chairman of the Center's board. Our thanks go to all these institutions and individuals, without whose support and assistance this volume would not have come into being.

We are also grateful to the University of Pennsylvania Press for its significant contribution in improving this manuscript, specifically to Janice Meyerson for her fine copyediting and to Erica Ginsburg and Jerome Singerman for their editorial guidance. Tamar Kaplan Appel provided us with an exemplary index. We would be remiss if we did not thank the two anonymous readers for the Press, whose comments helped make this a better book than it would otherwise have been. Finally, we acknowledge the efforts of all the contributors to the volume, along with the other participants in the Wolfenbüttel conference, in creating the community of scholars that made this collective project possible.